937.07

P9-DHF-846

29468

NERO

THE END OF A DYNASTY

To
JG, JBG, MCG, VTG
Nero's latest victims

NERO

THE END OF A DYNASTY

Miriam T. Griffin

Yale University Press
New Haven and London

First published in the United Kingdom in 1984 by
B. T. Batsford Limited
First published in the United States of America in 1985 by
Yale University Press

Library of Congress catalog card number: 84-51761
International standard book number: 0-300-03285-4

Printed in Great Britain

10 9 8 7 6 5 4 3 2 1

Contents

CONTENTS

List of Illustrations

Preface

In excusing the monotony of his narrative, with its concentration on imperial crime and cruelty, the historian Tacitus argued that to be wise in politics is to understand those who wield power according to the constitution of the time: in his own day, he claimed, that meant studying the character of the Princeps. As if in confirmation of his judgement, the genre of imperial biography was about to be inaugurated in Latin by his younger contemporary Suetonius and was thereafter to remain long in fashion.

This ancient defence of imperial biography is difficult to impugn. Yet it imposes no obligation to rewrite the works of the ancient historians and biographers which are accessible in excellent translations even to the general reader. Indeed recent scholarship tends to frown on the composition of imperial lives, favouring instead works that illuminate the general structure of the imperial system and the long processes that explain the development of the Empire. Yet even from this point of view, it sometimes matters that a particular man became Princeps at a particular time. It can be argued that, as Princeps, Nero affected cultural processes, namely the history of the visual arts and of Latin literature, and that, by failing as Princeps, he made manifest both the structural weaknesses and the practical necessity of the Augustan system.

This study is intended to be a hybrid, biographical in its concentration on the Emperor's personality and problems, historical in its analysis of his fall in terms of the interaction of that personality with the political system. Nero's reign is here examined from two standpoints: first, his own inclinations and the way his expression of them was affected by his particular circumstances and the advice of others; then the pressures inherent in the Principate, pressures which were bound to condition any ruler's conduct even if he was not continuously aware of them. In accordance with the latter focus, the excellent beginning of his reign is examined for signs of stress such as appear in his dealings with the Senate and his handling of his freedmen secretaries (chapter 6), while the latter disastrous phase leads to an extended post-mortem (chapters 11–15) covering the problem of the succession, the financial responsibilities of the Emperor, and two questions bearing on the appropriate image of the Princeps: the temptation of philhellenism and the need for military glory.

There are other problems and other aspects of the imperial image that could have been considered with profit had space permitted, but I hope these will at least suggest why it was so difficult to succeed as Princeps. If it is reasonable to think that a good political system can function reasonably well in the hands of mediocrities, then the Principate stands condemned, for it required men of exceptional and varied talents at the head. There is no need to exculpate the last of the Julio-Claudians or the folly and viciousness of other Emperors in order to see that the terrible instability that was to be manifested by the *novus status* of Augustus resulted in large measure from its original design.

The common fate of books that aim to suit different types of reader, from the general to the scholarly, is to please none of them. But the effort has been made, and its consequences should be stated. Only the odd phrase has been left untranslated; documentation being limited by considerations of space, I have chosen, in the interests of students and teachers, to cite more ancient evidence and less modern scholarship. I apologise to those whose work I have used but not expressly cited. It remains to add that the dossier was effectively closed in the spring of 1983.

In the years that have elapsed since the start of this project, I have incurred many debts. For chapter 8 in particular, I exploited the generosity of the scholarly world. As regards coins, Dr. Cathy King not only read and commented on my work but helped me to select the coins to be photographed. Through her good offices, Dr. C. H. V. Sutherland generously provided me with proofs of the second edition of Volume I of the *Roman Imperial Coinage*. And long ago Dr. D. MacDowall sent me material from the *Western Coinages of Nero* well in advance of publication. For the architectural section, first the late Martin Frederiksen and then Mr. Nicholas Purcell suggested bibliography and commented on drafts. The latter not only shared with me his new ideas on the Domus Aurea but provided the rough draft for the map of Rome. Dottoressa Laura Fabbrini graciously responded to requests for clarification of her new excavations and granted permission to reproduce her plans of the Domus Aurea. I am also grateful to the British Academy which in 1980 made me a grant from the Small Grants Research Fund in the Humanities thus enabling me to study at first hand the site of the Domus Aurea and the paintings from the Domus Transitoria, to view the remains of Nero's villa and harbour at Anzio, and to use the invaluable library of the British School at Rome.

Dr. Gillian Clark and Dr. Tessa Rajak have continued to query my logic as profitably as when they were subject to my tutelage; other colleagues, such as Dr. Simon Hornblower, furnished me with inscriptions and encouragement. Sir Ronald Syme has, as always, helped me in person and in print. The dedication perhaps suggests something of the long-suffering of my family but not enough of their help in the face of pessimism and proofs.

Somerville College   Miriam T. Griffin
Oxford   Summer 1984

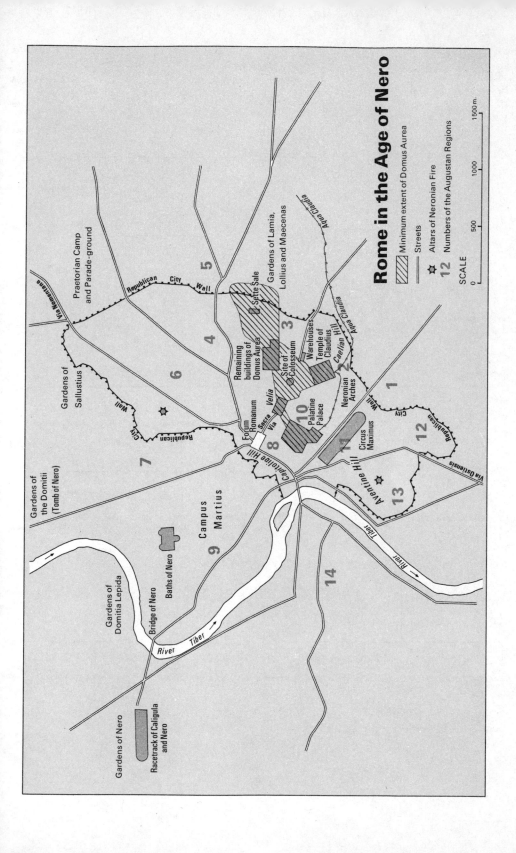

Rome in the Age of Nero

Minimum extent of Domus Aurea

Streets

Altars of Neronian Fire

12 Numbers of the Augustan Regions

SCALE
0   500   1000   1500 m.

Gardens of Nero

Racetrack of Caligula and Nero

Gardens of Domitia Lepida

Bridge of Nero

River Tiber

Baths of Nero

Campus Martius

9

Gardens of the Domitii (Tomb of Nero)

7

City Wall

Republican Wall

Capitoline Hill

Forum Romanum

8

Sacra Via

Velia

10

Palatine Palace

11

Circus Maximus

Aventine Hill

13

River Tiber

14

Via Ostiensis

City Wall

Republican

12

1

Neronian Arches

Caelian Hill

Aqua Claudia

2

Warehouses

Temple of Claudius

Site of Colosseum

Remaining buildings of Domus Aurea

3

Settte Sale

Gardens of Lamia, Lollius and Maecenas

Aqua Claudia

4

5

6

Gardens of Sallustius

Republican City Wall

Praetorian Camp and Parade-ground

Via Nomentana

STEMMA of
The Julio – Claudians

C. JULIUS CAESAR

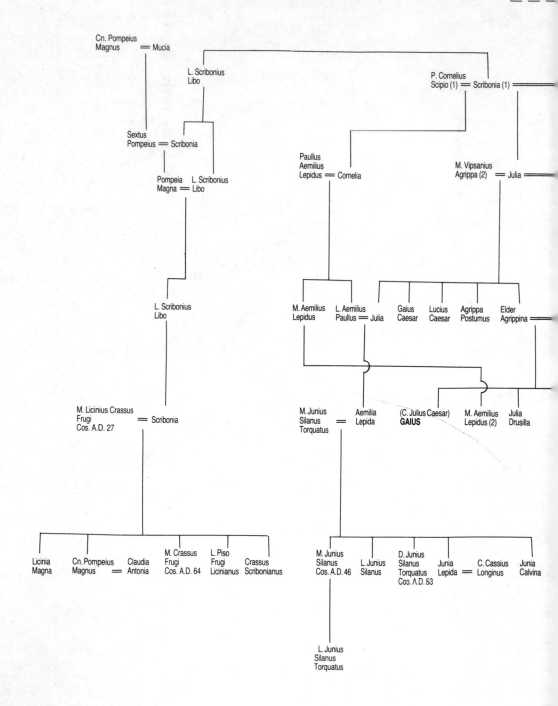

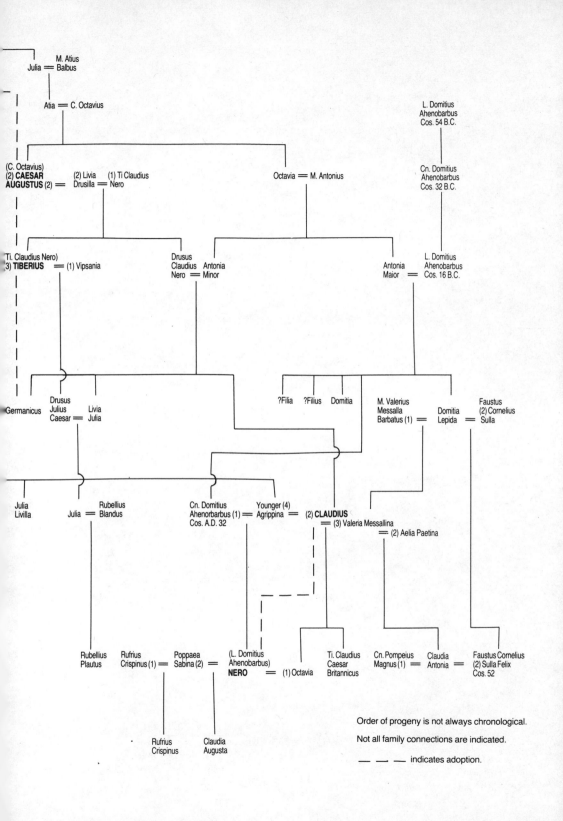

Order of progeny is not always chronological.

Not all family connections are indicated.

— — — indicates adoption.

ONE

Introduction

Commenting on the unanimity of opinion about the Emperor Nero that prevails among the ancient authorities, the historian Charles Merivale wrote, 'With some allowance only for extravagance of colouring, we must accept in the main the verisimilitude of the picture they have left us of this arch-tyrant, the last and the most detestable of the Caesarean family.'[1] Though there were historians who wrote laudatory accounts while Nero was alive, their verdict was overturned after his death and their works have not survived.[2] It could hardly be otherwise. For Nero was the first Princeps to be declared a public enemy by the Senate. Moreover, his failure as Princeps led to a series of bloody civil wars that recalled the death agonies of the Republic, which had continued to haunt the Roman imagination.

Nero's first historians wrote under the new dynasty of the Flavian Emperors, and they endorsed the official view that Nero had dishonoured Augustus and the rest of the Julio-Claudian line. It was they who first gave his tyranny the extravagant colouring familiar from our extant sources. Thus the Elder Pliny described Nero as 'the destroyer of the human race', 'the poison of the world'.[3] For the pagan tradition of Latin historiography, Nero was to become one of the canonical tyrants along with Caligula and Domitian, though his building projects still commanded admiration and the tradition of a decent start to his reign lingered on.[4]

The Jews, who rebelled against the cruelty of his procurators, and the Christians, who suffered undeserved punishment for the Great Fire of Rome, had their own reasons for hating Nero. Deliberately perverting the Greek hope that the philhellene Emperor would return, they portrayed him as an avenging spirit who would come back to punish the power that persecuted them. In the Jewish Sibylline Oracles, written not long after the destruction of Jerusalem in 70, Nero is the exile of Rome, the great king and criminal, who has fled to the Parthians and will cross the Euphrates with tens of thousands to destroy Rome and the whole world.[5] In comparable Christian outpourings, Nero is the Anti-Christ whose persecution of the Christians heralds the destruction of Rome. This view of Nero as Anti-Christ continued to be celebrated by the Church Fathers and by later Christian writers.[6] The picture of him as the incarnation of evil triumphed as Christianity triumphed.

In European literature Nero has served as the stock example of unnatural cruelty, a matricide in Shakespeare's *Hamlet*, a fratricide in Racine's *Britannicus*. The hero of the Marquis de Sade, he has fascinated decadent writers as the *incredibilium cupitor* longing to overcome human limits through extremes of luxury, cruelty and depravity.[7] Here and there a kind word is heard. Napoleon is reported to have said that the people loved Nero because he oppressed the great but never burdened the small.[8] But on the whole, in France, in Germany, and in England, the picture is the same. Certainly no serious historian has been tempted to whitewash the tyrant.

The last century, however, has seen a change of focus in the study of Nero's reign. Merivale's eloquent endorsement of the judgement of antiquity appeared in 1858 as a preface to an account of the vices of the Emperor and the humiliations of his subjects. Fourteen years later there was published in Germany what may be called the first modern book on Nero, *The History of the Roman Empire under the Reign of Nero*. In this work, dedicated to Theodor Mommsen and following his call for rigorous examination of the literary sources and serious attention to other types of evidence (notably coins and inscriptions), Hermann Schiller described the state of the Roman world at that period rather than the antics of the Emperor and his courtiers. This led him into a thorough analysis of the revolt in the provinces that brought Nero's reign to its chaotic close.

The picture that Schiller drew is, in the main, the one that appears in Bernard Henderson's *The Life and Principate of the Emperor Nero*: Nero's conduct did deteriorate, but the only real opposition to him came from the governing class in Rome. His overthrow was the result of a 'nationalist' rising against Rome by the Gauls, which was not provoked by his crimes at home nor undertaken in the interests of the senators of Rome. Henderson's work, which appeared in 1903, is still the most extensive account in English. That by Momigliano in *The Cambridge Ancient History* (volume x) which appeared in 1934, lays more stress on Nero's loss of prestige with the armies but takes a similar view of the Gallic rising. This diagnosis of Nero's fall has now been abandoned. Numismatists have demonstrated, and historians confirmed, that Vindex was acting not as a patriotic Gaul, but as a disillusioned Roman senator rousing the Gallic upper classes to revolt against an unworthy ruler whose rapacity they had already experienced. The most recent studies in English return to the view that prevails in the ancient writers, namely, that Nero's vices alienated his upper-class subjects and caused his overthrow. Warmington in *Nero: Reality and Legend* (1969) places the emphasis on his frivolity and ineptitude, while Grant in *Nero* (1970) blames his paranoid cruelty.

Whatever we may now think of his conclusion that Nero's crimes were not the cause of his overthrow, Schiller's work was a valuable contribution. The significance of Nero's reign to the historian of the Roman Empire, as opposed to the writer of literature or student of morality, does not lie wholly in Nero's character. For the historian, the most important event of

Nero's reign was its collapse. The dynastic link with the founder of the Principate was severed and his system placed in jeopardy. In surviving and ceasing to be the heritage of one family, the Principate was ripe for clearer definition as an institution. On the other hand, what had often been feared had now been demonstrated: the *novus status* created and accepted as a protection against civil war could not guarantee that result by its mere existence. For Nero's eventual successor, these were practical problems to be solved. For the later historian, there is an invitation here to exploit the benefits of hindsight and explore how the crisis occurred and how far the political system itself contributed to Nero's failure.

There is also a practical advantage involved in accepting this invitation. By keeping in mind the need to explain why Nero fell, we may avoid the two principal pitfalls that face anyone writing about an emperor and his reign. The first is an exclusive concentration on biographical material which, in this case, can simply result in a rewriting of some of the best narrative in Suetonius and Tacitus, an exercise as otiose as it is impertinent. The second is a tendency to see one's task as that of narrating all of the significant events within the chronological limits. Unfortunately, relations between Rome and Judaea or developments in Britain are not best understood by considering the period when a particular individual occupied the throne, for the problems endemic to any area of the Roman Empire mean that events there only become intelligible over a longer space of time. Similarly, the development of the imperial administrative or financial systems is not best illuminated when examined reign by reign. A better approach is to concentrate on Nero's own decisions and initiatives and on those aspects of the Emperor's behaviour that affected the stability of his position. In this way we may illuminate, not only Nero's ability as Princeps, but the difficulties of the Principate itself.

Did the rôle that Nero initially played so well embody conflicts that he ultimately found impossible to resolve? Did the system offer particular temptations to a man of his temperament? Was the more successful Vespasian simply an *empereur de bon sens* or was he less exposed than Nero to certain features of the Principate and more aware, because of recent history, of the need to change others?

TWO

The Making of a Princeps

Augustus once expressed in an edict his wish to be called the 'author of the best type of government' and to retain to the end the expectation that the foundations he had laid for the state would hold firm.[1] But the Principate was not a form of government created at one stroke; rather it had evolved as Augustus corrected past mistakes and faced new problems. The first major step was completed in January of 27 BC when Octavian was given various honours, including the title Augustus, for making certain moves whose effect he described thus: 'I transferred the state from my power into the control of the Senate and the Roman People. After this, I had no more power than my fellow consuls but I excelled all in authority (*auctoritas*)', *auctoritas* being a capacity to get one's own way, a political ascendancy secured by force of personality and excellence of achievement.

Even after the establishment of Julius Caesar's dictatorship in 49 BC, the old Republican institutions continued to furnish the forms and procedures of government: the Senate still passed decrees, the assemblies passed laws and elected magistrates. But the power of decision lay first with Caesar and then, after a short interval, with the Triumvirs, of whom only one remained in power after the Battle of Actium in September of 31 BC. When Octavian renounced his control in 27 BC and asked the Senate to resume responsibility for the army, the laws and the provinces, the Senate promptly offered him back the control of the provinces, which would have carried with it command of the armies. Octavian accepted only certain military provinces and for a limited period of ten years. In addition, he was elected consul every year.[2] For Augustus this remained the definition of his position that best accorded with his claim to be exercising certain traditional functions entrusted to him by the sovereign SPQR. That may be why the statement quoted above was left in its original prominent position, at the close of his account of his achievements, despite later changes in the definition of his power.

The consulship had long been the supreme magistracy of Rome. The power of the Triumvirs was described as equal to the consuls and Octavian held that office every year after Actium. Although such an arrangement showed a sensitivity to Roman tradition, it was awkward in other respects.

It was difficult for the Princeps to make plausible his claim that the only difference between himself and his colleagues was *auctoritas*, especially as he had an escort of troops in Rome, traditionally the privilege of Roman generals abroad. Then again, the ambitions of the sons of great families to become consul were substantially impeded by the tenure of half the available positions by the Princeps. Finally, the tenure of an annual elective office was not a permanent transferrable position, depending as it did on the personal ascendancy of a particular individual. The events of the year 23 BC showed up these disadvantages with unmistakable clarity. Augustus became seriously ill and nearly died, he clashed with his consular colleague who, though connected by marriage with Augustus' close associate Maecenas, then joined a conspiracy against the Princeps. As a result, Augustus resigned the consulship, to resume it only twice thereafter and then for only half the year on each occasion.[3] Senate and People voted him new powers: the *tribunicia potestas* for life which enabled him to adopt the stance of a champion of the lower orders and, through the tribunician veto, to say 'no' with an appearance of clemency rather than autocracy; and *imperium* at consular level which could be exercised in Rome and his own provinces, did not need renewal, and could be used to issue orders to governors of the provinces not allocated to the Princeps. This *imperium*, which came eventually to be called *imperium proconsulare*, and the tribunician power, reinforced by certain privileges of precedence in the Senate, became the legal basis of the Principate. They were powers traditional in appearance, yet, in fact, anomalous. Augustus had ample time to give his interpretation of them in the 36 years he lived to wield them.

By the time the first Princeps died in AD 14, it had been established that the provinces to be governed by legates of the Princeps' choice included all of the military provinces, though the proconsul of Africa retained control of one legion until the reign of Gaius. All triumphs belonged to the Princeps, though others could be granted triumphal insignia, and, after the reign of Tiberius, no general outside the imperial house could be hailed as Imperator.[4] This must have meant that all booty now fell to the Emperor, whose private wealth was in fact essential to the running of the state. The military and financial resources of the Princeps were what made him, in all but name, a monarch. It is not surprising that a law recording powers granted to Vespasian cites Augustus as a *de facto* precedent for this extravagant conferment: 'that he may have legal power to do what he deems to be in keeping with the advantage of the state and the dignity of affairs divine and human, public and private'.[5]

Augustus lived long enough to accustom men to the idea of dynastic succession without having to admit that he was a king. It had not been an easy idea to make acceptable to the governing class: in 23 BC he had read out his will to show that he had not included in it any request for a special position to be given to his young nephew Marcellus. Neither his nephew nor his grandsons survived him. But by the time Augustus died he had secured the succession, immediately for his stepson Tiberius Claudius Nero, and, eventually, for his own descendants, the children of his granddaughter Julia Agrippina.[6] In this way he founded the Julio-Claudian dynasty.

Augustus' wishes were fulfilled to the extent that Agrippina's youngest son Gaius eventually became Princeps. When he was murdered along with his wife and daughter, less than four years later, there were members of the Senate who thought that the opportunity for abandoning Augustus' system of government had come. But the Praetorian Guard had a vested interest in that system. They forced the Senate to recognise as Princeps Gaius' surviving male relative, his uncle Claudius. Gaius' sisters also survived his assassination. One of them was the younger Agrippina, great-grand-daughter of Augustus and mother of the future Emperor Nero.

Nero's Paternal Clan

Lucius Domitius Ahenobarbus, as Nero was called at birth, was also connected by blood with Augustus on the paternal side. Augustus' sister Octavia had produced two daughters by her marriage to Antony, and Nero's grandfather Lucius had been chosen as husband for the elder Antonia. His son Gnaeus – the name alternated with Lucius by family tradition – was selected by Augustus' successor Tiberius as a husband for the younger Julia Agrippina, and the future Emperor was the only child of the marriage.

The family of Domitii Ahenobarbi belonged to the Republican nobility. They could boast a line of consuls that extended back over two hundred years, while family legend traced their fame to the very infancy of the Roman Republic. Castor and Pollux, it was said, had foretold the Roman victory over the Latins at Lake Regillus to Lucius Domitius, providing proof of their divinity by stroking his cheeks and giving him the bronze beard that gave rise to the family's *cognomen*. A witty Republican orator found the name peculiarly appropriate to the consul of 96 BC, 'It is not surprising', he said, 'that he has a brazen beard, as his nerve is iron and his heart lead'. For the military achievements of the clan were matched by a tendency to arrogance and violence. The consul of 122 BC, without senatorial authorisation, had staged a kind of private triumph, riding through southern Gaul on an elephant after his victories there. Cicero's contemporary L. Domitius, described by him as 'consul designate from the cradle', put up a fierce struggle when Pompey and Crassus combined to deprive him of his birthright. His son, deemed by Suetonius the best of the family, was lucky to find an outlet for his aggression and ability in the Civil Wars, changing sides honourably but opportunely.

Nero's biographer Suetonius propounds the thesis that his subject degenerated from the virtues of his ancestors, yet reproduced the vices of each of them as if by inheritance! He gives a lurid picture of the qualities of

Nero's recent forbears, in whom the ancestral violence and pride were sharpened into cruelty and exhibitionism. His grandfather gave beast-baitings within the city as well as in the Circus Maximus and had suffered a reprimand, followed by a legal injunction from Augustus himself, for the cruelty of his gladiatorial shows. His father was said to have killed one of his freedmen for drinking less than he was ordered, and to have run his chariot over a boy deliberately. Less lurid items about these immediate ancestors suggest some of Nero's own predilections: both of these men were skilled and enthusiastic chariot-drivers, both were honoured by cities of the Greek East, and the grandfather produced a farce in which Roman knights and respectable women appeared on the stage.[7]

This Lucius Domitius Ahenobarbus, consul in 16 BC, also upheld the family military tradition, winning triumphal insignia for dramatic successes in Germany. He acquired from Augustus patrician status for his family and prestige for himself, for he was named as executor in the Emperor's will. Nothing comparable is known to the credit of Nero's father Gnaeus. The epithet 'illustrious' applied to him by the contemporary historian Velleius Paterculus is apparently a tribute to his descent alone, like the aristocratic candour ('nobilissima simplicitas') which the same writer attributes to father and son alike.[8] Gnaeus Domitius Ahenobarbus may have come to his consulship of AD 32 late and little is recorded of him after that, besides a reputation for idleness and a belated enthusiasm for declamation.[9] In the last year of Tiberius' reign, he was put on a commission composed of the husbands of Tiberius' granddaughters and charged with dispensing aid to those whose property had been damaged in a fire. Next he is found accused of adultery and treason but saved by the death of the Emperor in March of AD 37.[10] Nine months later, on 15 December AD 37, he acknowledged his son, the only child of his marriage to Agrippina, now in its tenth year.[11]

That Agrippina's pregnancy, following directly on the death of the tyrant, was the result of planning, not coincidence, is suggested by the family tradition of only sons, which had enabled the Domitii to maintain both standing and wealth.[12] Since the Romans did not acknowledge the rights of primogeniture, limitation of family was the only way of maintaining a concentration of property, while the tendency of the imperial system to divert the traditional senatorial sources of wealth (booty, legacies, extortion) into the hands of the Princeps aggravated the difficulties for the great families. The family resources that had enabled Nero's great-great-grandfather to raise troops in the Civil War for Pompey's cause, by promising them land from his own estates, were still renowned in the time of Nero's father. For, when he was involved in a legal dispute over money with his sister Domitia, her husband remarked in the course of pleading her case, 'There is nothing you both need less than what you are competing for'.[13] Sister and brother both had a reputation for meanness combined with contentiousness. He is said to have cheated bankers and withheld prize money, until moved by the ridicule of his sister Domitia. She is reported to have complained when a certain Junius Bassus accused her of selling her old shoes; his riposte was, 'I never said that she sold old ones: I said that she bought them'.[14]

The family preserved both their line and their wealth: it was their intimate link with the imperial house that was to bring them first the purple, and then extinction. Nero was to retain a close feeling of identification with his paternal clan after his adoption by Claudius had transferred him to the Claudian *gens*. His arranging for a statue to be voted in his father's honour on his accession can, of course, be explained as a mere gesture of *pietas*, a quality that was much admired by the Roman governing class. The same might be said of the sacrifices made, at Nero's request, by the Arval Priests each year on 11th December, his father's birthday, before the Domus Domitiana.[15] But, as late as AD 63, when Nero had ceased to care about respect for traditional sentiment, he chose to mark the birth of his daughter Claudia by circus games at Antium, in honour of the Claudian and Domitian *gentes*.[16] Even after 64 it is possible to discern another tribute to his paternal ancestry in the beard that figures on some of his coin portraits (figs. 18, 22). Nero had shaved his first beard in 59, and it is unlikely that he actually sported one at this date, for some of his coins of the same period omit the beard, as do sculptured representations. Moreover, the beard still appears on coins of 66/7, when one ancient writer specifically attests that he was clean-shaven. In these last years Nero was prone to embellish his coin portrait with various attributes. Perhaps he took the opportunity to recall the family name, similarly commemorated earlier by his great-grandfather, the Antonian admiral, who adorned his coins with a bearded ancestor.[17]

Even in the last year of Nero's life, when the leader of the rebellion against his rule referred to him in a public statement as 'Ahenobarbus', Nero defiantly declared that he would reject his adoptive name and resume that of his own family. The Emperor's attitude may explain why Lucan, in his epic poem on the Civil War, singled out, for lengthy celebration, the heroism of Lucius Domitius Ahenobarbus, Nero's Pompeian ancestor.[18] Yet it was the abusive use of his original name to cast doubt on his dynastic claim to the throne that continued after Nero's death. In fact, his own career led to his being judged unworthy of the Domitii by Juvenal, and, by a bitter irony, cast disgrace on the ancestor Lucan had honoured.[19]

In understanding Nero's personality, it is important to remember that he felt respect for his father's family, and that Romans traditionally regarded it as a duty to live up to the achievements of their ancestors. It is likely that Nero felt the burden of expectation imposed by the military glory of the Domitii, a burden which his accession to the purple will have increased. On the other hand, family tradition may have countered any inhibitions he was encouraged to feel about indulging his passion for chariots and the theatre.

Nero also retained a feeling of loyalty towards his birthplace. Antium was a seaside resort near Rome, frequented by wealthy functionaries and politicians, and described by Cicero as 'the quietest, coolest, pleasantest place in the world'. Nero's imperial predecessors had escaped there for short holidays from the pressures of the capital. He himself was to establish there a colony of privileged veterans and construct a harbour at great expense, as well as a magnificent seaside villa where his only child was born.[20] His uncle Gaius, who had also been born at Antium and had a special fondness for the place, may have been there at Nero's birth. For, at the purification ceremony, some nine days later, he is said to have suggested a name for the infant – that of his own uncle Claudius, an unprepossessing pedant and the laughing-stock of the family. This joke was later regarded as a bad omen attending the birth. Another was the father's reply to a well-wisher, 'Nothing born of myself and Agrippina can be other than odious and a public disaster'.[21]

The Ambitions of Agrippina

The birth itself was difficult, involving a breach delivery, not an uncommon occurrence in Agrippina's family. The Elder Pliny uncovered that nugget of information in the memoirs of Agrippina herself, probably composed in the latter part of Claudius' reign when she was contriving her son's succession. They may have contained the story reported by Suetonius that Nero was touched by the rays of the sun at the moment of birth, as well as the tale that serpents guarded him in infancy and saved him from assassins in the pay of Claudius' first wife Messallina. Whether or not Pliny also found there the detail that Agrippina had two canine teeth on the right side of her upper jaw, a feature which portended fortune's favour, it is clear that this work of propaganda expressed Agrippina's traits of consuming ambition and paranoid suspicion.[22] Years later the story was told that she consulted an astrologer about Nero's future and, when told that he would rule and kill his mother, replied 'Let him kill as long as he rules'.[23]

Agrippina's childhood and youth would have warped the most sanguine nature, as her prospects fluctuated between extremes. She had started life in happy circumstances as the eldest of three daughters born to Augustus' granddaughter Agrippina by her marriage to Germanicus. Her father was the son of Augustus' stepson Drusus and the adopted son of Tiberius, who had been Princeps for just over a year when she was born in November of AD 15. The birth occurred on 6 November, at Oppidum Ubiorum, the modern Cologne, for in these years her mother was travelling with Germanicus, first when he went to command the German armies, later on his mission to the East. One of Agrippina's earliest memories may have been her journey to Tarracina at the age of four: in the dead of winter, she was taken to meet her mother returning from Syria with the ashes of her father. The bereaved widow, accompanied on her return by the boy Gaius and the infant Livilla, moved all to tears by her look of exhaustion, grief and repressed bitterness. There followed all the horrors of a murder trial with the accused ending his own life, but not ending the rumours that Tiberius himself was ultimately responsible for poisoning Germanicus. The Emperor and his mother were conspicuous by their absence at the interment of his ashes in the tomb of Augustus.[24]

With the death of Germanicus in AD 19, the struggle for the succession had begun. Adoption had made him Tiberius' eldest son, and Augustus made his wishes clear when he arranged the adoption in AD 4 and, soon after, the marriage to his own granddaughter. But now, was Tiberius' natural son Drusus (and ultimately his descendants) to succeed when the ageing Emperor died, or the sons of the deceased Germanicus? In the next three years Drusus, by first holding the consulship with his father and then receiving the tribunician power, seemed clearly marked out as successor.[25] When he died in the autumn of 23 only one of his twin sons, born in AD 19, survived to remain a focus of plotting and suspicion. By then, the two eldest sons of Germanicus had come of age and received the right to stand for office before the legal age, an exemption by now traditional for princes of the ruling house.

Tiberius remained paralysed, caught between his almost superstitious reverence for Augustus' policies and his natural ambitions for the descendants of his blood. While his son Drusus lived, his fondness for Germanicus' sons seemed to point to adoption as the natural solution, a repetition of Augustus' arrangement for Tiberius and Germanicus.[26] But no adoption actually took place, and, after the death of Drusus, Tiberius presented Germanicus' adult sons to the Senate, asking that the Fathers themselves should look after them and remarking that their birth made their circumstances vital to the state. They seemed the obvious key to the succession, but in the very next year Tiberius warned the Senate against voting excessive honours to the young men.[27]

The family of Germanicus had in fact a powerful enemy in the Prefect of the Praetorian Guard, Lucius Aelius Sejanus. The death of Drusus had set him thinking. His hopes of continued, indeed increased, power and influence in the future lay with a youthful Princeps. Tiberius Gemellus, the surviving twin son of Drusus, would be a minor for another decade and Tiberius might well die soon, as he was now sixty-five years old and showed little sign of the will to live.[28] Tiberius took refuge, as so often, in delay. He avoided taking steps that would encourage or discourage either of the two ambitious mothers. In 25 Sejanus was refused permission to marry the widow Livia Julia, and, when, a year later, the widow Agrippina asked the Emperor to provide her with a husband, Tiberius walked away without a word.[29] Soon he turned his back on Rome itself, going first to Campania and finally, in 27, to Capri. There he continued to ignore the fact that Germanicus' third son, Gaius, was now old enough to assume the *toga virilis* until AD 31, when the boy was eighteen years old and a timely warning from Germanicus' mother Antonia persuaded him that the boy's life was in danger from Sejanus.[30] A dramatic incident in which Sejanus saved the

Emperor's life during a landslip in Campania had confirmed Tiberius' firm belief that his Prefect's motive was loyalty to himself.[31] By the time his eyes were finally opened in 31, the widow of Germanicus and her eldest son had been exiled to two bleak islands, while her second son, who had helped to incriminate them, was himself imprisoned in the palace in Rome.

For all his weaknesses, Tiberius still had enough grasp of affairs to see that he could not destroy all of Augustus' male descendants. The youngest son Gaius was summoned to Capri in 31, and the fall of Sejanus followed soon after, but his mother had been so brutally treated that Tiberius could not hope for peace if she returned.[32] Her eldest son had died shortly before Sejanus; the second was feared because of his vindictive disposition. Mother and son were left to starve in their separate places of imprisonment. The Elder Agrippina died fittingly on 18 October 33, the second anniversary of the death of Sejanus. Tiberius made the point when he reported to the Senate that she had taken her own life because of grief at the death of a lover.[33] That was the final humiliation for a woman known for her loyalty to her husband, alive and dead.

Tacitus describes the Elder Agrippina as 'intolerant of an equal, greedy for dominance, a woman who had abandoned the defects of women for the concerns of men'.[34] His account, even when read with caution, reveals her as ambitious and strong-minded, proud of her descent from Augustus and scornful of Tiberius. She clearly had the pride of her father Agrippa who scorned to use his family name Vipsanius because it revealed his humble origins.[35] She must have been the single most important influence on her daughter and namesake who was later to include in her memoirs a lurid account of what the granddaughter of Augustus had suffered at the hands of his successor. In 28, the year before the mother was finally denounced for arrogance in one of Tiberius' sinister letters from Capri, the Emperor himself had come to Campania with Sejanus and personally consigned the daughter in marriage to Cn. Domitius Ahenobarbus. The younger Agrippina was then thirteen years old.[36]

Right up to the end, Tiberius did not resolve his doubts about the succession.[37] In his will he named his grandson Tiberius Gemellus and Germanicus' son Gaius as his joint heirs. This was later taken as a declaration of his intention that they would rule jointly, but the fact that Tiberius neglected to introduce his grandson to public life, though he was seventeen when Tiberius died, suggests that he was simply avoiding making a decision.[38] The same paralysis of will is reflected in the story that he foretold Gaius' murder of his rival but felt helpless to prevent it.[39]

When Tiberius died and Gaius succeeded in March of 37, Agrippina's fortunes underwent a complete change. Gaius was well aware that the popularity he enjoyed rested on the reputation of his father Germanicus and on sympathy for the wrongs his family had suffered at the hands of Tiberius. General enthusiasm for his succession and the active co-operation of Sejanus' successor as Praetorian Prefect, Naevius Sutorius Macro, enabled

Gaius to have Tiberius' will set aside by the Senate. Though Gaius duly honoured Tiberius and publicly buried documents relating to the prosecution of his mother and brothers, he spared no energy in honouring his own family. Even in the funeral oration he delivered for Tiberius, he spoke at length about his descent from Augustus and the virtues of his father Germanicus.[40] He made a personal voyage to Pandateria and Pontia to bring the ashes of his mother and his brother Nero back to Rome, and then marched in a triumphal procession to deposit them in the mausoleum of Augustus.[41] His three sisters were exalted above the position previously accorded imperial princesses. Not only were they made honorary Vestal Virgins and permitted to watch the circus games from the imperial seats, but they were represented as allegorical figures on coins and included in the preambles to senatorial proposals, the annual vows for the Emperor's safety, and both the oath of allegiance to him and the annual oath to his *acta*. Inclusion in these oaths is the most significant honour, for it openly recognized them as part of a 'royal family'.[42]

It was in this heady atmosphere of the first year of the new reign that Agrippina gave birth to her son. The odds against his ever becoming ruler of Rome were formidable, for Gaius was young, and he had respected Tiberius' wishes in a modified way by adopting Tiberius Gemellus. For two years of the new reign the sun shone, and then history seemed to repeat itself as Gaius turned on his own family. In the autumn of 39 Agrippina found herself in exile on the island of Pontia from which her brother's ashes had recently been rescued. That sudden felicity and power after so much uncertainty and repression would prove too much for the young Princeps had no doubt been surmised by men of sense.[43] A mysterious illness late in 37 and the death of his favourite sister Drusilla in June of the next year, had led to increasingly erratic behaviour. Gaius had begun to experience the fears as well as the delights of absolute rule, and those nearest to him suffered first. Tiberius Gemellus, Macro, and his father-in-law M. Junius Silanus were all forced to commit suicide. Then in 39 Gaius turned his suspicions on the Senate and the high command. He revived the dreaded *maiestas* charge and he decided that the governor of Upper Germany was a conspirator with confederates in the imperial house. During his illness he had made Drusilla his heir, and on the husband he had found for her, M. Aemilius Lepidus, a great-grandson of Augustus, he had bestowed privileges that hinted of the succession. Now Drusilla was dead and the Emperor decided that this man and his two surviving sisters, Agrippina and Livilla, were linked in an adulterous confederacy to destroy him.

In September of 39 Gaius marched to Germany taking his sisters and Lepidus with him. By 28 October Agrippina was approaching Rome, forced to carry the ashes of her alleged paramour in a cruel parody of her mother's tragic return from the East twenty years before.[44] Gaius justified his condemnation of his sisters by producing letters in their hands that were supposed to prove adultery and treason. Other lovers of Agrippina, besides

Lepidus, were named, including Ofonius Tigellinus who later became Nero's Praetorian Prefect. It is impossible to know how much truth lay behind these charges, for adultery with women of the imperial house was regularly alleged where political ambitions were suspected. But some weight should perhaps be given to Tacitus' belief that Agrippina had compromised herself with Lepidus out of ambition, because he is so sceptical of allegations of adultery concerning her mother.[45] Her husband, it must be remembered, was a virtual invalid. Even if we suppose her too hard-headed for emotional indulgence, practical considerations might tempt her to a liaison with the heir apparent: there was the future of her son to be secured.

With the exposure (or fabrication) of the plot, Agrippina's hopes were blasted. Her property was confiscated and she herself sent into exile. Worse still, Gaius had just married his third wife, Milonia Caesonia, who had already proved her capacity for providing an heir by becoming pregnant. The child, born a month after the marriage, was a girl, but Gaius no doubt hoped that a son would follow.[46]

Agrippina's husband Domitius is attested at the meeting of the Arval Brothers a day or two before the sacrifices 'because of the detection of the wicked conspiracy of Cn. Lentulus Gaetulicus'. Unfortunately, the list of members attending that dramatic session is lost, but his absence from the meeting of 1 June 40 suggests that he left Rome with his son on the news of his wife's disgrace. Towards the end of the year he died of dropsy at Pyrgi in Etruria.[47] The young Domitius, now aged three, was sent to his aunt, Domitia Lepida. At her house the boy was 'brought up in actual want, under two tutors, a dancer and a barber'. Behind this typical Suetonian exaggeration lies the fact that, though he had been left heir to one-third of his father's estate, his uncle Gaius saw no reason to be content with the remainder and took the boy's share as well.[48] The period of time involved, however, was brief, probably only a few months, for on 24 January in 41 Gaius was assassinated, and the new Emperor, young Domitius' great-uncle Claudius, restored the boy's property to him and recalled his mother and her sister Livilla from exile.[49]

While her nephew had been living with her, Domitia Lepida had become a person of some consequence, for her daughter Valeria Messallina was the wife of the new Emperor. On 12 February 41 she bore Claudius a son, soon to be known by the cognomen Britannicus in honour of Claudius' conquest of Britain. Agrippina and her sister had recovered their property through Claudius' generosity, and Livilla's marriage, which must have been dissolved on her conviction for adultery, seems to have been declared valid again.[50] Agrippina, remembering the weakness of her mother's position after the death of Germanicus, set out to find a husband. She first set her sights on Servius Sulpicius Galba, who was later to succeed her son as Princeps. Well-born with a distinguished military career, Galba was also exceedingly rich and may have just received from Claudius a large bequest from Livia Augusta, which had been withheld by Tiberius.[51] Rumour had it that Galba's mother-in-law reproached the princess for unseemly flirtation. In any case, Galba escaped her allurements, continued to serve Claudius with honour in Britain and Africa, and lived quietly as a widower until, on Agrippina's death, Nero appointed him governor of Hither Spain, which became the base for his rise to power.

Agrippina now turned her attentions to C. Sallustius Passienus Crispus, heir to the fortune of Augustus' confidant, Sallustius Crispus. His capital is estimated by Suetonius at 200 million HS, a large fortune, though only half the amount traditionally credited to Claudius' outrageous freedmen.[52] The only obstacle to the plan was that Passienus Crispus was already married – to Agrippina's sister-in-law Domitia. He had defended his wife in her suit against her brother, but he was now willing to desert her for Domitius' widow. The marriage was fortunate for Agrippina. Passienus was a man of influence, who became consul for the second time in 44. He then died conveniently in, or before, the latter part of 47. In the very next year Claudius himself became a widower. Naturally, the fact that Passienus had named Agrippina and her son as heirs and then died opportunely led some to ignore this time interval and to suggest that Agrippina had aided nature with a little poison.[53]

In the very year of her return, Agrippina had seen her sister Livilla again sent into exile for adultery. The enemy now was Claudius' young wife Valeria Messallina who feared the influence of this beautiful young descendant of Augustus.[54] For Agrippina played up to her uncle and succeeded in keeping his favour. She may have had enough influence with him already in 41 to have persuaded him to ask the Senate for a modification of their original capital sentence in the case of Livilla's alleged lover, the senator and philosopher Lucius Annaeus Seneca.[55] Messallina's jealous hostility she parried by a work of propaganda, the memoirs we have already mentioned. She had the skin of one of the serpents that were supposed to have saved her son from Messallina's agents encased in a gold bracelet which he wore for all to see. And in 47, at the great Secular Games, when the offspring of the nobility rode horseback in the Game of Troy, 'the shouting of the populace showed how much sympathy they felt for the grandson of Germanicus and for his daughter'.[56]

Messallina was no match for her rival. She was somewhat younger than Agrippina, and, like her, had lost her father in youth.[57] Claudius, thirty years her senior, was physically repulsive and unpredictable in his behaviour. On his accession they had been married for two years, and Messallina, aged about twenty, was the mother of his daughter Octavia and, soon, of his son and heir. But Claudius had already divorced two wives who had borne him children, one on trivial grounds, and both had remained on friendly terms with him.[58] They were also possible rivals should Claudius tire of Messallina, while the daughter of Germanicus presented another temptation to her susceptible husband. The popularity of Agrippina's son was rightly seen by Messallina as a threat to Britannicus, but Claudius refused to be alarmed. In 47 she became involved in a scandalous affair with one of the consuls-elect, the ambitious and disaffected C. Silius.[59] While Claudius was fussing over his new harbour at Ostia, she went through a marriage ceremony with Silius in Rome, a prelude to the planned murder of Claudius and the adoption of her son Britannicus.[60] Claudius was awakened from his oblivion by the freedman Narcissus, Silius was condemned, and Messallina took her own life.[61]

Early in 49 Agrippina was married to Claudius, a senatorial decree being needed to legalise the union of uncle and niece, previously considered incestuous. The atmosphere of foreboding was intensified on the day of the wedding when a young descendant of Augustus took his life. Lucius Junius Silanus had been removed from the Senate and forced to resign his praetorship at the end of 48 by the censor Lucius Vitellius, one of Agrippina's new allies. The real objection to him lay in the fact that he had been betrothed to Claudius' daughter Octavia and was thus an obstacle in the path of Agrippina's ambitions for her son. That obstacle removed, Lucius Domitius was now betrothed to his cousin Octavia. As with the Emperor's marriage, Lucius Vitellius now secured a senatorial decree urging this course on the Emperor.[62]

Claudius was now approaching the age of 60. The freedman Pallas argued that the adoption of Domitius would strengthen the imperial house, whose future at present depended on Britannicus, a mere boy. Claudius consented and astonished the Senate by justifying a course of action that would effectively deprive his own son, younger than Domitius by three years, of the imperial throne. On 25 February 50 Domitius became, by law of the Roman People, Tiberius Claudius Nero Caesar or, as he is sometimes called, Nero Claudius Caesar Drusus Germanicus.[63] His triumph over Britannicus was publicly demonstrated in the next year when Nero was allowed to assume the *toga virilis* at the age of thirteen, a year before the normal minimum age. Distributions of money were given in his name to the people and soldiers, and his entry into public life given substance by his election to the consulship on 4 March 51. He was not to enter office for six years, when he would be nineteen. In this pre-election, as in his exemption from the lower magistracies and the grant of the title *princeps iuventutis*, Nero was being accorded the same privileges as Augustus' grandsons Gaius and Lucius had received. In addition, the Senate granted him proconsular *imperium* outside the city and he was co-opted into the four ancient priesthoods. He led the praetorian troops in parade and, at the games given in his honour, the contrast between Britannicus in his boy's toga and Nero, wearing the triumphal toga assumed by the Princeps on special occasions, made clear who was the heir to the throne.[64]

Nero's portrait now appeared on coins. In the Eastern and Danubian provinces coins celebrated both Britannicus and Nero, and one African colony put Britannicus on the obverse, Nero on the reverse – to show its loyalty to Claudius' natural son, or more probably, because it was out of touch with events in Rome. But from the official Roman coinage Britannicus now disappeared.[65] In 53 Nero married Octavia. Since Nero's adoption had made her his half-sister in the eyes of the law, she now had to be transferred out of her own *gens*, to which her husband now belonged.[66] Agrippina had achieved this dominant position for her son and herself by a web of political alliances. Of Claudius' friends, she had won over, besides the powerful Lucius Vitellius, three times consul and censor with the Emperor, his secretary in charge of accounts (*a rationibus*) M. Antonius Pallas and his doctor C. Stertinius Xenophon.[67] In addition, she secured the dismissal of centurions and tribunes of the Praetorian Guard who were thought to favour Britannicus, and in 51 she persuaded Claudius to replace the two Prefects whose preferences she suspected by one commander who knew well to whom he owed his promotion.[68] Sextus Afranius Burrus was to remain one of her key supporters when the transfer of imperial power took place.

The effect on the young Nero of the tense and sinister atmosphere in which he grew up can only be divined in part. Though the period of separation from his mother was short in the event, the circumstances of her absence and uncertainty about its duration must have contributed to that need for constant reassurance and demonstrated affection that he displayed in adulthood. His mother's immense ambition, and her ruthless methods must have made him associate political power with malice, intrigue and distrust. Through her he would have been aware that every advance in his position exposed him further to jealousy and disloyalty.

Yet the official portraiture is bland enough. The earliest identifiable statues of the young Nero probably date from his adoption by Claudius, for they show him still wearing the *bulla*, an amulet worn by free-born boys who had not yet come of age.[69] These statues accord well with Suetonius' description of him as having a handsome rather than a charming face.[70] The features are regular, the brow prominent, the eyes set deep and the ears rather conspicuous; the cheeks and chin appear small in comparison with the upper part of the face (fig. 1). With time the lower part of the face and the neck were to become so heavy as to change the proportions of his countenance entirely and lend it a coarse and vulgar appearance (fig. 3). But in youth the boy must have made an attractive contrast to the elderly spastic Claudius.

Suetonius describes Nero's hair as tawny (*subflavus*), a term too vague to reveal whether or not he had inherited the distinctive bronze-coloured beard of the Domitii Ahenobarbi.[71] In any case, however much he may have adhered, physically and sentimentally, to the tradition of his father's family, the dominant influence on Nero's life was his mother. There is no sign that he ever questioned the plans she laid or the methods she devised.[72] But she was less successful in focussing his affections exclusively on herself.

Despite the feud between his elder aunt and his mother, resulting from the transfer of matrimonial allegiance by Passienus Crispus, Nero seems to have been on good terms with Domitia.[73] Yet when his aunt died in 59 Nero suppressed her will, thus finishing his father's financial feud with her. Naturally, there were rumours of poisoning.[74]

With his younger aunt, Domitia Lepida, Agrippina also quarrelled. Lepida had been a favourite with her husband and continued to indulge the nephew she had looked after as an infant. It may have been on her estates in Calabria that Nero first met Ofonius Tigellinus, an unsavoury companion of his parents in better days who was to become one of his most detested minions in his later years.[75] As Lepida had quarrelled with her daughter Messallina, she did not take the part of her grandson Britannicus in the struggle for the succession, even while Messallina was alive. His aunt thus offered Nero a sweet and peaceful haven from the domineering methods of his mother. It was a pattern that was to be repeated after his accession, when Seneca and Burrus found him easy to manage as long as Agrippina was there to make their yoke seem light. But now, as later, Agrippina could tolerate no rival, and in 53 she persuaded Claudius to convict her sister-in-law on the charges of practising magic and of disturbing the peace by a failure to control her slave herdsmen. To please his mother, Nero gave evidence against his aunt.[76]

The principal scene of intrigue, however, was the palace itself, where Nero lived with his mother, at least from the time of her marriage to Claudius. Every day Claudius dined with his own children and the sons and daughters of the nobility.[77] There Nero may first have formed his friendship with the future Emperor Otho[78] and learned to dislike his future wife Octavia. There Britannicus may have provoked Agrippina's wrath by greeting him as 'Domitius', more than a year after his adoption.[79]

Nero, in fact, was brought up at the centre of real power in the state, for the palace was ceasing to be just a grander version of the house of a great noble. Under Gaius and Claudius court life had developed apace: imperial patronage, even access to the Emperor, lay in the hands of his family favourites and freedmen. Gaius had come to the throne young and without any experience of public life. Claudius, though a mature man on his accession, had spent most of his life in the palace: as the laughing-stock of the imperial family, he had been kept from the public gaze and denied experience of the Senate and of public office until his nephew Gaius had made him his consular colleague in his late forties. It is not surprising that neither of them ever understood the senatorial ethos and that, especially when frightened, they tended to rely not on members of the traditional governing class but on the court figures, particularly women and freedmen, whom they knew best. Nero witnessed such things as the title Augusta being conferred on his mother, a title that no imperial lady had acquired so young, and the Senate forced to vote marks of magisterial rank to imperial freedmen.[80]

Nero had not been exposed to the best models, though he had been spared the gloomy tyranny of Tiberius. His stepfather Passienus Crispus had said of Gaius 'No one ever made a better slave or a worse master', and of Claudius 'I would rather have approval from Augustus, but generosity from Claudius'.[81] Nero was to prove similar to Gaius in temperament and taste, and the Claudian style of government, though at first repudiated under the influence of his first advisers, was eventually to surface again. Meanwhile, Nero profited from the gullibility and undiscerning generosity of Claudius, which his mother exploited to the full.

After Agrippina's return from exile, Nero's education was supervised by two freedmen, Beryllus and Anicetus. He must have had a certain regard for them as, on his accession, one became his secretary for Greek correspondence (ab epistulis Graecis), the other the prefect of the fleet at Misenum.[82] But as her son approached the age of twelve, when the serious study of rhetoric customarily began, Agrippina decided to entrust his training to Lucius Annaeus Seneca, one of the best orators in the time of Gaius and now a celebrated author of Stoic philosophical essays (fig. 4). She prevailed on Claudius to cancel the sentence of banishment and confiscation passed on him in 41 and, in addition, to secure his election to the praetorship for the year 50. Seneca returned, well aware of Agrippina's ambitions for her son, and prepared to teach him practical wisdom as well as eloquence: philosophy was banned from the curriculum by Agrippina.[83] It was rare even for a prince to have a senator as tutor, and Seneca was, in addition, a distinguished literary figure. By contrast, the most loyal of Britannicus' tutors were condemned to exile or death and his education entrusted to minions of Agrippina, who would keep watch on him.[84]

Nero was also given the opportunity of demonstrating his rhetorical education. Two declamations are reported to his credit, and, in 51, he thanked Claudius in the Senate for the honours he had just received.[85] Two years later he addressed that body in Latin on behalf of the colony of Bononia which was in financial straits owing to a serious fire. He also performed in Greek, pleading with equal success in support of various privileges and concessions for the cities of Ilium, Rhodes and Apamea.[86]

Agrippina was near her goal. Nero had made a favourable impression when judging cases as Prefect of Rome while the ordinary magistrates were absent from the city at the Latin festival, and his popularity increased when he gave games in honour of Claudius.[87] But, in February of 54, Britannicus turned thirteen, the age at which Nero had been allowed to assume the toga virilis, and Claudius began talking about his advancement. He made a will, but as Nero later suppressed it, ancient writers were free to conjecture what it said.[88] In the event, Claudius died on 13 October 54 without taking any steps to strengthen Britannicus' position. The official story was that Claudius died of an attack of fever about noon while he was watching some pantomime actors, but the providential timing of his death naturally led to suspicions of poisoning by his wife.[89] Sceptics also claimed, with greater plausibility, that Agrippina concealed the fact of his death until the time was propitious according to astrological calculations, and until the Praetorian Guard could be alerted.[90]

At the right moment, towards midday, Burrus escorted Nero out of the palace and into the praetorian camp. There he was hailed by the Guard as Imperator, and responded with a promise of largesse. The Senate followed suit, voting Nero the necessary tribunician power and proconsular imperium and heaping honours on Agrippina.[91] Nero was now Princeps, but it was not yet clear who would rule.

PART ONE

NERO'S PRINCIPATE

THREE

The New Ruler

Our knowledge of Nero's reign derives principally from three ancient writers, the Roman historian Tacitus, the biographer Suetonius and the Greek historian Cassius Dio. The first two wrote their accounts in the early second century. The third was at work about a hundred years later, but his history is preserved, at this point, only in excerpts compiled in the Byzantine period. All three are agreed that a period of good rule preceded Nero's descent into tyranny. Their accounts are sufficiently independent of each other to show that this historical tradition goes back partly to oral report (in the case of Tacitus and Suetonius), and partly to common sources, namely the writers who first recorded these events under the Flavian Emperors.

The tradition of any early period of excellent government went on to enjoy a long life, as is shown by the way in which two fourth-century historians interpreted a cryptic anecdote about Trajan and his view of Nero. This Optimus Princeps, who reached adolescence while Nero was occupying the throne, was reported to have said that all other *principes* were surpassed by five years of Nero. Whether or not Trajan made such a statement, with its implication that Nero surpassed Augustus; what the statement meant to the original purveyor of the anecdote: these are riddles past solution. It is significant, however, that the two fourth-century writers to whom we owe its preservation assumed that the Quinquennium mentioned was the *first* five years of Nero's reign. Indeed one of them goes on to moralise about the easy corruption of youth, and both remark on the shocking character of the remainder of Nero's life.[1]

Such a universal and enduring tradition of an excellent beginning lends some substance to the proclamations of a Golden Age that we find in the poems of Nero's flatterers and courtiers. A passage from a pastoral poem by Calpurnius Siculus will show the general tone of these effusions:

> Amid untroubled peace, the Golden Age springs to a second birth; at last kindly Themis, throwing off the gathered dust of her mourning, returns to the earth; blissful ages attend the youthful prince ...

The poet goes on to celebrate the peaceful accession of the prince, his exercise of clemency in jurisdiction, the return of the rule of law, and the freedom of the Senate and consuls.[2] These contemporary laudations are too vague to reveal the characteristics of the early years of Nero's Principate, and the two late proponents of the Quinquennium Neronis offer only achievements in foreign policy and public building, most of which belong to a later period of the reign. To make matters worse, our three major authorities are not as agreed on the details as they are on the general idea. They present different views of the agents, the character and the duration of the initial good period of government.

In considering these discrepancies in the principal accounts it is well to start with the question of who was actually responsible for policy in the early years. Suetonius says that after his accession Nero left the direction of all public and private business to his mother. The period of time he has in mind is indicated only by his reference to the funeral and consecration of Claudius, which belong to the late autumn of 54, only a month or so after Nero's accession.[3] In any case, as is natural in a biographer, Suetonius quickly forgets this idea and presents his subject as the source of political activity throughout the rest of his reign. The only exception occurs in chapters 16 and 17 where his customary use of active verbs with the Emperor as subject is abandoned in favour of the impersonal passive voice. What is the significance of this change in style? It is difficult to believe that Suetonius means to credit Nero's mother or his advisers with the measures he here lists. Some of these reforms are known from Tacitus and Dio (who credit most of them to Nero) to have been instituted after Agrippina's death and the influential period of Seneca and Burrus, Nero's chief advisers. In any case, the importance of these two, or indeed of any advisers, is not attested by Suetonius.[4] The most likely explanation is that the biographer was trying to minimise the element of contradiction that these solid and unostentatious reforms, of which he clearly approved, would introduce into his portrait of Nero as a man who lacked any severity or concern with moral standards. The result of the passives is a vagueness of attribution rather than a clear suggestion of alternative authorship.

Cassius Dio has a clearer conception. Agrippina at first controlled Nero's personal life and managed the affairs of state. She did not lose her domestic authority until 55, when Nero embarked on a passionate love affair with an imperial freedwoman called Acte, thus openly insulting his wife Octavia and defying his mother's disapproval.[5] But her control of the business of government ceased at the end of 54, and in a most dramatic way. Some ambassadors from Armenia were brought before the Emperor, and Agrippina entered the Senate chamber and moved to join Nero on his dais. This was to claim a position visibly greater than that she had enjoyed under Claudius, when she had sat on a separate dais near the Emperor's at public spectacles and had once received obeisance from a vanquished enemy king. Nero was prompted by Seneca and Burrus to step down immediately and advance to meet her: the apparent gesture of respect averted a political disgrace.[6] In Dio's view, Seneca and Burrus now took over the control of government while Nero continued to indulge his pleasures without much interference from his advisers.[7]

Tacitus has a more sophisticated version than Suetonius or Dio. He believed that, on Nero's accession, Agrippina was able to order the imperial procurators in Asia to poison the proconsul of that province and to force Claudius' influential secretary Narcissus, to suicide. But Narcissus had already been incarcerated while Claudius lived and, in Tacitus' view, the imperial minions would assume, until the situation was clarified, that Agrippina acted with the knowledge and acquiescence of the Princeps, which in fact was missing.[8] While agreeing with Dio that Agrippina's personal dominance over her son only deteriorated when Nero began his liaison with Acte, Tacitus clearly mistrusted the apparent signs of her early political control over him. These signs, it must be said, were impressive. The historian himself mentions that Nero, after his salutation by the praetorian cohort stationed at the palace, gave the watchword 'Best of Mothers' (Optima Mater), and that the Senate followed suit by voting her an escort of lictors, as if she were a magistrate, and by making her a priestess of the new cult of Divus Claudius. He also notes that meetings of the Senate in 54 were held in the palace so that she could listen to the proceedings, discreetly hidden behind a curtain. Tacitus probably knew that in the early days Nero often walked beside the litter in which his mother rode. He may well have seen the coins issued in December of 54 on which the heads of Agrippina and Nero were shown facing each other and Agrippina's titles appeared on the obverse, Nero's being relegated to the reverse (fig. 14). Even in 55, when Nero was consul, the coins still featured Agrippina's head on the obverse, though now the two heads were parallel, with Nero's in front and the position of the titles reversed (fig. 15).[9]

Despite the outward signs, Tacitus was sceptical of Agrippina's apparent ascendancy even in the very early days. He prefaces his account of her privileges with the remark, 'In public, however, every honour was lavished upon her'. His reasons for scepticism are not difficult to guess. Tacitus knew that it was the influential Seneca, who had written Nero's funeral eulogy of Claudius, who also composed his opening address to the Senate deprecating the Claudian style of government.[10] Agrippina could not have inspired or even assented to that speech, any more than she liked the abrogation of one of Claudius' measures soon after. The historian several times draws the obvious comparison of Agrippina on the death of Claudius to Livia on the death of Augustus.[11] He clearly felt that, while Tiberius accorded his mother less in the way of outward signs of honour, his almost obsessive adherence to the policy of Augustus, as he understood it, would have consoled her; by contrast, Agrippina had to endure criticism, explicit and implicit, of her husband's method of government. Tacitus also inferred from Nero's dismissal, early in 55, of M. Antonius Pallas from the post of chief accountant (a rationibus) that Nero must have resented for some time the arrogance of this Claudian freedman who had long been a supporter of Agrippina.[12]

That Tacitus was right about Agrippina's insecure grip on power from the start is suggested by Seneca's *Divi Claudii Apocolocyntosis* (literally, *The Pumpkinification of the Divine Claudius*), a satire on Claudius' apotheosis, probably composed for the entertainment of the court on the holiday of the Saturnalia in December 54. The criticisms of Claudius' government offered there are a comic version of the promises in Nero's address to the Senate, as reported by Tacitus. For him, as for Dio, Seneca and Burrus acquired the influence Agrippina had lost, but the two authors differ in their view of the method used by these advisers to manage Nero. According to Tacitus they indulged Nero's desires up to a point, not in order to distract him from government but in order to counter the baneful influence of Agrippina. Accordingly, Tacitus shows them conniving in Nero's affair with Acte but has Nero himself defy Agrippina by dismissing Pallas. He implies that the method used by Seneca and Burrus was to let Nero see how much admiration he could win by showing tact and clemency to the Senate, and generosity to men of ability.[13] Tacitus' portrayal of Nero's activities in the *Annals* contrasts strongly with the picture of his predecessor Claudius, who is shown as a ruler so amenable to manipulation that he was only formally responsible for many of his political decisions.

This conflict in our sources over Nero's role is a matter of grave concern for our study of the interaction of Nero's personal defects with the system of the Augustan Principate. For it is obviously imperative for us to know whether or not Nero actually grappled with the system at all.

Shall we believe with Dio that Nero left the decisions to others, or with Suetonius that he was in full control, or with Tacitus that he was active under guidance? Tacitus had read authors who could have and probably did reveal the true situation in their histories of the period. He mentions Cluvius Rufus, who in Nero's reign was a senior consular with access to the palace, Pliny the Elder, a high-placed equestrian with court connections, and Fabius Rusticus, who was a protégé of Seneca. Yet at least some of these Flavian sources were also used by Cassius Dio and Suetonius, and, even if there are some indications that they handled them more carelessly and less critically, we cannot be sure that it is Tacitus who always conveyed what they said more accurately.[14] For it is likely that, as we surmised for his view of Agrippina's position, he used his considerable intelligence and imagination to interpret what he read.

Fortunately there is some evidence of an indirect kind that can be brought to bear on the question of Nero's role in government. First, it is worth considering the implications of Nero's cultural pursuits and his attempts to influence the art and sport of his time. Nero's tastes had been firm and individual from the very start of his education. In rhetoric, the staple ingredient of training for public life, he had little interest, though he was competent enough, as is shown by his ventures as an orator during the reign of Claudius. Tacitus notes with censure that the crucial political speeches of his early years as Princeps were written by Seneca, but it was probably the necessary experience and delicacy that Nero felt he lacked, rather than the basic skills of composition. Suetonius mentions that he declaimed in public after his accession, and we have, preserved on an inscription, his famous speech proclaiming the freedom of Greece. This oration was delivered in Greek in AD 67, two years after Seneca's death, and was probably composed by the Emperor himself. The speech is perfectly competent, even elegant at times, if idiosyncratic and somewhat wanting in tact.[15] Similarly, Nero is likely to have composed the oration he delivered at the funeral of his wife in 65 as well as his last political speech – an appeal to the people, presumably in Latin, written just before he fled Rome. It was never delivered but was found in his writing case after his death.[16]

Yet Nero's energies went mainly into the study of poetry, music (singing and playing the cithara), painting, sculpture and chariot-racing. For the last he was content to be a fan until the death of his domineering mother in 59 made him less willing to heed his advisers.[17] But Suetonius makes it clear that Nero received formal instruction in the other pursuits, all, except for painting and sculpture, traditional components of the liberal education designed by the Greeks and adopted with reservations by the Romans.[18] His love for music must have been particularly pronounced, to judge from the fact that Seneca chose to flatter him as the equal of Apollo the singer and lyre player soon after his accession.[19]

After becoming Princeps, Nero applied himself to these pursuits with even greater zeal. He held working dinners for poets: the malicious said his aim was to appropriate their lines. He took instruction from the greatest *citharoedi* of his day, Terpnus and Menecrates.[20] After Agrippina's death in 59 he even turned his attention to philosophy. Tacitus draws a cruel picture of the high-minded purveyors of morality disputing points at the Emperor's sumptuous board.[21] He even took up Greek athletics and dancing.[22]

Towards all the aesthetic and intellectual skills they learned from the Greeks the Romans had complex attitudes. While admitting that 'captured Greece took the victor captive', the Romans knew that devotion to these arts had not prevented the political downfall of Greece and suspected that they may have even contributed to it. They tended, often in the same breath, to assert the greater value of their own practical talents in war and government and then to claim equality in the acquired artistic and intellectual skills. For the Roman of high social status such pursuits were acceptable as training for public life, as relaxation after work in the Senate and law courts, and as solace when political activity was impossible. But the less relevance the discipline had to political life, the less it was deemed to deserve attention, and the more its practice was left to foreigners and slaves, which brought it into further social disrepute. Cornelius Nepos, writing in the reign of Augustus, noted that a Roman reader would feel that it detracted from the dignity of great men to record who taught them music and to praise them for dancing and playing instruments well – activities comparable with those other despised Greek habits of incest and pederasty.[23]

It is a measure of Nero's determination that he defied his mother and his mentors in following his enthusiasms, particularly his passion for music. However much Rome accepted music as a standard part of education,[24] there was no tolerance for a noble who was not content to be an amateur. Sallust had said of one of the Republican ladies, 'She played and danced more elegantly than was necessary for a respectable woman'. Nero showed no restraint in his zeal to achieve perfection. For the sake of his voice he would lie down with lead weights on top of him in order to strengthen his diaphragm; he subjected himself to purges and extreme dietary restrictions. The Elder Pliny notes that on certain fixed days of every month Nero lived exclusively on a diet of chives preserved in oil. He was prepared to acquire the habits of a professional charioteer, learning to drink a concoction of dried boar's dung in water, which was supposed to have a healing effect on the muscles.[25]

Nero not only aimed at a professional standard: he wished to race chariots in the circus, wrestle in the stadium, or sing and dance on the stage. As Nepos remarks, the Greeks regarded it as praiseworthy to win in the Olympic games or appear on stage publicly, 'but for us these activities are partly notorious, partly disgraceful and hostile to morality'. Indeed there was a tradition that the immediate cause of the assassination of Nero's uncle Gaius had been his proclamation of an all night vigil during which, it was rumoured, he intended to appear on stage for the first time.[26]

The Romans were here displaying their extraordinary talent for maintaining attitudes of disapproval towards practices that had long since become common. For Nero's exhibitionism was not a new or an isolated phenomenon in the Roman upper classes. From at least the time of Caesar the Dictator young nobles and knights had appeared at spectacles racing chariots, acting, and performing as gladiators.[27] Augustan legislation prohibited appearances in the arena and on stage by senators and knights, but the copious testimony to evasion of the ban, its renewal by Tiberius and its subsequent neglect, show that this measure, like Augustus' legislation on luxury, adultery and childlessness, had little chance of prevailing against fashion.[28] Its omission from the ban shows that chariot-racing was regarded as less disgraceful than acting or fighting as a gladiator: racing a chariot seemed to have some connection with aristocratic military prowess.[29] On the other hand, though gladiatorial contests might also seem to offer training for war and had long been traditional at Rome, it was thought worse for a person of status to appear in the arena than to appear on the stage, perhaps because assignment to the arena was a regular punishment for criminal slaves.[30]

Nero's mother and his advisers shared the conservative viewpoint of Augustus, Tiberius and Gaius' assassins, however liberal other members of Roman society may have become. At first Nero could not resist their combined, or rather coincident, pressure. But after his mother's death in 59 Seneca and Burrus could only effect compromises. In accordance with the order of prejudice that obtained, the Princeps was first allowed to drive chariots in a private circus, though an audience soon sought him out.[31] Then he sang and performed on the cithara at private games which had a link with Roman tradition in that they were intended to celebrate the shaving of his first beard, an important event in the young Roman's life. At these games, called the *Juvenalia*, a gymnastic show and a sacrifice accompanied the shaving of the beard, which was then dedicated in its gold and pearl box in the temple of Jupiter on the Capitoline. But the principal feature of the event was the appearance of the Emperor on stage, carefully tuning his cithara and testing his voice, then performing tragic arias. The praetorian officers in attendance were shocked, while their Prefect Afranius Burrus 'praised as he grieved', in the words of Tacitus.[32]

It must already have been clear that Nero would ultimately insist on performing on the public stage. Indeed by the end of his life he seems to have regarded himself primarily as a professional artist who could make his living by his art if deposed. His famous remark, 'Qualis artifex pereo', 'What an artist dies with me!' shows that he had come to think of himself first and foremost as a master *citharoedus*.[33]

We seem to have travelled far from our original question about Nero's political passivity, yet the evidence for Nero's determination in the arts suggests that he could not have been totally dominated by his advisers in other respects. By analogy with the compromise effected over his racing and theatrical ambitions, which lasted until 65 (when he finally performed in public in Rome), we should expect that his advisers could do no more than guide him in the right direction.

But was Nero interested in government? Perhaps he would have been only too glad to have been spared the duties of his position in order to indulge himself. That is indeed how Dio saw things. To take such a view, however, is to overlook an important aspect of Nero's activities, namely, his determination to enlist others in them. From the first he took the opportunity afforded by the classes that were held in the palace to communicate his enthusiasms to other imperial children and to the favoured offspring of the aristocracy. Suetonius has a charming story about Nero lamenting to his fellow pupils the tragic death of a popular charioteer and turning aside the reprimand of his *paedagogus* by pretending that their talk was of Hector in the *Iliad*.[34] Something more significant was involved when Nero as Princeps encouraged the participation of the upper classes in the performing arts and in public sport.

Our sources allege that the Emperor induced senators and knights to appear in the circus, on stage and in the arena, shortly before or very early in

59.[35] They suggest, and the history of early imperial legislation confirms, that bribery was not always necessary. In view of the Princeps' own eagerness to perform, it would be perverse to imagine that Nero's motive here was to humiliate the upper orders. Tacitus gives as his motive a desire to soften up public opinion for the disgrace of his own appearance. This explanation, and the equally obvious one that he wanted to make his shows as spectacular as possible, fits well with the inclusion of the arena in the initial invitations. For although Nero never aspired to the helmet himself, he was here encouraging a traditional Roman amusement. Yet it is well to bear in mind that Nero, while never completely losing interest in gladiatorial shows, gave very few in comparison with his other spectacles.[36]

In his arrangements for the Juvenalia, another motive seems to be at work, that of re-educating the public. For this festival members of the upper orders were encouraged by the Emperor to attend school and perfect their singing and dancing, and wearing of masks by performers was forbidden.[37] Tacitus makes Nero claim in defence that music was sacred to Apollo, and there seems no reason to doubt that he was already trying to revive the spirit of the ancient Greek games, where the noblest competed and where prowess in music, racing and athletics was highly regarded.[38] In the next year he actually introduced for the first time at Rome a quinquennial contest in the Greek mode called the Neronia. Men of high rank participated in contests of oratory, poetry, singing and playing the lyre. Consulars presided and the Vestal Virgins attended the athletic competitions (limited to professionals), just as the priestesses of Demeter customarily did at Olympia.[39] Nero did not himself perform on this occasion, which in itself suggests that his aim was re-education rather than self-justification. His seriousness of purpose was underlined by the exclusion of professional pantomime dancers from this sacred festival, a move that forfeited, according to Tacitus, the enthusiasm of the plebs.[40]

Nero also set himself to counter the Roman prejudice against Greek athletics, a contempt based on the belief that such exercising in the nude encouraged homosexuality and generally undermined the qualities essential in good soldiers. Thus Lucan makes Caesar say of Pompey's Greek soldiers, 'an army enlisted from the gymnasia, unmanned by practice in wrestling, scarcely able to carry their arms'.[41] In Nero's day professional gymnastic displays were no longer novel, but the introduction of the habits of the gymnasium into the private life of the upper orders was actively opposed not only by philosophers but by traditionalists. Claudius sneeringly described a condemned Senator as 'that wonder of the wrestling floor'.[42] If the strictures of Seneca and the Elder Pliny suggest that Greek athletics became more fashionable under Nero, the Emperor would have been the first to claim the credit. When Nero inherited his aunt Domitia's estates at Ravenna in 59, he proposed to erect a gymnasium there.[43] Then in 61 he dedicated his new public baths in Rome, a complex that included a gymnasium. He marked the occasion by a free distribution of oil to senators and *equites*, who were clearly meant to be attracted to athletics by the free offer.[44]

It is unlikely that Nero would have regarded the education of Roman tastes as wholly separable from his governmental policies. Though such a notion can scarcely be taken as typical of Roman rulers, it is not so far from the ancient conception of the work of government as it is from ours. Not only was the giving of games part of what the Roman people traditionally expected, first from its Republican magistrates, then from its *principes*; not only was less expected of ancient than of modern government in the way of grand policy-making and zealous administration;[45] the ruler was actually expected to exercise a moral influence, particularly by his own example. In urging Nero to practise clemency Seneca had written: 'The gentleness of your spirit will be diffused little by little through the whole body of the empire, and all things will be moulded to your likeness'.[46] Nero himself may well have seen his efforts at aesthetic indoctrination as a vital part of his work as Princeps. Certainly he was determined that his political advisers should be seen to support the Juvenalia. Seneca and Burrus acted as prompters and leaders of applause, and Seneca's brother Junius Gallio introduced Nero's own performances.[47]

Even a consideration of Nero's more personal motive for becoming a virtuoso, namely, his thirst for praise, can provide clues to his relations with his advisers and his attitude to government in the early years of rule. Suetonius states, 'Above all he was obsessed with a desire for popularity and was the rival of anyone who in any way stirred the feelings of the mob'.[48] If Nero craved admiration, a likely place to look for his aims as Emperor is in the praises of his admirers, for they would be concerned to hit the right note. One of the poets who hoped to gain the ear of the Emperor was Calpurnius Siculus, and what he chose to sing was not only praise of the young prince's beauty and talent but the return of legal forms, the freedom of the Senate, and the end of financial oppression.[49] The kind of flattery offered by Seneca is even more significant. The *Apocolocyntosis*, a satirical account of Claudius' deification, was clearly intended to please the young ruler, who enjoyed the satire of personal attack and had himself made Claudius' elevation the object of an imperial witticism. It is no surprise to find in this work of late 54 a comparison of Nero to Apollo in voice and beauty: more striking is the celebration of the return of the rule of law.[50] In fact, Seneca's flattery of Nero is largely indirect, for the attack on the abuses of the Claudian regime matched Nero's accession promises.

These indications that Nero did take an active interest in government on his accession are confirmed by the dry facts of prosopography. One of Nero's playmates in the palace, the future Emperor Otho, was married to a woman of high birth and rare beauty called Poppaea Sabina. The ancient authorities, titillated by the story of her flirtation with Nero, retail different versions of the way it began: did Otho marry her in order to make her available to Nero or did he, like Candaules in Herodotus, boast of his wife's beauty once too often?[51] Nero found himself Otho's rival and resolved the conflict in his own favour by appointing the troublesome husband as governor of Lusitania, though he was only twenty-six and had not yet held the office of praetor which was the normal qualification for the post. Plutarch says that Nero wished to destroy Otho altogether but was persuaded by Seneca to adopt this diplomatic solution. It was a solution he clearly found satisfactory, for Otho was sent out in 58 and was kept in charge of that distant province for the rest of Nero's reign.[52]

Two other appointments seem to be cases of the young Princeps finding jobs for his former tutors. Beryllus, who had been his *paedagogus*, was appointed his Greek secretary (*ab epistulis Graecis*) and was thought by the Syrians to be influential enough to be worth a bribe, for they succeeded in securing through him a benefit for the city of Caesarea: the date of the episode is unfortunately in dispute, but it could fall in late 55.[53] The appointment of another ex-paedagogus as commander of the fleet of Misenum can be securely dated before 59, since it was in that capacity that the freedman Anicetus advised Nero on the construction of a ship in which to drown Agrippina. He must have owed his post to Nero, as another commander is attested as late as 52, and such an established enemy of Agrippina is not likely to have been appointed in the last years of Claudius.[54] Anicetus was later called upon to collaborate in the disgrace of Nero's wife Octavia and then, suffering the common fate of becoming obnoxious to the instigator of his crimes, was sent into comfortable exile in Sardinia. From a psychological point of view it is interesting to observe here the tendency of Nero to remain attached to those who looked after him in early youth, when his mother was in exile or offering him a consuming possessiveness rather than ordinary maternal affection. He similarly retained an attachment for his nurses and for the man who served as his legal guardian after his father's death until he came of age.[55]

The case of Anicetus gives us grounds for surmising that Nero was also personally responsible for the posting to Sardinia of the man involved in his first crime as Princeps. Tacitus names a praetorian tribune Julius Pollio as Nero's agent in the poisoning of Britannicus. An inscription reveals a T. Julius Pollio as praesidial procurator (governor of equestrian rank) of Sardinia, and there is no obstacle to identifying him as the successor to Vipsanius Laenas, condemned for extortion in 56.[56]

Though one cannot prove that the initiative in making these appointments lay with Nero and not with Seneca or Burrus or even (in the case of Beryllus) with Agrippina, the intimate connection of these men with Nero, and his retention in office of at least one of them (Anicetus) into the period when his original mentors were losing influence, makes it perverse to assume his passivity in their original assignments.

Finally, we have some indications of the way in which Nero was actually handled by Seneca and Burrus. Tacitus describes their method as follows:

> In guiding the Emperor's youth with a unanimity rarely found when power is shared, they exercised equal but contrasting influence. Burrus contributed his military experience and severity of character, Seneca his

lessons in eloquence and dignified affability to the joint effort to control the perilous adolescence of the Princeps by measured indulgence, should he refuse real virtue.

Some years before Nero's accession Seneca had written in very similar terms of the middle way that must be used in controlling privileged children prone to anger, 'We must guide the child between the two extremes, using now the curb and now the spur'.[57]

Tacitus' idea that Seneca exploited the moral ascendancy of a former tutor is reflected in the tone Seneca adopts in De Clementia, written in late 55 or 56.[58] He set out ostensibly to hold up to Nero a mirror in which to view his own virtues, particularly clemency, which is celebrated as the quality most appropriate to men, and among men, to rulers. In fact, the work is a closely woven mixture of eulogy and admonition, for, as Pliny was to say to his Emperor Trajan, 'In a eulogy good rulers recognise what they do, bad ones what they ought to do'.[59] Seneca may exaggerate when he praises Nero's total innocence a year after the murder of Britannicus, and he is certainly appealing to his vanity when he tells him that he can surpass Augustus;[60] yet he does not mince words in warning Nero that virtue is not easy to maintain, and it is to his timidity that he appeals when stressing that the only security for a ruler lies in the love of his subjects.[61]

Can we assume that Seneca handled Nero like this from day to day, persuading him to adopt measures, make appointments, decide judicial cases, in accordance with the programme announced in his words to the Senate and with his model of the virtuous ruler? Tacitus says of an earlier speech on clemency that Seneca wrote it to demonstrate the excellence of his teaching or to show off his talent. Perhaps De Clementia is a pretence to convince the public that Seneca was training their ruler to be a philosopher king. Certainly there is a note of self-justification in the treatise, 'I know the Stoic sect has a bad reputation among the ignorant for being too rigid and unlikely to furnish good advice to principes or reges (kings)', though he implies that criticism fastens not on his failure to train and involve Nero in government but on his inculcation of the wrong precepts.[62]

There is no way of proving that Nero and Seneca really maintained the relationship depicted in De Clementia. But two episodes in the 'good period' of the reign lend plausibility to the picture of Nero participating in government business under guidance. A person under tutelage, who is neither by nature nor upbringing a promising student, is apt to make mistakes. In these episodes it is possible that we see the young Nero applying his lessons on the generosity and clemency befitting a ruler with singular ineptitude.

The first concerns finance. Complaints about the methods used by the tax-collectors in exacting harbour dues and other indirect taxes in Italy and the provinces reached the Emperor in the year 58, probably at the theatre or games when it was customary for the mob to enjoy such licence. Nero was moved to make a magnificent gesture: he would abolish all indirect taxes thus conferring the noblest possible benefit on the human race. Tacitus' account strongly suggests that the idea was Nero's own, for the trumpeting of his own generosity is strikingly similar to what he was to say in 67 when cancelling the taxes of the province of Achaea. Like the later gift, which the hard-headed Vespasian had to cancel for good fiscal reasons, this offer was wildly impracticable: the public treasury (*aerarium*) was chronically in the red and dependent on imperial subventions.[63] Rationalising interpretations that credit Nero with a plan for free trade throughout the Empire, or a scheme to increase direct taxation to compensate for the loss of revenue, run directly contrary to Tacitus' account, which is our only source.[64]

Nero's conduct becomes intelligible if we reflect that, although Seneca himself may well have joined the chorus of tactful but firm protest that greeted this particular scheme, it is more than likely that he did in general encourage Nero to be generous. At the beginning of the same year the young Princeps had granted annual subsidies to three impoverished nobles, without scrutinising too closely the habits that had led two of them into embarrassed circumstances. Tacitus found Nero's liberality on this occasion too indiscriminate, but he records no contemporary criticism from his advisers or others. This is not surprising, for Tiberius had roused deep resentment in the Senate by the humiliations he imposed on needy senators who requested subsidies. No doubt the majority of the Senate would feel that Nero had erred on the right side, and Seneca's outspoken comments on Tiberius' methods leave little doubt that here Nero acted with the approval of his adviser. 'I will speak my mind', Seneca writes in *De Beneficiis*. 'It does not befit the Princeps to give *ignominiae causa* (in order to inflict humiliation).'[65]

If Nero's inventiveness in the sphere of financial generosity was misguided, his later creation of opportunities for exercising clemency was immoral and ultimately disastrous. In 62 one of the praetors of the year, an unpopular senator, was accused before the Senate of treason by the son-in-law of Nero's favourite Ofonius Tigellinus, who was now holding the high equestrian post of Prefect of the Watch. Antistius Sosianus was alleged to have recited verses insulting to the Emperor at a party. Though his host denied having heard any such verses, the consul designate proposed the ancient punishment of scourging to death. When Thrasea Paetus, a man of strong principle, spoke against such a cruel sentence and carried the majority with him in his proposal that exile with confiscation of property be imposed as the penalty, the consuls referred the matter to the Emperor. He wrote back in terms that made his resentment clear: the man deserved the harsher punishment; had the Senate decreed what was fair, he would himself have modified its severity. Therefore he would not interfere with their moderation; let them acquit the man if they chose.[66]

Tacitus says that the general belief was that the whole case had been concocted in order to give the Emperor a chance of acquiring glory by vetoing the expected harsh senatorial sentence. The past record of the accuser, the weakness of the case, and the allusion in the Emperor's letter to his thwarted plans for pardon, clearly formed the basis of this inference, which Tacitus seems to have accepted. For he lays stress on each of these indications and on the fact that this was the first treason (*maiestas*) trial of the reign. His judgment has been questioned; but the clues, particularly the last, do strongly favour his conclusion. Since cases traditionally covered by this charge had been dismissed by the consuls earlier in the reign, in accordance with Nero's accession promises, the Emperor must now have changed his policy and encouraged, or at least consented to, the acceptance of the case.[67] As Tacitus reports Nero's letter (perhaps using the *acta senatus* – the official record), it does show that the Emperor was piqued by the Senate's failure to impose a heavy penalty, despite the weakness of the evidence. But might it not be legitimate to conclude that the Emperor simply wanted revenge for insults he was persuaded had been voiced and therefore resented the Senate's failure to exact it in full measure? Then why did he link with his expression of disappointment a reference to the clemency he would have liked to exercise? Tacitus notes later on that when more serious victims were involved Nero made similar statements of his merciful intentions after driving his victims to suicide.[68] Yet here the defendant was still alive and under lenient sentence, so that Nero could not have been trying to counter suspicions of cruelty. Tacitus was therefore entirely reasonable in concluding from the Emperor's letter and the circumstances of the case that Nero was disappointed in the failure of his plan to demonstrate his clemency.

Seneca had taught Nero that clemency could bring him glory, and, in his treatise, he had particularly pointed to its exercise in the sphere of jurisdiction. But he cannot have intended Nero to reintroduce charges for purely verbal treason – charges which he had abjured at the start of his reign and actually prevented during his first years of power – in order to practise the virtue. The case of Antistius Sosianus arose in 62. Though it falls outside the traditional quinquennium of virtue, it is used by Tacitus to open the year that he saw as the turning point of the reign. Its invocation in this attempted demonstration of Nero's participation in government during the good years of his reign leads naturally on to an examination, first of the character of that good period, and then of its length.

FOUR

The Golden Age

Despite their disagreement over the part Nero himself played, the historians Tacitus and Cassius Dio are in accord in maintaining that Seneca and Burrus exercised the dominant influence on government in the initial years of his reign. But they differ in defining the temporal limits of their ascendancy and, more radically, over the character of the government for which they were responsible. According to Dio, Seneca and Burrus made many changes in existing institutions and caused the enactment of new legislation, thereby winning general approval.[1] For Tacitus, the key to the principles of government lay in the speech Nero delivered in the Senate house on his accession, a speech written by Seneca in which the Emperor repudiated certain abuses of the old régime and promised to share his power with the Senate.[2] Suetonius also stresses Nero's accession speech, but he emphasizes, not so much the relations of Princeps and Senate, as the qualities of generosity, clemency and accessibility that affected all classes of society. Unlike our other two authorities, Suetonius, as we have seen, ignores the political role of Seneca and Burrus, though he mentions that both tutor and Prefect ended as Nero victims.[3]

Attractive as Dio's conception appears at first, it is extremely difficult to substantiate. Nowhere in the course of Dio's own account is there any example of such innovation or legislation. It is true that we are dependent for this part of his history on his epitomators, but, even so, it is hard to believe in a deliberate and systematic distortion of his account designed to omit all references of this kind. Tacitus' more detailed narrative does include measures of reform, but the author makes it clear that, in his view, Nero's first years did not owe their golden colour to such enactments. Some he treats with indifference; some he mentions as being more a matter of appearance than of substance. Even those he notes with approval, such as the measures to check misconduct by provincial governors, are not regarded by him as part of a consistent policy; on the contrary, he regards the government as lax in seeing that such abuses were punished.[4] As for the role Dio gives Seneca and Burrus, there is no evidence of their open support for any imperial edict or senatorial decree. Even a decree passed during Seneca's consulship in 56 comes down to us in the name of his colleague, Trebellius

Maximus, being cited consistently by the jurists as the *senatus consultum Trebellianum*.[5] Tacitus' narrative provides just one instance of alleged Senecan influence on a senatorial decision: an old enemy of Seneca is shown blaming him for a measure preventing advocates from receiving gifts. But Tacitus, who makes no mention of Seneca when he earlier records the actual passage of the decree, clearly means us to understand that the allegation, even if true, was of 'behind-the-scenes' influence.[6] And even such indirect influence cannot be taken as Seneca's usual mode of operation, for, as we shall see, there were very special reasons for him to intervene on that occasion.

On the face of it then, Dio's conception seems highly questionable. It may be that he gave his own content to the tradition of a period of good government, for Dio lived in the period of the Severan emperors when basic changes in the imperial system were taking place. His tendency to that kind of anachronism is suggested by a speech he attributes to Augustus' adviser Maecenas containing what appear to be Dio's own detailed proposals, financial, military and judicial.[7]

Tacitus relates how, after the Senate had voted Nero the powers held by his predecessors, Claudius was buried with due ceremony, including a panegyric written by Seneca and delivered by Nero. The period of mourning over, Nero entered the Senate chamber and delivered a political oration. In it he noted the support he had been offered by the Senate and soldiers, mentioned the respectable precedents he hoped to follow (notably that of the first Princeps), and then went on to say that he came to the throne with no factional prejudices and would take no vengeance for past wrongs. The importance of this promise became evident when he began to describe the principles by which he would govern, for he started with a renunciation of the most detested practices of Claudius. Clearly the promise of amnesty, like the deification of his predecessor, were necessary indications that the new Emperor's attack on the practices of the old regime was not to include an attack on those who had supported and profited from that regime. Nero ended his speech with a formula for a division of responsibility between himself and the Senate.[8]

The senators listening to this speech in the autumn of 54 would not have been altogether surprised by it. Most of them would have remembered the message sent by Claudius to the Senate from the praetorian camp, repudiating the harshness of his two predecessors, Tiberius and Gaius, and promising a government that would in name be his, but in reality belong to all. And some of them would have heard Gaius promising to share power with the Senate and denouncing the most offensive acts of Tiberius. They probably remembered too that Gaius and Claudius had claimed Augustus as a model.[9] They responded in kind, tastelessly but conventionally, decreeing that the speech be engraved on a silver tablet and read once a year.[10]

The one unusual thing about the Emperor's speech could not become evident until after its delivery: Nero kept his promises. So Tacitus tells us, going on to state that 'many things were determined by the will of the Senate'.[11] Tacitus' account of what happened in the years immediately following should illuminate what, in his view, the Neronian Senate understood by these promises and what they accepted as fulfilment of them.

The correction of Claudian abuses is easy to document. Tacitus' paraphrase of this part of Nero's speech runs as follows:

> He would not adjudicate all matters and allow a few individuals to wield power, by having accusers and defendants heard privately within the palace; corruption and favouritism would be excluded from his house; the palace and affairs of state would be kept separate.

The first point relates to Claudius' passion for jurisdiction that led him to take cases that would normally have come before other tribunals and to sit among the advisers when one of the ordinary magistrates did try a case. One unfortunate result of Claudius' zeal was that pleaders who had influence with the Emperor could now command large bribes. The first act of the Neronian Senate was to echo Nero's promise to end such improper influence by reviving the Lex Cincia prohibiting forensic orators from accepting money or presents in return for their services.[12]

Nero did, to some extent, cut down his personal jurisdiction. The exuberant Calpurnius Siculus sang of justice returning to the forum and the consul presiding over a tribunal no longer empty.[13] Tacitus provides evidence that more appeals in civil cases now came to the Senate, and that on two occasions, in 58 and 59, quarrels within and between Italian cities were handled by the Senate or its appointed representatives.[14]

When Nero did try cases himself, such as those involving men close to the Emperor, he no doubt avoided the irregularities in procedure for which Claudius had been ridiculed. It is not until the later part of his reign that we find the ancient authorities noting a lack of suitable advisers on Nero's *consilium* and the acceptance of insubstantial evidence of guilt.[15]

Nero introduced some innovations in legal procedure, according to Suetonius, but their date is not given and their significance is hard to assess. Instead of making continuous speeches, both parties to the case presented their arguments point by point,[16] and those sitting with the Emperor as his *consilium* were asked to write down their opinions on the case. Written opinions had been used on occasion in Augustus' time, and Suetonius implies that Nero departed from custom here only in that he did not read out the opinions before the *consilium* and the parties to the case: instead he read them in private and made his own decision.[17] Unfortunately it is not clear to what extent Nero, in giving himself the opportunity to avoid being bound by his *consilium*'s majority view, was violating recognised legal procedure. But, if Nero adopted his innovation early on in his reign, his motive may have been a good one – to ensure himself time for deliberation, so that the final decision was not made while emotions were still running high. Perhaps he also hoped to encourage free expressions of opinion by preserving the secrecy of his advisers' views.[18]

The emphasis in Nero's accession speech on trials within the palace shows his concern with a particularly offensive type of Claudian jurisdiction. Secret trials were not generally characteristic of Nero's predecessor; and trials within the palace were not necessarily resented (even Augustus came in old age to judge cases on a tribunal in the palace).[19] What Nero was forswearing in his speech were the dreaded political trials of prominent men that Tacitus describes as taking place 'behind closed doors (*intra cubiculum*), without access to the Senate'. These were cases in which a charge of treason (*maiestas*) figured and which senators believed should either have been dismissed, or heard in the Senate. The one certain example is the accusation by Suillius Rufus of Decimus Valerius Asiaticus who was charged in the year after his second consulship with adultery and treason. Tricked by his intimates, among them his wife Messallina, Claudius pronounced a sentence of death. Other political cases earlier in the reign may well have followed a similar pattern.[20] One morning in the year after Claudius' accession the ex-consul Appius Junius Silanus found himself sentenced to immediate execution on the evidence of dreams reported by Messallina and the powerful freedman Narcissus.[21] Other victims, whose names were cited (along with that of Asiaticus) in the Neronian trial which finally brought Suillius to justice, may have been dealt with by Claudius in similar secrecy.[22]

In accordance with Nero's promise no *maiestas* charges of this trivial type are reported under Nero until the case of Antistius Sosianus in the year 62, and that was tried before the Senate. Nero's original policy was to discourage such trials altogether, and two cases, involving a charge of support for Britannicus, are expressly reported to have been rejected in Nero's first year, presumably by the consuls in the knowledge that the Emperor would approve. In pursuing this policy Nero and his advisers were drawing the same conclusion from the judicial persecution of Tiberius' last years – 'a virtual epidemic of accusation', as Seneca called it[23] – that had led Gaius and Claudius to abjure *maiestas* charges at the start of their reigns, namely that the evil of such trials lay not so much in the punishment that sometimes resulted from them as in the acceptance of the charges. Such trials licensed slander, treachery and malice on the part of the accusers and encouraged feelings of paranoia on the part of the ruler. Both Gaius and Claudius appear to have gone back on their promise soon after it was made; Nero kept his for nearly eight years.[24]

The second item among Nero's promises was of a more general character: the Emperor's household was to be free from bribery and improper influence; the palace would not meddle in affairs of state. Nero was here alluding to Claudius' susceptibility to pressure from his wives and his freedmen secretaries. It was a theme well exploited in literary satire, first by Seneca, later by Juvenal. In the *Apocolocyntosis* Claudius gives an order, and Seneca comments, 'You would think they were all his freedmen, so little attention did they pay to him', and at the end of the piece Claudius is sentenced to serve a freedman as secretarial assistant concerned with judicial cases (*a cognitionibus*).[25]

The exchange between defendant and Emperor during the trial of Suillius Rufus is particularly revealing testimony to such household domination. Charged with malicious prosecution and judicial murder, Suillius alleged that he had acted under imperial orders. Nero interrupted to say that Claudius' notebooks showed that he had never instigated an accusation, but Suillius now alleged Messallina's orders. This more damning revelation of the methods of the last reign Nero did not contradict, but merely remarked that agents of crime who profited from it deserved punishment.[26]

The influence of Claudius' wives and minions extended to many of the Emperor's activities, not just jurisdiction. Tacitus ridicules their undue importance when he has Claudius call the three freedmen Narcissus, Pallas and Callistus *in consilium* to discuss his remarriage after the death of Messallina. They are asked to give their opinions and reasons formally just as in a proper meeting of the Emperor's friends and advisers (*amici*). Again, Pallas, when finally dismissed from office by Nero, is described by Tacitus as swearing himself out of office like a magistrate. According to Dio, it was Narcissus who harangued the legions on the eve of the invasion of Britain and dispelled their superstitious fears about crossing the channel; according to Suetonius, he was held responsible for Vespasian's appointment as legionary commander. Claudius himself once named Pallas as the author of the senatorial decree he was proposing.[27]

Modern attempts to reconcile the Claudius of the documents with the hen-pecked half-wit portrayed by the ancient authors tend to proceed by accusing the latter of misconstruing what was really the Emperor's organisation of a secretariat and development of a central administration.[28] Yet one cannot explain similar ancient allegations of uxorial influence by postulating the organisation of Claudius' wives into a ministry. Moreover, the instances recorded of the offensive activity of Claudius' freedmen seem to have little to do with their actual posts.

It was this political influence on the Princeps leading to bribery and favouritism that Nero promised to end. Most of the powerful Claudian freedmen had died before their master. On Nero's accession Agrippina drove Narcissus to his death, but there remained Pallas, whose arrogance was particularly offensive. He claimed never to communicate with his own freedmen except by nods, signs or in writing, avoiding personal contact altogether.[29] It is significant that we do not know for certain the name of his immediate successor as *a rationibus*, the important financial post from which Nero dismissed him. Not that the Claudian pattern was completely reversed even in the early years. Pallas still retained his immense wealth until his death in 62, and Doryphorus, who succeeded Callistus as *a libellis* (in charge of petitions), received lavish gifts; Pallas was able to secure his brother's acquittal on a charge of extortion brought by his Jewish subjects, while Beryllus, who looked after Nero's Greek correspondence, was able to secure the interests of his Syrian compatriots.[30] On the whole, however, we hear little of the activities of Nero's freedmen except in crises directly concerning the palace.[31]

The earliest episode noted in our sources as giving offence was the mission of the freedman Polyclitus to Britain in 61, where he was supposed to improve relations between the Emperor's appointed governor and his *procurator* or financial agent and instil tranquillity in the recently defeated British tribes. According to Tacitus, Polyclitus with his large retinue was a burden to the people of Italy and Gaul and a terror to the Roman army in Britain, but the enemy found him ridiculous, 'for they were still used to freedom and unacquainted with the power of ex-slaves'. After the exposure of a conspiracy in 65 Nero conferred military honours, appropriate to the upper orders, on his freedman Epaphroditus, whose arrogance as *a libellis* is vividly described by Epictetus.[32] By the end of the reign Polyclitus, Patrobius, Petinus, Helius, Halotus and Narcissus were hated names of the old régime. Nero's successor, in response to popular demand, led them in chains through the streets of Rome and then had them executed.[33] The degree to which the Emperor came to violate his accession promises is revealed in the words Tacitus uses to condemn the activities of Nero's freedman Crescens after the Emperor's death. Applying the lessons he had learned at that court, Crescens bypassed the authority of the proconsul and, in the civil war of 69, brought the province of Africa over to Otho. Whereas Nero had once pledged that palace and state would be separate, Tacitus remarks of Crescens, 'Such people in evil times make themselves part of the state'.[34]

More difficult to interpret than the specific renunciations of Claudian abuses is the general formula with which Nero closed his accession manifesto. 'Let the Senate keep its ancient functions; let Italy and the public provinces stand at the judgment seat of the consuls; he would look after the armies entrusted to his care.' This statement might seem to imply that the Senate would consider cases concerning Italy and those provinces whose governors it appointed; the Emperor would handle cases from the imperial provinces which were, in fact, the military ones. However, the general disavowal of interference in jurisdiction precedes the statement in Tacitus' version of the speech. Moreover, the historian's comment that the fulfilment of these promises led to the Senate's making important decisions points to a more general division of responsibility. Yet this interpretation too needs refinement, for Tacitus' own account shows that Nero cannot have kept his word if what he promised was some clear division of powers and functions between himself and the Senate.

First, as regards the division of the provinces, the Emperor passed edicts which affected all the provinces, not only the imperial ones.[35] In 57 he forbade provincial governors of all ranks to give gladiatorial games. A year later, after complaints about the farmers of Rome's indirect taxes, Nero issued an edict obliging provincial governors and the urban praetor at Rome to give precedence to all cases against these *publicani*.[36]

When we consider Italy we do find that Italian cities addressed complaints to the Senate. The council and people of Puteoli in 58 aired their grievances in the Curia, and C. Cassius Longinus, a prominent senator with connections in the area, was assigned to settle their quarrel. When he failed, two other senators, the brothers Scribonii, were sent with a praetorian cohort.[37] Then, a year later, a gladiatorial spectacle at Pompeii gave rise to a savage brawl between the townspeople and spectators from the town of Nuceria (fig. 6). The Senate banned games there for ten years and exiled both the ex-senator responsible for the show and those who had initiated the violence.[38] But it is notable that, in the second case, the complaint initially went to the Emperor, and, in the first, the despatch of a praetorian cohort shows that the Emperor was eventually consulted.

As for the cities of the public provinces, Syracuse in Sicily apparently approached the Senate in 58 in order to secure a decree permitting an increase in the number of gladiators that could take part in their shows. By contrast, the first priest of the cult of Nero in the city of Messene in Achaea recorded, on an inscription, that he had approached the new Emperor with requests 'on behalf of Hellas'.[39]

All but the last of these cases in which Nero seems to be crossing the demarcation line drawn in his accession speech, are reported by Tacitus, and reported without a hint of disappointment. Yet in the *Histories* he had noted, when Italian quarrels were heard in the Senate, that this was 'according to ancient custom', and earlier, in the *Annals*, he had called Tiberius' referral of provincial demands to the Senate an 'imitation of the past'.[40] Similarly, he appends no word of praise when he reports other Neronian incidents that might suggest the Senate encroaching on imperial territory. Thus his own narrative suggests that, in 56, an equestrian governor of Sardinia and, in 60, a governor of Mauretania of the same status were charged by their subjects with extortion before the Senate and condemned. Yet by Tacitus' own day trials of such imperial procurators invariably came before the Princeps.[41]

Another area in which demarcation between Senate and Emperor has been traditionally sought was finance. Nero's conduct in this sphere ought to be particularly relevant here, for his predecessor Claudius made changes in the management of the state treasury that have been construed as detrimental to the Senate's interest. The *aerarium* housed in the temple of Saturn was in the Empire, as under the Republic, the state treasury and record office. Augustus had arranged in 28 BC for the junior magistrates who had run the *aerarium* under the Republic to be replaced by more senior men. Instead of two quaestors there were to be two *praefecti*, chosen by the Senate from among those who had already held the praetorship. But evidence of electoral malpractice led him to transfer the treasury five years later to two serving praetors chosen annually from among the serving magistrates by lot.[42] Claudius returned the administration to two quaestors who served for three years but were then advanced immediately to the praetorship, so that they did not lag behind their contemporaries. To some modern scholars this change has appeared sinister: these young men, picked by the Emperor for the job, were, it is said, really imperial officials, through which the independence of the *aerarium* was to be changed to imperial subjection. The ancient authorities detect no great political significance in the change. Tacitus and Dio simply note that dissatisfaction with the conduct of the praetors led Claudius to return to the Republican tradition of quaestorian management.[43] Given that Claudius' antiquarian studies had given him a taste for tradition, the abuses of the praetors in 42 afforded him a welcome opportunity to return the treasury to quaestors in 44.

In any case, the officials concerned would not have been suitable instruments to ensure imperial control of the treasury, for they did not make fiscal policy but dealt with routine matters. The requisite qualities for the task were honesty, accuracy and diligence, and the difficulties of securing men of this type offer a sufficient explanation of the changes made in the method of selection. Tacitus regards administrative concern of this kind as Nero's motive for altering the Claudian arrangement. In 56 Obultronius Sabinus, a quaestor in charge of the *aerarium*, was charged by a tribune of the plebs with undue severity in collecting debts due to the treasury. Nero decided to revert to the Augustan scheme of *praefecti* of praetorian rank, but he retained the Claudian practice of direct imperial appointment and three year tenure of post. This system endured, and the shrewd eye of Tacitus would hardly have failed to observe any permanent change in constitutional balance that resulted from it. His indifference should warn us against seeing such significance in the change.[44]

The Senate and Princeps had always made financial policy jointly and continued to do so. It should occasion no surprise to find that a trial before Nero in 55, in which the accuser was exiled for malicious prosecution, also resulted in the destruction, on imperial orders, of the records of old debts to the treasury which this same man had cruelly exploited for profit.[45] On the other hand Nero's new *praefecti* seem to have lost the powers of jurisdiction their predecessors had enjoyed, for cases were removed from the *aerarium* to the forum and jurisdiction given, at least temporarily, to the praetor and *reciperatores*.[46] It is possible that Nero felt it to be inappropriate for men who were not serving magistrates to sit in judgment. A difficult passage of Suetonius that discusses this transfer of jurisdiction also suggests that appeals on treasury cases were now to go to the Senate.[47]

Coinage appears to give, at first glance, visible and unambiguous evidence of Nero's abdication of authority and the Senate's acquisition of power. Nero's precious metal coinage, for the first ten years of his reign, differs from all other imperial issues of gold and silver in that it carries consistently the formula EX S C (*ex senatus consulto*) meaning 'in conformity with a decree of the Senate' (figs. 13–17, 19). The related formula S C had appeared on the token or *aes* coinage from the time when Augustus began to strike bronze coins in Rome but had not adorned the gold and silver. The obvious explanation for the Neronian aberration is that the imperial Senate had up to now only been responsible for token coinage, but now Nero handed over to their control the minting of gold and silver.

The first doubt about this explanation arises when one looks at what these early Neronian coins depict. Gold and silver coins of 54 honour *divus Claudius* (fig. 13) or represent Agrippina and Nero facing each other with Agrippina's name and titles on the obverse, Nero's being relegated to the reverse (fig. 14). In 55 the busts of Agrippina and Nero again appear on the obverse (fig. 15), but now they are parallel to each other with Nero's head in front and around them his titles and powers. Then, from the end of 55 until 64, we have very austere obverses showing a bare-headed portrait of Nero, and around it 'Nero Caesar Aug(ustus) Imp(erator)', but no reference to his powers. With this new obverse there appears on the reverse, at first, the oak wreath (*corona civica*) that had been voted to Augustus by the Senate in 27 BC, with EX S C in the centre and, around it, Nero's titles (fig. 16). At the end of 60 the oak wreath disappears from the reverse and is replaced by allegorical figures, usually identified as Ceres, Virtus and Roma (figs. 17, 19, 26).[48] The idea of senatorial control of this coinage seems appropriate to the bare-headed *corona civica* coins which appear to advertise the Emperor's Republican spirit and admiration for Augustus, while the allegorical figures could be explained as colourless variations. But it is inconceivable that the Senate should choose to inaugurate this series with coins paying conspicuous honour to the hated Claudius and advertising the ascendancy of Agrippina over her son. Even if the senatorial control was really a sham, one would not expect the Emperor to insist on its being exposed as such immediately.

The authorisation explanation of the EX S C on early Neronian coins was formulated in the context of a general theory that the S C on the imperial token coinage showed senatorial sanction, while the Emperor regularly controlled the precious metal coinage unilaterally. But the general theory has been seriously and successfully challenged.[49] The young magistrates who were in charge of minting bear in their title of *tresviri aere argento auro flando feriundo* the names of all three metals, so that it is hard to believe that they received imperial orders for coins of gold and silver and senatorial orders for the bronze. Then, at Antioch in the imperial province of Syria, *aes* coins were struck with Augustus' head on the obverse and, on the reverse, S C in the oak wreath. Again it is hard to believe that we have an instance of senatorial authorisation, in a distant province under the Emperor's control. Alternative explanations of the S C on token coinage have been suggested, such as that the Senate controlled the state stock of *aes* and had to authorise its withdrawal for minting, while the Emperor controlled the stock of gold and silver. But the presence of s c on the Antiochene *aes* and later on Neronian bronze issued at Lugdunum in Gaul is hard to explain in this way.[50] The most plausible explanation so far suggested is that originally the s c indicated not senatorial sanction of the issue but senatorial conferral of the honours depicted on the coin. It originally appeared with the celebrated *corona civica*, the title of Augustus, and other honours known to have been voted to Augustus by senatorial decree. Thereafter the s c was retained by tradition on the token coinage, even when the types changed.[51]

Such an explanation can be successfully transferred to the Neronian gold and silver. The honours voted to Divus Claudius and the Augustan *corona civica* shown on the reverse of the early Neronian coins with the EX s c fit into the tradition. Even when we reach the allegorical figures, the explanation does not fail, for on those coins the Emperor's titles, his designation as *pater patriae* and *pontifex maximus*, as well as his tribunician power and consulships, continue to appear, as on the *corona civica* type, on the reverse with the EX s c.[52] Nero, then, could in these years have been emphasising the senatorial sanction that underlay these powers. The coins represent a gesture of deference, not a transfer of power.

This evidence showing that there was no devolution of power to the Senate in Nero's first years as Princeps can be further supplemented by the information about Neronian elections supplied by the ancient authors. In 60 Nero ended heated competition for the twelve praetorian places by appointing the three superfluous candidates to legionary commands. He is further said to have refused higher office to senators whose fathers were freedmen.[53]

There is no need to conclude from all of this evidence that Nero did not keep his accession vows or that Tacitus, who vouches for their fulfilment, gave an anachronistic interpretation of Nero's promises and of the expectations they would have aroused in Nero's audience. Tacitus was only an adolescent when Nero died, but he had been able to speak with men who had been in public life during his reign.[54] He will have seen in the attitudes of such men that recognition of and resignation to monarchy, however disguised, which he attributes in an earlier work to a senator of the reign of Vespasian. There the decline of eloquence is explained as the natural consequence of a change of political system: instead of the discord of a free state we now have obedience to the ruler; instead of being in the control of a large number of ignorant men the state is now run by one man of superlative wisdom.[55] The attitude existed even earlier than that. When Tiberius, on the death of Augustus, spoke vaguely of a division of powers, one senator opined that such a division was impossible as the state was one organism governed by one mind.[56]

It was the view of the great scholar Theodor Mommsen that Augustus created a dyarchy of Senate and Princeps, by which he meant not so much a balance of power but a co-existence of responsibility. In fact, the overwhelming military and financial power of the Emperor, in addition to his accumulation of powers (including a *maius imperium* over the public provinces), makes any idea of separate senatorial authority unreal. The theory of divided authorisation for the coinage is one of the last vestiges in modern scholarship of Mommsen's view of the Principate, which is now generally rejected. Yet it cannot be denied that Emperors often described the system in Mommsenian terms, that is to say, that Mommsen was accepting, as a reality, an ancient formula that Nero and his predecessors actually employed. Usually it took the form of a promise of partnership with the Senate, such as Gaius and Claudius offered on their accession. With Nero it took the form of a renunciation of palace rule, appropriate after the abuses of his predecessor. The Principate as a system of government could only remain efficient and secure if it had the consent and co-operation of the senatorial order: the price demanded of the Emperor was respect for constitutional forms, deference to the Senate as a body, and opportunity for the ambitious members of the upper orders. To make sense of Tacitus' view that Nero's early years of rule saw the fulfilment of his accession promises we have only to accept that Nero's formula for a division of responsibility was understood on both sides in this non-literal sense.

Examined from this point of view, the sources provide ample illustration of Nero's good faith. The Senate was immediately encouraged to demonstrate its new freedom by overturning two measures of Claudius. One was the imperial edict of AD 47 imposing a limit on gifts advocates could receive, which Claudius had substituted for the total prohibition that had been proposed by the consul designate and strongly supported by the Senate.[57] The proposer C. Silius had the very next year been involved in a treasonable intrigue with Claudius' wife, and Suillius Rufus, the chief offender, had continued to prosper. Now a total ban was imposed, and a senatorial decree which required the quaestors-elect to arrange for the giving of gladiatorial games, was rescinded.[58] This decree was proposed by a senatorial sycophant, also in AD 47, and was felt to demean the quaestorship by putting a price on it. The cancellation was rightly regarded by Agrippina as a deliberate repudiation of her spouse's acts. The point was brought home personally to her when she was denied the opportunity to attend the Senate and to share Nero's dais when he received foreign ambassadors.[59]

Yet, even as the Senate was encouraged in its freedom, a certain moderation and caution was imposed in accordance with Nero's promise not to show vindictiveness. No prosecutions are recorded under the revived Lex Cincia. Even Suillius Rufus was not tried until 58, and then only because he persisted in attacking the Senate's decree and its real instigator, Seneca.[60] As for the quaestorian gladiatorial games, a late biographer of the poet Lucan mentions that he gave such games with his colleagues in that office 'as was then customary'. Lucan was quaestor later in Nero's reign, and if this statement is correct the removal of the obligation was not accompanied by any effort to discourage the Claudian custom.[61] Finally, although Agrippina was not admitted into the Senate, at least the first meeting at which these measures she so disliked were passed was held in the Palatine Library, not in the Senate House in the forum. This was not without precedent: the Senate had met there under Augustus and Tiberius[62] – but on this occasion the site was chosen in order that Agrippina might discreetly observe the session, concealed behind a curtain in a specially constructed entrance. Similarly, as we have noted earlier, her desire to share Nero's dais was countered tactfully by an act of deference.[63]

To the governing class the good Emperor owed not only respect for their assembly and their order as a whole, but a willingness to open opportunities for achievement and then to acknowledge success. Pliny was to praise Trajan for offering the same rewards for virtue as had existed in the Republic, and that most reflective of Emperors, Marcus Aurelius, notes in his eulogy of his predecessor Antoninus Pius that he was not jealous of men of talent but gave them the chance to win honour.[64] Military talent was at once valued at Rome and daunting to an Emperor unsure of his position. When the notable general Cn. Domitius Corbulo (fig. 5) was recalled by Claudius from waging an offensive in Germany, he is reported to have sighed 'The Roman commanders of old were lucky'. He was regarded as a thorn in the flesh of the indolent Claudius, but his finest hour lay ahead. In Nero's first year as Emperor the situation in Armenia, which served as a buffer state between the Roman and Parthian Empires, sharply deteriorated. When the Parthian king became involved in a struggle for his own throne and withdrew from Armenia, the Senate voted the young Princeps extravagant honours. Tacitus notes that, despite the conventional flattery, they were motivated by genuine pleasure that Nero had entrusted the expected war to Corbulo: 'It seemed that there would be scope for merit'.[65]

In the next year, however, the enterprising governor of Upper Germany, L. Antistius Vetus, was baulked in his plan to use the legions under his command for an engineering project that would give Gaul a continuous inland waterway from the Mediterranean to the Channel. The governor of the neighbouring province of Belgica in Gaul complained that it was dangerous to bring German legions into another province and thus stir up the Gauls. Tacitus implies that Nero stopped Antistius' project because he was persuaded that a personal threat to him might be involved, presumably in the form of a Gallic revolt. But in this case Nero may have feared Gallic resentment of a legionary presence or wished to avoid strife between his commanders. In any case, Antistius was relieved of his German command after less than a year.[66]

Tacitus' interpretation of this incident highlights the particular delicacy with which those of high birth needed to be treated by a Princeps who desired the good will of the Senate. The descendant of a Republican consul or the son of an imperial consul was felt to deserve high office. This attitude, a legacy from Republican tradition, was adopted without demur by those who had worked their way to consular rank, such as Pliny, Tacitus, and, most relevant for Nero's reign, Seneca, who in his work *De Beneficiis* explains that the election to the consulate of a degenerate aristocrat is a just return for the virtue of his ancestors.[67] The chief prize for such men was the consulship and, in particular, the ordinary consulships of the year which would evermore be designated by those two names. It was important for the Princeps not to monopolise one of the two coveted positions every year, yet it would not do for the Emperor to disdain the highest Republican office altogether or to demean his own position by holding one of the suffect consulships later in the year. Nero's practice in this respect would clearly have been regarded as moderate and in accord with his assurances to the Senate: he held five ordinary consulships in fourteen years of rule, the last in 68 being an unpremeditated gesture of panic in the spring after the Vindex rising.[68]

Down until the year 61 the consular lists of Nero's reign bear, at the head of each year, the names of those whose ancestors had graced the Republican *fasti* or had attained the consulship under the Principate. The ambitions of new men were satisfied by suffect consulships, up to three pairs being accommodated in the six months that usually remained after the term of the *ordinarii*.[69] Nero further showed his respect for the office by forbidding his consular colleague in 55 to take the oath to uphold his *acta* when swearing to uphold those of past respectable *principes*, Augustus and Claudius.[70] And when a consul died on the last day of the year Nero showed his sensitivity to senatorial sentiment by refusing explicitly to repeat the notorious action of Julius Caesar who had appointed a man consul for a day.[71]

The same spirit explains Nero's refusal to accept the 'continuous consulships' offered him in 58, along with other extravagant honours, after Corbulo's dramatic victory in Armenia.[72] To accept would have meant curtailing the opportunities for the aristocracy to attain the ordinary consulships that they saw as their birthright. Even had Nero given up his other powers and rested his constitutional position on the consulship, the contrast between his real position and his theoretical equality with a magisterial colleague would have proved offensive and ultimately as unsuccessful as when Augustus had made that experiment between 28 and 23 BC.

Like Augustus, Gaius and Claudius, Nero postponed acceptance of the title *pater patriae* offered on his accession, and, in his first year, he refused gold and silver statues of himself and the honour of having the initial month of the year changed to December, the month of his birth.[73] The adjective for such modesty is *civilis* in Latin or *demotikos* in Greek: the virtue of avoiding outright autocracy, of behaving as an equal with one's fellow citizens and of encouraging freedom of speech and action.[74] It is the quality advertised by the bare-headed obverses and the recurrent EX S C of Nero's early gold and silver coins.

The biographer Suetonius also makes a brief reference to Nero's accession speech and to the implementation of its pledges, in a way that is different from, but not in conflict with Tacitus' account: 'He declared that he would govern according to the model of Augustus and he never missed an opportunity to show generosity, clemency or affability'.[75] This is obviously not a paraphrase, such as Tacitus offers, but an interpretation of the spirit of Nero's pronouncement, and the standpoint is moral, rather than political, and not exclusively senatorial. Suetonius proceeds to recount actions of the Emperor embodying these three virtues as they affected various sections of society, and his list of illustrations can be supplemented from our other sources. Unfortunately Suetonius does not date his examples, so that only those mentioned elsewhere can be used with confidence to augment our knowledge of the character and duration of Nero's initial good period of government.

As instances of generosity Suetonius mentions a distribution of money to the plebs, which Tacitus enables us to date to 57.[76] Tacitus also tells us of a distribution to the Praetorian Guard on Nero's accession, while Dio records another after Agrippina's murder in 59: Suetonius notes that in 65, after the Pisonian conspiracy, Nero gave the Praetorians a free monthly grain allowance.[77] He also records the generous annual subsidies that Nero granted in 58 to members of the ancient nobility.[78]

Suetonius also mentions that there were measures of tax relief: he probably means those which Tacitus reports under the years 57 and 58, remarking that most of them were ineffective or soon forgotten. In this last category Tacitus includes the imperial edict of 58 which aimed to correct the abusive practices of the *publicani* who collected various indirect taxes and which was substituted for the Emperor's original grandiose scheme of abolishing indirect taxes altogether.[79] Another measure, noted by Suetonius, was Nero's reduction by three-quarters of the rewards paid to informers against those who were liable under the Lex Papia Poppaea. Tiberius had earlier tried, by reinterpretation of the law, to moderate prosecutions, for this measure, which Augustus had hoped would provide an incentive to marriage and reproduction, actually resulted in the frequent imposition of the statutory penalties, to the enrichment, first of the *aerarium*, then of both *aerarium* and *fiscus*. By recording this move of Nero's in the context of his reduction of taxes and of his personal generosity, Suetonius implies that the effect was intended to be a reduction of prosecutions, and perhaps of penalties imposed, rather than the securing of a larger proportion of the penalties imposed to the treasuries. We do not know how great a difference Nero's measure made, only that prosecutions did not stop entirely and that Trajan tried to encourage confessions of liability, presumably to avoid the evils of delation.[80]

Evidence for generous legislation concerning treasure-trove has been found in a poem written to celebrate the prosperity and freedom of the new era. Whereas in the recent past, says the poet, men were frightened of discovering gold while ploughing, now they can keep it and use it without fear. These lines seem less likely to be an allusion to legal reform than a reference to change in imperial practice. It may be inferred that Claudius, like Domitian after him, had sought pretexts for claiming such finds.[81]

Suetonius might have listed Nero's more respectable building projects as further examples of generosity. In fact we know from Tacitus and Dio that some of his more important public buildings, the amphitheatre in 57, the market in 59 and the baths dedicated in 61 belong early on in his reign.[82]

Clementia had been one of the great imperial virtues since the start of the Principate. The propagandist use made of this quality by Julius Caesar in the preceding civil wars helps to explain its prominence: in the Republic the word had been used mostly, though not exclusively, of Roman treatment of conquered foreign nations. When in 27 BC the Senate conferred the title Augustus on the Princeps, a gold shield was also put up in the Senate House celebrating four virtues: *virtus*, *clementia*, *iustitia* and *pietas*. The placing of clemency between valour and justice points to its older associations with military conquests and its newer use to signify moderation towards political enemies, often in a judicial context. *Clementia* (and the related virtue of *moderatio*) appeared on Tiberius' coins, and the Senate voted that an altar of clemency be set up in his honour, in the hope of discouraging him from fomenting further political prosecutions.[83] Claudius promised to exercise the virtue but ended by neglecting proper judicial procedure and giving free rein to political prosecutions: he is held responsible in Seneca's satire for the deaths of 35 senators and 221 equites. According to Suetonius, Nero particularly singled out for criticism two qualities of Claudius, stupidity and cruelty, the opposite of clemency.[84]

It is therefore not surprising that *clementia* was one of the key themes of the new régime. Calpurnius Siculus, in his celebration of Nero's accession, sings:

> Clemency has broken the frenzied swords. No longer will the fettered Senate in funeral procession weary the executioner. No longer will the wretched Senate chamber be empty and the prison full.

Here not only is the association with jurisdiction clear, but the importance of clemency for the Senate in particular is stressed and the contrast with Claudius made explicit.[85]

In 55 Seneca composed and Nero read to the Senate an address on the subject of clemency. The occasion was the Emperor's restoration of Plautius Lateranus to senatorial rank, the status he had lost under Claudius after his involvement in Messallina's intrigue with C. Silius. Nero's implicit repudiation of Claudian practice here echoes that of the accession speech; later he was more explicit. After the murder of Agrippina in 59 he accused her, in a letter of reputed Senecan authorship, of being responsible for the crimes of the Claudian régime and of devising plots against prominent men. He then proceeded to demonstrate his clemency by pardoning various men and women of high rank who had suffered under Claudius from Agrippina's displeasure.[86]

The zeal with which Nero embraced Seneca's preaching of clemency was here inappropriately displayed in the context of matricide. It could also lead him, as we have seen, to the staging of a *maiestas* trial in order to exercise the virtue. Seneca could hardly have approved. His lengthy treatise on the subject, published in Nero's second year of rule, had shown that, for him, *clementia* presupposed a framework of justice, though it meant taking the mildest course consonant with it; moreover, the speech he had written for Nero's accession implied that treason trials based on such flimsy verbal charges were not the proper province of justice.[87]

In his first years, however, Nero had exercised clemency in a more orthodox fashion, first by pardoning Plautius Lateranus, then by vetoing in 58 an attempt to follow up Suillius Rufus' condemnation by indicting his son.[88] Nero went on to secure the acquittal, in trials before the Senate, of various members of the upper orders charged with forgery or extortion. In the forgery case of 61 the senator Asinius Marcellus owed the Emperor's leniency, in Tacitus' opinion, to his illustrious ancestry and respectable life. But in two of the extortion cases Tacitus believed that less reputable motives were at work. In 57 Nero saved Publius Celer, he suggests, in return for an opportune murder committed while he was procurator in Asia; in 58 Nero intervened on behalf of two proconsuls of Africa, one of whom he pardoned only because he enjoyed strong support in the Senate through his wealth and childlessness.[89] Similarly, the Jewish historian Josephus adduces the improper influence of Pallas and Agrippina to account for Nero's rescue of Pallas' brother Felix from the revenge planned by the Jews against their hated governor.[90]

The Senate would dislike this and the fact that, within five years of his conviction for extortion in 57, Cossutianus Capito had recovered his senatorial rank through the influence of his father-in-law, the hated Praetorian Prefect Tigellinus.[91] But Nero's general lack of rigour in seeing that delinquent governors were punished is in line with the Senate's own characteristic reluctance to punish their peers on the evidence of their subjects.[92] Tacitus, whose disapproval of such laxity is not typical, notes the misconduct of two proconsuls of Asia, Suillius Rufus and Salvius Titianus, governor in 64: neither Senate nor Emperor took any steps to punish them for their provincial crimes.[93]

The sole example Suetonius offers of Nero's clemency is his reluctance to sign a death warrant, expressed in the words, 'How I wish I had never learned to write'. This anecdote relates to the period before 56, because another version of it appears, appropriately enough, in Seneca's *De Clementia* which was written in that year. Here it is Burrus himself asking the Emperor to authorise the execution of two bandits which he, as Praetorian Prefect, must carry out. It is not clear here, or in the contrasting story that Suetonius tells of the Emperor Gaius (who referred to his monthly authorisation of executions as 'clearing his accounts'), how many cases had been tried by the Emperor himself. Presumably most of them came up from the ordinary permanent courts or from the tribunals of such officers as the *praefectus urbi* and *praefectus vigilum* who would deal with lower class offenders.[94]

Of the three virtues that Suetonius mentions, the first two, *liberalitas* and *clementia*, presuppose that the Principate was really a monarchical system in which subjects were dependent on the good will of their ruler. They are qualities that help to make autocracy bearable without concealing it. The third quality, *comitas*, is the social aspect of *civilitas*, an affability and accessibility that helps to conceal the fact of autocratic power. Suetonius' examples here include Nero's modest reply to an expression of gratitude by the Senate, 'When I have deserved it'. But he also notes Nero's ability to greet men of all orders by name from memory and his willingness to expose himself to the public gaze when he exercised, declaimed or read poetry.[95]

Suetonius agrees with Tacitus in seeing the key to the character of Nero's initial years of good government in the promises of his accession speech. He also shares with Tacitus, as against Dio, a lack of emphasis on legislation and reform. He does not, any more than Tacitus, fail to note such measures, but, where he explicitly ascribes them to Nero, he thinks of them as examples of the Emperor's virtuous behaviour, on a par with his popular remarks and his personal relations with his subjects, individuals and groups. Suetonius clearly takes it for granted that it was the character of the Princeps that counted. If we compare the kind of qualities for which Claudius was criticised by Seneca and the degree to which his manner of government was deemed to count for more than any reforms he introduced, we must conclude that Tacitus and Suetonius are judging Nero's reign by standards familiar to his own contemporaries.

Of the specific measures Suetonius mentions in this section of his *Nero*, none that can be dated, except the grain allowance to the Praetorians, fall after 60. Otherwise, Suetonius offers little help on the question of the duration of the good period. He is even less informative about the activities of Seneca and Burrus, to which we must now devote some attention. A study of their role will test Tacitus' conception of the excellence of Nero's early years of rule. Moreover, the definition of their period of ascendancy ought to contribute to the question of the duration of this good period.

FIVE

Partners in Power

Dio's conception of Seneca and Burrus as inspirers of legislation in a reforming régime is hard to credit, as we have seen. What can be put in its place?

Tacitus remarks that Seneca and Burrus were an unusual example of harmony in power. The two men were similar in age and background, but different in character and experience. Sextus Afranius Burrus was a native of Gallia Narbonensis, the oldest and most Romanized of the Gallic provinces, whose nucleus corresponded to the modern Provence. His family had probably been enfranchised during the civil wars: they adopted the name of one of Pompey's officers, Afranius, who had presumably secured the grant of citizenship for them. Burrus' career shows that they were prosperous enough to qualify as *equites*, for he did his military service as an officer, holding the post of military tribune. Then, from the reign of Tiberius until the last years of Claudius, he served as a procurator managing the estates of various members of the imperial family. It is reasonable to assume a date of birth somewhere in the decade 10–1 BC. The inscription which reveals his career was found at Vaison (the ancient Vasio) and is a dedication to him as the patron of the town.[1] This suggests that it was his birthplace and that he continued to keep a residence there and to maintain his local connections. Profoundly respectable as this background was, it gave no promise of the elevation that political circumstances were to bring to Burrus.

In the year 51, Agrippina was putting the finishing touches to the scheme whereby her son would succeed the ageing Claudius. He was already the affianced husband of Claudius' daughter Octavia and the Emperor's son by adoption and in this year he received honours that marked him out clearly as the heir apparent. Agrippina had created a nexus of political alliances, and she was gradually replacing those old friends of Messallina, now political allies of her son Britannicus, who occupied key positions.

The allegiance of the Praetorian Guard was crucial to her plans. These cohorts formed the principal bodyguard of the Emperor, guarding his chamber at night, escorting him in Rome even into the Senate House and accompanying him on journeys. They were under the direct command of the Princeps who gave them their password and appointed their higher officers, the tribunes and centurions, himself.[2] Augustus had retained the Praetorian Guard he had as triumvir, when he regularized his position as Princeps in 27 BC, but he only began to appoint special commanders for it, called *praefecti praetorio*, in 2 BC. From then on, it was customary for two men of equestrian rank to command the Guard and to serve the Princeps in an increasing number of ways, from guarding his person to appearing on the panel of advisers when he exercised jurisdiction. The double Prefecture, like the direct imperial appointment of the officers, was no doubt partly devised as a curb on the ambitious Prefect who might be tempted to use his command of the Guard against the Princeps. The two cases where Nero's predecessors are definitely known to have allowed one man to hold the post demonstrate the prudence of the normal Augustan arrangement: Tiberius had to remove Sejanus by a combination of stealth and force, and his successor Macro met a similar fate early in the reign of Gaius. Tiberius had also made the presence of the Guard and the power of his Prefect more obvious by allowing Sejanus to concentrate his nine praetorian cohorts in one camp on the outskirts of Rome. The arrangement endured, and by Nero's accession there were twelve cohorts controlling the city from their barracks on the Viminal Hill.[3]

At those moments when the security of the Emperor was most tenuous, the attitude of the Praetorian Guard and its Prefects would naturally be of crucial importance. Thus, at the accession of a new Princeps or when a serious conspiracy threatened the throne, the loyalty of the praetorians could determine the course of history. For this reason, they became involved in intrigue regarding the succession.

The two Prefects who succeeded Macro were sympathizers in the plot to murder Gaius, which was led by officers of the Guard. Claudius replaced them with two men whom he later put to death. One of these, Catonius Justus, is said to have owed his execution in 43 to Messallina whose misdemeanours he was about to report to her husband.[4] Their replacements, Rufrius Crispinus and Lusius Geta, enjoyed the reputation of being loyal supporters of Messallina and her son. When Agrippina became Claudius' wife, she determined to end the tenure of these two Prefects.[5]

The subordinate officers, however, were her starting point. She persuaded Claudius in 51 to remove the centurions and tribunes who showed pity for Britannicus.[6] Then she convinced him that two Prefects only interfered with guard discipline by their mutual rivalry. She produced, as a candidate for the single Prefecture, the irreproachable Burrus, known to Claudius as his financial agent, yet hereafter bound by loyalty to his wife who had raised him unexpectedly to such heights.[7] Lusius Geta was elevated to the post of Prefect of Egypt and Rufrius Crispinus was consoled with consular insignia. Burrus played his part to perfection at the moment of Claudius' death, escorting Nero out of the palace and prompting the cohort on duty to salute him and then accompany him to the praetorian camp.[8] It may have been on this occasion that he was granted the *ornamenta consularia* recorded on the Vaison inscription.

Agrippina, first as the wife, then as the mother of the Emperor, had her own praetorian bodyguard, which may have helped her to keep the loyalty of the Guard as a whole. In 55, angry at the dismissal of Pallas, she threatened to present Britannicus in the praetorian camp, and, after his death, she became noticeably gracious to praetorian tribunes and centurions.[9]

Nero now removed her detachment of praetorians (as well as her German bodyguard), but in 59, after the first attempt to murder Agrippina had failed, Burrus informed Nero that he could not ask praetorian troops to dispose of his mother. Though Burrus adduced the loyalty of the Guard to the whole imperial house and to Germanicus' family in particular, his attitude suggests that Agrippina had done her work of purging the Guard thoroughly, for a praetorian officer had disposed of Britannicus four years earlier without apparently causing any trouble in the praetorian ranks. Indeed six years after her death, one of the many officers of the Guard who joined the Pisonian conspiracy named Agrippina's murder as the first in the list of Nero's crimes that justified his own disloyalty, while one of the leading conspirators was Burrus' successor, Faenius Rufus, himself a protégé of Agrippina. According to Tacitus, his colleague Tigellinus poisoned Nero's mind against Faenius by saying he had been Agrippina's lover and wished to avenge her death. Some awareness of the feelings of the Guard may explain why, when Burrus died, Nero appointed two Prefects, his own favourite Tigellinus and Faenius Rufus, then still in charge of the corn supply, a post he had secured through Agrippina's favour.[10]

Agrippina had difficulties with Burrus after the accession, however, for he cooperated with Seneca in an attempt to free Nero from the Claudian habits of government. Though Burrus' attachment to Agrippina was still taken for granted by others,[11] he remained loyal to Nero after her death in 59, an occasion when his control over the Guard proved invaluable. The secret of Burrus' popularity with his men may lie in Tacitus' description of him as having a 'distinguished military reputation', although the inscription recording his career reveals no military experience apart from his service as military tribune. It is possible that Tacitus' phrase should be translated as 'a distinguished reputation with the soldiers', in which case it may be that his honest and upright character accounts for his hold on the loyalty of his men.[12] In any case, Burrus died like a soldier, his last words 'I am well', being an echo of those of the defeated general in the civil wars who said, as he fell on his sword, 'The commander is well'. In the customary manner, a rumour circulated that Burrus had been poisoned and that his last words, addressed to Nero, were meant as a reproachful contrast with the Emperor's diseased soul.[13] The kernel of truth behind this story is that, by 62, Nero was sufficiently irked by Burrus to find his death welcome.

Burrus' partner in power, Lucius Annaeus Seneca, was born about 1 BC, and like Burrus, came from an equestrian family in one of the oldest and most Romanized of the western provinces. Unlike the Afranii, however, who were Gauls enfranchised by a Roman commander, the Annaei (as their name indicates) were originally Italian immigrants to Spain, settling, as did so many Italians during the Republic, in the south – the modern Andalusia. But any cultural differences between the descendants of enfranchised Spaniards and those of Italian immigrants had largely disappeared by the Empire, within the rich and educated class to which Seneca belonged. The real difference between Seneca and Burrus lay in their chosen mode of life, for Seneca was a senator and an intellectual.

Though born in Cordova, Seneca had enjoyed an excellent education at Rome under the severe but loving eye of his father, a man whose principal interests were oratory and history. At the close of Tiberius' reign, when he was approaching ninety, the Elder Seneca acceded to his son's request to compile for them the best sayings of the declaimers of his time; this work has come down to us as the *Controversiae* and *Suasoriae*. Seneca was the middle son, the eldest being Annaeus Novatus, later immortalised under his adoptive name as 'careless Gallio' in the Acts of the Apostles.[14] The youngest son, M. Annaeus Mela, the father of Lucan, was the only one to remain equestrian in rank, but, unlike his father, he was to abandon the life of a gentleman and scholar for the lucrative position of procurator of imperial estates. He is described by Tacitus as a 'Roman knight of senatorial standing', and he must certainly have moved in senatorial circles, for his two elder brothers rose to be consuls. Yet when the younger of the two was approaching the age of forty, they had apparently not yet progressed beyond the first step of the senatorial career, the quaestorship, for which the minimum age was 25.[15] Both brothers were prone to chest ailments, and Novatus was, according to Seneca, a gentle man who disliked flattery, and was perhaps reluctant to enter public life.[16] Seneca himself had become immersed in philosophy of an ascetic kind in early adolescence,[17] the age when an ambitious young man might have been serving as military tribune, holding minor magistracies and canvassing for the quaestorship.

Both brothers had had every chance of early success in achieving senatorial status, for their mother's stepsister was married to the highest equestrian official of the Empire, the Prefect of Egypt, and he was probably a supporter of Sejanus, for he was recalled just as Tiberius' minion fell in AD 31. It was in fact his aunt's influence that eventually gained Seneca the *latus clavus*, the imperial permission to stand for office that was required for men of non-senatorial birth. But his aunt had by then been forced to wait for the end of the purge that followed the fall of Sejanus. That would explain why Seneca had only held the quaestorship and one more office, the tribunate or aedileship, by 41.[18]

In these years Seneca collected some influential friends – Cn. Lentulus Gaetulicus, aristocrat, consular and poet, and the sisters of the Emperor Gaius. He also became a successful orator whose style and success irked the new Emperor. Seneca thought it wise to abandon his forensic activity, just at the time when Gaetulicus was executed for treason and Gaius' sisters Agrippina and Livilla were punished as associates and sent into exile. Dio reports that Seneca only escaped death because one of the Emperor's mistresses told him that he would, in any case, soon be dead of consumption.[19]

With the accession of Claudius in 41, Agrippina and Livilla returned, but before the year was out, Livilla was banished again on a charge of adultery. The man selected by her rival Messallina to be punished as her partner was Seneca. Agrippina may have been responsible for his avoiding sentence of death, but it was not until he had endured eight long years on the island of Corsica that she was able to effect his recall.[20] In the third year of his exile he had written a grovelling appeal for mercy, disguised as a Consolation, to Claudius' freedman Polybius, but the appeal had not succeeded. Now Agrippina brought him home and secured for him a praetorship. Tacitus notes that Agrippina expected his recall to bring her popularity because of his literary eminence: before and during his exile, Seneca had published three consolation pieces, and at least one of his works on natural science, the lost treatise on earthquakes.[21] The lengthy treatise On Anger must now have been in progress.[22]

Agrippina did not intend Seneca to teach Nero philosophy, only rhetoric. She had in mind his considerable repute as an orator before his exile: the style of his works written in exile showed no diminution in rhetorical skill. Seneca's complaints of his declining fluency in Latin in the Consolation to Polybius were partly literary echoes of Ovid's laments from the Black Sea.[23]

According to Tacitus, Agrippina also wanted Seneca to advise her and her son on the way to achieve their ultimate aim. Seneca knew the ways of court and he could teach the young prince wit and charm as well as eloquence. If necessary, he could be expected to take their part against Claudius, because of his exile. For Seneca may have been sincere in depicting himself, in the Consolation he addressed to his mother from exile, as an innocent man, and he could not have written to Polybius appealing to imperial 'justice or clemency', if his guilt had been manifest and justice had unquestionably been done.[24] In any case, however much he protested that change of fortune mattered not to the Stoic, he had not enjoyed his stay on Corsica.

On Nero's accession to the throne, Seneca became known as amicus principis. This was not an official public position, like the praetorship he held in 50 or the consulship he attained in 56. Yet it could not be a purely private relationship. When the Emperor called someone his friend, it was virtually a title bestowing on its holder high social cachet, the attentions of people seeking favours through his influence, and the expectation of being asked from time to time to advise the Emperor as a member of his consilium. But neither his senatorial position nor this title indicate the special position that Seneca enjoyed. There were a large number of senatorial amici: Seneca's brother, L. Junius Gallio Annaeanus, who is called 'my friend' by Claudius in a letter inscribed at Delphi during his term as governor of Achaea, was a friend of Nero also, but he was not as close to the Emperor as Seneca.[25] The former tutor strove to maintain his influence as mentor, adviser, and confidant at the same, or at an even higher level, than it had been for the five years before Nero's accession. Seneca's detractors teased Nero with remaining under his tutor's instructions as Emperor, and Seneca himself, in Tacitus' account of his suicide, underlines the wickedness of Nero's condemnation of himself by speaking of the murder of 'his teacher and mentor'.[26]

Burrus was also an *amicus principis*, but his influence derived from his official position as Praetorian Prefect. Different in personality as well as position, the two *amici* exercised their influence in a cooperative but contrasting manner. Burrus possessed a moral severity that issued in telling looks and pithy disapproving remarks. Thus, in the few glimpses ancient writers give of his methods, we see him telling Nero, 'The guard will commit no crime against a descendant of Germanicus; let Anicetus fulfil his promise' (viz. to murder Agrippina); applauding but looking pained when Nero performed at his private games; snapping back when asked a second time for his opinion, 'When I have once pronounced on a matter, do not ask me again'; and opposing Nero's divorce from Claudia's daughter Octavia in the words, 'Well then, give her back her dowry', meaning the throne.[27]

Seneca, by contrast, was polished, charming and tactful: his indirect methods are reflected in *De Clementia*. It is true that on his death bed he claimed to have spoken frankly to his ungrateful sovereign, while the philosophical Plutarch shows him discouraging Nero's extravagance by lecturing him on true poverty. But in *De Beneficiis* he provides a description of the relationship of Agrippa and Maecenas to Augustus that shows a more realistic conception of his role as *amicus*. According to Seneca, Augustus came to regret his public fulminations about the disgraceful conduct of his daughter Julia: 'None of this misery would have come upon me if Agrippa or Maecenas had still been alive'. Seneca comments, 'Do not believe that Agrippa and Maecenas were accustomed to tell him the truth; had they lived they would have been among those who concealed it. It is the custom of kings to praise the dead and insult the living and to attribute the virtue of speaking the truth to those from whom they no longer have to hear it'.[28] How Seneca avoided confrontation with Nero is demonstrated by the way he dealt with the attempt of Agrippina to win over her susceptible son by demonstrations of affection suggestive of incest. Seneca sent the freedwoman Acte, who had long been Nero's mistress, to warn the Emperor that Agrippina was boasting of her power over him and that the soldiers would not tolerate such conduct.[29] Seneca dealt with other crises in the same direct way. When Nero in his first years of rule, feeling no affection for his wife Octavia, began the affair with Acte which antagonised his mother, Seneca asked his friend Annaeus Serenus, then Prefect of the

Watch and a familiar figure at court, to cover up Nero's intrigue by pretending to have an affair with the girl himself.[30]

As Seneca's story about Augustus and the scandal of Julia suggests, the *amicus principis* could have a role to play in managing crises at court. Though her protégés themselves, Seneca and Burrus realised that the baneful political effects of Agrippina's ambitions could only be averted if Nero was free to involve himself in the political programme he espoused on his accession. 'They both waged one crusade against the ferocity of Agrippina', as Tacitus puts it.[31] The subtlety of their approach perhaps owes less to Burrus than to Seneca, whose name is mentioned in more of these court incidents, but Burrus' control of the praetorians helped to assure Nero that theirs was the way to security, and, as in the warning about incest, could be used to threaten him.

Agrippina was a formidable adversary. She had political allies at all levels, acquired during Claudius' reign, and she knew how to exploit her Augustan lineage and descent from Germanicus to the full. Whether or not she finally resorted to seduction to control Nero, she certainly exploited the habits of obedience Nero acquired in childhood towards his sole parent, and she never hesitated to remind him of her efforts in securing him the throne. She intended to follow up the success of these efforts by eliminating any new rivals to herself or her son, being well aware that Nero's position was insecure because of his youth and the dubious means by which he had achieved power. At the time of her marriage to Claudius, she had rid herself of two members of a numerous family that could claim direct descent from Augustus through his daughter Julia: these were Lucius Junius Silanus and his sister Junia Calvina. Now, in 54, she had their elder brother Marcus Junius Silanus poisoned by the imperial procurators in Asia where he was proconsul, without the Emperor's knowledge, or so Tacitus and Dio allege.[32]

The conflict between Agrippina and her supporters on the one side and Nero's advisers on the other developed quickly. In 55 the Emperor began his love affair with Acte, assisted by Seneca and Burrus who realized that Nero was bound to find a substitute for Octavia and that this was a relatively harmless liaison.[33] Agrippina's jealousy and resentment decided Nero to undermine her position by removing Pallas from his post of financial secretary.[34] Pallas had held that post under Claudius, and had supported Agrippina at the time of Claudius' remarriage and afterwards. By humiliating Pallas, Nero demonstrated his conviction to reverse the Claudian style of government with its powerful wives and freedmen, as he had promised the Senate in his accession speech.

In her terror, Agrippina now endeavoured to threaten Nero into submission by supporting Britannicus as the rightful heir to Claudius' throne. She knew well how to alarm Nero but she underestimated how he would respond to such a threat. The timing was perfect, for Britannicus would celebrate his fourteenth birthday on the next day, 13 February 55, which was to mark his coming of age. But Agrippina had overplayed her hand, and Nero arranged to have Britannicus poisoned at the children's table in the palace. At this point Seneca and Burrus imitated the practice Seneca attributes to Augustus' senior *amici* – they pretended ignorance. They could plausibly do so, for the ancient authorities make it clear that the murder was carried out so discreetly that the official version, that Britannicus had had an epileptic fit, was credible. Dio, it is true, reports that the appearance of the body revealed the truth to spectators at the funeral, but this must be discredited because Dio himself reports that the funeral was sparsely attended and conducted in a driving rain, while Tacitus adds that it took place at night.[35]

Seneca and Burrus were no doubt among the powerful friends of the Emperor whose consciences were soothed by gifts of his property. They may have shared the view Tacitus mentions as current at the time, that the deed was inevitable given the hostility between the two princes and the fact that monarchy, by its very nature, cannot be shared.[36] Their main concern was with Nero's conduct of government outside the palace and with his treatment of his subjects, apart from his relatives. Nevertheless, in the next stage of the conflict between Nero and his mother, they did intervene. Agrippina responded to Britannicus' death by angry recriminations towards her son, expressions of affection towards Octavia and courtesies towards well-born senators and praetorian officers. Nero responded by removing her bodyguard and expelling her from the palace. These signs of her loss of influence made her an obvious target for the malice of those she had offended over the years. Junia Silana had been an enemy of Messallina and, at first, a friend of Agrippina, but rivalry over a man had poisoned the friendship. Silana now accused Agrippina of supporting another rival to the throne, Rubellius Plautus, whose mother was Tiberius' granddaughter. Tiberius' adoption by Augustus entitled Rubellius to regard himself as a direct descendant of Augustus, in the same degree as Nero. In his panic, Nero now wished to murder both his alleged rival and his mother. Burrus was summoned and shrewdly agreed to execute the crime if an inquiry proved Agrippina guilty.

It was not the intention of Seneca and Burrus that Agrippina should be removed from the scene. Their influence over Nero depended largely on the fact that they provided a refuge from her tactless and arrogant demands. Therefore, Seneca and Burrus listened to Agrippina's defence and persuaded Nero to see her. The result was a temporary improvement of their relations, and Agrippina was even allowed to place some of her favourites in important posts.[37]

For checking Nero's murderous impulses on this occasion, Seneca and Burrus paid a price. Already slightly distrusted by Nero as protégés of Agrippina, their defence of her now undermined their position with the Emperor. In his history, Fabius Rusticus reported that his patron Seneca had had to dissuade Nero from deposing Burrus from his praetorian command when the rumours of Agrippina's promotion of Rubellius Plautus first reached him. Tacitus was probably right to distrust this story, but he himself reports that when Burrus was interrogating Agrippina, some of Nero's freedmen were present as witnesses, which suggests imperial distrust.[38] Then, immediately after the reconciliation of mother and son, Burrus was charged, along with Pallas, with sponsoring yet another imperial candidate. In the event, Nero was not ready to abandon Burrus, who sat on his *consilium* for those parts of the proceedings that did not concern himself and had the satisfaction of seeing his accuser punished.[39] Seneca also was allowed to have his revenge some two years later, when Suillius Rufus attacked him for conduct incompatible with his philosophical pretensions (including, apparently, a hint of adultery with Agrippina).[40] But Nero was becoming less willing to accept his advisers' standards of conduct, and in the year 56, the Emperor first embarked on such antics as roaming the streets at night in disguise with a gang for the purpose of petty thieving and violence.[41]

The reconciliation of 55 with his mother did not last long. Nero was irritated, in general, by Agrippina's heavy-handed insistence on decorous conduct and, in particular, by her opposition to his new amorous entanglement with Poppaea Sabina which began about 58. Tacitus implies that Seneca and Burrus again favoured Nero's *amour* as a way of diminishing Agrippina's influence, but Poppaea was a more demanding lover than Acte, and Nero's desire to be free of maternal nagging was all the stronger for his extra years of maturity and exasperation.[42] Nero's own solution to the problem of Agrippina, murder, did not meet with his advisers' approval, and he knew enough not to ask her old clients to help dispose of her. Instead he applied to his old teacher Anicetus, an enemy of Agrippina and now prefect of the fleet at Misenum, who suggested a collapsible boat. Agrippina was to be drowned sailing across the Bay of Naples after celebrating the feast of the Quinquatria with her son at Baiae. The plan misfired; Agrippina swam to safety; Nero, terrified, now called in Seneca and Burrus. Burrus, as we have seen, refused to use the praetorians, and Anicetus was left to finish the deed by more direct methods. Agrippina is said to have asked the naval officer sent to kill her to direct his sword at her womb.[43] She was not surprised at Nero's ingratitude: the astrologers' prediction had come true.

Nero's confidence in Seneca and Burrus was never completely restored. It was now that they found themselves compelled to allow him to race chariots in a private circus and then to perform at private games. In 60 came the institution of the Greek games called the Neronia. By comparison with the bullying of his mother, the discipline imposed by his *amici* had seemed tolerable; but now there were more attractive alternatives of flattery and of self-indulgence. Nonetheless, by these concessions, they seemed to have bought Nero's acceptance of one of the points that had cost Agrippina her life: he must not divorce Octavia. It was only later, after Burrus' death and the removal of his rival Rubellius Plautus, that Nero gratified Poppaea's desire to become his wife.

If Seneca and Burrus were of little practical help to the Emperor in disposing of his mother, they did at least play their part in handling Nero's relations with the public. Nero had pretended that the messenger who came from Agrippina to tell of her survival was carrying a sword to use against him and that Agrippina had then committed suicide, feeling guilt at her intended crime. Now, after the summary funeral, Burrus had centurions and tribunes of the Praetorian Guard congratulate the Emperor on his narrow escape from assassination. His friends encouraged the Campanian cities to offer sacrifice in gratitude.[44] Burrus was probably among them, perhaps Seneca also, for he was generally believed to have composed the letter that Nero wrote from Naples to the Senate. According to this official version there had been a nautical accident, followed by Agrippina's attempted murder of himself and her suicide. The account was embellished with a list of Agrippina's faults and crimes which made the whole story tantamount to a confession.[45] Seneca and Burrus may also have been among the members of Nero's entourage who then returned to Rome to prepare a suitable reception for him.[46]

Though Burrus and other *amici* were clearly important in purveying and supporting the official version, it was Seneca who was the creator. In an interview between Nero and Seneca, composed by Tacitus to dramatize Seneca's withdrawal from active political life in 62, Seneca is made to compare his role with that of Agrippa and Maecenas. Tacitus no doubt knew the striking passage in *De Beneficiis* in which their difficult position was vividly described, but he makes Nero reinforce his arguments against Seneca's retirement by citing the example of Lucius Vitellius, who had remained Claudius' adviser until his death.[47] The comparison is not entirely flattering to Seneca, in that Vitellius' obsequiousness was notorious, but it does suggest an additional element in Seneca's role, for Vitellius had persuaded the Senate to approve Claudius' marriage with his niece Agrippina and to pass a decree legalizing marriages betwen an uncle and his brother's daughter. His speech then served as a model for that of the consul designate who was induced to propose Octavia's betrothal to Agrippina's son.[48]

Seneca carried this role of imperial propagandist further than anyone before him by writing Nero's major political speeches: the funeral oration for Claudius, the accession speeches to the Praetorian Guard and the Senate, speeches on clemency delivered in the Senate.[49] He may also have composed the simple edict in which Nero announced Britannicus' death. The letter to the Senate explaining the death of Agrippina was obviously a less satisfactory composition than the rest, but Nero's panic after the matricide was extreme, and he may have insisted on the indictment of his mother, which was the worst feature of the letter. In addition, the murder itself had been so clumsily carried out, that some attempt at explanation seemed necessary, for, in contrast to the secrecy that had attended Britannicus' demise, Anicetus had involved several of his naval officers, and the crowd which had gathered for the shipwreck had witnessed the arrival of Anicetus and his men at Agrippina's villa.[50]

About a year after Britannicus' death, Seneca composed a philosophical treatise which supported the official version of that event by proclaiming Nero's innocence of bloodshed, and tried to reassure the public that whatever struggles Nero might have with his relations, his principles of government would remain the same. *De Clementia* opens, to be sure, with the following statement of intention, 'I have undertaken to write about clemency, Nero Caesar, that I may serve as a kind of mirror and give you the supreme pleasure of seeing your own image'. Yet the treatise is not merely a personal message to Nero. There is a warning for all in the description of the blessings of the new régime: 'profound and deep security, justice elevated above all violation; before their eyes is the joyous spectacle of a form of government that lacks no element of absolute liberty except the licence to be destroyed'. The warning implied is spelled out later on:

> just so long will this people be free from danger as it will know how to submit to the reins; if ever it will break the reins or not allow them to be restored when dislodged by some accident, then this unity, this fabric of the mightiest of empires will shatter into pieces and the end of rule for the city will come with the end of obedience. Therefore it is no wonder that *principes* and rulers and guardians of the public order, by whatever name they are known, are loved above those to whom we have personal ties; for if public interests come before private ones for men of sound judgment, then it follows that he too is dearer upon whom the state depends. For Caesar and the state have for so long been intermingled that they cannot be separated without the destruction of both; for while Caesar needs strength, the state needs a head.[51]

Seneca here passes from the risk of attacking or deposing the ruler in a monarchical system to Rome's need to maintain its particular monarchical system. There can be no doubt that the treatise is of much greater general significance than an exhortation to loyalty after the death of Britannicus, as is made clear by the philosophical analysis of the virtue of clemency that occupies the whole of Book II. Seneca was taking publicity and propaganda to the level of political ideology. The emphasis on clemency, interpreted to suit the fluid procedures of imperial and senatorial jurisdiction, was a clear echo of the accession programme of the new government. But the treatise offers no parallel to the constitutional notion of power emanating from and shared with the Senate that Nero had proclaimed in the Curia. Instead, the role of Princeps is repeatedly likened to that of a king, and the safeguard of liberty offered is the virtue of the ruler: the rule of law is guaranteed by a ruler who behaves *as if* he were obliged to obey the laws.[52] Seneca may have been experimenting with a more realistic conception of the Principate, drawing on Hellenistic treatises on kingship. He may have been urging the upper classes to accept that Caesar's power was absolute and to concentrate their efforts on seeing that he was well-trained and well-provided with good advice.

The Preface to Book II of the work contains a story about Burrus, 'your Prefect, a rare man born to serve a Princeps like you'. He is shown fulfilling one of the routine duties of the Praetorian Prefect, presenting execution orders to be annotated and signed, albeit with reluctance. There is no reason to doubt Burrus' approval of the policy of clemency, but it seems a fair assumption that he played a subordinate role in formulating and promoting political ideology.

When we turn to another aspect of the role of *amicus*, that of patronage, the evidence raises difficulties. Although a man as close to the Emperor as Burrus might well be expected to have a hand in suggesting candidates for imperial appointments, there is only one case in which he is explicitly alleged to have done so. This concerns the Parthian crisis that arose a few months after Nero's accession. Tacitus reports popular rumour about how the young Emperor and his advisers Seneca and Burrus would cope with the crisis, and, in particular, whether they would appoint a good general. In the event, Domitius Corbulo was chosen, a man who combined military distinction with the virtue of having been insufficiently favoured by the last Princeps.[53]

For Seneca, the clearest evidence, apart from the Corbulo episode, concerns the appointment of Salvius Otho as governor of Lusitania in 58.[54] Tacitus also notes that the historian Fabius Rusticus prospered through Seneca's friendship, but we do not know whether anything beyond literary patronage was involved.

This slight, yet explicit, testimony to Seneca's patronage adds support to the natural assumption that known friends and relatives of his who are found holding significant posts during his ascendancy owed their success, at least in part, to his influence. Under Claudius, Seneca's patronage must have consisted primarily in suggesting names to Agrippina. She may well have regarded Seneca's friends as men likely to be loyal to her, in view of her role in his return from exile. It is in this period that we find Seneca's elder brother Gallio serving as governor of Achaea in 51/2, a promising post in view of Claudius' affection for Greece and Greek culture.[55] At the same time Seneca's father-in-law Pompeius Paullinus was serving as prefect of the corn supply, while his brother-in-law probably attained a suffect consulship.[56] His younger brother Mela was starting on the series of imperial procuratorships through which he achieved power comparable to a senator.[57]

On Nero's accession, Seneca acquired a more direct influence on appointments, as we have seen. His brother Gallio reached the consulship, probably in 55, preceding his younger brother in that office by a year.[58] Mela's son Lucan became quaestor in either 60 or 61.[59] The elder Paullinus was probably replaced late in 55 by Agrippina's candidate Faenius Rufus, but his son Aulus Pompeius Paullinus now became legate of Lower Germany.[60] He proved a competent governor and general, despite a weakness for luxury that led him to take his silver plate with him into the wilds of Germany.[61] His successor Duvius Avitus is the most plausible example of patronage exercised by Burrus. A native of Burrus' own city Vaison, he made notable progress in his career from about 52 when Burrus would have been in a position to advance him. Two equestrian friends of Seneca also prospered under Nero. Annaeus Serenus probably became Prefect of the Watch when his predecessor was sent to Armenia in 54 and died in post, probably before 62, after eating mushrooms with his officers at a banquet.[62] Lucilius Junior, the addressee of several dialogues and the famous series of moral epistles, did his equestrian military service and attained the procuratorship of Sicily.[63] More tenuously connected with Seneca is the consul designate of 62, Q. Junius Marullus: he may be identical with the Marullus to whom Seneca later sent a letter of consolation on the death of his son.[64]

Serenus and Lucilius were close friends to whom Seneca dedicated several philosophical works, while the elder Pompeius Paullinus was the recipient of *De Brevitate Vitae*, in which his onerous duties are described and his retirement from his post foreshadowed. Of the eleven surviving philosophical works that Seneca addressed to people outside his immediate family, seven are dedicated to these highly-placed equestrian officials and one to Aebutius Liberalis, another man of equestrian rank. These facts provide the key to understanding the success of Seneca's collaboration with Burrus: they both came from the same equestrian milieu and Seneca, through his friends and his brother Mela, retained strong ties with his social origins. The lack of evidence for his active participation in the Senate, and the view of the Principate that he takes in *De Clementia*, help to confirm that Seneca felt more comfortable with men who were not immersed in senatorial attitudes and traditions.

The activities that our sources attest for Seneca and Burrus – the management of court intrigue, the organization of public opinion, and the exercise of patronage – fit admirably with Tacitus' conception of the character of Nero's government in his first years of rule. If we accept the view of Tacitus and Dio (which stray allusions elsewhere support),[65] that Seneca and Burrus wielded decisive influence over the Princeps at first, then this conception of their activity helps in turn to confirm Tacitus' picture of the imperial programme: a promise of tactful behaviour towards the Senate and generosity towards all subjects, a reform in style, rather than content.

A word more must be said about Seneca's role as a high-ranking senator. According to Tacitus, public opinion credited Seneca, first, with Nero's laudable actions, and later, with his crimes, so that Seneca once tried to withdraw from public life, in 62, to avoid envy and finally did withdraw, in 64, to avoid blame.[66] But such vagueness suggests that it was difficult to link his name to any particular measure or decision and there is no direct evidence for Seneca's presence in the Neronian Senate. Indeed there is some indirect evidence against his regular attendance. For on two occasions, even before Seneca's first request to retire in 62, the consuls were afraid to put a motion from the floor to the vote without first consulting the Emperor. It is hard to believe that, had Seneca been present, the consuls and senators would not have had a fairly clear idea of imperial views.[67] One cannot, of course, rule out the possibility that some of the decrees passed were actually prompted by Seneca. But the common assumption that Seneca took practical steps to implement his philosophical views on provincial administration, on the treatment of slaves, or on gladiatorial games through legislation is very difficult to support. Nero's edicts prohibiting provincial governors from giving gladiatorial games, and putting an end to provincial deputations of thanks to Roman governors – measures passed in 57 and 62 with the aim of protecting provincials against exploitation – may have had Seneca's support; Nero's ruling that, in his gladiatorial games of 57, no one would be killed except in combat at least accords with Seneca's ideas of clemency. But, in the case of slaves and freedmen, it is easier to point to the senatorial decrees of 57 extending the practice of punishing the entire household of a murdered master, than to Neronian reforms improving their lot. Even in reporting at length the senatorial debate, held in 61, to consider the fate of the large household of the murdered *praefectus urbi* Pedanius Secundus, Tacitus records no speech of Seneca, not even his presence. In fact, the view that Nero adopted – that all of the slaves must be executed but that resident freedmen should not be punished, in excess of the law's requirement – cannot be said to conflict with Seneca's conception of clemency as a rational moderation opposed to both pity and cruelty.[68]

Tacitus does hint, however, at Seneca's presence among the *amici* consulted by Nero on a senatorial proposal of 56, which would have allowed patrons to revoke the manumission of ungrateful freedmen. Here arguments of a type similar to those found in *De Clementia* and *De Beneficiis* are used against the proposal, and Nero eventually advised the Senate to consider, as a body, the conduct of individual miscreants.[69] It would surely be assumed by Tacitus' readers that Seneca was also among the *seniores* (elder statesmen) or *senatores* (senators) who dissuaded Nero from abolishing indirect taxes.[70]

Even in the sphere of legislation then, it is Seneca's influence on Nero personally, not in the Senate, that is best attested, and even within the sphere of imperially sponsored legislation, there is little to suggest that his work was as important as the activities we examined earlier. The same is true, to a greater extent, of Burrus. What we can reconstruct of their role then seems to confirm admirably the Tacitean conception of the good period of Nero's reign.

It remains to determine how long the dominance of Seneca and Burrus continued. Here the implausibility of Dio's picture of their activities is clearly exposed, for he retires Seneca and Burrus from an active role in government early in 55, after the murder of Britannicus. He seems to have allowed Nero's advisers only a few months for their reforms, possibly because he could not find any content for this model of their activity. After Britannicus' removal, according to Dio, Seneca and Burrus were content to carry on the government with moderation, and to survive: they gave up any attempt to control Nero's conduct but were not without personal influence, for he notes that Burrus escaped prosecution and Seneca incited Nero to murder his mother.[71]

For Tacitus, the crises with Agrippina in 55 and 59 weakened the position of Seneca and Burrus, but the real end came early in 62, when Burrus died and Seneca asked Nero's permission to retire.[72] After Agrippina's death the Emperor had come more and more under the influence of Ofonius Tigellinus, who probably succeeded Annaeus Serenus as Prefect of the Watch some time before 62[73] when he and Faenius Rufus were appointed to fill Burrus' place as Praetorian Prefects.[74] Seneca's request to surrender his fortune and retire from his role as *amicus principis* was refused by Nero. Nevertheless Seneca, from then on, refused his usual crowd of morning callers, avoided his customary entourage of clients and kept himself out of Rome, ostensibly nursing his frail constitution and cultivating his love of philosophy.[75] In 64, after the Great Fire of July which led to Nero's ruthless pillaging of temples, Seneca was still regarded as close to the Emperor, for he now asked to be allowed to withdraw from the city, wishing to dissociate himself from these acts of sacrilege. Nero again refused his request, and Seneca withdrew to his chamber.[76]

Tacitus' version is confirmed in a number of ways. First, the Elder Pliny describes Seneca around 61–2 as 'foremost among scholars and possessed of excessive power which soon ruined him', a description which suggests that Seneca's political influence was still thought to be significant at that date.[77] Then, Seneca's *Letters to Lucilius* not only show him travelling in the spring of 64 in Campania, but also allude to official duties. Since Nero at that very time went with his entourage to perform in the theatre at Naples, it is likely that Seneca was part of that entourage: that would confirm Tacitus' view that Nero insisted on his remaining outwardly his *amicus*.[78] The *Letters* show Seneca visiting his villas at Nomentum and Alba in the autumn of 64: that is compatible with a later withdrawal to his room, after Nero's fund-raising measures were well advanced.[79]

Finally, the activities of some of Seneca's friends and relations confirm that, after 62, the public was meant to think that he was still influential. His friend Lucilius was in Sicily in the summer of 64 and Seneca speaks of urban duties to follow his procuratorship, perhaps an official post. His brother-in-law Pompeius Paullinus was appointed late in 62 to a commission of three consulars examining public revenues, and his brother Mela seems to have continued his procuratorial services.[80]

Despite appearances, however, Tacitus thought that it was the death of one of the partners in this extraordinary example of political collaboration that really marked the end of the other's influence with the Emperor. And he regarded that influence as so crucial for the maintenance of good government that its end marked the turning point of Nero's reign.

SIX

The Turning Point

Our three major authorities have now been scrutinised as to the balance of
activity between Nero and his advisers and the character of the government
in the initial 'good' years of the reign. But what years precisely are meant?
Neither Suetonius, Dio nor Tacitus yields anything so definite and crude as
a neat Quinquennium.

Suetonius the biographer is the least helpful largely because of his failure
to date incidents and measures when illustrating particular methods of
government or traits of character, though within categories he usually
preserves a roughly chronological order. Moreover, the *Life of Nero* is
constructed around a sharp division (at chapter 19) between blameless and
commendable acts on the one hand and shameful and criminal ones on the
other, but examples of each come from all periods of Nero's reign. Thus his
crimes include his excursion into hooliganism that Tacitus allows us to date
to 56, and, among his good works, a gift of corn to the praetorians as late as
65.[1] The episode of the Great Fire of 64 is listed under crimes, but the
subsequent punishment of the Christians appears in a catalogue of reforms
aimed at social abuses.[2] The balance throughout is clearly on the side of evil,
and even some of the items in the blameless chapters appear to carry implicit
criticism.[3] Suetonius finally introduces his account of Nero's demise by
remarking that the world had tolerated a bad ruler for 14 years – the whole
of Nero's reign. Yet, at chapter 26, the biographer indicates that the
manifestations of Nero's innate and hereditary vices became more and more
obvious and extreme. Suetonius thus recognizes a process of decline in
conduct, if not in character, but his mode of presentation precludes a
description of that process.

Tacitus, by contrast, appears to mark a clear turning point. After
describing the first *maiestas* trials of the reign in early 62 he introduces the
death of Burrus with the words, 'As the ills of the state grew worse, the
forces for good were declining'. The death of Burrus, he explains, broke
Seneca's power and Nero now listened to evil advisers while Seneca tried to
withdrew from public life. Tigellinus, one of Nero's new Prefects of the
Guard, grew in influence day by day and succeeded in making the Emperor
his collaborator in crime.[4] Explicit statements make it clear that Tacitus

83

singled out the year 62 as significant on three counts: the end of the patnership of Seneca and Burrus, the re-emergence of *maiestas* charges and the use of murder as a security measure, applied not merely to members of the imperial family but to possible rivals to the throne. According to Tacitus, this was the method favoured, and indeed implemented, by Agrippina at the start of the reign, but then repudiated by Nero under the influence of Seneca and Burrus.[5]

Cassius Dio, like Suetonius and Tacitus, holds that Nero had a natural inclination to vice. In his view, indulgence began at once, and Seneca's and Burrus' policy of allowing him to gratify his desires, as long as they did not damage public interests, only encouraged his passions. Although Dio's account is only partially preserved at this point, the principal stages of Nero's decline are clearly marked in what survives. First there is the murder of Britannicus in 55, which led Seneca and Burrus to limit their efforts to routine government and self-preservation; then, the death of Agrippina in 59, after which Nero lost all sense of right and wrong and listened to flattery with total credulity.[6] Dio's most thorough editor divined that his two Neronian books were divided so as to mark the importance of this second stage, Book LXII starting with the year 59.[7]

Tacitus also begins a new book at that point and indeed makes explicit the significance of Agrippina's removal for Nero's conduct: 'He plunged into all the excesses which a certain regard for his mother had up to now retarded but not entirely controlled (XIV. 13). In this analysis, Tacitus and Dio were following a tradition that had taken shape even before Nero's death, as Tacitus' own narrative makes clear. In recounting the uncovering of the Pisonian conspiracy in the spring of 65, Tacitus claims to give verbatim the reply of the praetorian tribune Subrius Flavus who was asked by the Emperor why he had betrayed his oath of loyalty: 'I began to hate you after you murdered your mother and your wife, and became a charioteer, an actor and an arsonist' (XV. 67). If we allow that October 54 to March 59 is roughly a quinquennium, we can see that this tradition, in a grossly exaggerated form, is the basis of the anecdote in which Trajan praises a Quinquennium Neronis as incomparable and then goes on to talk about his later moral decline. Aurelius Victor and the author of the *Epitome de Caesaribus* identified the period as the beginning of the reign, on the basis of this well-known tradition. They then attempted to justify Trajan's praise with building works and provincial annexations for which Nero was indeed famous, but which, did they but know, fell mostly outside the first five years.[8] Tacitus knew better and saw the five-year period as more negative in character – a *relatively* innocent time – and chose to concentrate on the year 62 when Nero began to break early pledges and carry his crimes outside his immediate family.

Tacitus' analysis is, however, *in its own terms*, vulnerable. Some have thought him unduly impressed with Seneca's importance either through personal sympathy or under the influence of the historian Fabius Rusticus who inclined to give his patron credit even where it was not due.[9] For, it can be argued, there is no sharp break at 62 if we reflect on the promises and practices already noted as characteristic of the good period of government. We have noticed damaging items before 62: it was early in 61 that Polyclitus was flaunting his power over the senatorial governor in Britain, and the same year may well have seen the conflict between Nero's freedman Acratus, sent to collect art treasures for Nero's first palace, and the esteemed Barea Soranus, the proconsul of Asia.[10] In 61 Caesennius Paetus became the first man of non-consular ancestry to hold the ordinary consulship under Nero, and Nero's early practice was finally buried at the beginning of 62 when two new men took office.[11] The gymnasium meant to establish Greek athletics in Roman upper class life was dedicated in 61, and perhaps opened the year before.[12] On the other hand, there is evidence that everything was not lost in 62. Towards the end of that year, Nero supported a worthy proposal of his later enemy and victim Thrasea Paetus which was designed to curb provincial governors. Continuity with the policy of the early years is demonstrated by the gold and silver coins which continue to bear the legend EX S C until the end of 64. It was not until that year that the Emperor appeared on the public stage at Naples, and not until 65 that the enormity occurred at Rome.

Finally, there is the test of contemporary reaction. If things were so bad in 62, why was there no serious conspiracy until the first half of 65? In the interim, Seneca had made his withdrawal from public life obvious, the Great Fire of 64 had seriously damaged Nero's moral reputation and financial viability, and a treason trial before the Senate had ended in the suicide of Decimus Junius Silanus Torquatus. That was more serious than the case of Antistius Sosianus in 62, for Torquatus was related to the Julian strain of the imperial house and designs on the throne were alleged.[13]

Though the case against Tacitus' analysis is not overwhelming, there is some sign that he himself was aware of its weaknesses. Thus Tacitus reports rumours that Rubellius Plautus was planning resistance with Corbulo, commander of considerable forces in the East, and rousing the people of Asia, where he was living in exile; also that his father-in-law was urging him to raise a civil war. The rumours, according to Tacitus, were idle, and the advice ignored, but the historian perhaps wished to suggest that even as early as 62 rebellion against Nero was a possibility. The same motive perhaps underlies the mysterious item with which Tacitus ends Book XIV: Seneca, accused of association with C. Calpurnius Piso successfully turned the charge against his accuser 'which alarmed Piso and caused the serious and disastrous conspiracy against Nero'. This notice, appearing under the year 62, is an absurdity, for Tacitus' own account shows that the conspiracy did not occur for three years, was not initiated by Piso, and that Nero was a trusting intimate of Piso at the time.[14] It may be that Tacitus would have removed the item in revision, but his original idea must have been to leave in the reader's mind the idea that Rome was already ripe for revolt in 62.

It is important to remember, however, that the incomplete state of the *Annals* probably makes Tacitus' analysis seem cruder than it was. When writing about Tiberius, Tacitus marked a sharp break in the reign at the year AD 23, praising the character of Tiberius' first nine years and noting that the death of his son Drusus unleashed the malign influence of the Praetorian Prefect Aelius Sejanus. The analysis has obvious parallels with the break at 62, marked by the death of Burrus and the appointment of the evil Tigellinus as Prefect, which ensured his ultimate dominance. This pattern is likely to be Tacitus' own because, as with 62, the break at 23 is a departure from the usual analysis of Tiberius' decline that we find in the other sources, the death of Germanicus in AD 19 being the principal point of change.[15] Tacitus, however, takes account of this tradition as well, when he comes to give his summary of the reign of Tiberius in Book VI.

The Neronian account is incomplete, Book XVI breaking off in the year 66: the rest was either lost or never composed. As with Tiberius, Tacitus might have appended a summary of Nero's decline that would have added nuance to his earlier break, perhaps even some discrepancy. It is true that he did not do so for Claudius at the end of Book XII, but then, for Tacitus, Claudius was not in control of events for at least the latter part of his reign. The historian had no comparable reason for omitting a final analysis of Nero.

Tacitus has another means of revealing his conception of the significant developments in a reign. The historical work we know as the *Annals* was in fact entitled 'From the Death of Divus Augustus': it combines the annalistic principle of arrangement with the division of the material into reigns. Thus the work begins with the accession of Tiberius, and the accession of each subsequent Emperor stands at the opening of a book. Within that larger structure, however, the material is arranged year by year, and each Tiberian book (except perhaps the last, which is imperfectly preserved) closes with the end of a year. But even here, the choice of the terminal year is meant to reveal Tacitus' conception of the development of the reign, as a comparison with the summary at the end of Book VI reveals. Book II closes with the year 19, in which Germanicus died; Book III opens with the return of his ashes to Italy and Book IV with 23, the year when Drusus died. Book V opens with the death of Livia in 29. Book VI ended either with the death of Sejanus or with the end of the year 31 in which he perished.

Even the one book division that survives for the Claudian account is revealing. By now, Tacitus had ceased to make the end of his books coincide with the end of calendar years. Book XI ends with the death of Messallina in the autumn of 48; Book XII opens with the intrigues of his freedmen culminating in Claudius' marriage to Agrippina.

If we examine Tacitus' account of Nero from this point of view, we find that the historian does indicate several significant points of crisis in the reign. Thus Book XIII opens with Nero's accession, Book XIV opens with the plot to murder Agrippina in 59 and closes half-way through the year 62 with the proleptic notice of the Pisonian conspiracy; and Book xv, the last complete book, closes with the end of the Pisonian conspiracy. As with Tiberius, it appears that Tacitus accommodated the traditional view of the turning point of the reign and was aware of a gradual decline. But he was impressed by the difference a powerful and evil adviser could make, and he used the point at which such a man came to predominate in the Emperor's counsels to give shape to his narrative.

Tacitus' assumption that vice appears when the restraints on a person are removed, thus releasing his true nature, is by no means peculiar to him. The idea of a permanent fixed character is found in the Neronian period itself in Seneca's *De Clementia*, where Seneca tells Nero that either one is good by nature or one acts a role which cannot be maintained.[16] Tacitus' notion of the evil genius, however, seems to spring more from direct reflection on politics, and on autocracy in particular. Despite the similarity of treatment that Tacitus accords Tiberius and Nero, he sees more contrast than similarity in their characters. Tiberius at last saw through and destroyed his Prefect, though he was more formidable and more deeply entrenched in power than Tigellinus. Nero did not, partly because he did not survive the death of Burrus by as many years as Tiberius outlived the death of Drusus, but, more important, because he was less experienced, and less intelligent.

Signs of Stress in the Good Years

The importance of Nero's personality in explaining the change in the character of his government must be given due weight. But before examining how his weaknesses led to the descent into tyranny, let us take a last look at the good period of government, in order to scrutinise some signs of stress already apparent in his initial and successful style of rule. These will make us more aware of the difficulties of being a good ruler within the constraints of the Principate, and better able to understand why Nero failed to maintain the excellent standard he at first adopted and why his misconduct eventually took the particular forms it did.

The most serious breach of the accession promises, before 62, was the excessive power and influence accorded the imperial freedmen Polyclitus and Acratus. Yet, even earlier, Nero had been unable to reverse the Claudian pattern completely.[17] The excessive influence of minions of inferior social status is not a hazard peculiar to the Principate: an autocrat whose power depends on the denial of power to those who would otherwise enjoy it, will tend to feel more confidence in those whose safety and position depend entirely on himself. But the fact that, in Rome, it tended to be slaves and freedmen who served as secretaries and agents of men in public life did mean that intense social prejudice was aroused when too much reliance was placed on these minions. And it may be that social prejudice had some real basis, for an institution which puts one man at the mercy of another is bound to warp the character, inculcating deceit and flattery as means of survival.[18] Even in the Republic, Cicero had warned his brother Quintus when serving as governor of Asia not to allow his slaves too much influence and to restrict what influence they had to domestic and private matters, not allowing it to impinge on affairs of state. He points out that the control over one's household is one of the key supports of *dignitas* — the prestige of magisterial rank and office.[19] For Tacitus, writing under the Empire, it was *libertas* as well that was at stake. 'The lower status of freedmen in comparison with freeborn and indeed aristocracy', he wrote, 'is a proof of liberty: in monarchy they acquire power, not only in the household, but in the state.'[20]

The Principate, in the form established by Augustus, gave maximum opportunity for influence to a particular group of freedmen, and maximum opportunity for resentment on the part of the upper orders. To quote a recent study of the Emperor's functions: 'That with the emergence of a monarch the freedmen of his household should exercise a real influence was an inevitable product of . . . the domestic setting of the exercise of power by Roman office-holders and the exiguous nature of the staff supplied to them by the *res publica*'. For the Princeps was, in theory, just a Roman senator and magistrate. Educated freedmen had always served as secretaries in the houses of Republican *principes viri*, and now they served in the *domus* of the Princeps. But the growing difference in power, status and responsibilities between the Emperor and the ordinary *nobilis* was bound to be reflected in the position of his freedmen, so that a difference of degree gradually became a difference in kind. Thus Junius Silanus Torquatus was suspected by Nero of having imperial ambitions because he let his freedmen have the same titles as those of the Emperor, titles which had once been traditional in noble houses.[21]

An intelligent Emperor could minimize, or conceal, the power of such men. Augustus was a kind master and patron, and he was prepared to seek solitude in his freedmen's villas: but he did not dine with them and he would not tolerate insolence, dishonesty, social misconduct or abuse of influence. Tacitus praises Tiberius for keeping their numbers down, although he was probably comparing his household with later imperial ones.[22] Even after Claudius, Nero did manage to keep his *liberti* out of the limelight. According to Tacitus, Nero likened the departure of Pallas from his post of *a rationibus* to the behaviour of a magistrate being sworn out of office.[23] But Claudius cannot carry all the opprobrium for the evils of a system that was bound to become more odious as the power of the Emperor and hence of his immediate agents grew. In the end, the only cure for the 'arrogance' of these freedmen and for the ill-feeling of the upper orders towards them, was to replace them by *equites*; at the start of the Principate, men of equestrian status would have thought these jobs beneath them.[24] Eventually, Domitian, Trajan and Hadrian, following a practice introduced by Vitellius in the abnormal situation of civil war, made the change. Vespasian had underlined the problem by adopting the opposite solution in the case of the father of Claudius Etruscus, a former slave of Tiberius, whom he elevated to equestrian rank while he was holding the post of *a rationibus*.[25]

Even after the *ab epistulis*, *a rationibus*, *a libellis* and *a studiis* were regularly *equites*, there were imperial freedmen close to the Emperor whose wealth and influence remained a focus of resentment. One indication of the high social status they claimed is the fact that a high proportion of imperial slaves and freedmen married freeborn women.[26] The skill required to keep them in their place can be inferred from the words of Pliny praising Trajan's success:

> Many principes, while they were masters of the citizens, were the slaves of their freedmen: they were governed by their advice and whim, through them they heard requests; through them they replied; in fact, from them praetorships, priesthoods and consulships were solicited. You treat your freedmen with the highest honour, but as freedmen, and you believe it is enough for them to be reputed upright and frugal. For you know that nothing so reveals that the emperor is not among the great, than that his freedmen are.[27]

Both the eventual change in status of the top posts in the imperial household and the evidence for the continuing need for control and caution by the Emperor, show what a difficult role the seventeen-year-old heir to the *familia Caesaris* (as the slaves and freedmen of the Emperor were called) inherited with them. The lack of discipline exercised by his two predecessors must have aggravated the difficulty. But Nero saw the need and made the effort. The incorrigible Pallas he dismissed, reserving his reliance on the loyalty of such men for intimate palace matters, including the murder of his mother.[28] It was only when the pacification of Britain after the serious revolt of 60 was being impeded by discord between the imperial legate and the imperial procurator that Nero fell back on the use of an imperial freedmen to observe and reconcile the senator and the knight.[29]

By 62 Nero was beginning to find the tactful handling of the Senate an unrewarding effort. Yet it was crucial to the smooth running of the Principate that the ancient assembly retain its prestige and dignity, for the upper orders, current and potential senators, set great store by this vestige of the Republic, and their consent in the new dispensation was absolutely essential. No man can rule alone, and the senatorial class was the repository of the political wisdom and administrative experience of Rome. But as long as the practice was maintained whereby the armies of the state were commanded and the provinces of the Empire governed by ex-magistrates, the most serious threat of revolt came from disaffected senators. Moreover, the corporate feeling instilled by membership of the Senate meant that such revolt could be widespread. A less dramatic but still serious threat to the system would result from apathy and depression in the senatorial class. Without its co-operation in assuming commands and governorships, there would be a shortage of administrative manpower which could only be met by retaining the willing in their posts for long terms, thereby increasing the chance of successful rebellion. This structure was to be maintained for two centuries after Nero, because the Emperors themselves were, and, for the most part, thought like members of the senatorial order, and because the Romans at all levels seem to have believed that the institutions of the Roman Republic were flawless in themselves and that the Civil Wars in which the Republic died were traceable solely to the vices of the last generations who lived under it and abused it.

Nonetheless, no Emperor could be unaware of the tension between his own authority and the theoretical sovereignty of the Senate (and even more theoretical rights of the popular assemblies). Nero was being perfectly logical when, late in his reign, he coupled his boast that no Princeps before had ever known what power he really had, with a threat to blot out the whole senatorial order and hand over command of the armies and provinces to equites and freedmen.[30] His reasoning was impeccable when he chose to express his attitude during the Greek tour in 66/7 by speaking of himself and the Roman people, without mention of the Senate. The traditional Senatus Populusque Romanus had implied senatorial command and the imperial Senate was the custodian of those vestiges of the Republic that still survived.

On his accession, however, Nero committed himself to achieving a *modus vivendi* with that body. Though his later attitude was the end result of a long process of imperial misconduct, senatorial resentment and mutual suspicion, it is possible to see, even in his early years, the difficulty of the task that Nero's well-intentioned advisers had set themselves and him.

On the practical level, it was not easy to make the Senate's deliberations interesting and important. The imperial Senate retained, and indeed improved on, the constitutional powers it had possessed under the Republic. Its decrees, formally expressions of advice to magistrates, began to assume the force of law, on a par with laws passed by the popular assemblies. It acquired the decisive power over elections to magistracies and it became an important criminal court. But, at the same time, the Princeps' pronouncements attained the force of law. He had great influence over candidature at elections and an independent jurisdiction and right to hear appeals. In fact, the Republican situation was now reversed. Whereas once the Senate had exercised a *de facto* control greater than its formal powers and its *auctoritas* was often contrasted with the people's *potestas*, its increased legal powers were now subject to the *auctoritas* of the Princeps.

One effect of this development was that, whereas all men valued senatorial rank and many valued the posts which it made available to them, meetings of the Senate itself became less attractive. Absenteeism had been common under the Republic, so a caucus ran affairs, but now it was essential that the Senate be seen to be well-attended and busy. Augustus and his successors imposed (but rarely enforced) penalties for non-attendance, yet still had to limit compulsory meetings to two per month and to reduce, more than once, the quorum required for valid decrees.[31] In 66 Nero was to complain of the tendency of senior senators to prefer their gardens to the Curia.[32]

Another effect was that senatorial meetings could be awkward to manage. True defiance was rare, as most senators had had to secure the Emperor's approval at some stage in their career: they were men who knew where power lay and why it was necessary that it should remain there. But how was the Emperor to ensure that the Senate could still deal with substantial business without inadvertently raising awkward issues and making unsuitable proposals or turning themselves into lackeys? Even Augustus, a consummate stage manager, had to resort to such tactics as calling on senators to give their opinions in an unpredictable order, so they could not rely on just agreeing with one of the early speakers.[33] But his principal inspiration was the creation of a probouleutic council to prepare business for the Senate's principal meetings. It was composed of the consuls (or the other consul, when the Princeps held the office), one of each of the other magistrates, and fifteen senators drawn by lot who changed every six months. The purpose of this rotating sample of the Senate must have been, as Dio says, to promote the notion that through them the whole body had some share in what was being proposed.[34] If he created the right atmosphere at this council, the Princeps could try out proposals and receive candid reactions and suggestions for improvement, which might give him the true range of response the proposal would find in the Senate as a whole. In return, the consuls would be able to try out on the Emperor proposals of their own or ones that had been mooted in senatorial debate, and other members of the council could suggest matters that they thought should come before the House. Then again, the members could prepare opinion for the coming proposals and explain that certain obvious objections and amendments had already been considered.[35]

The council did not survive Augustus. Tiberius, like a Republican magistrate, consulted with his *amici* and respected elder statesmen, the only unusual feature being that the latter were chosen for him by the Senate.[36] It may be that Tiberius' motive was to restore the authority of the plenary sessions of the Senate, but the lack of a probouleutic body to sound and prepare opinion led to awkward meetings. He also found it hard to convey his meaning to the Senate and was easily thrown off balance by unexpected remarks. But he thought it right to attend the Senate regularly, and he had matters of all kinds brought before it. It must have been, in large part, the strain of these debates that drove him after twelve years to flee first to Campania and then to Capri.

For Claudius, as one might expect, given the tyranny of Gaius and his own reliance on soldiers and court figures, the main problem was servility. A papyrus preserves a speech, usually and plausibly attributed to him, in which he puts various proposals affecting the standing courts to the Senate, in the traditional formula for inviting senatorial views: 'If you like my suggestion, agree, or, if not, find another, either now or at a later session'. But Claudius then goes on to gloss the traditional formula thus: 'It little befits the majesty of this order for only the consul designate to state his opinion, itself taken word for word from the consul's proposal, and for the others to say the word "Agreed" and then, when they leave, to remark, "We have stated our view"'.[37]

The ancient sources are of little help in revealing Nero's conduct of business in the Senate. Tacitus shows us that he often attended, at least in the early years,[38] making pronouncements there and intervening, sometimes by use of the veto, in criminal matters.[39] One incident, though difficult to interpret, seems to show up the problems posed by the end of Augustus' council, that is, Nero's proposal to abolish indirect taxes in 58.[40] According to Tacitus, Nero was moved by popular complaints but his extravagant proposal met with opposition from the 'senators.' From the use of this word, the senatorial context,[41] and the flattery with which the counter-arguments are introduced, it might seem that this took place in a senatorial meeting. Had the probouleutic council been involved, the Emperor might have been prevented from bringing such a silly proposal in that form and the more moderate measures he subsequently implemented by edict might have taken the form of senatorial decrees. But 'senatores' might mean the Emperor's senatorial *amici* convened by him (or Lipsius may have been right to read 'seniores' in the text). In that case, business that might have been dealt with by the probouleutic council and the Senate under the old system was here handled entirely by the Emperor and his intimates.

There is clear evidence of difficulties when the Emperor was not present, which was probably more often the case than under the conscientious Tiberius. One of the methods that Nero's predecessor had used to insure that debate in the Senate took the right turn was to prompt a senior senator, usually the consul designate, who would give his opinion first, if the consul presided, or first after the consuls, if the Emperor did. The possibility of prompting senior consulars was already a reality under Tiberius.[42] Tacitus reports two cases of the practice under Claudius, one when the Emperor was absent, the other when he was present. In the first, the consul designate was induced to propose that Claudius be urged to betroth his daughter Octavia to Domitius, the son of his new bride. Mammius Pollio used arguments similar to those recently heard in the Curia when Lucius Vitellius had persuaded the Senate to urge the Emperor to marry Agrippina. The Senate recognized the imperial inspiration and behaved accordingly.[43] Then, five years later, Claudius praised his freedman Pallas for being the true author of the senatorial decree he himself had just proposed and seen passed. The consul designate Barea Soranus, at the instigation of Agrippina, it is alleged, proposed elaborate honours and a bounty for Pallas, expressing gratitude for his services to the Princeps. Claudius then explained that Pallas would like the honour but refused the money, and the modified decree was passed and engraved for public consumption. Hence Claudius was able in one session to secure honour for Pallas and advertise his servant's honesty and parsimony.[44]

The method was precarious. In 62 Nero was eager to procure a heavy sentence for Antistius Sosianus against which he could exercise his clemency. The consul designate proposed the death penalty in the ancestral form of scourging to death. The more senior consulars apparently followed his lead, until Thrasea Paetus proposed the milder penalty of deportation and confiscation of property. His proposal prevailed in the division, but the consuls wrote to the Emperor for his consent and his ambiguous answer encouraged them to put the proposal in Thrasea's form, which the Senate passed.[45] Q. Junius Marullus, the consul designate concerned, was a man of no consequence who probably carried little weight in the Senate. Even if we assume that Marullus was one of the ambitious Spaniards who achieved high office through Seneca's patronage, the Senate had no reason, initially, to suppose that the palace was behind what appeared to be an obvious piece of opportunistic sycophancy.[46] It is likely that the senators, faced with the first treason trial of the reign, first failed to discern the imperial will and then failed to see how to put the blunder right, after Nero's letter had urged them, in injured tones, to persevere in their moderation.[47]

A surer method of conveying his wishes would have been to have Seneca attend the Senate. When L. Vitellius himself spoke to that body on the subject of Claudius' marriage, there was no doubt as to what was expected. But this method looked like direct autocracy and hardly preserved appearances.

The reluctance of the consuls to make the decrees final without imperial authorisation is a sinister phenomenon, demonstrating a lack of liaison between Emperor and Senate, which the probouleutic council might have prevented. Already under Tiberius, when matters arose without warning in senatorial debate, the consuls felt obliged to postpone the matter and consult the Emperor.[48] The earliest case under Nero arose in 56 when a lobby in the Senate demanded action against the insolence of freedmen towards their masters. The consuls were afraid to put the proposal to the House but wrote to Nero conveying the general opinion. The view that emerged in consultation with his *consilium* was that the Senate should consider re-enslavement in individual cases when charges were brought by patrons. Nero wrote to the Senate in that sense and no further action was taken.[49] Had the matter come up in Augustus's probouleutic *consilium*, it might only have reached the House as a proposal in its final form. The open avowal of senatorial dependence would have been avoided.

Another such case arose in 62, when the unexpected proposal arose from the right of any senator to speak on a matter outside the question put to the House and then demand that his item be made the subject of a formal proposal.[50] Tacitus reports that Thrasea Paetus had been criticised for not exercising this right in order to raise major issues although he was known to speak of the need for senatorial liberty. But in 56 a decree restricting the rights of tribunes had apparently originated in this fashion, and in 62 Thrasea did exercise the right. The Senate was voting on the penalty to be imposed in the trial of a prominent provincial, and Thrasea proposed that the Senate prohibit embassies of thanks being sent to Rome. The consuls refused to put the proposal to the Senate formally: it was only after Nero took the initiative himself that the decree was passed.[51] Had the matter arisen in Augustus' probouleutic council, the imperial initiative would not have been so blatant. It is not surprising to find that under Trajan, the practice of speaking outside the *relatio* (proposal before the House) was declining[52] and that in one case where it is attested, the senator uses the opportunity to ask the Princeps to make a ruling.[53]

The general process of degeneration of senatorial independence was well under way by then. Already under Tiberius, the Senate was reluctant to stay in session when the Princeps was out of Rome and voted to have the Emperor approve its decrees imposing capital penalties before they took effect.[54] Among the rights formally voted to Vespasian was that of clearing a proposed decree so that it could be put to the Senate, and all of the respectable early *principes* are cited as precedents.[55] Early in Vespasian's reign, Thrasea's son-in-law Helvidius Priscus tried in vain to persuade the Senate to take decisions of substance in the absence of the Princeps. Tacitus represents a senator in the time of Vespasian explaining that senators no longer need skill in speaking when men conduct themselves well and are prepared to obey the ruler, 'for there is no need to state one's opinions at length in the Senate when good men quickly agree'.[56] Finally, as the Senate lost the will to initiate business, so the Emperor tired of consulting them on anything important, and his attendance and that of the outstanding men declined.[57]

Nero's promises to the Senate about restoring their importance and prestige were what they wished to hear, and he tried to implement them. But it took a master actor such as Augustus to play that role, and Nero's dramatic talents were of a less subtle kind. The task was perhaps impossible anyway after the tyrannies of Tiberius and Gaius and the inadvertent autocracy of Claudius. The next civil war reminded senators of what the alternative to the Principate was, and the standards of senatorial independence dropped still further. The Princeps could only satisfy upper class sentiment by perpetual, exhausting and often thankless effort. That does not excuse Nero from giving up, but it shows how great were his efforts in the early years and what it would have cost to maintain them.

Ideological Tension

On an ideological level relations with the Senate also presented difficulties. Right from the start, flatterers had addressed the Princeps as an autocrat, and any adviser was bound to appeal to the traditional and real arguments for good behaviour, security and popularity, that had long been used for monarchs. As we have seen, Seneca's *De Clementia*, addressed to Nero, contains the most explicit statement of the view that the virtue of the Princeps is the only restraint on his use of power. In contrast with the vision of constitutional balance in the accession speech, Seneca takes the organic view of the Principate, with the Emperor as the soul or mind of the state. Indeed he goes so far as to call Nero *rex* by implication, urging: 'The Princeps should not only heal but leave no shameful scar; no glory comes to a king from cruel punishment', as well as rebuking his addressee with 'You think it hard that complete freedom of speech should be taken from kings'.[58] The Roman feeling against kings was traced by Cicero back to the expulsion of the Tarquins, and the use of the terms *rex* and *regnum* to indicate a man possessed of absolute power, rather than, as their Greek equivalents did, a good ruler as opposed to a tyrant. The words certainly retained their pejorative sense long after Nero's reign, during which Lucan could write, 'Of all the people who endure *regna* our lot is the worse, because we are ashamed of our slavery'.[59] Seneca, who elsewhere uses *rex* as a word of opprobrium, points up the novelty of his usage by speaking of '*principes*, *reges* and keepers of the public order, by whatever other name we call them'.[60] Seneca may have been trying, as we suggested above (chapter 5), to change that amazingly tenacious belief of the upper orders that only the Republican system was good and that the Principate could only be accepted to the degree that it approximated to the old system. He did not succeed.

Yet Seneca was only carrying to its natural conclusion one strain in the ambivalent ideology of the Principate. A Tiberian senator had already described the state as an organism whose mind was the Princeps: soon a Trajanic senator would describe the system as rule by one wise man, and the ruler as a beneficient source from which trickles of business might find their way to the Senate.[61] Nero was experiencing senatorial enthusiasm for his liberality and clemency, qualities which presuppose the inferior position of those they benefit. Now Seneca seemed to suggest that the Princeps could present himself in a monarchical light. What of his obligation, as expressed in his accession speech, to be a *civilis princeps*?

For Nero, being re-educated after the bad examples of Gaius and Claudius, but still inexperienced in senatorial ways, it must have seemed an insoluble problem to adopt the right stance. His mentor had set before him the two contrasting sides of imperial ideology: the Republican facade of the Augustan Principate and the virtues of a benevolent autocrat. In that Nero eventually found the monarchical model more congenial, Dio had cause to call Seneca 'a teacher of tyranny'.[62]

One way in which the Princeps became acutely aware of the ambiguity of his status was in facing the problems of the succession, for he found himself ruling by virtue of powers granted by Senate and People, but in reality selected through his family connection with the ruling house. This situation produced two immediate problems for the new Princeps: the complex attitude to Claudius that had to be maintained and the use by Nero's mother of possible rivals to the throne in controlling him.

Attitudes to Claudius

In his accession speech Nero promised to remedy certain abuses of his predecessor's government. But, while adopting Augustus as his model, he indicated clearly that there would be no reprisals for past conduct. Nero had already delivered a eulogy of Claudius in which he praised his achievements and qualities as a ruler: now his predecessor was voted a most lavish public funeral and declared a god by the senate.[63] The promise of amnesty towards those who had prospered under Claudius was good political common sense: no Princeps could afford to reject all of those who were well advanced in their careers and experienced in government. It is true that an Emperor who came to power after an assassination or a rebellion could make an example of some of the most powerful associates of his predecessor. But Nero had come to power as Claudius' chosen heir, in so far as there could be an heir to the position of Princeps. Claudius had adopted Nero, who thus became his elder son. The political significance of the will is demonstrated most clearly by its repression, either because it favoured Nero, and thus would remind men of the injustice done to Britannicus, or because it did not, and would leave Nero's position open to challenge.[64]

As Nero's claim to power rested partly on his relation to Claudius, he could hardly discredit him in public without weakening his own position. Instead, he styled himself 'divi Claudi filius' and advertised continuity in personnel, while promising to change the style of government. The balance was not easy to maintain. When Nero spoke of Claudius' *providentia* and *sapientia*, a titter spread through the audience, so Tacitus reports. No doubt Claudius' lack of foresight and prudence in providing for the security of Britannicus was uppermost in their minds. Nero's own party jokes about Claudius ranged from hits at his stupidity and cruelty to allusions to his death from mushroom-poisoning: 'Mushrooms were the food of the gods,' he said, 'since Claudius was made a god by eating one'. But when Pliny later remarked that Nero had deified Claudius in order to laugh at him, he was probably thinking particularly of Seneca's farce, the *Apocolocyntosis*.[65]

The title is a play on the Greek word *apotheosis* and the form is a Hellenistic type of satire in which prose and verse were combined. Seneca gave the satire a political twist in mentioning Claudius' neglect of proper judicial procedure, the venality of his court and the power of his freedmen and in having Augustus veto Claudius' deification because of his cruel murders. Like Nero's own jokes, the work combines an attack on the evils Nero had repudiated in the Senate with ridicule of the honour Nero himself had secured for Claudius. The work would have made the greatest impact soon after Claudius' death, on 13 October, and the consecration, which must have followed within a month. Allusions to the Saturnalia in the work might suggest that the author had this holiday in view: that would place the performance in mid-December, within two months of the funeral. The farce must have been intended for a limited audience, probably for performance at court, because it clearly contradicted the message of the funeral and deification. The Saturnalia was a season of unrestrained hilarity and frank speech: it was during these same festivities that Britannicus, at a palace drinking party, sang of the loss of his father's throne.[66]

Some have been tempted to see some serious political purpose in this farce.[67] A favourite suggestion has been that Agrippina is being attacked as the organizer and priestess of the cult of Claudius, but the fact that the official version of Claudius' death is presented stands against this, for Claudius' murder was the most notorious of her alleged crimes. Further-more it is unlikely that the decision to honour Claudius can be traced to Agrippina alone, though she seems to have been responsible for starting the construction of a temple to him.[68] For, as Tacitus observed, the attacks on Claudius' style of government in the accession speech suggest that Agrippina by no means dominated all decisions at the end of 54, and Nero had sound political reasons for honouring his adoptive father: he was thereby demonstrating *pietas* and celebrating his own status as *divi filius*.

Another view is that Britannicus' position is being attacked through this satirical portrayal of his father, because the deification had in fact done more for his position than for Nero's. Hence Claudius is reproached by Augustus for his murder of members of the Julian house and his claim to Trojan descent is impugned in an attempt to show that only Nero can justly be credited with Julian ancestry.[69] In favour of this argument is the fact that Nero made a lot of his descent from Augustus. Yet his genealogy, attested at various dates throughout his reign, combines both claims: it begins 'son of the deified Claudius', then (switching to the maternal line) 'grandson of Germanicus, great-grandson of Tiberius and great-great-grandson of Augustus'.[70] Moreover, the obvious way to attack Britannicus would have been to attack his mother Messallina, yet she is nowhere blamed for the deaths which other sources ascribe to her initiative, though many of these murders are mentioned among Claudius' crimes.[71] Instead, she is named by Augustus among the victims.[72] These features have given rise to another view, that the work is written not by Seneca, but by some promoter of Britannicus' claims. The simplest explanation may well be the best, that Seneca was here entertaining the Neronian court with a farce in which nothing except the young Princeps is treated seriously, – not Augustus' *Res Gestae*, not history, not philosophy, not his own *Consolation to Polybius* whose flattery of Claudius is cruelly parodied.[73] We must remember that Seneca is elsewhere credited with light verses and a gift for mockery.[74]

Nero and his friends may have enjoyed a release of feeling against Claudius in private, but the policy proclaimed on accession was maintained. Although Suillius Rufus complained that Seneca was hostile to friends of

Claudius, it is notable that no charge was preferred against him until he attacked Seneca.[75] There is no sign that those whom Claudius had elevated to the patriciate were denied advancement. Indeed, the future Emperor Otho was among Nero's closest friends at first and Otho's older brother became proconsul of Asia after the normal interval of eleven years. T. Sextius Africanus was consul in 59 and then put in charge of the Gallic census in 61, while Quintus Veranius was chosen by Nero to initiate his offensive in Britain in 57. Some of Claudius' closest associates continued to prosper: Lucius Volusius Saturninus was retained as Prefect of the City until his death in 56 and then granted a public funeral by the Senate at Nero's request; in 59, L. Julius Vestinus was made Prefect of Egypt: his son went on to achieve an ordinary consulship in 65.[76]

As for Claudius' consecration, it is clear that Nero's interest declined as time went on, but the honour was never cancelled. At first, Nero called himself DIVI F(ILIUS) on coins. Some issued in 55 celebrate the deification itself, showing, on the reverse, statues of Divus Claudius and Divus Augustus(?) being drawn in a car by elephants (fig. 15), and others of the early period, are devoted entirely to Divus Claudius, his head appearing on the obverse (fig. 13).[77] Though the filiation disappears from coins after 56, it was retained on the official records of the Arval Brothers priesthood until at least 60 and appears on less official inscriptions still later.[78] Nevertheless, there is some truth behind Suetonius' statement that Vespasian restored to Claudius the honour of apotheosis that Nero had neglected and annulled, for the temple that Agrippina had started to build for Claudius on the Caelian Hill was destroyed by Nero and rebuilt by Vespasian. But Nero did this in the course of clearing the ground for the Domus Aurea, the great palace begun after the Fire of 64, as a poem of Martial makes clear.[79] We need not suppose that Nero's purpose was to slight the memory of Claudius, though it is clear that he no longer gave high priority to its cultivation. That there was no deconsecration is also suggested by the fact that, just after Nero's death, officials in Egypt and Rome still gave Claudius his title of *divus*.[80]

Nero knew that he could not afford to drop his piety towards Claudius altogether: his claim to legitimate succession via the Claudian, as well as the Julian, line enabled him to outclass his rivals on either side.[81] Agrippina showed her awareness of the Claudian basis of his claim in threatening him with possible rivals: thus she gave her support to Britannicus, then to Rubellius Plautus. The importance of the Claudian claim lies behind the charge brought against Pallas and Burrus of promoting Faustus Cornelius Sulla Felix, the husband of Claudius' daughter Antonia.[82]

It is again the vital link with Claudius that explains Nero's delay in divorcing Claudius' daughter Octavia, though she was both uncongenial and sterile. Nero murdered his mother in order to marry the beautiful Poppaea who had proved her fertility in her first marriage.[83] Yet it was not for another three years that the divorce of Octavia and Nero's remarriage finally occurred.[84] Although Agrippina's death allowed him to enjoy his liaison with Poppaea, it did not remove the real obstacle to the divorce. Not until Nero had the courage to rid himself of the two men he most feared as possible claimants to his throne, Cornelius Sulla and Rubellius Plautus, did he finally make the break.

It was sound political sense on the part of Tacitus that led him to recount these murders just before the divorce in the crucial year 62. With similar acumen, he had noted the earlier exile of Sulla in 58, immediately after describing the start of Nero's liaison with Poppaea, and presented the exile of Plautus in 60 as Nero's response to the appearance of a comet, which was believed to foreshadow a change of ruler.[85] On the other hand, it is culpable negligence on his part to do no more than hint that at the time of the divorce Poppaea was known to be pregnant. Nero must have counted on this strengthening of his position, to counterbalance the crimes by which he first removed his rivals, and then severed one of his links with Claudius.[86]

Tacitus gives a pathetic description of this girl of nineteen (Octavia was actually 22 years old, at least)[87] being accused of adultery with a slave and defended by her maid under torture, then divorced on grounds of sterility and sent off to Campania under military guard. The public outcry led Nero to accuse her further of adultery with Anicetus, commander of the fleet at Misenum, as part of an attempt at revolution. Octavia was then confined to the island of Pandateria under armed guard and finally killed a few days later: her veins were opened under duress, in order to give the appearance of suicide. As the historian remarks, 'Octavia's wedding day had been her funeral'.

SEVEN

The Descent into Tyranny

The fate of Octavia and the marriage of Poppaea, as well as appealing to the historians, struck the imagination of a dramatist. These events of the year 62 form the subject of the *Octavia*, the only Roman historical drama to survive complete. The play is preserved with the tragedies of Seneca, but not in the earliest surviving manuscript and apparent allusions to events after Seneca's death, particularly to the death of Nero, make his authorship highly questionable.[1] A date of composition close to the events, however, is suggested by the author's thorough knowledge of the historical circumstances. Yet it is hard for us, at this distance in time, to distinguish personal experience from mere erudition. A more compelling argument for an early date is the author's grasp of Seneca's thought and style, for by the reign of Domitian there was a reaction in taste which Tacitus had to allow for in praising Seneca's eloquence.[2]

Nero is presented in the *Octavia* as a tyrant who explicitly rejects Seneca's teachings about clemency and self-restraint, and who aims to rule by fear. Just as he contracts the events of some months into three days,[3] the tragedian foreshortens the process of change in Nero's conduct: he is thoroughly wicked by 62. Poppaea's pride and her influence over Nero are lamented by Octavia; her beauty and the passion she inspires are proclaimed by Nero. But when she actually appears she is a pathetic bride, terrified by bad dreams and bent on appeasing the gods. The unnamed Prefect of the Guard, charged with suppressing the riot over Octavia's divorce and then sending her into exile, is presumably Tigellinus, but he is a colourless figure, afraid to carry out such unpopular orders, yet unable to make his views prevail with Nero. Nero is, in fact, the proverbial tyrant, robbed of any personal characteristics, a mere incarnation of the will to evil, unaffected by advice or influence.

The New Advisers

In the ancient historians, the picture of the position enjoyed by Poppaea and Tigellinus is quite different: more what one would expect from a young prince who had been used to heeding, albeit with growing irritation, a great deal of advice. Tacitus describes the pair in 65 as 'intimate counsellors of the Princeps' cruelties';[4] he and Dio show Poppaea persuading Nero to kill his mother and punish his wife, and Tigellinus inciting him to murder and debauchery.[5] The Prefect is able to secure the return to senatorial standing of his son-in-law within five years of his conviction on a capital charge, and to ensure the punishment of those who brought charges against himself.[6] This conception of Tigellinus as a powerful influence on Nero is found in other writers, for Plutarch says he was the most hated of Nero's adherents, and Juvenal imagines him able to requite insult with death.[7] There is earlier evidence too: when the people demanded the blood of Nero's adherents after his death, Tigellinus was singled out as the teacher and tutor of the tyrant.[8]

Josephus, writing before Tacitus, confirms Poppaea's influence on the Emperor when he ascribes to her the success of his own mission in 63–4: he secured the release from custody of some Jewish priests and the overturning of a decision by the procurator of Judaea in favour of King Herod Agrippa. Poppaea is described by Josephus as $\theta\epsilon\sigma\sigma\epsilon\beta\acute{\eta}s$, a word which seems to signify respect for religion though not actual adherence to Judaism.[9] But the other example of Poppaea's influence that Josephus cites turned out to be disastrous for the Jews. As a friend of the wife of Gessius Florus, she is said to have secured him the post of Procurator of Judaea in 64. His conduct in that office brought Jewish unrest to its climax in the great revolt of 66. Poppaea probably did not intend to give the Jews such an offensive governor, but, given the high level of anti-Semitic feeling among Greeks under the Principate, the appointment of a resident of a Greek city, married to a Greek wife, was not the most promising idea.[10]

It is Poppaea's beauty and extravagance, however, that receive most mention in the ancient writers. The Elder Pliny, who tells us that Nero celebrated her amber-coloured tresses in song, remarks that the mules which drew her carriage were shod in gold, and that five hundred asses produced milk for the daily bath that preserved her complexion. She clearly set the tone of the Neronian court in the latter part of the reign, providing a standard for others to imitate: Juvenal gives her name to a fashionable beauty preparation.[11]

Poppaea had always been ambitious. Her father T. Ollius was of non-senatorial ancestry and had only reached the quaestorship before he died as an adherent of Sejanus in 31; his daughter was therefore at least six years older than Nero. In view of her father's disgrace, it is not surprising that she preferred to take the name of her grandfather C. Poppaeus Sabinus, who, despite undistinguished origins, had achieved the consulship and triumphal decorations. He ended by serving as the governor of the important province of Moesia for twenty-four years. Not even the fate of his son-in-law could shake the trust of Tiberius in this man, described by Tacitus as 'equal to his responsibilities but no more'.[12] Poppaea inherited her beauty from her mother, who had eventually escaped from her inglorious widowhood into a union with the ancient family of the Cornelii Scipiones. The Elder Poppaea was one of the victims of Messallina, by whom she was accused of adultery and then driven to suicide by threats of imprisonment.[13]

That was in 47, when the younger Poppaea must have been of nubile age. Her first husband was one of those honoured by Claudius on the occasion of her mother's condemnation, the Praetorian Prefect Rufrius Crispinus. We do not know just when the marriage took place, only that before 58 she had divorced her husband, and that their son had not yet reached puberty when Nero had him drowned, probably after mid-66. After divorcing Crispinus, she married Salvius Otho, and so entranced the young Princeps by her coquetry that in 58 he had her husband sent off to govern Lusitania.[14]

Poppaea's face was not the whole of her fortune. Aside from intelligence and charm of conversation, she had wealth, inherited with her high social standing from the maternal side. Inscriptions reveal that the gens Poppaea owned at least five houses in Pompeii, including the celebrated House of the Golden Cupids and the House of Menander. In addition, a wax tablet found at Herculaneum refers to brick works in the territory of Pompeii owned by the Empress herself, while recent excavations have revealed that one of the villas at nearby Oplontis belonged to Poppaea. That we are dealing with a leading family of Pompeii is also apparent from the Ludi Poppaeenses mentioned in inscriptions.[15]

It is likely that Pompeii was Poppaea's birthplace, especially as her father's family, the Ollii, also owned property and perhaps originated there.[16] Just as Agrippina's birthplace oppidum Ubiorum had been made a colony after her marriage to Claudius, so Pompeii received this status from Nero. The honour is all the more striking in that the town had incurred displeasure at Rome in 59 because of a bloody riot in the amphitheatre: the Senate had banned all gladiatorial shows there for ten years and dissolved illegal collegia.[17] But inscriptions show that the ban was lifted by 65, and sometime after January of 63 the town became a colony 'by the judgment of Nero and Poppaea Augusta'.[18] Nero founded several colonies in Campania. Of those mentioned in the literary sources, Capua and Nuceria, founded in 57, actually received veteran soldiers as new settlers, like his colonies at Antium and Tarentum; Puteoli was merely given the status of colony in 60 with the title Colonia Claudia Neronensis Puteolana. The inscription that reveals the change to colonial status of Pompeii (and also of Tegeanum, an obscure town in Lucania) does not make clear the nature of the privilege or the titles they received. What Pompeian inscriptions do show is the profound gratitude of the town. In addition to gladiatorial games given 'for the safety of Nero in the earthquake', we find attested a flamen Neronis and the use of the name Neroneus for the month of April, decreed by the Senate after the Pisonian conspiracy.[19] The games show that Pompeii adopted and celebrated Nero's own interpretation of the earthquake that destroyed the theatre in Naples just after his performance there in 64. The Emperor took the escape of performer and audience as a sign of divine favour; others, says Tacitus, thought the collapse signified divine displeasure.[20]

The dating of Pompeii's elevation to 63 or later derives from the title Augusta that accompanies Poppaea's name on an inscription plausibly connected with the grant of colonial status.[21] Agrippina had received that title when her son was adopted by Claudius, just before she secured the colonial title for her birthplace. Poppaea was rewarded for the birth of her daughter, who was born at Antium on 21 January 63: the child also received the title, being called Claudia Augusta, and it may have been on this occasion that Poppaea's birthplace was honoured as well. Claudia Augusta died after four months and was deified.[22] When Poppaea herself met her death two years later, she was given a public funeral, her body being embalmed and buried, rather than cremated in the Roman fashion. She was deified, and a shrine erected which took three years to build. Poppaea had once said that she did not want to outlive her beauty: she had her wish, and she kept her hold on Nero's affections until his death.[23]

Poppaea's actual position could only distantly approximate to Agrippina's. She was far inferior in birth, and she had not the time, nor probably the skill, to build up a nexus of political support. No ancient author suggests, for example, that she had any particular allies among the imperial freedmen to balance the hostility of Doryphorus, or that she had established links before her marriage with praetorian officers or with either of the Guard Prefects.

Ofonius Tigellinus, too, represented a come-down socially from the eminently respectable Seneca and Burrus. Tacitus describes him as 'obscure in parentage and debauched in early life'. The scholiast on Juvenal supplies details of both charges: his father came from Agrigentum in Sicily but was relegated to Scyllaceum in south-east Italy; his son was therefore poor and without prospects. Relying on his good looks, however, he secured access to the households of Cn. Domitius and M. Vinicius, with both of whom he is said to have had sexual liaisons while, at the same time, enjoying adulterous relationships with their wives, Agrippina and her sister Livilla. Clearly there are gaps in this story. Tigellinus' father must have had some fortune and some friends in high places, for his son to be able to attract the notice of aristocrats and princesses. Dio adds support to the next episode of the scholiast's story: Tigellinus was relegated for adultery with Agrippina in 39. He then, continues the scholiast, plied a banausic trade in Greece and, on receiving an inheritance, was granted permission by Claudius to return, on condition that he kept out of the Emperor's sight. He bought some land in Apulia and Calabria where he raised race-horses and cultivated a friendship with the young Nero, whose passion for the sport he encouraged. By the time Tigellinus had become Prefect of the Watch he had achieved or recovered equestrian fortune and status.[24] His connection with Nero brought him not only great wealth but, especially after his appointment as

Prefect of the Praetorian Guard in 62, considerable influence and status. After the exposure of the Pisonian conspiracy in 65 he was granted triumphal decorations and a statue on the Palatine. These were greater honours than Rufrius Crispinus or Burrus had received as Guard Prefects: they show that Tacitus' implicit comparison of him to Sejanus is not entirely vain.[25]

The background of these key figures has been described in some detail because it contributes to the understanding of Nero's later reign. By virtue of their lower social standing, Poppaea and Tigellinus were more dependent on imperial favour than their predecessors. It is therefore not surprising that they gave Nero different advice and used different means to hold his favour.

Personality and Principate

Among the characteristics of Nero noted by Tacitus and Suetonius, two are particularly emphasised and illustrated: his desire for popularity, and his fear and insecurity.[26] Seneca had played on just these qualities when he urged Nero to practise clemency in order to win the love of his subjects, the only true guarantee of safety for a ruler. The policy which Nero carried out under his guidance could be summed up in the word *civilitas*. As a method of achieving popularity and security, it required self-control as well as a real, or well-feigned, desire for that degree of equality with the upper orders that the Emperor's position permitted. As we have tried to show, the policy burdened the Princeps with what was often a hypocritical and unrewarding task. After Burrus' death and Seneca's withdrawal, Nero was no longer deterred from satisfying the demands of his personality in other ways. Tigellinus and Poppaea encouraged exhibitionism as a means to popularity, and repression as an antidote to fear.

Nero had always found it congenial to strive for popularity with the Roman plebs: it was easy to achieve for a young, handsome prince who carried the blood of the revered founder of the Principate. In itself, such popularity was not a contemptible aim. It had been recognised as necessary by Augustus and, as practised by him, it was not incompatible with acceptance by the upper orders. Trajan was to achieve the same combination. As Fronto was later to observe, scarcely anyone excelled or even equalled Trajan in practising the arts of peace, for he knew 'that the Roman people are kept loyal by two things, the corn-dole and the shows; that government is judged successful as much for its amusements as for its serious activities; that neglect of the serious things brings greater damage, but neglect of amusements greater resentment'. The bread and circuses that Juvenal sneered at are here elevated as 'the loftiest principle of political wisdom'.[27]

Seneca was no less aware of their importance. In *De Brevitate Vitae* he describes what would have been the result of Gaius' neglect of the corn supply, had he not been killed when there were still eight or nine days' supply left: 'destruction, famine, and what follows famine: overthrow of all government. Those in charge would have been faced with stones, sword and fire.'[28] As for games, Seneca advanced against the combats of gladiators and wild beasts the usual philosophical objections to their cruelty and their bad effect on the morals of the spectators.[29] Yet he shows anything but approval of Tiberius, when noting how the scarcity of his games led the gladiator Triumphus to lament 'How fair an age has passed!'. In any case, Nero's liberality was principally lavished on spectacles of a less bloody variety.

Burrus too appreciated the importance of courting public opinion. He probably helped to organise a favourable popular reaction in Campania and Rome after Agrippina's murder.[30] Nero's behaviour then, like his earlier appeal for popular sympathy after the death of Britannicus, shows how sensitive he was from the start to his standing with the populace. A more respectable expression of that concern was his care of the corn supply.

Bread . . .

Responsibility for the organisation of the supply of corn to Rome had been assumed by Augustus only late in his reign and with considerable reluctance. The capital had long ago outgrown its hinterland, and, in any case, water transport was much cheaper than land transport, so that by the end of the Republic the city of Rome was largely dependent for corn on imports from Sicily, Sardinia and Africa. After the Battle of Actium, Egypt was added to the Roman Empire and became a major supplier. In 22 BC, at a time of famine, Augustus had agreed to become *curator annonae*. Although the responsibility brought with it so much power that the Senate had voted in 43 BC that no man should ever be given it again, the odium that failure would bring made him reluctant.[31] In AD 6, when there was famine again, Augustus set up a commission of ex-consuls to oversee the marketing of the corn, and in the next year he named two ex-consuls *curatores annonae*.[32] Only after this did Augustus finally decide that a permanent post was necessary.[33] The Princeps appointed the equestrian Prefect, and he accepted that the ultimate responsibility was his. It was he who was shouted at in the theatre when prices were high; it was he who was pelted with stale bread when scarcity was rumoured.[34]

Augustus' first Prefect of the Corn Supply was C. Turranius, who had served as Prefect of Egypt and was an authority on the geography and crops of Spain and Africa.[35] He was as tenacious as he was knowledgeable, serving until the latter part of Claudius' reign, when Pompeius Paullinus replaced him. Seneca shows us the Prefect at work checking the condition and weight of the corn as it is unloaded from ships and stored in granaries.

He notes that through diligence and honesty Paullinus is winning affection in a position where hostility is difficult to avoid. Tacitus testifies to similar success for Paullinus' successor Faenius Rufus who, after seven years in the post, was promoted to the Praetorian Prefecture 'because of his popularity, for he had managed the corn supply without personal gain'.[36]

Of Rufus' successor we hear nothing,[37] but Nero's own continuing concern with the provisioning of Rome is well attested. In 62, when a storm had destroyed two hundred corn ships in Ostia harbour and a fire had ruined a hundred other vessels bringing corn up the Tiber, Nero prevented a panic by having spoiled corn dumped in the river as a sign of confidence. He also kept the market price down, probably by granting subsidies to corn dealers out of his own funds. Two years later he cancelled a trip to Alexandria because he had a seizure in the Temple of Vesta, which he took as a warning from the protectress of the City. He announced that he must put the Roman people first and stay to protect them against adversity: Tacitus comments that the principal reason why this decision was welcome to the plebs was that they feared a corn shortage while he was away.[38] Later in 64, when the Great Fire had reduced the city to chaos, Nero had supplies brought in from Ostia and neighbouring towns and again lowered the market price of corn. It was only in the panic of his last days that, according to Suetonius, he was thought to be neglecting his people's sustenance, using ships to transport sand for the court wrestlers when the price of corn was soaring in a time of scarcity.[39]

The state's responsibility as regards corn was most direct in the case of the *frumentationes*, the free distributions which were made every month to approximately 200,000 male citizens. In the Republic great political capital had been made out of the twin issues of the scale and financing of these distributions. This is probably why Augustus, when he took on the care of the corn supply in 22 BC, entrusted the task to senators chosen by lot from a list of nominees drawn up by the magistrates. The duties of these ex-praetorian officials, the *praefecti frumenti dandi*, were regulated by senatorial decree, and EX S C follows the name of the post on inscriptions. Yet there could be no rigid separation of this aspect of the corn provisioning from the rest: the *praefectus annonae* made the contracts with suppliers, checked the shipments, and kept the accounts, which no doubt explains the need for honesty so emphasised in the sources.[40] It was in this area that the Emperor was most likely to incur expense, for the distributions, provided out of tithes in kind from the provinces or corn bought with taxes in money, had to be maintained, even if the sources fell short. Augustus records how he supplemented them in 23 and 18 BC out of his own granaries and treasury.[41] The Emperor also contributed staff. His minions carried out the actual distributions, for which the senatorial prefects took responsibility and credit.[42] In 64, according to Cassius Dio, Nero discontinued the corn dole after the Fire. This is most plausibly construed as an emergency measure which enabled him to keep the market price of corn low by releasing stored corn onto the market, including that bought for the state distributions.[43] There is no reason to think that the dole was not restored as soon as possible. In 65 the praetorians were added to the list of corn recipients.[44]

Claudius wished to put the corn supply of Rome on a more secure footing by improving the harbour at Ostia. The Tiber mouth did not allow shelter for larger corn transport ships, and, in winter, riding at sea was hazardous. Claudius developed a natural bay into an artificial harbour, of which the left mole was an extension of a large sand bank and carried a lighthouse. The sinking of a monstrous ship in which Gaius had had an obelisk transported from Egypt provided the foundation.[45] The Tiber was joined to the harbour by canals, as is recorded on an inscription near the site of the Claudian harbour dated to AD 46. This was four years after the start of the project, and much had clearly been accomplished; but a magnificent picture of the harbour on Nero's coins has suggested to some scholars that it was left to him to put the finishing touches to Claudius' project. Tacitus' account of the loss of two hundred ships within Ostia harbour shows that the harbour was in use by 62, while the coins on which the harbour appears are the large brass *sestertii*, none of which were minted before late 63 (fig. 24). It is possible that Nero completed some harbour buildings, but the coins could simply celebrate his concern for the corn supply of Rome, as do others of the same period which feature the goddesses Annona and Ceres (fig. 23).[46]

Nero showed his interest in finding long-term solutions for the problems of supplying Rome in other ways. Like Julius Caesar, who is credited with plans for building a harbour at Ostia, he was concerned with the difficulties of water transport to the City itself and the dangers for ships presented by the western Italian coastline. Caesar proposed, according to Plutarch, to run a canal from the Tiber immediately below Rome to the coast at Terracina, thus providing a safe passage to Rome for traders not bound for Ostia. With the acquisition of Egypt, however, the role of eastern corn had greatly increased.[47] These corn ships put in at Puteoli, much further down the coast than Terracina, for Puteoli offered a good natural harbour and storage facilities. The corn then had to be reloaded and shipped up the coast in smaller vessels. In 64 Nero was forcefully reminded of these hazards, first by the need for rapid movement of supplies after the Fire, then by the loss of several ships from the imperial fleet at Misenum which were caught in a heavy storm between Formiae and Campania. He may already have built the artificial harbour at Antium, which has been interpreted as a move to ease this situation. (In fact, the remains do not suggest a commercial harbour but rather an amenity provided for his veteran colony and for his own magnificent villa there.)[48] In any case, his ultimate plan was a canal even more ambitious than Caesar's, one which took into account the importance of Puteoli.

Work was begun in 64 on a waterway to run all the way from Lake Avernus to Ostia, securing safe passage for ships and draining the coastal marshes. It was abandoned, but the resistance to the scheme still echoes in our sources. The Elder Pliny blamed the work for the decline of Caecuban wine; Tacitus thought the plan both impractical and hubristic.[49] In fact, large engineering works were often greeted with opposition of this kind. Claudius had faced great resistance to his Ostian harbour, which may explain why he (and Trajan) publicly and implausibly claimed that the canals they ran from the Tiber to their harbours would free Rome of the danger of floods.[50]

Suetonius, though more sympathetic than most ancient writers to engineering projects, also regards this construction as a reckless extravagance, but he is more sympathetic to another plan of Nero's. He notes, after mentioning the plans for rebuilding Rome after the Fire, that Nero had also intended to move the walls of Rome as far as Ostia and to bring the sea to the 'old city' from there by means of a canal.[51] The quick movement of supplies from Ostia to Rome after the Fire may well have demonstrated the well-known disadvantages of the Tiber's winding channel and strong current. Had his two canals been constructed, Nero would have provided safe transport from the Campanian coast all the way to Rome. Presumably the Ostia–Rome canal was to follow the Avernus–Ostia channel: the completion of the first and the start of the second were both prevented by the Emperor's financial and political difficulties in his last years.

The problems of supply required not only the modification of nature but the encouragement of men. Rome depended on private traders even for the state corn that was distributed. Claudius personally guaranteed to traders their profits by underwriting losses incurred in storms, and he also held out to those who built corn ships of a certain minimum size legal privileges augmented by Nero, who released provincial importers from various harbour dues and their ships from property tax.[52] He may also be responsible for a more formal organisation of grain imports from Egypt, for Seneca, in recounting events of late May or early June 64, gives us our first explicit reference to the *classis Alexandrina* arriving at Puteoli.[53]

Finally, Nero may have tried to develop a new source of supply in the Black Sea area on which the Greek cities had long depended. The only explicit evidence is the *elogium* of Ti. Plautius Silvanus Aelianus which gives the details of his public career, including his term from 60 to 66 as governor of Moesia, the province between the Danube and the mountains of Bulgaria.[54] After various military exploits, the record states, 'He was the first to relieve the corn supply of the Roman people by a great shipment of wheat from that province'. Where exactly the Moesian wheat came from is not clear, but the Dobrudja has been suggested; it is a fair conjecture that the shipment was meant to ease the emergency created by the Fire of 64. Other events of this period suggest Nero's plans. In 61–2 came the military occupation of the Cimmerian Bosporus kingdom on the northern shore of the Black Sea, in connection with Aelianus' own defence of the Crimean city of Heraclea Chersonensis. There followed the subjection to direct

Roman rule of the kingdom of Pontus on the south side of the Black Sea. As Nero's last plans included a great expedition to the Caucasus, it is reasonable to think that he was planning to make the Black Sea 'a Roman lake';[55] whatever other considerations weighed with him, the attractions of a new source of wheat would not have been overlooked. It is even possible that the unfinished Corinthian canal begun in 67, another idea taken over from predecessors, was partly intended to facilitate commerce generally and corn transport in particular.[56]

Tiberius was prepared to remind the Senate how heavy a burden the Princeps carried in ensuring that the city was properly fed.[57] Nero knew better how to make the populace aware of his concern, as is shown by the publicity he gave the postponement of his trip abroad in 64 and by his coins celebrating the theme. Also advertised on his token coinage of 64 is the great *macellum* or market dedicated in 59 and located on the Caelian Hill (fig. 28).[58] After the Fire he not only saw to it that food was provided for the populace as a whole but arranged shelter for the homeless in his own gardens across the Tiber and in the buildings with which Agrippa had adorned the Campus Martius.[59] There is no sign that he ever abandoned this concern for the material welfare of the people of Rome and the popularity it brought. Even in 68, the corn shortage for which he was blamed was probably not due to his own neglect or profiteering but to the revolt of Clodius Macer in Africa which cut off supplies to Rome from that key province.[60]

. . . and Circuses

Three hundred years after Nero's death and the senatorial condemnation of his memory, those who attended the games were still receiving mementoes displaying the head of the greatest showman of them all. In addition to the gladiatorial games, the Juvenalia and the Neronia, Suetonius mentions chariot races, elaborately staged plays and the Ludi Maximi at which the crowd was showered with tokens redeemable for such lavish items as precious jewels, horses, slaves and houses.[61] He knew how to turn any public event into a show – his return from Campania after his mother's murder, or his return from Greece after his tour of the festivals. Suetonius points out that even the reception and crowning of Tiridates as king of Armenia can be considered one of his spectacles. The prince was exhibited in the forum and there made obeisance to Nero in the presence of the Praetorian Guard, the Senate and other citizens drawn up in formal array, while the rest of the population roared from the roof tops. Then he was led into Pompey's theatre whose stage and interior had been gilded for the occasion. Finally, Nero gave a public performance on the lyre and finished by driving a chariot in full charioteer costume.[62]

Nero also contributed buildings. In 57 he had an amphitheatre constructed on the Campus Martius, the foundations built of stone faced with marble, the main structure of wood surmounted by an awning the colour of the sky and studded with stars.[63] The poet Calpurnius Siculus describes the effect on a rural swain of the ivory and gold trimmings and of the exotic beasts that fought there, and he makes an elderly citizen of Rome remark, 'All the shows we saw in former years now seem shabby to us'. The Elder Pliny reports that for one of Nero's gladiatorial shows a Roman knight was sent by the organiser of the show to the Baltic Sea to bring back amber, which was used to trim the safety nets, weapons and coffins.[64] Pliny elsewhere mentions the Vatican circus of Gaius and Nero, presumably started by the one and finished by the other. The occasion for this construction is known from Tacitus who tells us that when Nero could no longer be deterred from racing and acting after his mother's death, Seneca and Burrus persuaded him not to appear in public. So he raced his chariot in the Vatican valley across the Tiber where an enclosure was built. For the Juvenalia of 59 he built a personal theatre in the gardens across the Tiber, which probably formed a complex with the circus.[65] It was probably in connection with the Neronia of 60 that Nero had his baths and adjoining gymnasium built.[66] The speed of this building programme and of its individual items, one year for the amphitheatre, one or two years for the gymnasium and baths, testify to the importance Nero attached to his entertainments.

The most important function of the games was to allow the populace at large to see their Emperor and to make their feelings known to him, for they had few other opportunities for contact with their sovereign. In the Republic the informal meetings at which magistrates harangued the crowd and the public assemblies for elections and legislation gave opportunities for the expression of public opinion. But with the end of free political activity, only the games were left as a regular place where popular enthusiasms and grievances could be aired without counting as civic disorder. Nero was following the best traditions when he introduced reforms after protests at the games about the practices of tax-collectors.[67]

At the games the Emperor's *civilitas* was displayed to the whole Roman people. Pliny in his Panegyric of Trajan notes how important it was for the Emperor to be visible at the circus, not shut up in a box as Domitian apparently was. Nero's viewing habits at the circus are not recorded, but in the theatre, according to Suetonius, he sat on the top of the proscaenium right over the stage. Here he was generally visible, though on some occasions he seems to have entered secretly and remained hidden from view.[68] At the amphitheatre, Suetonius notes that he witnessed the games from a raised platform close to the arena, at first looking through shutters but later in the open: Calpurnius Siculus has his rural spectator see the Emperor's face from afar. The use of a box by Nero is at first glance surprising, for he loved applause and admiration: he even allowed the plebs to watch him exercising on the Campus Martius. But the key to the puzzle may lie in the fact that the most dangerous contests, those involving gladiators and wild animals, were held in the amphitheatre, and excessive enthusiasm on the part of the Emperor had in the past been construed as bloodthirstiness. As Nero was particularly careful at first to parade his clemency, as a contrast to Claudius' cruelty, he may have felt that men would be watching his face closely at the arena. Indeed even the pyrrhic dances performed there could be hazardous: on one occasion Nero was spattered with blood when the flight of Icarus ended in an accident.[69]

It was not easy for the Emperor to avoid criticism. He had to appear to enjoy the games while not losing his dignity or being excessively moved. It was acceptable for Nero to favour the Greens among the four circus factions, those companies of professional charioteers whose masters hired out horses, equipment and drivers to those who put on the games.[70] But when he took sides in the strife between fans and rival pantomime actors he was clearly going too far. He allowed these brawls free reign by ending military supervision at the theatre, with such terrifying consequences that the soldiers had to be recalled in 56 and the pantomime actors themselves banished for four years.[71]

Sometimes Nero attended the theatre unannounced, sometimes he remained concealed. The ancient writers say that he wanted to see what was going on unobserved and to contribute to the disorders without inhibition. Should we rather see in this practice the estimable desire of a young ruler, normally escorted everywhere by guardsmen and lictors, to find out for himself what his people really thought? For Nero not only visited the theatre *incognito* but wandered around the streets, taverns and brothels of Rome in disguise, indulging in brawls and petty thieving. Shakespeare's Prince Hal could reasonably claim that he was thus preparing himself for the throne. Yet a reigning monarch ought to sound opinion more in the manner of his Henry V before Agincourt. Whereas Germanicus, when a prince, knew how to test his soldiers' feelings with discretion and dignity, Nero's conduct when Princeps was neither discreet nor dignified.[72] Besides encouraging public disorder, it could at times have more serious consequences. A senator resisted attack by the Emperor in disguise; later he revealed by apologising that he had recognised his assailant; the imperial displeasure drove him to suicide. Afterwards Nero kept a band of soldiers and gladiators near at hand. Clearly his conduct was not intended to serve the ends of statesmanship; it belongs more to that *nostalgie de la boue* which often affects young aristocrats, and which is vividly attested for Rome by Juvenal. Among Nero's companions on these sorties were the future Emperor Otho and his successor Vitellius. It may have been in Nero's company that Vitellius acquired his notorious taste for taverns and for the company of gamblers, dancers and charioteers.[73]

Nero needed to learn that without some moderation and self-control he might even lose the favour of the mob. Earlier he had chosen to ignore lampoons about his mother's murder; later he was to take little notice of insults aimed at his singing and his building operations.[74] But in 62 it was impossible to ignore a frantic mob invading the palace to protest against the divorce of Octavia. As she was led away into military custody a crowd gathered to protest, and Nero's reaction generated a rumour that he had changed his mind. According to Tacitus, the mob first climbed the Capitol to give thanks to the gods, then overturned statues of Poppaea and placed those of Octavia in the forum and temples. Finally they broke into the palace, where Nero turned the soldiers on them. Poppaea was understandably alarmed about what Nero would do. He had shown signs of wavering earlier and now he was clearly stirred when he saw how much love and sympathy were roused by Octavia's innocence and mistreatment and how much dislike by Poppaea's arrogance and immorality. Tacitus makes her appeal to Nero's timidity by turning his fears in another direction: Octavia's clients and slaves had organised this rebellion against the Emperor, who would be in even greater danger if Octavia were recalled to lead them. If he were firm, she argued, he could regain his security: the crowd was not the true Roman Plebs and it had been easily controlled.

Nero took her advice, but even now he was concerned to justify himself to his people. Anicetus was induced to testify to his adultery with Octavia before Nero and a council of intimates; an edict explained that Octavia had been found guilty of attempts on the loyalty of the fleet at Misenum, seducing its commander and then destroying the fruit of her adultery by abortion. When Octavia left for Pandateria she inspired pity but no further resistance.[75]

Subsequent events showed that this case of repression had not seriously damaged the Emperor's popularity. It may even have been true that the demonstration was not entirely spontaneous: Doryphorus, Nero's *a libellis*, was put to death soon after as an opponent of Poppaea's marriage and could have helped to organise discontent. In 64 came the most serious threat to Nero's popularity when the Great Fire broke out. It was widely believed that Nero first used the blaze as a backdrop for a virtuoso performance and then restarted it to clear the ground for his reconstruction of Rome. This time, force was used on a despised minority, the Christians, who were burned alive to illuminate circus games. Tacitus reports that, hated as they were by the Roman mob, their suffering aroused pity.[76] Yet the plebs were loyal to the end: even at these games held in his Vatican gardens Nero felt he could wander freely among them, and, in his last extremity, he was thinking of appealing to them from the rostra in the forum and asking for their support.[77]

First without Equals

The popularity that Seneca had promised Nero was general, but the sort of favour that he was later encouraged to pursue led inevitably to the alienation of the more traditional upper class elements. It was not that his spectacles were not enjoyed by senators and knights, who also gloried in being one of the sights the crowd came to see. The equestrian order received the honour of separate seats in the Circus Maximus, an extension of the privilege they had enjoyed in the theatre since the Republic. Augustus had, on one occasion, provided separate seats for senators and *equites* at Circus games, and a custom of separate seats developed, but Claudius first made the practice formal for senators. In 63 Nero abolished the trench around the Circus Maximus, which protected spectators, in order to provide a row of special seats for the knights.[78] This respect for the hierarchical character of Roman society was absolutely in accord with the ideas of the founder of the Principate.

Some members of the upper orders were more directly involved with Nero's games, serving as organisers, just as they had under other Emperors. In 55 the knight Arruntius Stella was put in charge of theatrical and circus shows, and Claudius Iulianus, who dispatched the Roman knight to collect amber for a gladiatorial show, may also have enjoyed that status.[79] Finally, the ex-consul and future governor of Britain, Quintus Veranius, is described on an inscription as 'presiding, at his own request, over the Emperor's Ludi Maximi at which he was the agent of his generosity'.[80]

Participation was also encouraged by Nero, especially in the musical and gymnastic competitions, and bribery or compulsion was not always necessary, as Tacitus himself suggests.[81] Nero's friend and later rival C. Calpurnius Piso had been heard to sing tragic parts, though his eulogist does not make it clear if this was in public. But the crowd certainly had opportunities to see their betters perform, and Nero enhanced their pleasure by forbidding, on at least one occasion, the wearing of masks.[82] More conservative elements were affronted and felt that Nero thus demeaned the upper crust of Roman society.

Even in his insistence on personal performance Nero had encouragement from persons of rank; Calvia Crispinilla, the future Emperor Vitellius and perhaps even the historian Cluvius Rufus, who served as herald at the second Neronia and later on his Greek tour.[83] Indeed Nero enrolled a gang of ambitious equestrian youths under the title of *Augustiani* to follow him around, applauding him in the most extravagant way. Dating from 59, this arrangement seems to combine the idea of a bodyguard with that of the Augustan *iuventus* (youth) organisation, now adapted so as to stress not the traditional military exercises but Nero's beloved music. In 64 this equestrian escort was enlarged by the addition of five thousand other citizens. The whole troupe was arranged in groups and taught to produce the rhythmic clapping that had enchanted Nero when some visiting Alexandrians had applauded him in the theatre at Naples.[84]

Tacitus notes that Roman knights, as well as Italian and provincial visitors to the capital, detested the spectacle of the Emperor performing in Rome in 65, and that the Senate tried to avert the disgrace by offering him the crowns for singing and oratory, as had been done successfully at the first

Neronia.[85] Nero's failure to win over the more conservative and respectable elements to his Greek contests was partly due to his impatience: he would not allow enough time for the change of *mores*, expecting Roman resistance to evaporate with imperial pressure and encouragement. His personal performances made the conversion of the upper classes more difficult, for they were the most obvious sign that his pursuit of popular favour took a form ultimately incompatible with the demands of *civilitas*. Nero did not want merely to be loved, he wanted to be uniquely loved, and he wanted to be applauded even by those he should have treated as his peers. The imperial friendship came to be offered or refused according to a man's degree of zeal in clapping, and he came to regard as a rival anyone who enjoyed popularity of any kind.[86]

From the very inception of the Principate no other aristocrat could compete with the Princeps in his ability to acquire popularity by largesse and other benefits. The founder had put an end to triumphs outside the imperial house and thus secured a monopoly of booty as well as military glory, while political power attracted gifts and legacies. But he intended that the members of the upper orders should help distribute his favours and thus maintain their superior standing in the state. His later dynastic successors went further towards monopoly. Tacitus maintains that conspicuous consumption and consequent favour with plebs or provincials had only brought destruction on noble houses.[87] Under the last of the Julio-Claudians the prestige of the aristocracy was thoroughly eroded, even in its more trivial aspects.

Nero's extravagance made it difficult for the ordinary magistrates, not only to give comparable games but, in the case of chariot races, to give them at all. He had the number of prizes increased, so that more races were added and the managers of the factions refused to produce drivers except for a full day's racing. Aulus Fabricius Veiento when praetor had the courage to refuse their terms and to train dogs to run instead of horses. His 'strike' induced the leader of the White and Red factions to back down, but the Greens and Blues refused to participate until Nero himself contributed extra prizes. Veiento no doubt had the confidence to behave like this because he was an intimate of Nero (indeed he was finally banished in 62 for selling the patronage of the Emperor). The date of the racing episode is uncertain but clearly before 62, possibly as early as 54.[88] Nero's generosity, reminiscent of Augustus' giving of games in the names of other magistrates, expresses the attitude of his early years of rule when Otho was allowed to chide him for meanness and outdo him in displays of extravagance.[89] The story in Suetonius that Britannicus was killed because Nero was envious of his voice transfers to his first years his later attitude, which led to the death of the pantomime actor Paris during the Greek tour and inspired Helius to execute Sulpicius Camerinus and his son: they refused to give up the ancestral name Pythicus which seemed to detract from the glory of Nero's victories at the Pythian games.[90]

Nero's intolerance of rivals was not confined to the sphere of entertainments: it ultimately invaded every area of public life. On his accession he promised to rule on the Augustan model and maintained privileges conferred by his predecessors, leaving it to Seneca to proclaim his superiority to Augustus.[91] But by 67, in his speech on the liberation of Greece, he was boasting of the uniqueness and superiority of his gift in comparison to the generosity of earlier *principes*. The Greeks, who had long been calling him the 'greatest of Emperors', must have felt surprised to have their own flattery echoed and surpassed.[92] In 66 the Prefect of Egypt was relegated for having used some baths that had been specially built in Alexandria for the projected visit of the Emperor,[93] and in the two preceding years members of the noble family of the Junii Silani had been convicted of revolutionary designs, the evidence being their generosity and their habit of giving their freedmen secretaries the same titles as were used for the imperial freedmen.[94]

The deterioration in Nero's attitude to well-born and able senators led to a narrowing of the opportunities for talent that had been a feature of the period of concord with the Senate. The first sign of that early policy had been the appointment of Domitius Corbulo, a man of proven military ability connected by marriage with families thought worthy of unions with the imperial house.[95] When Corbulo was sent to command in the war against Parthia, the elderly legate of Syria, Ummidius Quadratus, was retained: it would not do to reverse all of Claudius' decisions at once and a more dynamic appointment might have made even more difficult the co-operation that geography and strategy required of the two generals. In Britain, the elderly A. Didius Gallus was similarly kept in post, as he had military successes to his credit and was clearly well able to handle the consolidation that was now required after the energetic conquest carried out under Claudius.[96] But when Nero resolved to mount an offensive into Wales, probably in 57, he chose Q. Veranius, a man of senatorial family and military accomplishment who had been honoured by Claudius with an early consulate and patrician status. Veranius was a highly ambitious man who arranged to marry his daughter into one of the most illustrious clans of the Republican nobility, but he also possessed the graces of a courtier. When he died after only one year in his province, he left a will in which the boast that he would have conquered the province within two years was combined with lavish flattery of the Emperor.[97] His successor in Britain, C. Suetonius Paullinus, was popularly regarded as Corbulo's greatest rival because of his successful campaigns in Mauretania under Claudius.

In Germany, although engineering and pacification were now the main requirements, the large number of legions (now seven) stationed there since the Varus disaster under Augustus made Emperors anxious about the two consular governors in charge. Tiberius had left two commanders related by marriage there for too long, and his successor had to remove them by force. Nero chose for Lower Germany two able provincials, first Seneca's brother-in-law Pompeius Paullinus, then Duvius Avitus, a native of Burrus' home town. In Upper Germany, he at first appointed an enterprising man of consular family, L. Antistius Vetus, but he was removed after less than a year, probably because of friction with the governor of neighbouring Gallia Belgica.[98] That Nero was still pursuing his original generous policy afterwards is shown by the appointment in 59, or soon after, of two brothers of high birth and great wealth to the two German commands. Sulpicius Scribonius Proculus in Upper Germany and Sulpicius Scribonius Rufus in Lower Germany were retained for eight years. They were clearly men of authority and diplomacy, for in 58 C. Cassius Longinus had suggested that the Senate dispatch them to restore civic order in Puteoli, after his own efforts had proved too harsh to be effective: they succeeded by exemplary punishment and the use of a praetorian cohort. While Proculus was governor, an impressive column was erected at Mainz in fulfilment of a vow taken by the settlers around the legionary camp for the safety of the Emperor: the occasion was probably either the alleged plot of Agrippina in 59 or the Pisonian conspiracy in 65. A similar monument was apparently set up in his brother's province. These were men who deserved advancement, for loyalty as well as talent.[99]

On the Danube Nero's first governors are unknown, except in the case of Moesia. There Flavius Sabinus, the brother of the future Emperor Vespasian, was retained from Claudius' day until 61 when he became Prefect of the City and was succeeded by Ti. Plautius Silvanus Aelianus, one of the patrician Aelii Lamiae adopted by a brother of Claudius' first wife, Plautia Urgulanilla. His appointment to this vital military command on the lower Danube suggests that the few cases in which generals of note suffered some interruption in their careers in the early years of the reign are not to be explained by the Princeps' own fear of birth or talent.[100]

Servius Sulpicius Galba of the Republican nobility had governed Upper Germany with distinction under Claudius, accompanied him to Britain and was then given a two-year, rather than the usual one-year, term as proconsul of Africa in 45–7. Despite triumphal honours and a reputation for justice, he was then in retirement until, in 60, Nero appointed him governor of Hispania Tarraconensis. As Plutarch says, this was before Nero became afraid of those whose standing was high. The clue to his period of idleness is his rejection of Agrippina's advances in 41 and 42: when she became Claudius' wife, Galba could expect no further posts until her death in 59.[101] Suetonius explicitly attests a similar fate for Flavius Vespasianus, a new man who owed to Narcissus a legionary legateship in Britain and a suffect consulship in 51, but was then in retirement through fear of Agrippina, until her death, when he became proconsul of Africa.[102]

In another case, it was the favour of Agrippina that stood against a man. Anteius Rufus was promised the governorship of Syria as part of Nero's reconciliation with his mother at the end of 55, but Nero probably did not wish to give a protégé of his mother the chance to detract from Corbulo's lustre, so Anteius was detained at Rome. Corbulo himself took over the Syrian command in 60, and Nero then had found a more innocuous replacement for Syria than Anteius, who was finally condemned for treason in 66. By 65, if not already in 63, Syria was under the control of Cestius Gallus, a man whose consulship lay more than twenty years in the past.[103] When serious insurrection broke out in Judaea in May of 66, he borrowed a legion from his superior, Corbulo, and took charge. But, despite his four legions, he suffered a crushing defeat in November and died in the winter of 66/7, 'carried off by fate or ennui'.[104] By then Corbulo too was dead, but he owed his demise directly to the hostility and anxiety of Nero who summoned him to Greece with fair words and then had him greeted on landing with an order for his execution. Corbulo, who had probably been expecting a further command in Judaea or further east, stabbed himself muttering 'deserved'.[105] Syria's last Neronian governor was C. Licinius Mucianus, a man whose origins were probably provincial and who had commanded one of Corbulo's eastern legions and then the difficult province of Lycia-Pamphylia adjacent to Corbulo's domains. Meanwhile a separate command had been established to deal with the Jewish war, and for that Nero selected from his own entourage in Greece the future Emperor Vespasian, whose origins were non-senatorial and whose last post in Africa had earned him little credit.[106]

The Scribonii were summoned to Greece in 67 by Nero, on the pretext that he wished to consult them, and were then driven to suicide. Nero could count on such men leaving their armies and coming without suspicion because he was known to be planning expeditions to Ethiopia and the Caucasus and might well require able generals and military advice.[107] Scribonius Rufus was replaced by Fonteius Capito who left his suffect consulship in June before his term was over. Fonteius was of consular family, but, according to Tacitus, a man of low character. His partner in Upper Germany, Verginius Rufus, was, by contrast, of the highest character but of equestrian origins like Vespasian.[108]

Finally, in 69 two elderly men of equestrian family were in charge of the Danube provinces of Dalmatia and Pannonia. Tacitus is scornful of their age and lack of energy. One of them, Pompeius Silvanus, had been narrowly acquitted on an extortion charge in 58 through imperial intervention. He was probably free to take up the post in 66 but may only have replaced A. Ducenius Geminus, also a new man, somewhat later.[109] He and his colleague, Tampius Flavianus, probably also in his sixties, might well have been appointed by Nero. In Moesia the successor of the illustrious Plautius Silvanus Aelianus was Pomponius Pius, probably of undistinguished background.[110]

If the origin and age of these late Neronian governors suggest a deliberate policy of safe appointments,[111] they do not thereby demonstrate imperial negligence. It was only a man of Galba's lineage who would feel it necessary, when in post, to seek safety in inactivity. Licinius Mucianus,

Flavius Vespasianus and Verginius Rufus were men of undoubted capacity and energy. Even Tacitus' 'rich old men' were not contemptible soldiers. Pompeius Silvanus had held two legionary commands in youth, instead of the customary one, and Tampius Flavianus while in Pannonia subdued and transplanted hostile tribesmen across the Danube, for which he received triumphal honours from Vespasian.[112]

That these were delayed honours for a success actually achieved under Nero is suggested by the resemblance between Tampius Flavianus' account of his exploits on an inscription and the record of the achievements of Plautius Silvanus Aelianus in Moesia in the sixties. In the latter case the inscription notes the grant of triumphal honours by the Senate and cites Vespasian's words on that occasion: 'He governed Moesia with such distinction that the conferment of his honours should not have been left to me'.[113] This implicit reproach testifies to the way Nero had changed his attitude and departed from his early promises. The military victories of Corbulo and Duvius Avitus had been applauded by Nero, and he took imperial salutations for them. Even Suetonius Paullinus, who was recalled in 61 after suppressing Boudicca's revolt in Britain, had his earlier successes and this victory commemorated in such a fashion as well as being honoured by a special distribution to the plebs on his return home.[114]

Nero did not put the provinces at risk by appointing incompetent governors. But he did put the confidence of the Senate at risk through his growing unwillingness to trust its aristocratic members and to reward military achievement. Instead Suetonius' elderly successor, Petronius Turpilianus, received his triumphal ornaments for helping to repress a conspiracy.[115] Ultimately, all Nero's army commanders came to feel insecure as well as unappreciated, and it was only a matter of time until one of them initiated or supported an attempt at revolution.

EIGHT

The Tyranny of Art

The mere possession of regal power is enough to encourage a taste for unique adoration. Artistic achievement, too, especially in the performing arts, tends to breed a desire for unrivalled applause. Ultimately, Nero was to be at once a tyrant and a prima donna, and to become, as might be expected from that combination of roles, jealous and vain, suspicious and vindictive.

In order to do justice to the importance of Nero's artistic streak in the evolution of his Principate, we must consider more than its final manifestation, the Emperor singing and acting on the Roman stage before a terrified captive audience. That Nero had a genuine passion for the visual, musical and literary arts, emerges even from the prejudiced accounts of the historians. Nor would it be right to consider this interest as just a consequence of his philhellenism. On the contrary, his admiration for the Greeks was founded in large measure on his attitude to the arts: he respected the high value they placed on them and the high level of achievement that was the result. For Nero was no slave to Greek ideas, even where Greek inspiration was most obviously present. Thus his Greek games were named the Neronia in contravention of Greek precedent: even Domitian was later to observe the convention of honouring the gods when he called his games the Capitolia, after Jupiter Capitolinus. In addition, Nero repeated his games at an interval of five years, perhaps observing the traditional Roman *lustrum* but, in any case, not in accordance with the Greek penteteric and trieteric intervals (intervals of four and two years) used for the four great Greek festivals.[1] These are trivial points, but there is something more important: it is possible to show that in his aesthetic ideas Nero was advancing further in the direction of the most characteristic Roman developments.

Two areas in which artistic enterprise touched traditional concerns of government were coinage and architecture. The exceptionally high level of design and execution found in Nero's coins and in the remains of his buildings at Rome has naturally led scholars to feel that Nero himself must be responsible for these high standards, and to lament the general lack of evidence for direct imperial intervention in these undertakings.

The assumption is in fact less rash in the case of Nero than of other

Emperors, even if we leave aside his well attested artistic interests. For Suetonius, speaking of Nero's victory celebrations that attended his return from the Greek tour, notes that he set up statues of himself dressed as a lyre player and struck a coin with the same device. Copper and brass coins of one of the lower denominations (the *as*) do show on the obverse, the head of Nero and his titles and, on the reverse, Apollo dressed in flowing robes and playing the lyre (fig. 31), but Suetonius' report is inaccurate in two respects. First, comparison with Augustan coins depicting Actian Apollo in similar guise shows that the god, not the Emperor, is actually depicted on the coin; then the form of Nero's name dates the coins before 66; therefore they were not struck after Nero's return from Greece in 68.[2] But there is no reason to doubt that the coins were intended and understood as an allusion to the Emperor's performances: his voice and looks had been compared to Apollo's by Seneca and Calpurnius Siculus at the start of his reign, and he had been hailed as Apollo by the audience at his first appearance on stage in 59. What is significant is the way Suetonius takes the Emperor's choice of type for granted, and indeed, given the implicit identification with Nero, it would have required extraordinary courage on the part of anyone else to have authorised such a type without at least obtaining imperial consent.[3]

As for the role of the Emperor in building his palaces in Rome, we have the first-hand evidence of Philo, who describes how some Jewish envoys were made to follow the Emperor Gaius around as he discussed building improvements with the curators of the Lamian Gardens.[4] In the case of Nero, Tacitus represents the architects, Severus and Celer, working directly with the Emperor. Moreover, he and Suetonius attribute to Nero not only projects of which they disapprove, namely the Domus Aurea and the Avernus Canal, but also the sensible safety requirements for the rebuilding of Rome after the Fire of 64.

Numismatic Innovations

It seems reasonable then to assume that where we find evidence of striking artistic innovation in the coinage or city architecture, Nero is to some extent responsible. For the coins, the radical improvement of aesthetic quality is considerable. 'It is during the Nero period that the coins of the Roman Empire unquestionably reach their highest point of artistic excellence.' This verdict of Sydenham, author of the first systematic study of the Neronian coinage, has never been impugned, nor has his analysis of its merits in terms of a combination of Greek technical skill and Roman pictorial realism.[5]

The gold and silver coins of the first decade, whose reverses feature the EX S C that advertises concord with the Senate, show no great advance on the coinage of earlier Emperors (figs. 13–17, 19). Nero's portraits, showing the subtle signs of physical maturation, are realistically and skilfully done, but the civic crown design gave little scope for innovation on the reverse and the allegorical figures that later take its place are rather stiff and show little modelling. But about the year 64 Nero's coinage underwent dramatic changes. The mint now issued, for the first time in this reign, large quantities of token coinage in the full range of denominations: the sestertii, dupondii, asses, semisses and quadrantes that traditionally provided the smaller units of the monetary system. The semis had not been issued by the Roman mint under the Augustan arrangements, and it was not the only innovation. The surfaces of the large coins, the sestertii and dupondii, had only been exploited in earlier reigns to a limited extent, while the brass or orichalcum (an alloy of copper and zinc) in which they were traditionally issued had been declining in quality and appearance. Nero's brass, by contrast, is a beautiful bright golden-yellow colour and it was now used for the smaller denominations as well, which had previously been issued in the less esteemed copper. As these developments suggest the discovery of a new metal source, it is natural to connect them with the Elder Pliny's statement, written in the 70s, that zinc ore had recently been discovered in Germany.[6]

On the larger of these handsome coins the beautifully executed portraits of the Emperor, characteristic of all the later Neronian coins, are best displayed (figs. 18, 22, 27, 30–1). The increasingly bloated look of Nero's face and neck, in combination with facial detail and expressions familiar from the earlier portraits, argue for realistic portrayal; yet an element of idealisation has been detected in the slight upward tilt of the head and the deep setting of the eyes, which owe something to Hellenistic inspiration.[7] Again, Nero's hair-style with its stiff row of curls, flat on the forehead, then waved high behind, was not pure stylisation on the coins, for Suetonius tells us that Nero took to wearing his hair 'arranged in steps'. This coiffure was clearly modelled on that of charioteers and actors, and it is worn by Apollo when he is represented as Apollo Auriga or Citharoedus.[8] Similarly, the later style he affected on the Greek tour, with the hair growing long at the back, is shown on coins of that date. Yet realism cannot explain the beard that often appears, for Nero was clean-shaven: it may be symbolic of his paternal ancestry.[9]

The reverses of the later coins, however, represent the clearest advance on earlier types. There appear all at once a range of designs, all finely executed and showing a great variety in conception. Elegant single figures, reminiscent of Greek statues in their general posture and fine drapery, represent Roma (fig. 26), Victoria (fig. 30), Securitas (fig. 29), Apollo Citharoedus (fig. 31). Greek inspiration shows most clearly in these figures and in those that occur in groups on the Annona and Ceres coins (fig. 23), the *adlocutio* type where Nero is shown addressing the Praetorian Guard, the *congiarium* design where he distributes largesse, and the *decursio* coins where he exercises on horseback (fig. 25).[10] But the composition of these groups is a new development going beyond anything found on earlier coins, Greek or Roman. Finally, the Roman passion for architecture and realism issues in the wonderful diagram of the port of Ostia (fig. 24), and in fine and detailed sketches of the temple of Vesta, the gates of Janus (fig. 21), Nero's elaborate market (fig. 28) and his triumphal arch (fig. 27).

The relevance of these types to the years from 63 to 66 when they were issued is not always clear. The Securitas coins may be directly related to the suppression of the Pisonian conspiracy in 65. But some coins apparently advertise earlier benefits of the Emperor: the first *congiarium* in 57, the institution of the Greek quinquennial games in 60 (fig. 32), the building of the market in 59 and of the triumphal arch, voted in 58 and erected in 62. Others may just proclaim his continued concern for the corn supply, or his willingness to heed the warning he received in the temple of Vesta. On the other hand, it may be that Nero actually completed some of the harbour buildings at Ostia, and that the temple, the market and the arch required some rebuilding after the Great Fire.[11] The Janus coins present a different problem, for Suetonius dates the closure to the visit of Tiridates in 66, while some of the coins are dated as early as 64/5. Suetonius may be in error. The closure could have taken place earlier, as the diplomatic arrangements for Tiridates' coronation at Rome, which ended the conflict with Parthia, were made in 63. Alternatively, it is conceivable that the coins were planned and issued in advance of the actual ceremony, for Tiridates delayed, and his arrival was probably later than Nero originally hoped.[12]

What is clear is that the types themselves lend support to the notion that Nero chose them. The only military achievements explicitly celebrated concern Armenia, which also received the greatest prominence in the Emperor's imperial salutations. Also stressed are the corn supply, building projects, and imperial generosity. The Greek games are commemorated, the smallest coins (semisses and quadrantes) being exclusively devoted to them. Finally, Nero's personal performances are celebrated on the Apollo coins and on one of the Victoria types: this has a Victory with a palm branch and statuette of Minerva on the reverse and, on the obverse, Nero wearing a garland of bay, olive and perhaps pine, both sides commemorating the triumphs of the Greek tour.[13]

The latest date on the series of gold and silver coins carrying the unusual 'EX S C' is *tribunicia potestas* x (December 63–December 64). The other precious metal coins from Nero's reign bear no specific dates but are sharply distinguishable from these in portraiture and type. In these respects, moreover, they resemble closely token coins that carry dates of *tribunicia potestas* XI and later. This hint of a chronological break in the gold and silver issues fits well with other indications of a sharp change: the undated coins do not carry the 'EX S C' and are lower in weight than the dated. The silver coins show in addition a notable decrease in the percentage of pure silver.

The other changes concern the token coinage. The introduction of brass for the lower denominations brought with it a reduction in the size of the as, semis and quadrans, since copper, in which they had previously been struck, was regarded as lower in value. To clarify the new system, token coins issued from about mid-64 display marks of value: the as is marked I, the dupondius II, the semis S (figs. 30–2). More traditional was the S C that all the denominations bore (figs. 24, 26–8, 30–2), a characteristic of the token coinage from Augustus' time. Finally, as careful analysis of iconography and technique reveals, some of the later token coinage was being produced by some other mint besides the one at Rome (figs. 27–9). There is widespread agreement that this mint was the one at the Roman colony of Lugdunum, previously used by Augustus and Tiberius for the production of gold and silver but no longer operative since Gaius.[14] The lower denominations in brass seem to peter out about a year later.

How are all these changes related, and what were they meant to achieve? Except for the reduction in the weight of the aureus, which is noted by the Elder Pliny, they are not mentioned by any ancient author.[15] For the reduction in the metal content of the gold and silver, the obvious explanation is financial stringency. The government could stretch its bullion reserves to meet its obligations in this way, and, provided the change was not so drastic as to drive the older, heavier coins out of circulation, it could make a considerable profit in recoining the old coins as they came in through taxes or other payments.[16] The date of late 64–5 for the change naturally suggests some connection with the Great Fire of July 64. The financial strain involved in providing emergency food and shelter, and then in implementing Nero's ambitious plans for rebuilding the city, provides an obvious motive for the government to reduce the metal content.[17]

No such obvious explanation suggests itself for Nero's introduction of a general brass coinage. Recent work seems to have weakened some of the most favoured hypotheses. Some variation in the relative weights of the brass and copper coins under Gaius and Claudius prompted the idea that it was difficult to adjust the coins to the market price of the two metals, and that Nero's plan was to eliminate the problem by coining only in brass. But it now seems likely that the general brass coinage was preceded in late 62 or 63 by an issue of copper asses, semisses and quadrantes, which followed the weight ratio that had obtained under Claudius, and that, after the abandonment of the general brass coinage, all denominations were struck again in the two metals, at a lower weight but with much the same ratio. There is thus little reason to think that Nero felt this ratio to be problematic. Another idea that enjoyed a great vogue was that Nero the philhellene was trying to relate the Roman token coinage more closely to the various systems existing in the Greek cities of the eastern empire. But, while later Emperors seem to have produced asses in orichalchum for distribution in the East, Nero's asses, semisses and quadrantes in the metal were struck at the mint of Rome and circulated principally in Italy.

After the issue of small copper coins (which do not carry s c) Nero seems to have introduced first a general brass coinage without s c (figs. 23, 25, 29) or marks of value in late 63–64. Then in mid-64 and early 65, a large number of coins of all denominations were produced with s c and marks of value and, at the end of that issue, the weight of all the denominations was reduced by 5–10%. The use of brass instead of copper for the lower denominations could have been of some financial advantage to the mint, in that the coins could be lighter, and so more could be produced from the same amount of copper. But the financial gain was small, not at all comparable with that involved in recoining gold and silver, and would probably not have been worth the trouble. The subsequent fine adjustment of weight downward is best explained as a way of restoring the old relation between the precious metal coinage and the token coinage when the weight of the former was changed.[18] It is possible that the production of large quantities of token coinage is related to government spending after the Fire, but if the first introduction of the general brass coinage comes before late 64 it is hard to think that it was introduced suddenly without a good deal of prior planning.

Yet the Fire may still have some connection with this general brass coinage. This large undertaking may well have required an expansion of the organisation at the mint which was probably still located, as in the Republic, in the temple of Juno Moneta on the Capitoline Hill. This district was probably one of those only partially affected by the Fire, but, since we know that by the reign of Trajan the mint was in Region III, one of those demolished by the Fire, it seems reasonable to suggest that it was Nero who transferred the mint when its new location on the Caelian Hill became available.[19] The move may have facilitated the production of the principal brass issue with s c in 64–5, yet the principal effect of the Fire on the new brass coinage was probably to end it altogether. By 65 the full extent of the financial resources needed to rebuild the city will have been realised. The renewed production of gold and silver meant that the mint now had to abandon the elaborate scheme for the token coinage: both at Rome and at Lugdunum, the older system of larger denominations in brass, smaller in copper, was reintroduced for token coins, which by now were in short supply.[20] The older explanations of the abandonment of the experiment, namely that the smaller brass coins proved unacceptable, or that the system was too complicated, are less plausible, especially in view of the orichalchum asses circulated in the East by later Emperors.

If the general brass coinage does not seem to have been called forth by a financial emergency, or by practical problems of bimetallism, or by philhellenism, how shall we explain it? Given that there had been a long gap since the last token issues, Nero must have realised that there would be a need to issue some sooner or later. But the use of the new and beautiful alloy in such an imaginative and systematic way suggests one aspect of the artistic temperament. It was not a totally new idea; in fact, Corinth, and perhaps other Greek cities, had already produced a complete range of token coinage in brass. The idea of a set of coins that looked fine and matched in colour and design must have appealed to Nero, who liked carrying things out in a whole-hearted way, without compromise. Nor was it an impracticable idea. Indeed, some features of the scheme endured: the new weights of the coins, like those of the gold and silver, were maintained by later Emperors, the Roman mint remained on the Caelian Hill, and the mint at Lugdunum was kept open into the reign of Vespasian.[21]

We may have some reflection of Nero's attitude to his new coinage in a curious passage of Suetonius, explaining how Nero raised money for an expedition against Vindex and Galba in 68. One of his measures was to demand that all citizens make a contribution from their capital, and that all tenants of private houses and flats pay a year's rent to his treasury, instead of paying their landlords. He insisted 'with great fastidiousness and rigour' that these payments be made in 'new coin, refined silver and pure gold': the demand for new coin is usually aesthetic, as in its use for gifts.[22]

It will be convenient to raise here a question about the later coinage that relates to our preoccupations in earlier chapters.[24] How are we to explain the abandonment of EX S C on the late gold and silver, and the initial omission of S C on the token coinage, followed by its restoration on the final issues? We have already noted that the presence of EX S C until late 64 blurs Tacitus' turning point of 62. Apparently, Nero felt no desire until then to withdraw this early gesture of respect to the Senate. It therefore becomes hard to explain the omission of the traditional S C on the token coins as a deliberate affront to that body, for these coins seem to have been issued during the last two years of the initial gold and silver. Nero might have wished to maintain the old distinction between the two types of coins without altering his arrangement for the precious metals and so, in a sense, maintained it in reverse. But with his plan to interrupt the issues of gold and silver in order to devote the energies of the mint to the general brass coinage, he may have decided to awaken earlier tradition and restore the S C. The emergency gold and silver subsequently required was not in the original plan, and so the EX S C was now omitted and the distinction between precious metal and token coinage reinstated in the traditional form. On this view, the prolonged presence of EX S C was far more significant than its later absence.

Architecture and Town Planning

Nero's building projects exhibit some of the same characteristics as his later coinage. In design they are advanced, but again it is the most distinctively Roman developments that they carry further. Severus and Celer, the chief architects and engineers for Nero's palaces, and probably for other projects, were not Greek by origin, to judge by their names. Indeed, the Romans had long felt particularly at home in architecture and engineering, so much so that by Trajan's time, Pliny had to be reminded that the Greek cities of his province of Bithynia abounded in competent architects, and that many of those working in Rome came from the Greek world.[23]

Even the decoration shows no slavish adherence to Greek taste. Its designs and mythological scenes belong to a fashion long current in the city and also known at Pompeii. This is not to deny that many of the techniques used, and many of the artists employed, originated from the Greek East, but only to argue that Nero's architectural ambitions are not to be understood as an aspect of his philhellenism. Indeed, his chief painter Famulus, whose name does not suggest Greek origin, clearly regarded himself as a Roman of the deepest dye. According to the Elder Pliny, most of his work was in Nero's palace, the Domus Aurea, where he painted for a few hours every day 'with dignity, dressed always in a toga even when using scaffolding'.[24] Pliny contrasts his severe and dignified carriage with his painting, which he calls *floridus, umidus: floridus* appears to relate to his use of expensive pigments of red, blue, gold and purple, which only a rich patron could supply.[25] The style found in the Golden House is identified as the impressionistic ivth Pompeian style, and the summary execution and smallness of the designs, in comparison with the size of the rooms, has been subjected to sharp criticism from students of Roman painting in this century. Its decorative qualities were better understood by the Renaissance artists who climbed down into the rooms of the Domus Aurea, left their names scratched on the walls, and adopted the style they discovered there. The grotesques, as the designs were called from the grottoes in which they were found, were then more numerous and better preserved than they are now: they provided the inspiration for the painting in the Vatican loggia by Raphael and his assistants. Even now the originals, if understood as a kind of sophisticated wallpaper (a white ground is favoured in what were probably the darker rooms), give an impression of grace and elegance despite their poor state of preservation (figs. 7–8).

Famulus was perhaps ahead of the artists at Pompeii in his adoption of the ivth style, and his version of it shows some individual characteristics in tonality and organisation of space. But art historians are agreed that the only major innovation found in the Domus Aurea, and perhaps attributable to him, is the use of vault mosaics. One clear example survives on the vault of a room in the west wing identified as a nymphaeum: here, set against the reddish background of the vault, is an octagonal shape in white with two dark figures on it. The limitation to two colours clearly suggests the model of floor mosaics and supports the notion that this is one of the first ventures in applying mosaic technique to vaults on an extensive scale, a technique which was to become so important in early Christian art.[26] Nero also added to the repertoire of decoration new examples of the coloured marbles long admired in Rome, including porphyry from Egypt and serpentine from Laconia.

Nonetheless, the innovations in decoration are less impressive than those in architecture and engineering. All the remains of Neronian buildings show an adventurous use of vaults, domes and arcades, precisely those shapes that represent the most important advance made on Greek design by Rome. There is a reliance on concrete faced with brick, the principal Roman contribution to building materials.[27] These features are matched by an enthusiasm for engineering feats which could challenge the obstruction of nature. We have already noted Nero's canal projects in which, following Caesar and Claudius, he applied this type of ingenuity to the practical purpose of improving corn transport. But Nero's delight in such virtuosity for its own sake was in tune with Roman tradition, though this 'lover of the incredible', as Tacitus calls him, showed a new ardour and fresh imagination, especially where luxury and pleasure could be enhanced.[28] By AD 60 Nero had exploited the natural beauties of the upper Anio valley to build a lovely villa at Sublaqueum (modern Subiaco). Showing his well-attested fascination with water as a decorative element, he had an enormous dam constructed which caused two of the three lakes to join into one narrow lake with two basins.[29] Among the schemes unfinished at his death was a great covered pool several miles long, surrounded by colonnades extending from Misenum to Lake Avernus, and fed by the hot springs around Baiae. The work reached a sufficiently advanced stage to feature on glass flasks of the third and fourth centuries made in the region of the Bay of Naples, perhaps as a touristic novelty: a sketch of the coast from Misenum to Baiae engraved on the flasks shows various monuments including this *stagnum Neronis* (Nero's pool).[30]

It was in Nero's palaces, the Domus Transitoria ruined by the Fire of 64 and the Domus Aurea that he did not live to complete, that all of these features reach their culmination. There survives under the remains of Domitian's palace on the Palatine a complex of rooms belonging to the Domus Transitoria. Several richly decorated chambers open off a nymphaeum with multiple cascades spilling behind an ornate podium, whose architectonic decoration is reminiscent of the stage (fig. 12). This is a summer apartment receiving air and light indirectly from a court-yard, and supplied with hypocausts and air spaces to protect the structure from the dampness of the fountains.[31] Finally, the Domus Aurea presents a wealth of architectural innovation including an exploitation of the dome to create a new conception of internal space: we can still appreciate the type of effect in a later building, namely the Pantheon as rebuilt by Hadrian.

Nero's projects for building also recall the spirit of his general brass coinage in their uncompromising and systematic character. If so many of these schemes were unfinished, that was not because he tired of large projects, or shrank from the difficulties, but because he died at 31, earlier than he or anyone else would have predicted.[32] The splendour of the early works, the amphitheatre, the market, the bath-gymnasium complex (an innovation in Rome), show how determined he was to create the best buildings that Roman technology could produce. But they were also useful buildings, in the tradition of imperial contributions to the amenities of Rome. Even the *arcus Neroniani*, which supplied the lake for Nero's last palace, was built earlier and with more general uses in mind: it was an extension of the Claudian aqueduct westward to the Caelian, Aventine, Palatine Hills, and the area across the Tiber.[33]

The imperial residence he built or was building for himself before the Fire seems to be at once more unorthodox and more selfish than these utilitarian constructions. All Tacitus and Suetonius tell us of the Domus Transitoria was that it was designed to connect the Palatine Hill with the Gardens of Maecenas on the Esquiline. Until very recently the only remains that archaeologists could attribute with confidence to the Domus Transitoria were on the Palatine. Now its extent has been confirmed by fresh investigations of the remains of the Domus Aurea on the Oppian Hill: the older palace, it appears, already occupied this same site near the Gardens of Maecenas.[34] The most likely interpretation of Nero's plan is that it was a scheme to connect the major imperial properties in Rome, the more official quarters on the Palatine with the more comfortable gardens and villas near the edge of the city, the Maecenatian, Lamian and Lollian Gardens.

The Emperors conducted business, as Roman magistrates had always done, in their own residences,[35] but since these tended to increase by inheritance from one Emperor to another in no very systematic way it must have been difficult to co-ordinate their official activities: the archive rooms, assembly halls and offices of their minions were scattered over a wide area. The original imperial residence was Augustus' house which, like those of many other nobles, was on the Palatine. Augustus himself and his successors expanded the Palatine buildings. The fact that even the parsimonious and conservative Tiberius built a palace there suggests that there must have been some need for expansion.[36] Gradually the Hill was to become identified with the imperial position, though some private houses were still found there after Nero's time.[37] Nero's addition to these buildings on the Palatine was then entirely in accordance with precedent and not to be assumed irrelevant to his imperial duties, even if the most striking remains found under Domitian's later palace rather suggest, as we have seen, the purposes of leisure. But without knowing the nature of the connection made across the valley of the Colosseum, it is hard to say if the Domus Transitoria broke sharply with earlier imperial practice by interfering with pre-existing buildings or roads, and thus disrupting the life of the capital. Several strands of evidence, however, suggest that it did not. Though both authors are eloquently hostile towards the Domus Aurea, Tacitus scarcely mentions the earlier palace which it replaced, and Suetonius comments only on its cost. Furthermore, an anecdote in Suetonius shows that Nero himself was held to be dissatisfied with the earlier scheme, since he is said to have remarked of the Domus Aurea that at last he was beginning to be housed like a human being. It seems likely then that, despite his architectural imagination and ambition, Nero at first accepted the limits set by tradition on the kind of building and the limits set by existing conditions on its extent. But he may well have grumbled more than Augustus, who made his forum narrower than he had planned because he preferred not to resort to confiscation or compulsory purchase.[38]

The Great Fire of 64 presented Nero with new opportunities for freer building, just as it may have increased the opportunities for innovatory

1   Statue of the young Nero (*Musée du Louvre*)

2   Bust of Nero in the Terme Museum, Rome (*Deutsches Archaeologisches Institut, Rome*)

3   Late bust of Nero (*Worcester Art Museum, Massachusetts*)

 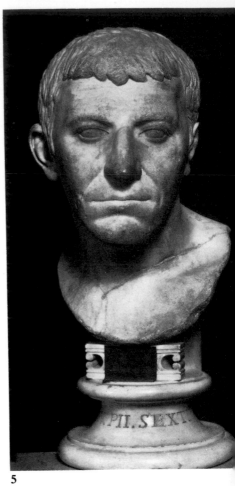

4   5

4   Seneca, from a double herm of Seneca and Socrates (*Staatliche Museen, Berlin*)

5   Bust of Domitius Corbulo in the Museo Capitolino, Rome (*Mansell Collection*)

6 Fresco of the riot in the amphitheatre at Pompeii in AD 59 from the Museo
Nazionale, Naples (*Mansell Collection*)

7

8

7 Fresco from the
Sala degli Uccelletti in
the Domus Aurea
(*Fototeca Unione*)

8 Corridor of the
Domus Aurea (*Fototeca
Unione*)

9   The dome and openings for lighting of the octagonal hall in the Domus Aurea (*Fototeca Unione*)

10   Octagonal domed hall in the centre of the Domus Aurea (*Fototeca Unione*)

11   Eastern part of the northern buttresses of the temple terrace, Temple of Divus Claudius (*Fototeca Unione*)

12   Eastern side of the nymphaeum intersected by a foundation wall of the Domus Aurea (*Fototeca Unione*)

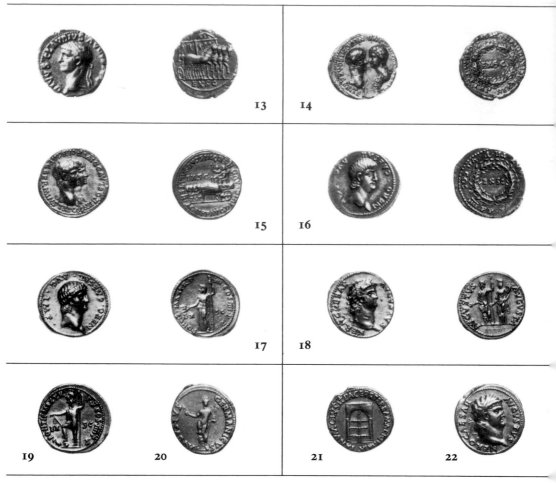

13 14

15 16

17 18

19 20 21 22

Aurei and Denarii (actual size) (*Ashmolean Museum, Oxford*)

13   *Obv.* Divus Claudius laureate. *Rev.* Quadriga EX S C [*RIC²* Nero 4; *BMC* I Nero 4]

14   *Obv.* Busts of Nero and Agrippina (facing). *Rev.* Nero's titles EX S C [*RIC²* 1; *BMC* 1]

15   *Obv.* Busts of Nero and Agrippina (jugate). *Rev.* 2 radiate divi EX S C [*RIC²* 6; *BMC* 7]

16   *Obv.* Nero bareheaded. *Rev.* Oak-wreath EX S C [*RIC²* 21; *BMC* 23]

17   *Obv.* Nero bareheaded. *Rev.* Ceres EX S C [*RIC²* 23; *BMC* 25]

18   *Obv.* Nero laureate, bearded. *Rev.* Augustus Augusta. [*RIC²* 44; *BMC* 52]

19   *Rev.* Virtus EX S C [*RIC²* 40; *BMC* 45]

20   *Rev.* Augustus Germanicus (Nero radiate). [*RIC²* 46; *BMC* 56]

23 24

25 26

27

21 Gates of Janus. [*RIC*² 50; *BMC* 64]

22 *Obv*. Nero laureate, bearded [*RIC*² 52; *BMC* 67]

Sestertii (actual size) (*Ashmolean Museum, Oxford*)

23 *Rev*. Annona Augusti Ceres. [*RIC*² 98]

24 *Rev*. August (i) Por (t) Ost (i) s c [*RIC*² 181; *BMC* 134]

25 *Rev*. Decursio. [*RIC*² 107]

26 *Rev*. Roma s c [*RIC*² 274; *BMC* 178]

27 *Obv*. Imp Nero Caesar with globe (Lugdunum mint). *Rev*. Triumphal Arch s c [*RIC*² 500; *BMC* 333]

28 | 29

30

31 | 32

Dupondii, As and Semis (actual size) (*Ashmolean Museum, Oxford*)

28 *Rev.* Mac (ellum) Aug. s c [*RIC²* 402; *BMC* 336]

29 *Rev.* Securitas Augusti. [*RIC²* 519; *BMC* 342]

30 *Obv.* Nero radiate. *Rev.* Victoria Augusti s c. Mark of value: ii. [*RIC²* 199; *BMC* 219]

31 *Obv.* Nero radiate. *Rev.* Apollo with lyre s c. Mark of value: i. [*RIC²* 211; *BMC* 256]

32 *Rev.* Cer (tamen) quin (quennale) Rom(a) Co(stitutum) s c. Mark of value: s. [*RIC²* 233; *BMC* 261]

coinage. Though Rome was regularly subject to fires as a consequence of overcrowding, timber construction, and inadequate fire-fighting apparatus, there was nothing routine about this blaze. It broke out in the early hours of 19 July and lasted for six days, only to be renewed for a further three days: it effectively levelled three of the fourteen regions (3, 10, 11) into which Augustus had divided Rome, leaving only four untouched (1, 5, 6, 14).[39] The first outbreak started in some shops to the south of the Palatine around the Circus Maximus, and spread north along the east side of the Palatine, through the Colosseum Valley to the lower reaches of the Esquiline. The second outbreak started to the north of the Capitoline Hill but apparently did not spread to the Campus Martius where buildings were opened to homeless inhabitants of the city.

The Fire destroyed shops, tenements, large private houses and temples in the heart of the city, and thus gave the artistic Emperor an opportunity to rebuild Rome nearer to his heart's desire. Unfortunately, it is very difficult to recover Nero's intentions because this scheme, left incomplete, was soon abandoned by his successors. Indeed, much that had been finished was undone in the reaction that began under the Flavian dynasty, so that, for architectural remains, we are left only with what survived in the basements of other men's buildings. Again, Nero's plans attracted the attention of our literary sources precisely because they affected people intimately and hence produced strong and biased reactions. These feelings are reflected in our sources and render them suspect.

It was, in fact, not so much the general reconstruction plan as its crowning feature, Nero's new palace, that attracted strong hostility. When discussing the general rebuilding of the city Tacitus and Suetonius manage to give some dispassionate detail intermixed with cool criticism and even tepid approval on social and aesthetic grounds. Indeed Tacitus, as well as Dio, looks with favour on the controlled rebuilding which Nero initiated, in comparison with the haphazard reconstruction of Rome after the Gallic sack four and a half centuries earlier.[40] This same explanation (certainly false) of the irregularity of early Rome is found in Livy who speaks of the result of the early rebuilding as 'a city filled up rather than laid out': he no doubt reveals the attitude of the Augustan age, which may still have been the attitude of Nero's contemporaries. Certainly the historians attest that coincidence of date between the Fire of 64 and the Gallic sack was noted at the time, which makes it likely that their comparisons of the two reconstructions also go back to 64. The anonymous epigram that circulated at the time, 'Rome will become one house; move to Veii, citizens, if that house does not take over Veii too', recalls with irony the suggestion made on the earlier occasion, according to tradition, that Rome's inhabitants move to Veii rather than rebuild their city.[41] This time, it is suggested, the rebuilding itself was to cause the migration. Yet the epigram helps to confirm that hostility was directed at the Domus Aurea rather than at the general plans for urban reconstruction.

Nero introduced new building regulations in the hope of preventing such devastating fires in the future. He revived the Augustan limit on height, which had been ignored, and laid down rules against timber construction and shared walls: fire-resistant stone was to be used. The streets were to be wider and regularly laid out, and tenement congestion was to be reduced by the provision of both internal courtyards and porticoes on the ground floor facing the street, which could also serve as protection against falling debris in the event of fire. To government control was added government help. Probably as a protection against looting, debris was to be left untouched until removed free of charge and carried down the Tiber by returning corn ships. The availability of public water was to be protected by supervisors. Finally, Nero contributed out of his own funds to the building of the porticoes.[42]

The actual rebuilding was mostly left to private initiative: the cleared areas were restored to the owners of the tenements, and rewards were offered to those who built private houses or tenements within a limited space of time. The jurists preserve one example of these incentives that shows Nero closely following Claudian rewards for building corn ships: a Junian Latin who invested at least 100,000 sesterces in building a house in Rome would obtain Roman citizenship.[43] The task of rebuilding was immense. It was not finished within the four years that remained to Nero, though the poor state in which Vespasian found Rome owed something to the later fire of 69, and to the presence of armies in the city during the Civil Wars that followed Nero's fall.[44] The only criticism Tacitus records of the new plans seems reasonable to us: the inhabitants would be more exposed to the heat of the sun.[45] But other periods have had to learn the shortcomings of town planning by bitter experience, and Tacitus himself does not subscribe to the view.

So far, Nero's intentions do not seem to transcend pragmatic reconstruction; but more ambitious designs probably went with his vision of a Rome of spacious avenues. Suetonius notes in connection with the building code, in the part of his biography that is supposed to contain blameless deeds, an unfulfilled plan to extend the walls of Rome as far as Ostia and to connect the old city with Ostia by a canal. The two schemes form a whole, for the canal, which would have facilitated the supply of corn to the city, would have been particularly necessary should the expansion of the city bring with it, as must have seemed likely, an increase in population. Though the extent of the expansion may be exaggerated by Suetonius, the existence of such a plan gains some plausibility from Tacitus' remark that the rubble from the fire was to be used to fill the marshy land of the coastal plain behind Ostia.[46] Nero's schemes for widening the streets, controlling building heights, and creating open spaces, would in themselves have helped to create a housing shortage, to say nothing of his plans for the Domus Aurea, which was to cover some heavily residential and commercial areas.[47] If Nero avoided expropriation, as his promise to return cleared tenement sites to their owners suggests, he may have been hoping to persuade owners of damaged sites near the centre to sell them and to buy in the new area opened up for development. Thus an extensive enlargement of the city is not out of keeping with the general tenor of Nero's plans, which were rational and practical, however imaginative and ambitious.

The only feature of Nero's plans for Rome that smacks of megalomania is the popular belief, reported by Tacitus without corroboration, that Nero wanted the glory of founding a new city to be named after himself. Suetonius, who vouches for the intention, gives the new name as Neropolis.[48] What value are we to attach to this story? When Commodus later espoused such a plan he is said to have favoured the name Colonia Commodiana; earlier the Senate had made the more modest proposal that the Mons Caelius, after a fire there, be renamed the Mons Augustus in honour of Tiberius' generosity to the distressed.[49] Is the choice of a Greek name supposed to suggest Nero's beloved Greek city of Naples (Neapolis), or worse, the type of Hellenistic self-glorification expressed in the name of Alexandria? Previous Roman Emperors, like the Roman generals before them, had christened cities of the East Pompeiopolis, Sebasteia, Claudio-polis. Yet in Italy towns usually took colonial titles, as did Nero's colony of Puteoli. The important thing to remember is that Tacitus does not give the form of the name, nor does he vouch for the story of the proposed change; while, in Suetonius, it occurs in a hostile chapter about Nero's preposterous lust for eternal fame, along with other alleged changes of name probably not instigated by him.[50] In such a malicious anecdote a Greek form of name would be chosen to suggest Nero's absurd philhellenism.

The only other sign of megalomania at this time is the bronze colossus, a statue of Nero about 120 Roman feet high intended to be placed on the Sacra Via in front of the Golden House. The colossus was certainly a piece of self-glorification, even if one rejects theories that it showed Nero wearing a radiate crown, or represented as the Sun-god. The most likely interpret-ation of the confusing evidence is that Nero intended the statue to depict himself, that Vespasian left it *in situ* but had it redesigned and dedicated to the sun, and that Hadrian finally moved it near the Colosseum when he built his temple of Venus and Rome at the end of the Sacra Via.[51] There had long been statues of the Emperor and members of his family set up in Rome, but the size of this monument clearly made a different impact, for colossal statues were traditionally reserved for the gods. Indeed Zenodorus had made such a statue of Mercury, which led to his employment by Nero. The imperial commission resulted in an object of artistic beauty, worked in the material preferred by the sculptor, not in the gold and silver Nero offered, and designed on a scale to match the entrance to Nero's own palace.[52]

The rumour about renaming the city was not based only on what the colossus seemed to show of Nero's attitude. Great programmes of urban building had long been associated with self-advertisement. We have only to think of Sulla, Pompey and Caesar in the Republic, and then of the first

Princeps. If Nero, who had always loved acclaim, had ambitious plans for rebuilding Rome, no quantity of sober rules and practical provisions could obscure the obvious truth that the Emperor was seeking to create a focus for eternal applause.

But the rumours went further than megalomania. Imperial arson is alleged by Suetonius and Dio, and, even earlier, by the Elder Pliny.[53] But the belief in arson was already current in Nero's reign, for one of the praetorian officers who joined the Pisonian conspiracy reproached Nero with burning Rome.[54] Tacitus indicates that the story was actually contemporary with the event itself by ascribing to Nero's awareness of such a rumour his decision to find a scapegoat in the Christians: they were accused *en bloc* of incendiarism and visited with the punishment that fitted the crime, being used as living torches to light Nero's circus games.[55]

The scale and fury of the Fire naturally prompted the desire to blame someone, and suspicion of Nero was increased by the fact that the second outbreak began on Tigellinus' estates. Suetonius and Dio, like the author of the *Octavia*, imagine Nero indulging in an act of wanton and malicious destruction. Suetonius in fact says that the *pretext* (presumably more respectable than the real motive) was Nero's distaste for the ugliness and chaos of old Rome.[56] No doubt Nero's feelings about the city were well known, especially his dissatisfaction with the limits of his own palace, the Domus Transitoria. The idea of his aesthetic glee also seems to lie behind the story that Nero, when he returned to Rome from Antium on hearing the news, recited the 'Capture of Ilium' as he watched the flames: Tacitus gives this as a contemporary rumour and locates the performance on a private stage; Suetonius and Dio treat it as fact and locate it in public with the Emperor dressed in stage costume.[57]

The rumours of arson were natural enough, especially among those who already distrusted and disliked the Emperor. Tacitus is sceptical, and he seems in this to be not only unique but also just. The Fire, after all, did not start, or restart, in the area Nero ultimately developed for the Domus Aurea. It damaged his own newly-built apartments on the Palatine and Oppian Hills and, though he was to change somewhat the orientation of the rooms there, the similar style of painting and wall decoration together with the emphasis on fountains and pools in the Domus Aurea show that these rooms, and not just their location, must have continued to please him.[58] Indeed, in the Palatine wing some of the marble wall decoration seems to have been stripped for immediate use in the new structure built there at a higher level after the Fire.[59] In addition, a fire on this scale was bound to involve a great deal of unpopularity and expense for the Emperor, as past history showed. Finally, it has been calculated that the moon was full on 17 July in 64, just two days before the outbreak of the Fire, so that no worse time could have been chosen if arsonists going about with torches were to escape detection.[60]

Nero first attempted to quash the rumours by religious ceremonies designed to appease the supposedly angry gods. But, according to Tacitus, that was not enough, so he decided to fasten guilt on a human culprit, the Christians. The reason for choosing this unpopular group in particular is not recoverable. No doubt they had not participated in the preceding acts of worship, but then neither had the Jews: the clear distinction now made between these two detested sects, and the decision to punish only the younger offshoot, has been attributed to the influence of Poppaea who was a Jewish sympathiser. Nero did not succeed in suppressing the rumour of his personal responsibility for the disaster. It was probaby spread in the initial panic by some victims of the Fire, kept going by those whose losses were made permanent by Nero's building projects, and intensified by resentment at the fact that the extension of Rome, which would have afforded some relief, was never carried out.

The loss of housing for the plebs does not seem to have seriously impaired his popularity with them, even in the short term.[61] But there were owners of large houses who suffered, and they belonged to the section of society that had begun to fear the worst from the young Emperor after the divorce of Octavia, the elimination of Rubellius Plautus, Cornelius Sulla and D. Junius Silanus Torquatus, and Nero's public performance at Naples.

Of the area that we know to have been occupied by the Domus Aurea much was already in imperial hands, such as the parts of the Palatine and Esquiline Hills already used for the Domus Transitoria. Nero may have occupied the sites of some of the grand houses on the Palatine that had been damaged by the Fire, though some were still in private possession later on.[62] In the valley of the Colosseum, where he had his famous lake, there might previously have been shops of the kind the Fire destroyed when it started in the adjoining area to the south. The likelihood that this was, at least partially, a commercial area is increased by a plausible identification of the *horrea* or warehouses whose destruction Suetonius dramatises as a work of organised demolition: they could be those found under the nave of the Church of S. Clemente not far to the east of the Colosseum.[63] To the north, the Flavian poet Martial indicates that houses of the poor were sacrificed to Nero's park in the area, covered in his day by Titus' Baths. And here, on the Oppian Hill, next to the extant portions of the palace, have been found the remains of private houses of Republican date with various kinds of mosaic flooring indicating that some of them were quite modest dwellings.[64] To the south, Nero used the site of the temple of Divus Claudius, which he had authorised while his mother was alive, and on which much work had already been done.[65]

It is clear then that some private owners, rich and poor, saw the great palace and its parks laid out over the places in which they had lived and worked. It was traditional to approve of utilitarian building, but even public buildings whose purposes were not clearly for the public good could be criticised. All the more vulnerable then was Nero's Golden House. It could still be adduced half a century later in distant Bithynia as an example

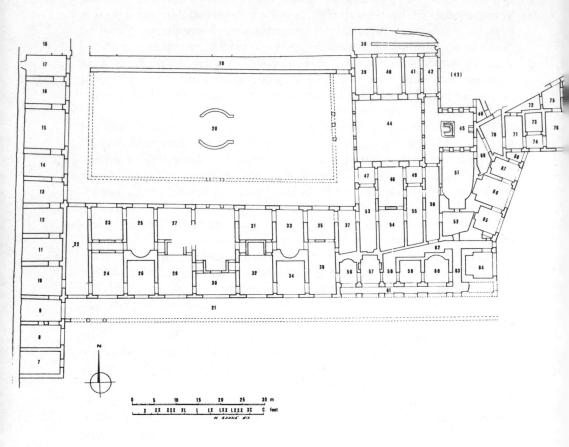

1   The lower floor of the Domus Aurea building in the light of recent excavations. The Octagon Room (no. 128) was probably the centre of a symmetrical plan, as suggested by the two trapezoidal courts. (Courtesy Laura Fabbrini)

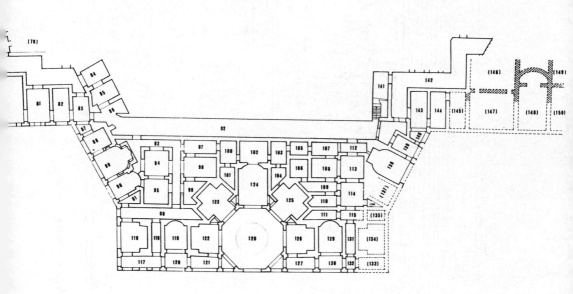

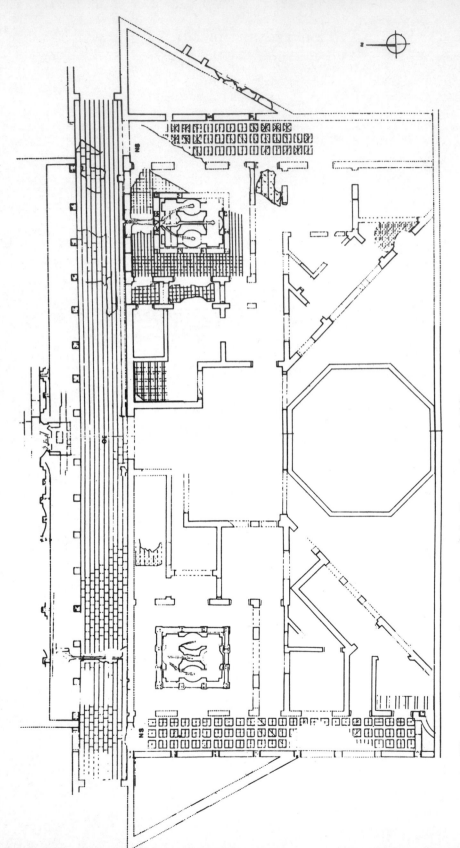

2　The recently-excavated upper floor of the Domus Aurea building on the Oppian Hill. (Courtesy Laura Fabbrini)

of selfish building to which citizens might reasonably object, in contrast with 'lofty edifices worthy of a great city'.[66] By that time successive Emperors had covered the major areas of the palace with public buildings of undoubted utility: the temple of Divus Claudius rebuilt by Vespasian, his great amphitheatre The Colosseum and perhaps a temple of the Sun for the redesigned Colossus;[67] then came the Baths of Titus, the gladiatorial school (the Ludus Magnus) of Domitian, his imperial residence of the Palatine, and finally Trajan's Baths. Except for Domitian's palace, all of these were meant to advertise the genuine public spirit of these Emperors, in contrast with Nero's selfishness. Vespasian had also made a point of moving the art treasures that had adorned Nero's palace into the temple of Peace.

Nero's selfishness as it damaged the interests of the public at large was the theme particularly developed by the Flavians, who did not wish to restore so much imperial property to its original owners. But selfishness was not all that worried Nero's contemporaries: at least among the upper orders there was a feeling that the Domus Aurea rendered visible a more monarchical conception of the Principate.[68] No one who saw the entrance of the palace could have doubted that self-glorification played a part in its conception. On the summit of the Velia, the hill that rose to the north of the Palatine and west of Nero's lake rose 'the hated entrance hall of the cruel king', in Martial's words. It was decorated with gold and precious stones, and surrounded by a triple colonnade. In front, just north of the later arch of Titus, where the path to the Palatine turns off at right angles from the Sacra Via (the main avenue of the forum), stood the bronze Colossus, facing the forum and no doubt visible from many parts of the city. The Sacra Via was widened and straightened and given a steeper gradient as it rose towards the entrance to the palace. All along it were arcades and, behind them, great pillared halls 'giving the imperial palace what it had never had before, and was never to have again, a worthy entrance from the forum Romanum', as one archaeologist has put it.[69] And when one looked across Nero's lake one saw the one monument to his deified predecessor converted into an ornamental nymphaeum – Nero's glory was not to be shared!

What was Nero's Golden House intended to be, and what place was it intended to have in Nero's reconstructed Rome? Suetonius concentrates on its luxury, emphasising the gold and jewels that adorned it, and the devices for showering flowers and perfumes from the walls of the dining rooms. Indeed, the luxurious taste of the time was in evidence in the name of the palace, derived from the generous use of gilt inside and probably on the façade too. But Tacitus says explicitly that the wonders of the palace were not so much its jewels and gold, which were by then commonplaces of luxury, as its fields and lakes, and the impression of unspoiled nature created by its woods, open spaces and long vistas.[70] Suetonius elaborates on this aspect as well, noting the different kinds of animals and specifying that there were tilled fields, vineyards and meadows. Both authors remark too on the display of technical ingenuity. Suetonius speaks of the fountains and pools, and of the moving panels and spraying pipes of the dining rooms, adding that the most impressive of these rooms was round and rotated constantly, like the world. The material remains support the Tacitean emphasis on layout, structural innovation and elegance, even delicacy of taste, as against sheer opulence.

Finally, both Suetonius and Tacitus lay particular stress on the size of the Domus Aurea, which is also the point of the contemporary epigram about moving to Veii, and of Martial's line 'one house took up the whole of Rome'. The current modern interpretation of the Domus Aurea as a rural villa in the centre of Rome accords with this dominant strain in the ancient criticism. It is a conception sufficiently grandiose and perverse in itself to explain the hostility engendered by Nero's building operations.[71] We do not need to follow scholarly flights of fancy and see, in the eventual design of the Colossus as the Sun and the rotating dining room that could have represented the heavens, hints that the Domus Aurea was planned to symbolise the rule of Nero the new Sun-god, making visible his association with Apollo and the Golden Age that had been celebrated at his accession.[72]

It has been pointed out that the standard attacks on luxury that resounded through the Roman schools of declamation and filled the pages of Roman poets and philosophers had long included criticism of spacious country villas, of town houses that took up too much city land, and of technical ingenuity that subjected nature to luxury. Neronian literature itself abounds in such diatribes: in Lucan, in Petronius, and particularly in Seneca. It may have been the building of the Domus Aurea itself which was the occasion for some of these generalisations, but they are so conventional that we should hesitate to infer from them that the palace was really excessive in opulence or colossal in size.[73]

The starting point in estimating the extent of the buildings and park of the Domus Aurea is Martial's poem, written in the reign of Titus:

Here where the heavenly colossus has a close view of the stars
And high structures rise on the lofty road,
There once shone the hated hall of the cruel king
And one house took up the whole of Rome.
Here where rises the huge mass of the awesome amphitheatre
In sight of all was Nero's pool.
Here where we admire the baths built so quickly for our benefit
A proud park deprived the poor of their houses.
Where the Claudian temple spreads its wide shade
Stood the last part of the palace.
Rome is returned to herself and under your rule, Caesar,
The delights of their master have become those of the people.

(*Liber de spectaculis* 2)

We learn from this that the Domus Aurea extended from the summit of the Velian Hill (part of which was destroyed around 1930), across the area of the

Colosseum, taking in the northern slope of the Caelian Hill and the slope of the Oppian. Evidence is also provided by the remains on the Oppian Hill west of the Sette Sale where the two large wings under Trajan's Baths have recently been more thoroughly excavated; those on the south-east of the Palatine under Domitian's palace where walls of the second Neronian palace cut into the remains of the Domus Transitoria; those just east of the Colosseum, in the valley between the Caelian and the Esquiline, where some rooms have been discovered.[74]

The estimates of the extent vary considerably, but all agree that it covered a larger area than the Vatican city, which embraces about 110 acres. A conservative estimate is 125 acres; the one most widely accepted now gives the extent as 200 acres, about the same as that of Hadrian's villa at Tivoli.[75] Yet the important question is the nature of this imperial property: a private residential estate in the heart of the city, however large an extension Nero planned for Rome, would still have created problems for the movement of traffic. In making his calculations for the larger estimate given above, van Essen worked on two premisses: that Nero would follow the terrain as much as possible, and that he would want to be isolated. This led him to suggest that the Domus Aurea was a natural basin, with the lake at its centre and the summits of the surrounding hills for its limits, except on the east and south-east where it went up to the surviving section of the old Servian Wall of Rome.

The first premiss overlooks Nero's willingness to rearrange nature, as demonstrated at Subiaco and in the remains of the palace itself, which show that the Oppian Hill was trimmed to receive the northern and western rooms at least, while the Velia was cut and buttressed to accommodate the entrance hall. As to the second premiss, van Essen was prepared to use it, against the evidence of Martial, to extend the estate beyond the temple of Divus Claudius up to the summit of the Caelian Hill: Nero would not be overlooked from higher ground. But, even in its own terms, the argument is faulty, as the high podium of the temple seems designed to neutralise the slope of the hill (fig. 11). The question of being overlooked would not arise when Nero's nymphaeum was placed there: indeed it has been suggested that on the south side, facing the Colosseum, cascades were arranged so that the maximum effect was derived from the elevation and the draining of the new branch of the Claudian aqueduct into Nero's lake.[76]

It is time, however, to consider the theory of privacy. We have already remarked that, in accordance with Roman tradition, the Emperors conducted business in their own houses and villas. Now certain features of Nero's plans suggest that the Domus Aurea was not intended to be a private precinct. The Elder Pliny says that Nero rebuilt the temple of Fortune, originally consecrated by Servius Tullius, in a newly-discovered type of translucent marble and 'included it in the Golden House'. It must have been one of the buildings in the park, and, as a temple, it can hardly have been without public access.[77] When Gaius, as is alleged, took over the temple of

Castor and Pollux in the forum as the entrance to his palace, his intention was that people would come there and worship him. And when Augustus bought up houses on the Palatine to enlarge his own, he promised to turn the property to public use, and built there the temple of Apollo.[78] Moreover, Nero is thought to have rebuilt the temple of Jupiter Stator which stood just south of his entrance hall and had been destroyed in the Fire of 64. What privacy would he have had with people attending the temple next door? And what of his expanded Sacra Via, which finished at his front door? One can hardly assume that the forum was to remain out of use, nor is it unlikely that the arcades and halls were to be used for commercial purposes, as had long been the case along the avenue. Then, on the east, we have already noted that the Domus Aurea may have been next to a rebuilt warehouse (see note 63) – at least the land was not confiscated for another use – and beyond that, in the Piazza S. Clemente, a new building for the official mint may have been built in Nero's time. Not far away to the south stood Nero's grandiose market on the Caelian.

As part of his general reconstruction of Rome Nero could have had the idea of embellishing the central area with parks, groves and fountains. Here in his complex of imperial buildings he could hear audiences and do business, while his people would have access to him and to some of the buildings and grounds. Nero's *comitas* and *popularitas* must be remembered: he was not a man to deprive his public. Shortly before the Fire he held a public banquet in which he extended to the people pleasures normally confined to the few. Tacitus' sneer on this occasion, 'He used the whole city as his house', reminds one of the squib 'Rome will become a house'.[79] Nero may have felt he was opening his house to the citizens, while his critics felt that he was excluding the citizens from their city. After the Fire we find him offering public entertainment in his Vatican circus and adjacent gardens, dressed as a charioteer and mixing with the plebs.[80] When the conspirators of 65 were planning Nero's assassination they considered killing him, according to Tacitus, in the hated palace or in public, or when he was visiting the Campanian villa of Piso, where he frequently went without his guards. Yet Tacitus says that it was because the Emperor did not often leave his house and gardens that the conspirators eventually decided on the circus games, which the Emperor regularly attended, and where he could be easily approached in the holiday atmosphere. Tacitus appears to contradict himself here over the Emperor's general accessibility, but he probably had particularly in mind, in the second passage, the fact that Nero no longer attended the Senate regularly, for the Senate house would have been the expected venue for a tyrannicide modelled on the murder of Caesar. The conspirators may also have considered, as the assassins of Gaius had, that the crowds at the circus made the Emperor's guards less effective than when he was in his palace or in the Senate.[81]

In any case, nothing suggests that Nero meant to shut himself up in the Domus Aurea. One of the problems for the Pisonian conspirators may have been that after the Fire, with his palace damaged and under reconstruction, Nero was spending his time in imperial properties that were more private, such as the Servilian Gardens.[82]

Thus the Domus Aurea park need not have prevented movement through the centre of the city, though doubtless the routes were changed. Even on the Palatine only a cryptoporticus connected the various imperial buildings: there was no need to weld them all into one enclosed complex, and they may have been intended to remain separate.[83]

The Golden House was, nonetheless, an ambitious, probably an over-ambitious, project. Observers would have gained the impression that a vast complex was in hand, because the work did not proceed area by area. Though never finished, a vast number of buildings were started all around the central lake. Nero no doubt spoke with enthusiasm of the technical marvels that were in hand. The unsympathetic may well have reacted as one scholar who wrote, 'The Fire gave a mortally egocentric autocrat the chance to demand a unique monumental expression of what he considered his worth and position to be'.[84]

The large remains on the Oppian Hill have by now lost most of their decoration. The grand apartments have been plunged in darkness since the foundations were laid for Trajan's Baths. Even before that, Vitellius and his wife were disappointed by the lack of decoration and the mean equipment of the palace. The Domus Aurea was left unfinished when Nero died, and the alterations made by Otho interfered with the grand architectural conception of its creator.[85] Even so, the construction and design still excite the admiration of architects and engineers by reason of the new exploitation of space and the creation of internal vistas. Two features, in particular, impress by their artistic and architectural originality: the five-sided trapezoidal court in the west wing, which was once matched by a similar one in the east wing, and the domed octagonal room in the centre with its five rooms radiating from it symmetrically. As the new excavations show, the palace originally had two floors, each of which displayed east-west symmetry and was interrupted by the two open trapezoidal courts. The two courts framed the central complex of rooms around the octagon which extended through the upper storey and could probably be viewed from the adjacent upper rooms as well as the lower ones (pp.134–6).[86]

The octagon room thus formed the focus of the whole building. It is usually identified with the main circular dining room described by Suetonius, though there is no agreement on what elements rotated. It is notable, however, that the inside of the dome shows no traces of decoration, and that the water that ran into the room to the north came in at a steeper gradient than would be necessary for a nymphaeum. Hence the suggestion that some of the water turned a device suspended through the opening in the dome, representing the changes of seasons on the vault. The two grooves on the outer surface of the dome will have served as tracks for the suspended device (figs. 9–10).[87] Whatever the explanation, the study of the Domus

Transitoria and the Domus Aurea shows, to an even greater degree than our examination of the coinage, that Nero was an enthusiast who threw himself into grand projects and put at their service the latest Roman technology and the most advanced artistic ideas.

Nero's zeal for the arts, however, did not stop at patronage and planning. If his aim of professional performance was more acceptable to the Greek way of thinking, his desire to achieve that standard in all the arts at once would strike even a Greek as absurd. Dio Chrysostom, having explained that no one can be superior in all *technai* (skills), says of Nero:

> And yet a certain king of our time had the ambition to be wise in this sort of wisdom, believing that he knew a great deal – not, however, such things as are not applauded by men, but those for which one can win a crown, i.e. acting as herald, singing to the cithara, reciting tragedies, wrestling, and being in the pancration competition. Besides he is said to have painted and sculpted and played the pipe: was he not then a wise man?

To the standard contrast of true and technical knowledge Dio here adds ridicule of the claim to master many techniques 'when it is difficult to be thoroughly proficient even in one', and scorn of Nero's obsession with the performing arts.

Nero the informed patron and Nero the jealous practitioner were to play decisive but conflicting roles in the artistic achievements of the period. Of his personal participation in the visual arts, mentioned by Dio Chrysostom, we hear nothing more. But in music his performances became notorious, and though he worked seriously for his victories and suffered real anxieties, he found real rivals increasingly difficult to endure.[88] The great literary achievements of his time owe much to the Emperor's patronage, but his own desire to excel in an area where competition came mostly from members of the upper orders was disastrous, both in artistic and in political terms. As patron and entrepreneur Nero could have no rival; as performer and writer he knew that he did. Unlike Frederick the Great, who despite growing autocracy remained aware that his verse was inferior to Voltaire's, Nero found it harder and harder to endure the superiority of anyone, and gradually took refuge in a combination of oppression and self-deception.

NINE

The Artistic Tyrant

The Literary Renaissance

Readers of Latin literature are accustomed to think in terms of a classical period in the late Republic and the reign of Augustus, followed by a barren period of nearly half a century, which ends with the flowering of Silver Latin under Nero, the Flavians and early Antonines. As regards writers of prose this impression does not stand up to reflection. Seneca, the versatile genius of the Neronian age, has left several works written under the Emperors Gaius and Claudius, while the great Silver Latin prose authors, Tacitus and Pliny, come long after Nero, with only the didactic writers Columella and Quintilian to speak for the Neronian and Flavian periods. But in poetry and the mixed genre of Menippean satire the impression is largely true. In epic we pass from Virgil and Ovid direct to Lucan, in pastoral from Virgil to Calpurnius Siculus and the Einsiedeln Eclogues, in verse satire from Horace to Persius, and in Menippean satire from Varro to Seneca's *Apocolocyntosis* and Petronius' *Satyricon*.

The composition of these works can be firmly dated to Nero's reign. Lucan, who was fourteen when Nero became Princeps, can hardly have written even his juvenile works earlier; and what ancient testimony there is for Persius, who was nineteen at Nero's accession, suggests that at least the one work we have was composed after that event.[1] The pastoral works are dated by internal evidence to Nero's reign.[2] Petronius is traditionally identified with the ironical courtier in Tacitus, who, after his consulship, became one of Nero's intimates and his *elegantiae arbiter*. Anecdotes in the Elder Pliny and Plutarch suggest that he is also their 'T. Petronius consularis'. That may permit a further identification with (?T.) Petronius Niger, now clearly attested as consul in the latter part of the year 62.[3] The composition of the *Satyricon* may well have started before Petronius joined Nero's entourage, for his literary gifts were probably among the forms of 'sophisticated luxury' which, according to Tacitus, first attracted Nero. On the other hand, the inclusion in the *Satyricon* of a lengthy hexameter treatment of the Civil Wars may point to some acquaintance with Lucan's epic, which only began to see the light just after the first Neronia in 60.[4]

Research into lost writers helps to modify the idea of a fresh start with Nero. For prose, the names of lost technical writers, including the encyclopaedist Cornelius Celsus, close the gap before Seneca's writings on natural history and Columella's agricultural treatise, while in philosophy at least Seneca's teacher Papirius Fabianus was thought worthy of stylistic analysis by both Senecas, father and son.[5] But it is in history, biography and autobiography that we seem to have lost most in quantity and quality. In addition to the memoirs of Tiberius and Claudius and the historical works of the latter Emperor, there were the historians praised by Quintilian and Tacitus: Aufidius Bassus and Servilius Nonianus for their style, Cremutius Cordus for his courage.[6] As for poetry, the Claudian tragedian Pomponius Secundus is celebrated by the same exacting critics, while Pliny testifies to the continuity of light verse.[7]

Yet scholarly rummaging among fragments and lists of names does nothing to close the chronological hiatus in the poetic genres of satire, pastoral and epic. Quintilian, it is true, admits to leaving out good writers in his account of Greek and Latin literature in Book x, because he is only discussing those literary genres that contribute most to the perfecting of oratorical skill. But he clearly canvasses the principal genres to which Roman writers had contributed, and his selection of the best makes the pattern that emerges all the more significant.[8] Of epic poets he lists none between Ovid's contemporary Cornelius Severus and four writers, Serranus, Saleius Bassus, Lucan and Valerius Flaccus, who wrote under Nero and Vespasian; in satire he names no one between Horace and Persius; in Menippean satire he lists only Varro, who established the form in Latin, but that is because the versatile Seneca is reserved for the end of the whole discussion.[9] The Flavian critic allows us to add another genre to those that were revived under Nero, for he can find no lyric poet worthy of mention between Horace and his own time, except Caesius Bassus. Though he notes the inferiority of Bassus to his predecessors and successors, in general Quintilian rates the Neronian writers he mentions high. Finally, when we come to elegy we find that no post-Augustan writer appears in Quintilian's catalogue, although Martial tells us that Nero celebrated the future Emperor Nerva as the Tibullus of his time. Nero's judgment does not of course guarantee the quality of Nerva's verses, but Martial's evidence at least suggests that elegy too was revived in his reign.[10]

Nothing in literary history is more difficult than to explain why writing flourishes at one time and declines at another. Is the Neronian renaissance an accident, or an example of cultural energy reviving after a lull? The second merely offers a description in the guise of an explanation, the first denies that there is an explanation at all. Most scholars have found it more satisfactory to give Nero at least some of the credit.

'All hope and purpose in the literary arts lies with Caesar alone.'[11] So Juvenal was to say under Hadrian; so poets hoping for praise or money had said earlier. That the Emperor would take an interest in literature was a natural expectation, for, like any other member of the governing class at Rome, he was assumed to be able to speak and write well. According to Tacitus all the Julio-Claudian Emperors except Nero composed their own speeches, and all of them are credited by Suetonius with some literary accomplishment.[12] Some of these works sprang directly from their imperial occupations, such as the autobiographies of Augustus, Tiberius and Claudius, but others were genuine examples of *belles-lettres*.

Augustus composed in prose and in verse. His own taste ran to improving literature and to moderate style, but he listened to compositions of all sorts.[13] While his encouragement of literature was managed by Maecenas, the imperial touch was light, though the *recusationes* of Horace already attest to the Emperor's concern, later remarked by Suetonius, to be written about in a serious manner.[14] By the end of the reign after the disgrace and death of Maecenas, his direct patronage had led to the burning and banning of books and the exile of writers.[15] Yet the change in atmosphere had been gradual and the net contribution to literature remarkable.

Tiberius wrote verse in Latin and Greek, particularly favouring the learned works of the Alexandrian poets as models. Some effect of his tastes can be discerned: scholars wrote commentaries on those Greek poets to please him, and Germanicus' translation of Aratus' astronomical work suits Tiberius' interest in Greek poetry and in astrology. Valerius Maximus, who composed a handbook of memorable words and deeds for use by orators, appeals to Tiberius' punishment of vice and encouragement of virtue in his invocation.[16] But there is little evidence for encouragement of literature by Tiberius while Emperor, despite the escort of writers that Horace attests for him earlier. Even the sycophantic historian Velleius Paterculus, writing after fifteen years of Tiberius' reign had elapsed, thought that four major genres of Latin literature were now in decline, tragedy and oratory having reached their peak in the Republic, history and poetry having come to the end of an eighty-year period of efflorescence around the time of Augustus' death.[17]

What scant testimony there is to Tiberius' grants of money and friendship to writers is more than balanced by the examples of persecution attributed to the latter two thirds of his reign. Julius Montanus was a good poet, known for Tiberius' friendship and then for his displeasure.[18] Clutorius Priscus had been rewarded by Tiberius for a poem on the death of Germanicus, but he was put to death in 21 by an anxious senate for composing another such poem in anticipation of the death of Drusus.[19] Even the Greek grammarians and scholars who entertained the Emperor had to watch out for the inadvertent allusion.[20] The powerful influence of his praetorian prefects, first Sejanus, then Macro, was equally baneful. One claimed as victim a notable historian, Cremutius Cordus, the other a blue-blooded writer of tragedy, Mamercus Aemilius Scaurus. Even a freedman writer of fables on the model of Aesop suffered exile because Sejanus suspected disagreeable references to himself.[21] What one had to do to please

Sejanus and his master is clear enough from the effusions and distortions of Velleius Paterculus.[22]

Gaius abused Virgil and Livy and threatened to remove their works from the libraries in order to enforce his tastes, but his only real interest was in oratory, for which he had a genuine gift. Since, however, he could not stand competition from other able orators, his influence on literature was totally negative.[23]

Claudius' interests were also narrow, but took a different direction, towards history and antiquarian research. He gave recitations of his historical writings in Latin and Greek, and he was apparently prepared to listen to others, for Pliny tells of his being lured by the sound of applause to a recitation by Servilius Nonianus.[24] Seneca ridicules the taste for antiquarian scholarship which flourished during Claudius' reign and which doubtless owed something to his inspiration.[25] Yet it is characteristic of Claudius that the only explicit references to encouragement of literature in his years of rule concern his freedmen secretaries. Polybius is depicted by Seneca in 44 as surrounded by admirers who make copies of his great works, a translation of Homer into Latin and another of Virgil into Greek. Seneca urges him to write an account of Claudius' achievements, using the Emperor both as his subject and as his model in historical writing.[26] A few years later, the medical writer Scribonius Largus is found thanking Claudius' secretary in charge of petitions for his previous encouragement and for bringing his work to the attention of Claudius, who had rewarded him.[27]

Neronian Patronage

The evidence for Nero's patronage affords a contrast in quantity and in kind. There is direct testimony from writers not only to his personal support but to the patronage of members of the senatorial class in favour with the Emperor: their role is commonly compared to that of Maecenas.

Of the Emperor's own generosity the clearest evidence comes from Lucillius, a writer of Greek epigrams. In dedicating his second book to Nero, he writes, 'Olympian Muses, daughters of Zeus, I would be finished had not Nero Caesar given me cash'. In other poems he addresses 'Lord Caesar', once pretending to show him the plight of a mutilated boxer, once ridiculing the lethal skills of a doctor.[28] Three other poems support the idea, already suggested by the unusual specification of the Emperor's name in the dedication poem, that the epigrams belong to the earlier part of the reign. In one of these the poet makes fun of an inept dancer in three roles – Niobe, Canace and Capaneus – of which the first two are mentioned as roles Nero sang after the second Neronia in 65.[29] In Nero's last years a writer eager for imperial support would surely have avoided criticism of these roles, even though they were apparently sung and played, rather than danced, by the Emperor. The second poem offers a firmer indication: here a singer named

Hegelochos is said to have sung the role of Nauplius in a Greek city, thus making Nauplius again a bane to the Greeks. Now Nero not only sang the role of Nauplius, but banished the Cynic philosopher Isidorus for taunting him 'because he sang well of the ills of Nauplius but made ill use of his own goods' – a gibe that should belong to the period of heavy expenditure after the Great Fire of 64.[30] Finally there is the piece in which Lucillius expresses his hatred of those who despise young poets even if they stick to Homer as a model. This would come best from an author still at the start of his career, addressing a very young ruler known to be a poet himself.[31]

Imperial interest in Greek epigrammatists is nothing new, but pro-Greek sentiment may lie behind the other pieces of explicit testimony to Nero's encouragement of literature – indeed, it may be the foundation for an audacious invention. At an unknown date, perhaps in the early third century, a certain Septimius produced a Latin translation of a 'Diary of the Trojan War' written in Greek.[32] In the Letter of dedication he explains that the work was based on an eye-witness account written down in Punic letters by Dictys of Crete, who actually served on the Greek side in the war. The Prologue explains that shepherds found the account when the tomb of Dictys collapsed in the thirteenth year of Nero (66/7), and their master showed it to Rutilius Rufus, the Governor of Crete, who sent it to Nero; he put the work in a library, and rewarded the master handsomely with gifts and the Roman citizenship. The bogus claim to great antiquity and the romantic circumstances of discovery can be paralleled in other works of the Empire, but it is less easy to decide how much of the rest of the story is fantasy. Papyri have now made it clear that there was a Greek original that Septimius translated, and that it could belong to the reign of Nero. On the other hand the governor is called Rutilius Rufus, which is probably a tribute to the famous upright legate in Asia in the first century BC, as there is no known Neronian consular of that name. The date of 66/7 is that of Nero's Greek tour, but the story does not make clear whether Nero received the work in Rome or in Greece. Nero's role in this tale could be real; his credulity is demonstrated by his belief in another Punic story, about Dido's treasure. Or it could be a fiction suggested by the Dido story and by Nero's well-known interest in Greece, in literature generally, and in the theme that he chose as the subject of his own epic, the *Troica*.[33]

The return to the early Augustan pattern of literary patronage is celebrated explicitly by Calpurnius Siculus and the author of the *Panegyric on Piso*, who may indeed be identical.[34] In addressing Piso the young poet asks for support, spiritual and material, such as the well-born orator and poet has given to writers and other needy clients. This birthday ode is a foretaste of the renown his poetry can confer on Piso as his Maecenas, and Piso is reminded that Maecenas supported not only Virgil, but Varius Rufus and Horace as well.[35]

In Calpurnius Siculus' *Eclogues* the significance of the parallel with Maecenas is more fully spelled out. Three 'political' poems are placed at the beginning, the middle and the end of this collection of pastoral poems. In two, we hear of Corydon's patron Meliboeus. At the end of his first Eclogue, in which the accession of a young prince is celebrated in the form of a prophecy,[36] the poet Corydon says: 'perhaps Meliboeus will bear this song to our prince's ears'. In the fourth Eclogue Corydon has become more optimistic: 'Times have changed, and our god is not the same' (v.30), and he aspires to singing of the Golden Age and the Emperor as did Tityrus (Virgil); Meliboeus, he notes, has already saved him from hunger and indeed from having to grind out a living at the ends of the earth where the prince could not hear him sing (vv.31–49). His patron is an expert in weather lore but also writes tragic and lyric verse, and he is now asked to correct Corydon's poem. Meliboeus duly listens and praises his song, whereupon, amid hints about Corydon's desire to own a farm, he is asked to take the poem to the Emperor, 'for you have the right to visit the inner shrine of Palatine Phoebus. Then you shall be to me as he was who brought Tityrus, the sweet singer, from the woods to the queen of cities' (vv.147–161).

The Piso of the *Panegyric* is probably C. Calpurnius Piso, later the leader of a conspiracy to unseat Nero and make himself Emperor. Tacitus notes his high birth and aristocratic connections, and remarks that he had a great reputation because of his virtues or apparent virtues. He used his eloquence to defend his fellow-citizens, was generous to his friends and accessible to strangers, lived magnificently and sang tragic roles – qualities that fit well with what is said in the *Panegyric*, which can add to these attainments, skill at singing to the cithara and improvising verse.[37]

Meliboeus has been variously identified, the most popular candidates being Piso again, or Seneca. But whether one person or two, Meliboeus and Piso exemplify the high-ranking independent men close to the Emperor who set the fashion for writing and encouraging poetry. The generosity of such senators was celebrated by later poets as one of the glories of a past age. Juvenal names Seneca, Piso and Cotta: the last is clearly the Aurelius Cotta of whom Tacitus reports that he dissipated his ancestral fortune by luxurious living and then accepted an imperial allowance.[38] Martial names Piso and Seneca, whose help he enjoyed, and adds Memmius and Crispus, who can perhaps be identified as the Neronian consulars C. Memmius Regulus and Vibius Crispus, the latter known from Tacitus as a gifted orator.[39]

More is known of Seneca's protégés than of the men helped by the others.[40] Tacitus tells us that the historian Fabius Rusticus benefited from his friendship in youth, and Seneca's friend Lucilius, who may have owed his appointment as procurator to Seneca, wrote a poem on Sicily and celebrated Stoic doctrine in poetry and prose. We know of these works from Seneca himself, who wrote letters encouraging Lucilius to compose them, and who read them carefully.[41] He may also have taken an interest in

Columella's work on agriculture, and the tenth book of that work, a poem on the cultivation of gardens, is said to have been requested by Seneca's brother Gallio.[42]

These men, including Martial, were *equites*, members of the social class into which Seneca and his brother had been born. Seneca's relationship with them was that of a social equal, modified by his own outstanding wealth and his senatorial rank. Seneca and Piso, along with such literary senators as Nerva, Petronius and Lucan, stood in a similar relationship to the Emperor. Calpurnius Siculus and the author of the *Panegyric on Piso*, however, appear as would-be financial dependants of their immediate patron and of the Emperor. To some extent the difference may be only apparent – even equestrian poets like Martial and Juvenal grovel and complain of poverty in their poetry[43] – but there is likely to be a real difference, in distance from the Emperor at least, between the senatorial writers on the one hand and Calpurnius Siculus and Lucillius on the other, a difference that is worth bearing in mind as we consider what kind of influence Nero can be said to have had on the literature of his time.

The flattery of the 'court poets' does not reveal any literary direction from the throne: the admiration for Homer and Virgil that they display was universal, and almost the same standing can be claimed for Horace, who is mentioned in the *Panegyric*, and for Ovid, who is praised by Calpurnius Siculus.[44] In the poems addressed to Nero Lucillius makes fun of bad tragic singers, bad pantomime dancers, a mutilated boxer, and people who despise young poets. His epigrams as a whole reflect the Greek milieu of Rome – its astrologers, doctors, grammarians and athletes. No doubt his many poems about the Greek festivals (including the Sebasta at Naples), and his constant allusions to the technical language used in these contests, pleased Nero; but there were also the tastes of many other Romans who read Greek poetry.[45] There is little sign that the Emperor's tastes for literature were considered: at most, his prediliction for writing and hearing lampoons may have encouraged Lucillius to address epigrams of this type to him. More typical is the flattery of another Greek epigrammatist of the period, Antiphilus of Byzantium, who celebrates Nero's generosity to the city of Rhodes.[46] In another epigram Puteoli boasts of her harbour, challenging even Rome to admire its size. The poem can be construed as a tribute to the favour Puteoli had found with Nero, from whom it received in 60 colonial status and a new name.[47]

Calpurnius Siculus' flattery of Nero does emphasize the Emperor's interest in poetry and his connection with Apollo as patron of the arts, but otherwise he concentrates on his peaceful accession, his abolition of the abuses of the previous reign, his maintenance of world peace, and the return of the Golden Age: all themes reminiscent of Seneca's *Apocolocyntosis* and *De Clementia*. Then in his last political poem, the seventh *Eclogue*, the poet celebrates what became even dearer to the Emperor's heart – his new amphitheatre and his magnificent shows. Occasionally, too, he mentions conventional imperial achievements which were ultimately to prove of less interest to Nero − oratory and martial success.[48]

In the first of the anonymous pastorals known as the Einsiedeln Eclogues, the poem on the fall of Troy written by the Emperor himself is praised, and Homer and Virgil are shown conceding its superiority.[49] But neither here nor in the rest of Neronian 'court poetry' is there any reason to think that Nero's *literary* tastes suggested to the authors the kind of work they should write. Even if we could be sure that the work purporting to be written by Dictys of Crete was sent to Nero, it would be rash to suggest that Nero's interest in the theme of the Trojan War was known to the author and inspired his choice of subject. For the theme was a perennial favourite among Greeks, because of veneration for Homer, and among Romans, because of esteem for Virgil as well. In addition, as we shall see, the pro-Greek, anti-Trojan bias of Dictys' account is against any close connection with Nero's tastes.

By contrast, when we turn to those writers who did not simply gaze on Nero from afar, we do seem to see in their works obvious reflections of the Emperor's own literary enthusiasms. It is easy to see why this might be so. Nero gave recitations of his poems in public, but it was no doubt at his recitations at home, and even more at his working dinners with other poets, that his enthusiasms were most clearly communicated. Tacitus, who mentions these occasions under the year 59, describes them with a fine malice. 'He gathered together those with some talent for verse but who were not yet famous. They sat together and dined and strung together verses they had brought along or made up on the spot, and they filled in the Emperor's own lines. Inspection of his poems alone shows this, for they do not flow with vigour, inspiration or uniformity of style.'[50] Suetonius countered the allegation of plagiarism by examining Nero's manuscripts, which convinced him that the changes and additions made were the sort that a writer makes in the process of composition.[51] The dinners themselves should be real enough, however Tacitus may traduce their purpose, and one may question whether young writers were invited for such a low reason, or those who had already gained a reputation really excluded, since Tacitus' point about the restriction is linked to his charge of plagiarism.

What kind of literature did Nero himself favour? Martial mentions *carmina* (songs or poems) of Nero, and Suetonius notes a collection of songs for the cithara, called *The Master's Book*, which probably included words as well as music.[52] Dio tells us that at the Juvenalia in 59 Nero performed a piece called *Attis* or *The Bacchants*, yet he does not indicate that the composer was the Emperor, as is usually assumed.[53] Nero's choice for performance, nonetheless, shows the Alexandrian direction of his taste.[54]

Nero is mentioned by Pliny as a composer of light verse. Martial knew that he addressed playful lines in youth to a perfumer, and we hear of verses attacking two senators. The ex-praetor Claudius Pollio was ridiculed in a poem called 'The One-Eyed Man', while Afranius Quintianus was so offended by an improper poem taxing him with effeminacy that he joined the Pisonian conspiracy.[55] Another poem included disparaging remarks about a King Mithridates and his delight in chariot-racing.[56] But Nero's verses did not all serve such negative ends. In one poem, he celebrated Poppaea's amber-coloured hair, and another was composed in 64 to give thanks to the gods for preventing loss of life when the theatre at Naples collapsed after he and his audience had left. A half-line of hexameter verse, 'You would think it (had) thundered underground', cited by Suetonius in his Life of Lucan, may·come from this poem.[57]

With the exception of the last piece we cannot even guess the metre used in the poems mentioned so far.[58] But a taste for satire (in the non-technical sense) and for lyric poetry in the Alexandrian taste seems clear. It is worth noting that the lyric poet Caesius Bassus, 'a learned and scholarly man' according to the ancient grammarians, dedicated one of his works on metre to Nero, whom Martial calls 'learned' in speaking of his poems.[59] It is likely that Nero tried his hand at tragedy. According to Tacitus one of his reasons for resenting Seneca by 62 was the belief that his old teacher had increased his output of verse after Nero had acquired a love for writing poetry. Though Seneca wrote light verse, the reference is likely to be to the tragedies, the poetic compositions for which he was renowned.[60]

The imperial ventures about which we are best informed, however, were in epic poetry. At the second Neronia in 65 the Emperor recited from a work of his called *Troica*. The poem is mentioned in the first Einsiedeln Eclogue:

> You too, O Troy, raise your sacred ashes to the stars
> And show this work to Agamemnon's Mycenae.
> Now has the reward for disaster proved great! rejoice, you ruins
> And praise your pyres: your own son raises you up. (vv.38–41)

Here it is the burning of Troy that is particularly mentioned, which would have been a tactless and dangerous tribute after the rumours that Nero sang the *Capture of Troy* during the Fire of 64. But the poet may be writing earlier about performances of part of the epic given before the Fire. Indeed, these performances may be the basis of the hostile rumours.[61] Nero's interest in sympathetic treatment of Troy goes back to his successful speech on behalf of the city in 53. As for the subject of this epic, we know only that it treated Paris as the bravest of the Trojans, who surpassed even Hector at a Trojan contest. The scholiast on Lucan preserves some hexameter lines from 'Nero's First Book' which are plausibly assigned to the epic. They describe the course of the River Tigris and show an interest in geographical description and rhetorical antithesis reminiscent of Lucan. Another hexameter line, quoted by Seneca and possibly from *Troica*, exhibits an exotic word and elaborate sound patterns.[62]

After *Troica* Nero contemplated a large-scale Roman epic celebrating 'the deeds of the Romans'. He was much exercised over the question of the proper number of books. When flatterers suggested four hundred, the Stoic philosopher and scholar Annaeus Cornutus objected that no one would read so many. Someone retorted that the Stoic Chrysippus had written many more than that. 'But they are of benefit to the conduct of men's lives', Cornutus replied, a remark that brought him fame and banishment.[63]

The few surviving lines of Neronian verse tell one little of its quality. *The Master's Book*, which to judge from its title (*Liber Dominicus*) was probably compiled in Nero's lifetime, was still in circulation in 69 when Vitellius called for a song from it.[64] Vitellius had political reasons for showing enthusiasm for Nero, but Martial and Suetonius indicate that his poems were still known in their times. Even Juvenal's lines comparing the two matricides: 'At least Orestes never sang upon the stage/nor wrote an epic on Troy' seem to be aimed at the fact of the epic's composition, not at its quality, just as they damn the fact of performance rather than its incompetence. Similarly Quintilian's failure to mention Nero's compositions may be a judgment on his tyranny, not his talent.[65] Except for the strictures of Tacitus mentioned above, strictures which Suetonius' rebuttal of the charge of plagiarism does nothing to answer, hostile criticism tends to focus on Nero's voice, which is described as weak and husky and which moved some of his audience to laughter and others to tears.[66]

Seneca's praise of Nero's poetry in the *Apocolocyntosis*, and later in the *Natural Questions* written in 62–4, can hardly be used as evidence of its quality, but it is some indication that literary men among Nero's intimates were supposed to take serious notice of the Emperor as a fellow-practitioner. When we recall how strong-minded Nero was from the start about imposing his own cultural notions, it seems reasonable to look for signs of his influence on the literature of the period.

No significance can be attributed to the fact that Pliny names Seneca, Nerva, and Verginius Rufus as writers of light verse, for Nero's own interest in such compositions was by no means distinctive.[67] The *Apocolocyntosis*, however, does seem to reflect Nero's taste for personal attack in its coarse ridicule of Claudius. Indeed, Dio mentions Seneca's *Pumpkinification* as just one example of the court jokes, including one by Nero, that were generated by Claudius' elevation to divinity.[68] The atmosphere of the court is suggestive too for Petronius' great work, which is also, in form, a kind of Menippean satire. What we have of it reflects not only the raillery of the palace but that *nostalgie de la boue* that Nero and his intimates expressed early in the reign in the form of street brawls. Through the low class characters of the *Satyricon* and their lewd adventures, Petronius provided his hearers with a literary form of slumming. The work also reflects the philhellenism of the Emperor. Not only is it set in Croton and in an unnamed City on the Bay of Naples (probably Puteoli), but it displays literary affinities with the *Odyssey* and the Hellenistic novel, of which it provides a kind of comic version: the hero's adventures are tied together by the theme of the wrath of Priapus; the romantic interest consists mainly of pederastic intrigues.

In addition to this generic literary allusion, there are clear echoes of Virgil and much talk about oratory, painting and poetry, put in the mouth of a teacher of rhetoric and a poet.[69] Poems of varying length occur, the longest and most notable being a treatment in iambic senarii of the *Capture of Troy*, and a hexameter sample of the theme of the Civil War. The second, introduced as it is by a lecture which seems to be aimed at Lucan, is probably a semi-serious critique of his epic on that theme.[70] The temptation is therefore strong to relate the first to Nero's *Troica*; but the temptation should be resisted, for the metre used by Petronius is that of tragedy, not epic, and the episode related is not the notorious burning of Troy but that of the Trojan Horse. Other targets have been suggested, such as Lucan's early poem the *Iliacon*, and Seneca's tragedies, some of which concern the Trojan war. The poem, which purports to describe the theme of a painting, probably reflects the general interest of that theme at the time, an interest shared by the Emperor.

Nero's own Trojan slant on the theme may be reflected in Lucan's lost *Iliacon* which treated the death of Hector and the ransoming of his body by Priam, and in the *Ilias Latina*, a potted translation of the *Iliad* into Latin hexameters, datable to this period and stressing the importance of Aeneas as founder of a second Troy and author of the noble gens of the Julii (899f.).[71]

We have already noted Nero's connection with the lyric poet Caesius Bassus, who dedicated to him a work on metre. Further hints of Nero's direct stimulation of lyric poetry are provided by Calpurnius Siculus, who tells us that Meliboeus, an intimate at court, wrote lyric poetry; and by the *Panegyric on Piso*, whose subject seems to have improvised lyric verse.[72]

Of the genres that revived during Nero's reign none can have owed more to his inspiration than epic. Lucan wrote the first three books of the *Bellum Civile* while he was in high favour with the Emperor. The opening eulogy, however tasteless it seems, must be accepted as serious flattery of the kind that Octavian had been offered by Virgil, with whom Lucan compared himself when introducing a recitation of the epic.[73] In these opening lines Lucan hails Nero as a suitable divinity to inspire a Roman poem. Though it was not until some years later that Nero was to embark on his own Roman epic, his general interest in hexameter verse and his work on *Troica* before 64 make it likely that he encouraged Lucan's ambitious effort to take up the genre where Virgil had left it. Both types of epic that interested Nero, the traditional and the Roman, continued to flourish, to judge from the *Argonautica* of Valerius Flaccus, Silius Italicus' *Punica*, and the *Thebaid* and *Achilleid* of Statius. These were all composed under the Flavians, but two of the authors, Silius certainly and Valerius Flaccus probably, grew to maturity in Neronian Rome.[74]

Tragedy did not need reviving, and Seneca had probably composed dramas before Nero became Emperor. But the gibe that he had begun to write more poetry after Nero became interested sounds like a hostile interpretation of the fact that he was inspired to write more by the enthusiasm of his literary pupil. Seneca's nephew Lucan left an incomplete tragedy about Medea, and Lucan's friend Persius had written a tragedy on a Roman theme.[75] Though tragedy, like history, had long been one of the standard genres for upper class writers, some account should be taken of the stimulus offered by an Emperor who performed as well as wrote.

Even philosophy, not only the sort that Seneca and his protégé Lucilius wrote but the more austere treatises in Greek by Annaeus Cornutus and lectures in Greek by Musonius Rufus, must have been encouraged by Nero's interest after his accession. Tacitus notes under the year 59 the after-dinner debates that the Emperor arranged, commenting cynically, 'There was no lack of those eager to have their solemn expressions on show among the diversions of the court'.[76]

As with the visual arts, the effect of Nero's influence was not to make Latin literature more Greek than it already was. He himself chose to write in Latin, and the forms that flourished in his reign included Roman epic and both forms of satire which Quintilian was to claim as 'all our own'. It was Lucilius who inspired Persius, Virgil that Lucan set out to surpass and Tibullus to whom Nero compared Nerva. The literary contests that featured in the Neronia were Greek only in the importance they accorded to art: it was at the first Neronia that Lucan, that most Roman of poets, won a crown for verse eulogy in Latin, and the Emperor was presented with the crown for Latin poetry.[77]

The Neronian impetus, and many of the Neronian writers, survived the upheavals of 69 and went on into the period of the Flavians. But the greatest authors did not outlive Nero. Though Persius was carried off by a stomach complaint, Seneca, Lucan and Petronius owed their demise directly to the Emperor. Lesser literary lights also suffered death, like Thrasea Paetus and Calpurnius Piso, or exile, like Musonius Rufus, Annaeus Cornutus and Verginius Flavus. The fact that so many of these literary victims were senators, and that others, mostly *equites*, were closely associated with senators, makes it possible to view their ruin as just one aspect of the general breakdown of Nero's concord with the Senate and the upper orders generally. Lucan was a participant in the conspiracy which aimed to set the poet and patron C. Calpurnius Piso on the throne, and he, Seneca and Petronius were all sentenced to death in 65 and 66 on charges of complicity. Musonius Rufus and Verginius Flavus, the first certainly, the second probably a knight, influential teachers in philosophy and rhetoric respectively, were sent into exile in the aftermath of the conspiracy, and a year later the two senators Thrasea Paetus and Curtius Montanus were condemned for political disaffection.[78] Conversely, those literary men of high rank who survived had given the Emperor open political support. Silius Italicus offered his services as an accuser with no appearance of reluctance;[79] Cocceius Nerva must have served Nero well in the exposure of the Pisonian conspiracy, for he not only received, while only praetor designate, triumphal decorations along with a senator of consular rank and Tigellinus, but was singled out, again with Tigellinus, for the honour of a statue on the Palatine.[80] Cluvius Rufus, orator and historian, apparently kept clear of political activity but served as Nero's herald on the Greek tour, and, appropriately enough, wrote a work on actors.[81]

Yet it is natural to ask if the Emperor's displeasure fell on writers only as senators and associates of senators, or if they presented a particular threat as writers. Indeed it has often been suggested that Nero faced a literary opposition.

The Theory of a Literary Opposition

This notion has usually been accompanied by the view that there were in Neronian Rome literary circles in which contrasting styles of writing accompanied contrasting political ideologies and even contrasting philosophies. Nero's conflicts with contemporary writers are then seen in terms of the support and hostility of particular groups.[82]

That there were circles in Rome where literature was fostered and discussed is a reasonable assumption. Tacitus has Tiberius speak of the gossip 'at banquets and in circles', he shows Petronius' friends reciting light verse to each other, and Seneca mentions reading philosophy with friends. Indeed the whole practice of recitation presupposes meetings, large, small, formal, informal, covering the whole range from soirées to public performances.[83] It is equally likely that the Neronian writers knew each other, at least those of the higher social orders. But as in any relatively small society, friendships did not always go with coincidence of opinion.

One example will suffice to show how complex the picture is. If we start with Seneca, we note a close acquaintance with C. Calpurnius Piso by 65; but Seneca did not join the Pisonian conspiracy, though he seems to have known a great deal about it.[84] His nephew Lucan, whose welcome into Nero's circle in the first years of the reign can hardly be dissociated from his uncle's position of influence,[85] was a close friend of Persius at this time, both being students of the Stoic Annaeus Cornutus; Persius, however, only met Seneca towards the end of his life in 62 and was not impressed by him.[86] Cornutus is shown by Dio to have been enjoying access to court as late as 65, and at some time he addressed a work on Virgil to Silius Italicus, who maintained good relations with Nero until the end, being *consul ordinarius* in 68; but Lucan had lost the Emperor's friendship by 64, while Persius was closely associated from 52 on with the Stoic senator Thrasea Paetus who had difficult relations with Nero from 59.[87]

What evidence can we use to identify the supposed coteries? Literary judgments are no guide to alignments. Everyone professed to admire Virgil and Horace, declared themselves against archaism, neologisms and excessively high-flown expressions, and advocated straight clear diction.[88] More precise criticisms of particular writers or more specific recommendations, such as the demand, made by Petronius' hero, for divine intervention in epic, tell us more, but not enough to enable us to assign writers to different stylistic schools. Mutual allusions are likely but seldom subject to proof; for too much literature has been lost, and what survives shows a great similarity of themes, preoccupations and effects. This feature is doubtless related to the training of the declamatory schools, where the emphasis was on using familiar arguments in a more interesting way.[89] It makes it difficult to distinguish variations on a common theme, or on the writer's own earlier efforts, from deliberate imitation or challenge of particular writers. Then, too, when the particular writer can be identified as a contemporary – and not Virgil or Horace or Ovid, as is more usual – we rarely have the clear evidence for dates of composition and publication that would tell us who could be alluding to whom.[90] Even where we feel some confidence in detecting allusions – as in Petronius' poem on the Civil War – the spirit of the reference eludes us, – hostile or complementary, serious or ironic. And even if we could identify rivalry, we would not have evidence for the existence of permanent coteries, still less for their association with distinct political views.

Philosophical allegiance is often uncertain. It is, in any case, an unreliable guide to literary affinities, for the basic tenets of the major philosophical schools were universally exploited for literary effect. As for associating different philosophical beliefs with different political views, it is a fact that the most interesting contrasts of political ideology in this period are those found among the adherents of orthodox Stoicism. On the other hand Persius, a fervent Stoic, discusses political life purely in terms of Greek democracy and the winning of mob popularity.[91] A literary opposition conceived in terms of factions locked in political conflict with each other as supporters and opponents of the Emperor cannot be established for Nero's reign.

There remains, as a method of detecting a literary opposition, the identification of hostile allusions to Nero in extant contemporary works. There is no reason to doubt that such allusions exist, some intended by the author, some invented by malevolent readers or imagined by the Emperor himself. The types of composition in which hostile references to those in power were traditional at Rome were tragedy, on Greek and Roman themes, and history.[92] But Neronian historiography is lost,[93] and Seneca's tragedies, though full of vitriolic attacks on tyranny, yield no clearly identifiable allusions to particular events. In other kinds of literature, allusions would be occasional and not easily recognized by the reader, then or now.[94]

The favourite hunting-ground for attacks on Nero has been the poems of Persius and Lucan, where the ancient biographers and scholiasts have led the way. The Life of Persius states that the satires contained attacks on the poets and orators of his day and on Nero, adding that Cornutus altered the line 'King Midas has donkey's ears' to 'Who does not have donkey's ears?' in the first satire, so that Nero might not think the remark was made of him. The scholiasts pick up this change and find, in addition, numerous unflattering references to the Emperor and to his verses.[95] Their view is incoherent, for if Cornutus thought it necessary to make one change, why did he leave all the other supposed insults standing in the text? And the alleged change itself is implausible in literary terms, as the whole of the first satire leads up to the question in line 121 'Who does not have donkey's ears?', starting from line 8: 'For who is there at Rome who does not – ah, if only I could say it'.

For Lucan the case is more serious, because he wrote his epic on a political theme and died for joining a political conspiracy. Moreover, there is not only the evidence of Suetonius' hostile biography of the poet, which mentions his ridicule of Nero's verses and a poem defaming the Emperor and his most powerful friends, but the testimony of the eulogizing Statius that Lucan wrote a prose work about the Great Fire blaming Nero for the disaster.[96]

Lucan was born on 3 November 39 and attracted Nero's attention through his Greek and Latin declamations at the time he assumed the *toga virilis*. He must then have been about fifteen, and the year 54, 55 or 56. His first real literary success came at the First Neronia in 60, when he recited a verse eulogy of Nero, for which he was crowned. After this he published three books of the epic (presumably the first three). By his success, according to the favourable 'Vacca' Life, or his vanity, according to Suetonius, he offended the Emperor on various occasions. Finally he was banned from reciting or publishing poetry and from pleading cases.[97] Not much trust can be placed in Dio's mention of the ban under the year 65, for his chronology is inaccurate (at least as it emerges from his Epitomators) for this part of the reign; and the story seems to be introduced as a companion piece to the tale of Cornutus' banishment, to which the date may really belong.[98]

Within this vague chronology it is difficult to locate the most significant marks of imperial favour Lucan received, the quaestorship held before the legal age and the augurate, one of the major priesthoods. After assuming the *toga virilis* and studying with Cornutus Lucan seems to have gone to Athens, only to be recalled by the Emperor and given the quaestorship. The recall must be before the first Neronia in 60, but neither of the biographers who mention it places it in relation to his literary activities. The normal age for the quaestorship was 25, though that was held to include the twenty-fifth year, which Lucan reached in November of 63. As he had no child to earn him a year's remission, the earliest Lucan could have taken office, by the normal rules, would have been in December of 63 for the year 63–4.[99] But princes of the imperial house were regularly advanced to the first senatorial magistracy five years in advance, and others of high birth and particular favour enjoyed lesser exemptions, though they are only vaguely indicated in the sources.[100] Lucan was only of equestrian birth, but his father and particularly his uncle were close to the Emperor. A parallel with Salvius Otho, another of the Emperor's youthful comrades, suggests itself. When Nero became Otho's rival for Poppaea Sabina he had him sent out to govern the imperial province of Lusitania, a post usually held by a senior ex-praetor who would be in his mid-thirties or older: Otho was only 26 and an ex-quaestor. Seneca's influence on Otho's behalf is alleged by Plutarch, and the incident belongs in 58, even earlier in the reign than Lucan's elevation. It is also instructive to note the charge that was brought against another confidant of the Emperor in 62, when Fabricius Veiento was accused of making a profit out of his ability to influence the Emperor in making appointments and granting the right to stand for public office.[101]

There is then nothing implausible about the idea that Lucan took office even four years before the normal age, in December of 59, when Nero would be consul in his year of office. It is a pleasing thought that Lucan may have read out the Emperor's speeches as his quaestor and in the same year sung his praises at the first Neronia. But perhaps December 60–61 is a better suggestion, as it was in 61 that Nero ceased to uphold senatorial tradition in its most conservative form by reserving ordinary consulships for men of consular family.

The ban might be better placed in 64 than in 65, Dio's date. This would allow both for the gradual building up of bad relations between Lucan and Nero after the quaestorship in 60 or 61, and also for the indications in Tacitus and the Vacca Life that the ban was the immediate cause of Lucan's joining the Pisonian conspiracy, as a founding member, early in 65.[102] The Suetonius Life does not mention the ban but makes Lucan's attacks on Nero a reaction to a slight by the Emperor not mentioned elsewhere: Nero 'froze' one of Lucan's recitations by calling an emergency meeting of the Senate. The likelihood is that it was the *Bellum Civile* Lucan was reciting, as that was the work which Suetonius clearly regarded as his masterpiece and which, according to the Vacca Life, most aroused Nero's jealousy. It is clear then that Lucan's satiric attacks on the verse and friends of the Emperor came only after Nero had publicly demonstrated his hostility to the poet, and the same could be true of the work on the burning of the city, if it blamed Nero for the Fire.[103]

There is a difficulty in supposing that it was the *content* of Lucan's epic that angered Nero. The first three books Nero allowed to be published after they had been recited in public.[104] It would have to be the recitation of the later books that offended him. Yet, although some increase in pro-Republican and anti-imperial sentiment can be detected in the later books, it is a difference of degree, not of kind. The epic opens with a eulogy of Nero, based on Virgil's praise of Octavian in the *Georgics*, but even more high-flown, so as to be positively grotesque at times.[105] Lucan says that if Fate found no other way for Nero to come, all the crime and guilt of the Civil Wars were worth the price. This fits the spirit of the *Laudes Neronis* delivered in 60. But already in the first three books there are passages reversing this idea and stating that civil war, even its prolongation, would be worth it, but only to avoid the end of freedom and the rule of one man.[106] The famous line 'The victor's cause pleased the Gods, but that of the vanquished, Cato' (1.128) rejects bland acquiescence in the outcome. Why should Nero have first reacted to Lucan's political views only after the first three books? Moreover, what Lucan expressed throughout, even in the violent passages of Book VII[107], was the common senatorial view, shared by the imperial members of that body too, that the Republic and *libertas* were preferable but that the Principate was a practical necessity for stability and peace. Rhetorical exaggeration of both ideas in Lucan should not have surprised or worried Nero.

The sources, both hostile and favourable to the poet, are unanimous in ascribing the poet's breach with Nero to the Emperor's jealousy of his poetic talent, aggravated by Lucan's vanity and self-advertisement. The fact that, unlike Nero, he excelled in oratory as well will have heightened the Emperor's feeling, as is reflected in the ban on pleading cases as well as reciting and publishing poetry.

As for Lucan's attitude, if we suppose that the vehemence of Book VII was not conventional sentimentality for the Republic, but 'literary opposition' to the Emperor, we shall have to accept that Lucan's political views were seriously inconsistent, for the poem cannot be a manifesto for the conspirator. Love of the Republic was not to be served by replacing Nero with another stagestruck aristocrat, and indeed, the conspirators, according to Tacitus, did not invite a consul of the year to join them, because he might urge the restoration of the Republic.[108] In fact, there is little reason to think that even Lucan's participation in the conspiracy sprang from serious political conviction. The historian contrasts the personal pique that drove Lucan to conspire with the love of Rome that moved one of his fellow conspirators.[109] Suetonius too speaks of revenge and notes remarks about the *glory* of tyrannicide. The poet died reciting a passage from the *Bellum Civile*; not however a denunciation of tyranny, but a purple passage describing a lingering death in battle, with which he compared his own enforced suicide. The concentration on himself, and on the means rather than the end, do seem to be common features of his life and his work.[110]

Rome did know writers who expressed political hostility to the régime obliquely in their writings. Curiatius Maternus, the tragedian, is clearly depicted as courting ruin in Tacitus' *Dialogue on Oratory*. Ovid had offended Augustus by the moral views he expressed in his poetry. But to Nero his art and the fame it brought came first, above ordinary politics and ordinary morality. In the case of Curtius Montanus, Lucan, and Seneca, his jealousy of their literary eminence is specifically attested. For Petronius, who avoided the higher forms of poetry that Nero most cultivated, the trouble came from the envy of Nero's favourite Tigellinus. Petronius had clearly not attacked the Emperor in the *Satyricon*, or Nero completely failed to realise that he had, for Petronius was in high favour with him down to 66, when Tigellinus reminded his master that Petronius had been a friend of one of the dissolute ringleaders of the conspiracy and bribed one of his rival's slaves to support his story.[111] To his will Petronius appended a list of the Emperor's sexual perversions complete with names and sent it to him. As Nero was astonished by his knowledge and set out to find his informant, it is unlikely that the *Satyricon* was already full of allusions to Nero's practices.[112]

The Emperor who at first did so much to encourage literature ended by attacking it at its root. His feud was not with what writers said or how they wrote, but with their excellence and success. It is difficult enough to produce good literature when the content is circumscribed, but it is impossible, according to the rules of logic as well as those of human nature, when it is quality itself that is proscribed. Some writers survived, those who were less gifted or more pliant or both. It is not surprising that Martial says of Nerva, who earned Nero's praise, that modesty restrained his talent, and that he did not give full sail to his fame.

The Emperor on the Stage

The practice of recitation allowed the writer to experience some of the public acclaim of the performing artist. Therefore Nero's competitive attitude to literature has a closer affinity with his acting and singing in public than may at first appear. But it was only through these theatrical arts, particularly when displayed at musical competitions, that Nero could earn the applause of a large audience and defeat his rivals in public. He could thereby maintain the politically important pose of 'first among equals' by competing with his social peers on equal terms and in accordance with the rules, and, at the same time, prove, at least to himself, that in the artistic sphere his primacy was real.

At first Nero made concessions to decorum. He performed only in his private circus and on his private stage. Even at the first celebration of his new festival, the Neronia, in August of 60, he did not participate in the musical competitions or the chariot-racing along with the senators and *equites* who were encouraged to do so.[113] But the judges rejected as unworthy all the entries for lyre-playing and offered the crown to the Emperor who had it laid at the foot of Augustus' statue. He actually accepted the crowns for oratory and Latin poetry which were offered to him at the request of the winners, although Lucan received a crown for his verse eulogy of the Emperor.[114]

In 63, after the birth of Poppaea's daughter in January, the Senate included in its honorific decrees provision for a Greek festival on the model of Augustus' periodic spectacles in honour of the Battle of Actium. The plan was apparently abandoned when the child died in April or May and it is uncertain if musical competitions would have been included or if the

Emperor intended to participate himself.[115] In any case, by 64 he had decided that he was ready for his public debut. Nero judged that it would cause less offence if he performed first at Naples, long regarded as a true Greek city where the most restrained Romans could relax in Greek clothes. It was the site of the only sacred quinquennial Greek games on Italian soil, the Italica Romaea Sebasta Olympia, established in AD 2 in Augustus' honour and recognized in Greece as equal in prestige to the four ancient festivals.[116]

For the imperial performance, the theatre was filled with citizens of Naples and the neighbouring towns and members of Nero's entourage, including a contingent of praetorians.[117] The Emperor addressed his audience in Greek and revelled in the rhythmic applause of some visiting Alexandrians, whose techniques were adopted by his own clique, now enlarged to five thousand. Even the collapse of the theatre, as the result of a minor earthquake, was taken by the Emperor as a sign of divine favour, for it was empty at the time. He celebrated the event in a poem.[118]

On leaving Naples, Nero had planned to go to Greece to compete in the great festivals, and his first stop on the journey was at Beneventum. But he gave up the plan and returned to Rome where he decided on a visit to the eastern provinces, particularly Egypt. That project too he abandoned and on the very day of departure. That is what Tacitus tells us, but the plan to visit Greece at this stage has been doubted because of evidence that the eastern visit was not a sudden whim but a well-planned scheme. Thus the Prefect of Egypt is said to have constructed special baths for Nero's visit, and Dio reports that Nero intended to accompany the expedition against the Parthian king, for which Corbulo was reappointed in 63.[119] Yet the baths could belong to preparations for a later visit and Dio dates his dubious item to 64. The visit to Beneventum on the main route to Brundisium, the principal departure point for Greece, remains suggestive. But it may be that Nero was originally planning to go to Greece and then on to places further east, just as on his actual visit to Greece late in 66 he was intending to visit Alexandria and supervise military expeditions to Ethiopia and the Black Sea.[120]

Nero's experience in the Temple of Vesta persuaded him to cancel the eastern visit in 64, and he consoled himself with a great public banquet. There followed the Great Fire, after which he held circus games in his Vatican gardens, striding around in the garb of a charioteer if not actually performing himself.[121]

The summer of 65 brought with it the repetition of the Neronia and the Emperor's first public stage performance in Rome. Had he been strict in following the example of the quinquennial Greek festivals, of course, he should have celebrated the Neronia in 64.[122] But Nero was no slave to Greek conventions, as is clear from his naming of the festival after himself rather than a deity. His cavalier way with festival dates was to be well illustrated on his Greek tour.[123]

The Senate tried to avert the disgrace of Nero's participation by offering him the crowns for singing and oratory, but Nero was determined to win a real contest. First he recited part of his epic on the Trojan War and then, as he left the theatre, he was recalled by his public who urged him to display his other talents as well. The *Augustiani* and the praetorians no doubt led the audience in this, while one of the presiding consulars, the future Emperor Vitellius, urged Nero to return to the theatre and perform on the lyre. Tacitus and Suetonius embellish their accounts of this occasion with horrific details: the Praetorian Prefects carrying the lyre, the soldiers compelling men to applaud. By 66 failure to listen to the imperial singing and strumming or to sacrifice to his heavenly voice could be mentioned in the Senate as an indication of disloyalty. Nero was performing frequently now, not only on the stage, but as a charioteer in the Circus Maximus.[124]

By this time, the old policy of seeking popularity and security by pleasing all sections of society had given way to exhibitionism and repression, the serious conspiracy that broke early in 65 having left the Emperor in no doubt about the hostility he aroused in some members of the upper orders. Nero knew where true enthusiasm for his art was to be found. Some Greek envoys who presented him with the crowns offered in their ancient festivals asked him to sing at dinner, and as Nero listened to their effusive applause, he remarked 'The Greeks alone know how to appreciate me and my art.'

Suetonius, who tells this story, remarks that Nero set out for Greece immediately, but there is clear evidence of careful planning beforehand. Buildings were constructed and improved at Olympia and Corinth, and many of the festivals were rescheduled so as to allow the Emperor to win all of the crowns in one year.[125] In the case of the Olympic games, held every four years, the celebration due in the late summer of 65 was postponed until his visit in the next year. Plans for his tour must have been made at least a year in advance, for the Arval Brothers took vows for the safe return of the Emperor and his wife on 25 September 66, presumably near the time when they embarked at Brundisium for Greece.[126] The organizers of the Olympic games also had to arrange for musical competitions to be held in addition to the athletic and chariot events which alone were traditional.

Only two of the major festivals were actually due to be held in the year of Nero's visit, the Isthmia at Corinth in April–May of 67 and the Pythia at Delphi in August of 67, but Suetonius says that all of the major festivals were held during that year, some even being repeated. The Isthmia may have been the games that were held twice, because Nero paid at least one visit to Corinth before performing the crowning act of the whole tour, the liberation of Greece, at a special celebration of the Isthmian Games on 28 November, 67.[127] At the end of August or earlier, he had inaugurated the cutting of the Isthmus canal in person, a ceremony that could have been timed to follow the normal celebration of the Games.[128]

The only other indications of the order in which the Games were held in 66/7 come from very poor sources. They show only that the Olympic games came first, the Pythia perhaps second, while considerations of geography may suggest that Nero took in the Actian Games right after his landing on Corcyra in October of 66.[129]

The accounts we have of Nero's performances, hostile as they are, show that he took his art in deadly earnest. He obeyed all the rules, never clearing his throat and wiping his brow only with the sleeve of his gown. He showed fear of the judges and their verdict, though the decision was always the same: 'Nero Caesar wins this contest and crowns the Roman people and his world empire'. Once, when he fell from his chariot at Olympia, the Emperor's life was in jeopardy, but never his crown. After landing at Puteoli, Nero celebrated his homecoming in four processions, at Naples where he had first performed, at Antium where he was born, at Alba Longa where he had his favourite imperial residence, and finally at Rome. His entry into the capital was his last great show. Dressed in a Greek cloak, wearing the Olympic crown and carrying the Pythian, Nero rode in Augustus' triumphal chariot; he entered the city not through the usual triumphal arch, but through a breach in the walls, as was the custom for the Greek *hieronica* or victor in the sacred games. Before him were carried, not the names of the cities he had conquered, but his crowns with the record of his victories and his songs. Behind came the Augustiani, instead of legionaries, and the procession finished its route at the Temple of Apollo on the Palatine, not that of Jupiter on the Capitoline.[130] This was the triumph of an artist.

TEN

'What an Artist Dies With Me'

That Nero escaped more and more into a world of fantasy from the time of the second Neronia is a conclusion difficult to resist, even allowing for malicious distortion in our sources. There had always been a tendency for the theatre to invade his life, as when a collapsible boat used on stage showed him how to murder his mother, or when a podium reminiscent of architectonic stage décor was used to adorn a nymphaeum of his first palace (fig. 12).[1] Insulated from facts by flatterers, more and more convinced of his musical talents, Nero made of the trip to Greece a physical demonstration of his mental withdrawal from the tensions and compromises demanded by political life in Rome. From his belief in real competition, which led him to fear his judges and bribe or slander his rivals, to his neglect of Helius' warnings about disaffection at home, a crescendo of illusion was rising to a climax in his paralysis after news came of Vindex' rebellion, his subsequent address to his body of advisers on the subject of water-organs, and his final panic after the defeat of the rebel.

In order to understand the form that political opposition to Nero eventually assumed and the nature of his reaction, we must return to the point when his performance as Princeps ceased to attract applause.

One of the leaders of the conspiracy that was hatched early in 65 reproached him with these crimes: the murder of his mother in 59 and of his wife in 62, his performance as a charioteer and actor, and the burning of Rome in 64. According to Dio, the conspirators could no longer endure Nero's shamelessness, licentiousness and cruelty.[2] The last vice had been demonstrated much earlier, while the first example of open sexual depravity had come in 64 when Nero celebrated his marriage to the freedman Pythagoras at a public banquet.[3] His shamelessness had not yet emerged: Nero was still sensitive and responsive to public opinion. He had not yet performed publicly at Rome but had chosen for his début in 64 a Greek city where Romans traditionally relaxed their standards. Even when he arranged for the prosecution in his absence of D. Junius Silanus Torquatus, on a charge of harbouring imperial ambitions, he was careful to say that he would have exercised clemency had the accused not forestalled condemnation by suicide.[4] He was still concerned to justify his sexual excesses on the ground that no man was chaste or pure, and even as late as 66 he was shocked to discover that his activities were known to Petronius. His behaviour after the Fire of 64 showed clearly how eager he was to dispel the rumour of imperial arson. Even after the conspiracy of 65 he was concerned to present proofs of its existence to the Senate and to counter the suspicion that he was punishing innocent men out of envy and fear of their distinction.[5]

Even if not dead to shame, however, Nero had by 65 given alarming indications that his tendency to fear and insecurity, especially when aggravated by disapproval, could lead to the total disappearance of his earlier *clementia* and *civilitas*. The murder of his mother had filled him with deep feelings of guilt that never left him. According to Suetonius, he believed he was haunted by her ghost and by the avenging Furies. The truth of the story is suggested by his failure, when in Greece, to visit either Athens, which had harboured the Furies, or Eleusis where a herald ordered the godless and wicked away before the performance of the Mysteries.[6] Just after his mother's death, when the soldiers, the Senate and the people were all acquiescing in the official version that the Emperor had been saved from a plot against his life, Nero had his first encounter with the displeasure of P. Clodius Thrasea Paetus, a senator of considerable moral influence with a numerous band of loyal associates.

Thrasea was the first senator in his family, but he had married the daughter and assumed the cognomen of Caecina Paetus who, as governor of Dalmatia, had led an armed rebellion against Claudius. Consul in 56, thereafter governor of a province, he had respected Nero's efforts in the early years to encourage senatorial initiative and free speech: he had participated even in minor senatorial debates and assisted provincials in the prosecution of a corrupt governor. But the servile conduct of the Senate after Agrippina's murder was too much for him: he made a dignified exit from the House, and later in the year, at the Juvenalia, he showed his disapproval of the performances given by the Emperor and his own peers. Then in 62 he cunningly thwarted Nero and demonstrated his power to carry the Senate with him, at the trial of Antistius Sosianus for treason. But Nero was still on amicable terms with him at the end of that year.[7]

The first open sign of his irritation with Thrasea came after Poppaea gave birth to a daughter in January of 63. Nero was elated, for the birth gave him a daughter to use in dynastic marriages and, more important, hopes of an heir that would more than compensate for the divorce of Octavia in consolidating his position on the throne. The Senate was invited *en masse* to Antium, but Thrasea was asked not to attend. When the infant died within four months Nero's grief was as intemperate as his joy had been. He no doubt grieved for the damage to his political prospects as well as for his personal loss, and, regretting his earlier display of pique, he was reconciled with Thrasea.[8] For Nero, Thrasea Paetus represented those who were hardest to please among the senators, and 'EX s c' on his gold and silver coins still advertised his intention to please.

The disappointment of his hopes for the succession revived fears that his mother had implanted in him years before. It was now that he reverted to her remedies and disposed of the prominent descendant of Augustus, whose brothers, Lucius and Marcus Junius Silanus, had been among her victims. He was now afraid to leave Rome and offered the plebs a grand public banquet to underline his message that it was concern for them that had led him to abandon his travelling plans.

Then came the Fire – a disaster for Rome and for the Emperor, whose relations with his subjects were becoming precarious. The rumours of his responsibility showed him, once and for all, how fragile was the popularity of a ruler. The long-term consequences of the Fire – loss of property and financial exactions by the government – aggravated the hostility of the upper orders in Rome and was eventually to turn the most powerful and prosperous of the provincials against the Emperor.

The Pisonian Conspiracy

The first plot to overthrow Nero, however, seems to have been planned without any connivance from governors, armies or subjects outside Rome. Like Caesar's assassins, like the murderers of Gaius, those who conspired to kill Nero on 19 April 65 had made no contact with sympathetic generals, though they clearly expected the armies to welcome, or at least accept, the deed. Our only reliable account of the Pisonian conspiracy comes from Tacitus who had read the reports of at least two historians contemporary with the events and knew what some of the participants said when they returned to Rome from banishment.[9]

The cast of characters included senators, *equites*, praetorian tribunes, centurions and eventually one of the Prefects. The list resembles closely that of the assassins of Gaius in January 41, except that no imperial freedmen are named. The plan was modelled closely on the murder of Caesar: the senator Plautius Lateranus, who had earlier enjoyed Nero's clemency, was to present a petition to the Emperor and, by grasping his knees, prevent him from avoiding the daggers of the others. Lateranus had signified his intention to present the petition in advance, if one can connect with this episode an anecdote recounted by the philosopher Epictetus: when asked by Epaphroditus, Nero's secretary in charge of petitions, what the cause of his confrontation with the Emperor was, Lateranus replied, 'If I wish to discuss it, I will do so with your master'.[10] In all three plots, some participated out of patriotism, others out of pique, and the various conspirators reacted to various wrongs. Lateranus, a patriot according to Tacitus, is made to allude, in Epictetus' story, to the resurgence of the power of the freedmen; the freedwoman Epicharis was to adduce, in addition to Nero's crimes, the fact that the Senate had no power; the praetorian officers stressed Nero's domestic murders, public performances and attempt to destroy the capital.[11]

The plot to kill Gaius had succeeded, but many of Piso's allies, who had been at the theatre, or at least in Rome, on that day, were keenly aware of the weaknesses of planning that had nearly led to chaos and disaster. Gaius' assassins, like Caesar's, had made no plans for government after the tyrant was dead. Even in 44 BC it had been rash to assume that the machinery of the Republic would automatically resume operation; in AD 41 it was a monstrous folly. There had been a prolonged struggle between the ringleaders of the conspiracy, acting in concert with the Senate, and the urban troops who finally prevailed, but not before leading senators had started bidding for the throne in an unseemly competition.[12]

In 65 the plan provided for the replacement of the dead Nero by C. Calpurnius Piso, a descendant of the Republican nobility who enjoyed widespread popularity. He himself had been in exile when Gaius was killed, but he was well aware of the possibility of rival candidates.[13] Tacitus notes that he feared the ambitions of L. Junius Silanus, and that M. Julius Vestinus Atticus, the consul, was not informed of the plot lest he favour a return to the Republic or give his support to another candidate. (In 41 the consul had made a lengthy speech celebrating the restoration of the Republic while Claudius was already being hailed Emperor in the praetorian camp.) Piso refused to have the murder carried out at his villa at Baiae, ostensibly because it would taint him with sacrilegious disregard of the duties of hospitality and remind men that the Emperor trusted him as a friend. It would also have allowed others to take control of the situation in Rome – his real motive, according to Tacitus.

Nero was to be attacked when attending chariot races at the Circus Maximus, just as Gaius had been killed on his way to a theatrical performance. Access to the Emperor at such a time was easy and Nero's movements would be restricted by the crowds. The lesson about securing the allegiance of the Praetorian Guard as a whole had been learned: no Claudius was to be found by the soldiers behind a curtain and spirited off to the camp. Piso himself, right after the murder in the Circus Maximus, was to be escorted from the temple of Ceres nearby to the praetorian camp by Faenius Rufus and other officers.

There had been some delay and hesitation, but Tacitus states firmly that the whole conspiracy was both conceived and hatched in 65, though he mentions a report that the praetorian tribune Subrius Flavus had been tempted to kill Nero earlier during a stage performance or in the confusion of the Fire the year before.[14] Why 65? If Tacitus is right to name praetorian officers among the initiators of the scheme, it seems remarkable that they waited so long after Nero had murdered his mother.[15] Yet until 62 her two former protégés, Burrus and Faenius Rufus, Prefects in succession, had been able to control what resentment there was among the praetorians. After that

Faenius steadily lost influence with Nero as the other Prefect Tigellinus ingratiated himself. Then there were fresh insults to the traditional sentiments of the Guard, as when a detachment accompanied Nero to Naples in 64 and watched him sing in public. Again, with regard to the senatorial ringleaders, Lucan may only have been banned from writing and publishing his poetry in 64, while the poem in which Nero offended Afranius Quintianus may have been of recent composition.

When the consuls took office in 65 the immediate future held the second Neronia at which Nero clearly intended to perform. Another consideration may have been the fact that Poppaea was pregnant again, if the fact was known. For the birth of an heir, now a distinct possibility, would certainly encourage Nero to throw off what inhibitions remained, and would also cause complications for any later assassination: not even the most vehement enemies of Gaius can have been pleased to see his infant daughter murdered in 41.[16] But if Poppaea's son was to be spared, it would be better to have Nero's successor safely installed before its birth.

In the event the scheme was a dismal failure. It foundered on the disloyalty of a freedman of the senator Flavius Scaevinus, who reported his patron's suspicious preparations to the Emperor; it was finally wrecked by the indecision of Piso, who immediately lost heart and could not be persuaded to appeal to the praetorians and people and seize the city. Abject confessions and dishonourable accusations followed, and Nero learned with growing alarm what numbers were involved. The disloyalty of the praetorian officers was particularly distressing: Nero could only trust new or recent recruits to deliver the death order to Piso, and, after the revelations and punishments, he felt it necessary to buy the loyalty of the Guard with a handsome donative and a free corn allowance.[17] In addition to the tribune Subrius Flavus and the centurion Sulpicius Asper, who were guilty and suffered execution, four praetorian tribunes were dismissed. Two other tribunes were spared for co-operating in the punishment of their fellow conspirators, but killed themselves.[18]

According to Tacitus, many innocent men were punished on inadequate evidence: some, like Vestinus Atticus, Seneca and Rufrius Crispinus, because Nero had personal reasons for hating them; others because they were falsely accused by conspirators trying to help themselves by giving information. Yet Nero had powerful support in uncovering the plot: the consular Petronius Turpilianus, the praetor-designate Cocceius Nerva, the loyal Prefect Tigellinus and the imperial freedman Epaphroditus all received honours befitting a military victory. Although the Emperor treated the exposure and punishment of the conspirators as a serious war, he still retained his balance: some of the accused were pardoned, others ignored. The Senate felt confident enough to stop the malicious prosecution of Seneca's brother Gallio by one of its members, and Nero refused a temple to himself, an unprecedented honour for the living Emperor at Rome.

It was only later in 65, after the death of Poppaea and her unborn child, that the unprovoked persecution of influential senators on treason charges began in earnest. Before that gloomy event, Tacitus' narrative is enlivened by the story of a bogus treasure hunt and incidents of the second Neronia. A Roman knight from Carthage dreamt that the gold brought by Dido from Troy when she founded the new city was buried in a cave on his estate. He bribed his way in to see the Emperor and prevailed on him to send soldiers and ships to find and carry off the treasure without any preliminary investigation of his claim. After the shock of the Pisonian conspiracy Nero may have seized on this sign of divine favour. The historian recounts with malicious glee how eulogies of the Emperor celebrating a literal age of gold were recited at the second Neronia (thus telling his readers – if they needed to be told – how he regarded the earlier effusions of Calpurnius Siculus and Seneca). But he has also a financial point to make: 'Nero's expectation of wealth contributed to national bankruptcy'. Tacitus may be unfair to trace heavy spending in 65 to unscrutinised hopes, as Nero had long-standing commitments in the second Neronia and the preparations for Tiridates' visit. And the historian himself rejects a story that the unfortunate dreamer, Caesellius Bassus, was imprisoned when nothing came of the treasure hunt and released when his property had been confiscated as compensation.[19]

Yet, as an omen, this story was accurate enough, for Suetonius notes that accusations and confiscations followed the fiasco, while Tacitus detects financial motives behind some of the political convictions that followed Poppaea's death later in the year.[20] Moreover, while Seneca had already been forbidden to change his will which was doubtless favourable to Nero, it was in 66 that the condemned were advised to make the Emperor or Tigellinus part heir in order to save the rest of the estate for their families.[21]

Poppaea's extravagant funeral must have added to the state deficit: she was not cremated as was customary but embalmed, and her public obsequies involved the burning of quantities of oriental spice. There is no reason to doubt that Nero's personal grief was intense, despite the widespread belief that her miscarriage and death were caused by a kick from her angry spouse. Not only was she given divine honours: Nero demonstrated his sexual dependence on her by having Sporus, a young freedman who resembled her, castrated and using him as a substitute, even going through a marriage ceremony later on the Greek tour.[22] In the eulogy he pronounced at her funeral, however, Nero lamented not only her beauty but the fact that she had once given him a child. The loss of his second child and possible heir must have contributed greatly to his grief: it also explains why he was to marry again within a year.[23] But for the moment he was consoling himself in Naples, from which letters were sent to the Senate ordering prosecutions for treason.[24]

Once again the well-born Silani, potential claimants to the throne, paid for his anxiety. Lucius, the son of Marcus Silanus, who had died in 54 when his son was still a boy, had been brought up in the house of the famous jurist Cassius Longinus by his aunt Junia Lepida. Now Cassius Longinus was first fobidden to attend Poppaea's funeral and then accused of harbouring seditious intentions. These he supposedly manifested by honouring his ancestor C. Cassius the tyrannicide, whose statue he was alleged to have inscribed 'to the leader of the cause'. The practical aim of his disloyalty, it was claimed, was to elevate his nephew, the descendant of Augustus, to the throne; Lucius Silanus himself was accused of showing his imperial ambitions in the same way as his paternal uncle Decimus, who had been convicted the previous year. The sentence of banishment sufficed for Cassius, a concession to his age; his nephew was killed by a centurion.[25]

It is not clear whether or not Nero believed that Lucius Silanus had been considered as a possible alternative to Piso earlier in 65, but other prosecutions at this time seem linked with even earlier anxieties of Nero. The next to be accused were a trio: L. Antistius Vetus, his mother-in-law Sextia and his daughter Antistia Pollitta who had been the wife of Rubellius Plautus. She had been with her husband when he was murdered three years before, and since then she had practised the ostentatious widowhood that was so fashionable in the Early Empire.[26] After she had gone to Naples and addressed pleas to Nero that proved vain, the three anticipated condemnation by suicide. There was no shortage of senators willing to turn up and condemn their peers.[27]

The next case had roots in the past, but also reflected Nero's new fear of able military men, and his increasing greed. The wealthy Anteius Rufus was accused by Nero's old victim Antistius Sosianus, still in exile, of consulting an astrologer about the death of the Emperor. Antistius also implicated Ostorius Scapula, a war hero of the Claudian conquest of Britain, who had refused to give hostile evidence at Antistius' trial in 62.[28] There followed addenda to the punishment of the Pisonian conspirators, which also brought testamentary profits. Annaeus Mela was accused of association with his son Lucan in conspiratorial plans, Petronius was similarly linked with Scaevinus, while Rufrius Crispinus, who had been exiled at the time of the detection, was now sentenced to death.

Tacitus' history of the period breaks off with the deaths of Barea Soranus and Thrasea Paetus, men whom Nero had long distrusted. Barea was accused of treasonable collusion with Rubellius Plautus. Against his daughter who was implicated in a further charge, that of dabbling in magic, it was recalled that her husband Annius Pollio had been exiled as an associate of Piso. Thrasea's seditious designs were inferred from the campaign of abstention in which his long feud with the Emperor had culminated: general non-attendance at the Senate since 63; non-participation in the senatorial oath taken every 1 January to uphold the acts of past and present Emperors; absence from his priestly college when vows for the Emperor's safety were taken each 3 January; absence from Poppaea's funeral and consecration in 65.[29]

The Persecution of the Stoics

Nero's desire for revenge against Thrasea was, according to Tacitus, stimulated by Cossutianus Capito, who reminded the Emperor that Thrasea was an adherent of the Stoa, a sect hostile to authority, and that he and his followers openly disapproved of the Emperor's conduct. These charges might be considered just an hysterical allusion to Thrasea's biography of the younger Cato, by now a Stoic saint, were it not for other attacks on adherents of the sect around this time.[30] Thrasea's son-in-law Helvidius Priscus and his friend Paconius Agrippinus, who were put on trial with Thrasea and relegated, were also prominent Stoics; Barea Soranus was accounted a disciple of Stoic philosophers, one of whom, the eminent Musonius Rufus, had been a companion of Rubellius Plautus,[31] himself accused of displaying Stoic arrogance and seditious Stoic convictions. When Musonius Rufus was banished as an accomplice in the Pisonian conspiracy, Tacitus states that the real ground for his conviction was his fame as a philosopher.[32]

The punishment of these Stoic adherents, when combined with other facts – that the Stoic Lucan was in the conspiracy, that the Stoic Seneca was alleged to have been, that Lucan's Stoic teacher Cornutus was banished, that the Stoic Arulenus Rusticus offered to use his tribunician veto in the Senate on Thrasea's behalf, that Demetrius the Cynic, who comforted Thrasea in his last hours, suffered banishment[33] – have suggested to many that there was a Stoic opposition under Nero. This philosophical opposition, it is argued, continued under the Flavians and provoked the trials of Stoic senators and the expulsions of philosophers attested under Vespasian and Domitian.

In examining this important idea, we must first note that on every occasion the punishment suffered by Stoic adherents was shared by others who cannot be connected with the sect. Thus the death of Rubellius Plautus coincided with that of Cornelius Sulla, who is not credited with philosophical interests. There is no evidence that C. Calpurnius Piso himself or any of the senators, *equites* and praetorian officers who planned the conspiracy with Lucan were also Stoics. While Lucius Silanus is described as a pupil of Heliodorus the Stoic, there is nothing to suggest that Cassius Longinus was an adherent of the creed: indeed his ancestor Cassius, whom he revered, was an Epicurean at the time of Caesar's murder and, on his mother's side, the Aelii Tuberones could claim an Academic more recently than a Stoic.[34] Finally, of the victims that perished in 66 before Thrasea Paetus and Barea Soranus, none, not even Seneca's brother Annaeus Mela, is attested as a Stoic.[35]

It is clear then that the Stoics who were condemned were thought both to have shared sentiments and to have concerted action with those who were not. Indeed, under earlier Emperors, men who were Stoics had been condemned on political charges, but without any significance being attached to their creed, as far as we know.[36] Yet it cannot be denied that under Nero the doctrines of the Porch themselves were brought under suspicion. What then was believed to be distinctively Stoic about the opposition, real or alleged, with which these men confronted the Emperor?

The accuser of Thrasea Paetus claimed that the Stoics were hostile to any ordered system of government, and that, if they destroyed the Emperor's power, they would go on to attack the Republic afterwards.[37] Tendentious as this argument is, it is at least accurate in not describing Stoicism as specifically hostile to the Principate or monarchy in general. Seneca, in a work of Neronian date, accuses Brutus of departing from Stoic precept in that he feared the name of king: 'for the best condition for a state is to be under a just king'. Seneca is probably distorting, for the sake of his argument, the more complex view of the Stoa in Brutus' day, namely that kingship was the best of the *simple* forms of government but inferior to the mixed constitution by reason of its tendency to degenerate.[38] And this preference may even have been current among the founders of the school, linked with admiration for Sparta whose system was often analysed in these terms.[39] But early Stoics had certainly shown no doctrinaire hostility to monarchy: three of them are known to have written treatises on kingship for various Hellenistic monarchs.[40] Hence the Stoic tradition was sufficiently diverse to justify a change of direction when the fall of the Republic made men lose faith in the mixed constitution. Not that there was a distinctively Stoic theory of kingship. The only central doctrine touching on forms of constitution was the paradox 'only the wise man is a king', from which it seemed reasonable to infer, as did Musonius Rufus, that the king should be a wise man, an idea that went back to Plato.[41]

Seneca and Marcus Aurelius exhibit the proper Stoic emphasis when they discuss how the Princeps, from the monarchical position he occupied, could practise Stoic virtue. In *De Clementia* Seneca calls Nero *rex* by implication. He also applies to him as Princeps many of the admonitions that philosophers had offered Hellenistic kings: the king's position as parallel to that of the gods whose vice-regent he is (1. 7); monarchy as a glorious servitude (1. 8, 1); the monarchical constitution as comparable to the organisation of bees (1. 19, 2). Seneca uses this last parallel to point out that nature's conception of king, as in the case of the bees, excludes a sting: he does not argue that nature has revealed, through the bees, that monarchy is the perfect form of government. In this he shows a typical Stoic concern with the moral exercise of power rather than its constitutional forms. Stoicism had enjoyed a long history because it remained applicable in different political circumstances, being in essence not a doctrine for states but for individuals, not for political man but for moral man. Indeed Cicero remarks that the second century BC Stoics were the first to deal with politics in a detailed and practical way at all: the main doctrines of the Porch had been developed long before that.[42]

These considerations are enough to render extremely implausible the ascription of specific constitutional doctrines to the Stoics of the Empire, such as the once popular notion that they advocated succession by adoption rather than by birth.[43] The Stoa, in common with all the dogmatic schools since Plato, condemned tyranny and distinguished it from kingship, not by any constitutional criterion but by the moral character of the ruler. Thus the moral disapproval evinced by Thrasea Paetus, Helvidius Priscus and Paconius Agrippinus towards Nero's conduct was in a sense political, for if the qualification for kingship was virtue it followed that Nero was a tyrant and had no right to his throne. And, though the targets of their disapproval were not distinctively Stoic targets, adherents of the sect manifested their distaste by a characteristic display of arrogance and censoriousness. Seneca warns his disciple Lucilius against those familiar and irritating qualities, and they were freely ascribed to Thrasea who, better evidence suggests, was actually a tolerant man with a sense of humour.[44]

Disapproval is not yet opposition. Everything depends on how that disapproval is implemented, and Stoicism, like the other philosophical schools, offered no clear guidance on this point. Cassius the Epicurean and Brutus the Academic, when they instigated Caesar's assassination, were not moved by doctrine. Indeed each had earlier shown a tendency to justify acquiescence in the rule of the dictator by reference to their philosophical beliefs.[45] What all of these schools recommended was refusal to compromise one's virtue, but this could take many forms. The defiant freedom with which Demetrius the Cynic addressed Gaius, Nero and Vespasian followed a long and hallowed tradition of free speech to which Seneca and Thrasea laid claim.[46] Refusal to co-operate in a tyrant's crimes was another traditional pattern, sanctioned by Socrates and adopted by Thrasea, who would not join the Senate in applauding Nero's murders or condemning innocent men.[47] To commit suicide in order to avoid evil actions or even the recognition of illegal power was orthodox Stoic conduct, as exemplified by Cato.[48] The Stoics emphasised too that obligations differed according to external circumstances, the role one played in society and one's past conduct: thus, according to Cicero, it had been right for Cato to commit suicide, but right for others with him to refrain.[49] Therefore, though many Stoics admired Brutus and Cassius, it could hardly be said that their school offered a clear directive to follow their example. On the other hand, tyrannicide could be justified in Stoic terms as one of those duties imposed by special circumstances, like suicide. The tyrant, it could be held, disrupted the natural bonds of human society that man is bound to uphold, so that this clear obligation could on occasion justify homicide, an act normally held to violate it.[50]

Given this complexity in the Stoic position, it is not surprising that the inspiration behind the Pisonian conspiracy cannot be shown to be Stoic. In fact, the only trace is the philosophical justification offered to Nero by the centurion Sulpicius Asper: 'There was no other way to cure your many vices'. For this idea is found in the writings of Seneca, and Seneca is alleged by Dio to have been a participant.[51] Moreover, Tacitus, who regards him as innocent, supplies disquieting evidence: that Seneca returned to his villa near Rome on the very day set for the murder 'by chance or intention'; that he had come from Campania (where Epicharis had attempted to corrupt the imperial fleet); and that he admitted to an exchange of messages with Piso through the conspirator Antonius Natalis, in which he showed previous friendship with Piso and a disinclination to have him call at the time. A later source identifies Epicharis as the mistress of Seneca's brother Annaeus Mela.[52] But these facts indicate at most that Seneca knew of the conspiracy, not that he was a member. He, in fact, denied having written to Piso in the treasonable terms alleged by Natalis: 'That their mutual interests would not be served by frequent meetings but that his safety depended on that of Piso' (the phrase about safety here was reminiscent of the oath of loyalty taken to the Princeps by soldiers and civilians).[53] Aside from this, there is only the evidence of rumour to set against Tacitus' verdict of innocence. He himself reports a story that had great currency, namely that the praetorian officers, with Seneca's knowledge, planned to kill Piso after disposing of Nero and then to make Seneca Emperor: Subrius Flavus was supposed to have remarked that the disgrace would remain if the lyre player were replaced by a tragic actor.[54] Although Sulpicius Asper's idea that it is justifiable to kill a man who is vicious beyond redemption occurs several times in Seneca's works, we must set against this Seneca's view of the murder of Caesar as a folly, his failure to participate in the murder of Gaius (which he regarded as justified) and his horror of civil war, always a possibility to be reckoned with when a ruler is assassinated.[55]

Asper's remark, without clear evidence of Senecan inspiration, would not have been construed as a distinctively Stoic justification for tyrannicide. The idea that punishment and death provide the only remedy for incurable vice is found in Plato, with the tyrant being a prime example: it was probably a philosophical cliché by this period.[56] Stoic inspiration for the Pisonian conspiracy cannot then be established, though Lucan was not in contradiction with his sect in supporting tyrannicide.

Censoriousness alone has so far emerged as a distinctively Stoic characteristic ascribed to real or alleged opponents of the régime. Another identifiable Stoic trait was *constantia*, that is, imperturbability and fidelity to principle even in the face of exile, torture or death. Tacitus says of Helvidius Priscus that he devoted his notable talents while still young to elevated studies 'which fortified him against the hazards of fortune met in public life. He followed those teachers of wisdom who hold that virtue alone is good, wickedness alone is bad, while power, birth and all other externals are neither good nor bad.' Epictetus records the impassiveness with which Paconius Agrippinus accepted his sentence: 'You are condemned by the Senate.' – 'In good time: now it's the hour for exercise.' – 'You have been condemned to exile.' – 'What about my property?' – 'It is not forfeit.' –

'Good! Then let us leave and have lunch at Aricia.' Yet the Stoics had no monopoly of courage or panache.[57]

Since Stoic teaching appears to offer little support for political sedition, the allegations made against the sect in this period require explanation. The first time that we find adherence to the Stoa explicitly cited as an indication of treasonable sentiments is in 62 when Tigellinus was warning Nero about Rubellius Plautus. Tacitus, by omitting any mention of Stoicism when Nero exiled Plautus two years earlier, seems to indicate that this was a device first used by Tigellinus after he had succeeded Burrus as Praetorian Prefect. Nero was no doubt tired of the Stoic advice he had received from Seneca: indeed Tigellinus by his sneers at Nero's 'instructor' had helped to effect Seneca's withdrawal from court.[58] Stoicism must have seemed a promising charge with which to rouse Nero's hostility and timidity.

Tacitus hints at the sophistries employed in these attacks. Tigellinus claimed that Stoicism made Rubellius Plautus dissatisfied with retirement, restless and eager for political activity; his son-in-law Cossutianûs Capito alleged that Thrasea's abstention from the Senate showed his adherence to the defiant example of Cato.[59] The sophistry lies in simplification, not in misrepresentation, for these apparently conflicting precepts could find support in Stoic doctrine. The Porch was in general in favour of participation in public life, and, in the popular imagination, it was opposed to Epicureanism and its doctrine of quiet existence.[60] But it was frequently remarked that none of the masters of the Old Stoa, Zeno, Cleanthes, Chrysippus, had entered politics,[61] while the Stoic and Epicurean doctrines in this area were complex and not so starkly contrasted as in the popular mind: Epicureans held that the wise man would not take part in politics unless some special reason intervened; the Stoics held that he would take part in politics unless something stood in the way.[62] The range of permissable exceptions to the rule of participation was extensive: a particular gift for philosophical investigation, or unsuitability with respect to temperament, talents, social position, or financial resources. There were also reasons for abstention connected with the moral condition of the state. Thus the wise man might find himself unable to exercise his exclusive competence to rule in a state dominated by evil men, and he was not expected to participate in a corrupt state unless it was making moral progress.[63]

This issue of participation in politics appears frequently in Seneca's essays of Neronian date. One unexpected theme that recurs again and again is the invalidity of reasons for abstention based on the condition of the state. In the surviving fragment of his work *On Leisure*, where he is considering the justification of abstention from politics *ab initio*, Seneca produces arguments based on the basic doctrines of his school, e.g. that a man has an obligation to benefit humanity in general, not just his fellow countrymen; that even a lifetime of study is inadequate to achieve the highest good, namely life according to nature (*De Otio* 4–5). While allowing arguments of personal unsuitability, Seneca points out that the exception based on the condition of the state, in effect, turns the traditional conditional prescription to enter public life into a self-contradictory proposition, for no actual state can ever be worthy of the wise man. The Stoic prescription to participate would become in effect an injunction to abstain: 'It is like saying that the best thing is to set sail except in seas where there are apt to be storms or shipwrecks: that amounts to praising sailing and forbidding one to weigh anchor' (8). In his treatise *On Peace of Mind*, where one of the topics considered is retirement from a political career, Seneca suggests that no state is so bad as to prevent a man in public life from continuing to serve the state in some way. He advocates a gradual and partial withdrawal into a mixture of leisure and activity, if chance obstacles or the condition of the state make full participation dangerous or impossible. The prime model here is Socrates, who served as an example of freedom to his fellow citizens, under the Rule of the Thirty Tyrants, and survived (4–5).

In the *Letters to Lucilius*, Seneca returns to this question of the correct motive, manner and pace for political retirement. One must withdraw gradually and unostentatiously (22), preferably offering excuses of ill-health, weakness, or even laziness, not boasting of one's decision to devote oneself to philosophy and moral improvement (68. 1, 3–4) or incurring the resentment of others by turning one's own virtue into a reproach (19. 2, 4; 103. 5). In retirement one must be inconspicuous and not offend the authorities (14. 10–11, 14). Particularly striking is Letter 73 where Seneca denies that philosophers are contumacious and scornful of rulers but stresses their gratitude for the stability and peace government provides.

Seneca's concern is so insistent that it seems to spring from immediate experience, his own and that of those around him. He himself followed his own precepts to the letter, withdrawing by stages, alleging ill-health and old age. But his repeated rejections of abstention or retirement on the grounds of the condition of the state suggest that others were employing the Stoic formula in this form.

The accusers of Thrasea Paetus urged that his absence from the Senate was a silent condemnation of all that the Princeps did. Thrasea had first employed this form of protest when he stalked out of the Curia in 59; Helvidius Priscus, his son-in-law, held no office under Nero after his tribunate in 56.[64] Their grounds for disillusionment with the government, namely the moral conduct of the Emperor and the decline of senatorial independence, were not new, nor was their form of protest. L. Calpurnius Piso had threatened Antony with abstention and another Lucius Piso had told Tiberius that the cruelty of accusers would drive him to leave the Senate and Rome. His father had abstained from standing for the higher magistracies until induced to take the consulship by Augustus.[65] Caesar had expressed his resentment of this form of protest to Cicero, and Tiberius had complained to the Senate of the reluctance of the able to shoulder the responsibilities of government. As Nero wrote in his speech of prelude to Thrasea's trial, such desertion of public duties was particularly odious because contagious, and an epidemic could bring the necessary operations of government to a halt.[66]

'The wise man will take part in politics unless there is an impediment'. Seneca's evidence suggests that in his day Stoics were using the traditional formula to describe their protest, accepting as an impediment the corrupt condition of the state. It is suggestive that, in Tacitus' account of Thrasea's last hours, he is found advising his young friend Arulenus Rusticus to consider carefully what course to adopt in public life *at such a time*. This may well derive from the biography of Thrasea that Rusticus later wrote. Thrasea's own biography of Cato is probably the source of the story in Plutarch that Cato on his deathbed forbade his son to engage in politics, 'for it was no longer possible to do so in a manner worthy of Cato and to do so otherwise was dishonourable'.[67]

The defects that Thrasea and Helvidius Priscus condemned in Nero's government were not to be found set down in Stoic teachings. The remedy they adopted was not unique to Stoicism or the only one consistent with the doctrines of the school: under Vespasian, when Helvidius thought the time was propitious, he first fought explicitly for senatorial independence and then, when disillusioned, chose a more outspoken and provocative way of fulfilling his senatorial duty than abstention.[68] It was when men like this had judged, as Roman senators, that Nero had deserted his early programme and that the Senate had lost even that modicum of freedom compatible with the Principate, that they employed the language of Stoicism to formulate their moral choices and justify their decisions. A subtle and complex body of doctrine that has survived many vicissitudes is unlikely to provide unambiguous answers, but it can provide the categories and terms in which to think and talk: Tacitus makes Thrasea speak of his obligation not to desert the way of life he had long followed as a senator; the same appeal to *constantia* is attributed by Epictetus to Paconius Agrippinus who said that he would not perform on the stage because consistency to his own chosen role (or *persona*) would not permit it.[69] Seneca had feared with justice that if political disapproval and defiance were cast in Stoic language the sect itself would be persecuted. For there was that degree of substance in the suspicions that caused Musonius Rufus and Demetrius the Cynic to be expelled from Rome by Nero and later led to the expulsions of philosophers under Vespasian and Domitian. But then too, it was a question of particular Stoics, not of Stoicism, for these expulsions were linked to political trials of men related by birth and doctrine to Nero's senatorial victims.[70]

The Vinician Conspiracy

Nero can hardly have believed that Stoicism alone would ever rob him of his throne. What the Pisonian conspiracy had demonstrated was the potential danger of the old Republican nobility. That section of society contributed several victims in the next two years: M. Crassus Frugi, Antistius Vetus and Sulpicius Camerinus.[71] But Nero also began to take seriously the potential threat from commanders of the provincial armies. Already in 62 Tigellinus had suggested that Rubellius Plautus in Asia might seek the support of the eastern armies, and Cornelius Sulla in Marseilles that of the Rhine legions. Tacitus regards these charges as absurd, as well as the more specific rumour about Plautus that he was in contact with Corbulo. Nero clearly ignored these stories at the time: Corbulo and the Scribonii brothers who governed the German provinces were only removed in the winter of 66/7. But in 66 one of the charges against Barea Soranus that led to his conviction was that he had tried to rouse the province of Asia to sedition when he was proconsul. This is perhaps to be linked with another charge, namely friendship with Rubellius Plautus, for Barea had been proconsul in 61/2 and Plautus was executed in Asia about the close of his term.[72] Tacitus does not point out additional facts that may have made the charges seem more substantial to the Emperor: Antistius Vetus, Plautus' father-in-law, who, the historian says, urged Plautus to resistance in 62, was himself proconsul of Asia in 63/4 when Corbulo was still in the east; Annius Pollio, the husband of Barea's daughter Servilia, was also the brother of Corbulo's son-in-law Annius Vinicianus. They were both sons of that Annius Vinicianus who was active in the plot against Gaius and afterwards instigated the armed revolt of the governor of Dalmatia against Claudius.[73]

Corbulo must have felt the net closing in on him for some time. His father-in-law Cassius Longinus was condemned in 65, one son of his half-brother had been exiled with Annius Pollio after the Pisonian conspiracy, and another perished probably in 66/7.[74] With the loss of Tacitus' account of these years we can only surmise that this last death may have had some connection with the conspiracy that probably led directly to Corbulo's execution. For the mysterious *coniuratio Viniciana* is mentioned only by Suetonius, who merely says that it was conceived and detected at Beneventum. The biographer supplies no indication of date, except that the plot came after the Pisonian conspiracy. The Arval Brothers offered thanks 'for the detection of a wicked plot' at some date after mid-May and before taking the vows for Nero's safe return on 25 September 66 when he departed for Greece.[75] The location at Beneventum suggests that the plot involved attacking the Emperor on his way to Greece, for he would naturally break his journey there.[76] It is tempting to infer from the name Suetonius gives the conspiracy that it was led by Annius Vinicianus, the son-in-law of Corbulo. Though not yet of senatorial age, he was given command of one of Corbulo's legions in 63, a sign of imperial confidence, according to Dio, who adds that, by the time he was sent to escort Tiridates to Rome, Corbulo felt the need to reassure the Emperor of his loyalty and sent the young man as hostage. When he arrived in Rome before the middle of May in 66, the trials of Thrasea Paetus and Barea Soranus were in progress.[77] If Vinicianus was not already harbouring disloyal sentiments, the plight of the two esteemed senators and his young sister-in-law Servilia, in contrast with the extravagant display of Nero's reception for the Armenian king, must have decided him to attempt in earnest the treason for which his brother had been unjustly exiled. As Nero's plans for the Greek tour were made well in advance, the conspirators could have known when he would leave Rome and when he would arrive at Beneventum.

Following the detection of the plot, Nero regarded the whole of the senatorial order as his enemy. He had found it difficult to keep up the pretence of senatorial independence; he had often felt threatened by individual senators; but now, according to Suetonius, he began to speak of blotting out the whole order and handing the provinces and armies over to Roman knights and imperial freedmen. Aquilius Regulus, who earned his spurs as an accuser in these years, was said to have taunted Nero with laziness because he was destroying the senators one by one, when the whole body could be wiped out with a word.[78] In Greece one of his entourage regularly amused him by saying 'I hate you, Caesar, for being a senator', and the Emperor himself, when formally inaugurating work on the Corinthian canal, prayed that the outcome might be successful for himself and the Roman people, deliberately omitting the Senate from the traditional formula.[79]

Why, given his awareness of senatorial hostility, did Nero not cancel his Greek tour after the detection of the Vinician conspiracy? In 64 he had abandoned his travel plans, but that was because he was afraid that his absence would displease the Roman populace. Now, after his triumphant exhibition of Tiridates, he was feeling confident in the support of the Roman plebs. From the praetorians and the upper orders in Rome he apparently refused to consider any threat except personal assassination, which his absence would prevent: he would deal with the generals he distrusted while in the east. He was eager to escape from Rome. Fame and glory, both military and artistic, were waiting for him in Greece.

It was more than twenty years since an Emperor had ventured out of Italy, the last occasion being Claudius' participation in the conquest of Britain in 43/4. The contrast between the two expeditions shows Nero's diminishing hold on political reality. Although Claudius had also experienced sedition the year before, that had been an armed revolt in a province, not a plot at Rome, and Claudius was going to strengthen his position by making a military reputation for himself, whereas Nero, whatever his ultimate plans, was certain to aggravate grievances already felt about his theatrical enthusiasms. Claudius had probably not planned to stay away longer than the six months he actually spent away from Rome, whereas Nero's complex arrangements seemed to portend a much longer absence. Finally, Claudius had taken with him many of the men who might be a threat to him in his absence and he had left in charge of Rome an experienced senator of proven military ability, namely Lucius Vitellius, fresh from his second term as ordinary consul.[80] Nero, by contrast, left his freedman Helius in charge, with power to confiscate, banish and execute men of all ranks, according to Dio. Moreover, though the same historian says that Nero took many of the foremost men to Greece in order to kill them, the only senators he names, Vespasian and Cluvius Rufus, were both new men and complaisant. Another senatorial member of his entourage, Paccius Africanus, is known only because he informed against the two Scribonii.[81] He was rewarded by being sent home to hold the consulship in July of 67, while his colleague Annius Afrinus apparently held office while in Greece.[82] One Praetorian Prefect would naturally command the Emperor's praetorian escort: Dio tells us it was Tigellinus. His absence, along with that of one consul in the latter part of 67, added to the low standing of the man Nero left in charge of Rome, allowed the other Prefect, Nymphidius Sabinus, to achieve the control of the Guard he was soon to demonstrate.

Aside from Nero's sinister wardrobe mistress Calvia Crispinilla and his new wife Statilia Messallina,[83] most of the members of the imperial entourage whose names are preserved were freedmen. This was natural, for wherever the Emperor was there were embassies to be processed, letters to be received and replies to be written. Although our sources do not mention Epaphroditus the *a libellis*, Phaon the *a rationibus* or the unknown *ab epistulis*, but maliciously preserve only the names of those like Phoebus, Sporus and Pythagoras who served his more disreputable needs,[84] it is clear that Nero did not entirely neglect his imperial duties. Governors were appointed to replace Corbulo and the Scribonii, consulships were arranged and a special commander was put in charge of the Jewish War after the defeat of the governor of Syria on 8 November 66.[85] But Nero was insulated from unappreciative audiences and candid advisers. The feeling that freedmen and flatterers ruled the Empire must have contributed to disaffection at home and among his high command: the old days of respect for the Senate and its leading members must have seemed very far away.

In the end Nero was recalled by Helius who went to Greece himself when the Emperor refused to take his many letters seriously. Helius, according to Dio, reported that another great conspiracy was developing at Rome. This may have been the one way he could find of persuading the Emperor to return, for Nero seemed to think he could adequately prevent revolt in the provinces by summoning suspected commanders to Greece and executing them.[86] Nothing more is heard of this urban conspiracy: it is possible that what had really alarmed Helius were the first rumblings of revolt in Gaul. Julius Vindex, the praetorian governor of Gallia Lugdunensis, had apparently approached various provincial governors, most of whom sent the letters to the Emperor. Sulpicius Galba, the consular governor of Hispania Tarraconensis, had simply ignored them, and Nero must have received some hint of this, for Galba is said to have intercepted orders for his own death sent by Nero to his procurator in Spain.[87] As all this must have occurred before Vindex finally rose in arms just before the middle of March in 68, it is possible that the revolt was planned for the first of January when the armies took their oaths of loyalty. So it was to happen in 69.

When the news of Vindex' rising came on the anniversary of his mother's death, Nero was in Naples: he did not even write to the Senate for eight days.[88] This was not wholly irrational: Vindex had no legions and there was no reason to doubt the loyalty of the urban cohort stationed at Lugdunum. Moreover, Gallic rebellions were the principal responsibility of the governor of Upper Germany, and Nero had appointed to that post only a year ago the new man Verginius Rufus.[89]

When the post brought only insulting missives from Vindex, Nero did write to the Senate asking them to stand by him, and at last he returned to Rome and summoned a meeting of his *consilium*. But at the meeting water-organs were in the forefront of his mind.[90] Within three weeks or so of the news about Vindex came more alarming information: Galba was not dead. He had heeded a second invitation from Vindex, and on 3 April had declared himself legate of the Senate and Roman People. Though he had only one legion, Spain had a large citizen population from which he began to recruit another. He was supported not only by his own legionary commander T. Vinius but also by Otho, then governor of Lusitania, and by the quaestor of Baetica.[91] Nero was badly shaken and at last seems to have taken some action. He deposed one of the consuls and assumed the office himself to signify his real leadership of the state and his decision to take the field. He had the Senate declare Galba a public enemy and declared his goods forfeit. He summoned home units from Illyricum, Germany and Britain that were already on their way east for his projected campaigns. He recruited a legion, the First Adiutrix, from the fleet at Misenum and other troops in Rome. All of these forces were then stationed in northern Italy under the command of the trusted Petronius Turpilianus, who had brought peace to Britain after the big revolt and had recently helped in the uncovering of the Pisonian conspiracy.[92] But Nero did not himself leave Rome to lead his armies.

The sequence of events from mid-April, when these preparations must have been made, up to the day of Nero's death on 9 June is difficult to reconstruct. At some time after he learned of Galba's defection Nero was informed of the revolt of Clodius Macer, the legate of the single legion in Africa, who similarly proclaimed himself the champion of liberty and began to raise auxiliary troops. This defection, engineered by Nero's old ally Calvia Crispinilla, contributed to the Emperor's unpopularity at Rome, for it threatened the essential corn shipments from Africa.[93]

The fatal blow came paradoxically in the form of a victory. Sometime in May the legions of Upper Germany, reinforced by detachments from the Lower German army, finally moved against the important stronghold of Vesontio and defeated the forces of Vindex, who committed suicide. The troops, however, were so elated at their victory that they offered to make their commander Emperor. Verginius refused, maintaining that the choice of Princeps must be made by the Senate and People, and he kept his word.[94] But this victory depressed Nero as well as Galba. He apparently sent out a second commander, Rubrius Gallus, to northern Italy, but even now he did not take command of his forces himself, though news of the troops in Italy brought him little joy. The Legion XIV Gemina seems to have been prevented from taking effective action by its Batavian auxiliaries, who were perhaps sympathetic to the Batavian supporters of Vindex and later claimed to have wrested Italy from Nero.[95] In addition, the conduct of their commander Petronius Turpilianus was ambiguous. Though later executed by Galba as a 'Neronian general', he is said by Dio to have taken up Galba's cause: the truth may be that he delayed, as had Verginius in dealing with Vindex, hoping for word from Rome that Nero was deposed. At some point, too, the Illyrican troops in Italy hailed Verginius Rufus as Emperor, though this may only have happened after Nero's death.[96]

The news about Verginius and the rumours about Petronius convinced Nero that the rest of his army had defected. Believing that all was lost, he began to think of flight – and in all directions. He finally fixed on Alexandria as his destination, probably unaware that the loyalty of the Prefect of Egypt was already wavering.[97] Nero failed to persuade tribunes and centurions of the Praetorian Guard to accompany him, but it was only after Nero was believed to have left Rome that their Prefect Nymphidius Sabinus brought the Guard to declare for Galba.[98] Tigellinus, now ill and hence playing a subordinate role, had already secured his safety by ingratiating himself with Galba's legate Vinius, but his caution may only have turned to disloyalty after his colleague's initiative.[99] And it was only that initiative that finally brought the Senate to declare Nero a public enemy and confer on Galba the powers making him officially Princeps.[100]

Nero was now a hunted outlaw skulking in Phaon's villa outside Rome with only four attendants, all freedmen. With the help of one of them, Epaphroditus, he finally managed to stab himself just as the horsemen arrived. To the very end his aesthetic sense remained with him: it was while he was ordering his grave to be decorated with any bits of marble that could be found that he uttered his famous lament, 'Qualis artifex pereo!'. At the last he extracted a promise from his minions that they would not allow his body to be mutilated.[101]

PART TWO

POST-MORTEM ON THE FALL OF NERO

ELEVEN

Why Did It Happen?

Nero's personality has dominated our study so far. It is time to turn to the difficulties inherent in the political system of the Principate, difficulties which this young, vain and insecure Princeps tried but eventually failed to surmount. This programme, outlined at the start, has received preliminary treatment in the context of the early reign, but it embodies presuppositions about Nero's fall that we are only now in a position to scrutinize.

First, is it right to assume that the collapse of the last of the Julio-Claudian rulers was anything but an accident, the outcome of superficial incidents, trivial in themselves but grossly mismanaged? For there are clear indications that Nero overestimated the defections of 68 and over-reacted by fleeing Rome when his doom could still be averted. Indeed Tacitus tells us that he was driven from his throne 'by messages and rumours, rather than by force of arms'.[1] His initial inaction in the face of the rising of Vindex was not wholly without justification, as we have seen. There may have been hesitation by the governor of Upper Germany, but neither he nor his colleague Fonteius Capito failed Nero in the end; and the seven legions belonging to the two German commands proved loyal until after the defeat of the rebels under Vindex at Vesontio. Even then, Verginius Rufus was able to bring the troops back to their allegiance by refusing the Empire for himself. Had Nero himself appeared before the German troops or his forces in northern Italy, his resolution might well have inspired more prompt and decisive action. Of these forces, he had recruited I Italica less than two years before and I Adiutrix for the present crisis; the British legion XIV Gemina was famed for its loyalty to him even after his death.[2] Nothing suggests that these legions favoured Galba over the descendant of Augustus, while their commanders, Verginius and Petronius, were apparently unwilling to seduce them away from Nero, until word came from Rome.

In the capital too, Nero could have controlled the situation. The Senate had obediently declared Galba a public enemy: it only reversed its position, condemning Nero and proclaiming Galba, after the Praetorian Guard had shown the way. But the Guard itself 'long accustomed to swear allegiance to the Caesars had been brought to desert Nero more by deceit and incitement than by its own inclination', in the words of Tacitus.[3] The

Emperor's vague design of sailing to Alexandria was known: it was enough for Nymphidius Sabinus to tell them that he was as good as gone and to promise a substantial donative in Galba's name to start the defection. Nero was already in flight from Rome when he heard the acclamation of Galba in the praetorian camp as he approached the north-east gate.[4] Had he been more determined and confident in the face of the crisis, the Guard would hardly have been swayed by a Prefect who had betrayed praetorian officers in the Pisonian conspiracy some three years earlier.[5]

It is possible that some of Nero's freedmen revealed his hide-out at the end, but that was only when his want of resolution had already ensured his defeat.[6] The plebs were loyal to the end and beyond, for Otho and Vitellius both thought it worthwhile to appeal to their nostalgia. A year after his death, Otho took his name, resumed work on the Golden House and courted his widow. Vitellius erected altars to Nero and had his songs performed.[7] Tacitus, it is true, remarks that the better sort of plebeian, specifying those connected with the great families, the clients and freedmen of Nero's upper class victims, were given hope by Nero's end. It was no doubt these same people whom Suetonius describes as putting on liberty caps and running about in their joy. But the *plebs sordida*, who missed his games and largesse, decorated his tomb with flowers, erected statues of him in the forum and posted up his edicts in hope of his return. Even Nero himself, in his last panic, thought that if he could reach the forum unharmed and deliver an appeal to the people, he might yet be forgiven his crimes.[8] It is hard to avoid the conclusion that if Nero had not allowed the odour of failure to envelop him, he could have retained his position at home and have suppressed the revolts of Galba and Clodius Macer, who were not acting in concert and had no forces of any size.

Yet accident and panic do not wholly explain the sequence of events. Support for the various rebel leaders was considerable. Vindex claimed to have 100,000 men under arms, and even if this was an exaggeration designed to persuade Galba to join him, he did lose 20,000 at Vesontio.[9] Galba was able to recruit a legion and auxiliary forces from the people of his province as well as creating a 'senate' and equestrian bodyguard from the top social stratum. Clodius Macer had done the same in Africa.[10]

There must have been substantial reasons for disaffection on this scale. Schiller and historians influenced by him have claimed that the cause of Nero's fall was Gallic nationalism, pointing to the attempt of some of the Gallic tribes to found an Empire of the Gauls two years later. This diagnosis has long been discredited. It is impossible to demonstrate tribal unity at any one time, and the leaders of the revolt of AD 70 were precisely those tribes who had not supported Vindex. Moreover, the coins and literary evidence for Vindex' programme show that he was demanding a return to Roman government on the Augustan model, liberation from tyranny not from Rome.[11] What moved the followers of Vindex, Galba and Clodius Macer was the harshness of the present régime: Dio notes heavier taxes and forced levies in Gaul and Britain; Plutarch observes that Galba could only sympathize with those oppressed by Nero's procurators in his province; the Elder Pliny remarks that Nero put to death six landowners in Africa who together owned one half of the land of the province. In addition, the sufferings of Judaea at the hands of Gessius Florus, of Egypt through the exactions of Caecina Tuscus and of Greece through the collections of Acratus show up the spuriousness of the defence of Roman rule that a Roman general was to offer the rebellious Gauls: 'Cruel Emperors only harm those close to them'.[12]

What differentiated the last rebellions against Nero from the British revolt of 61 and the Jewish rising of 66 was the connivance, indeed initiative, of Roman commanders and officials in the provinces.[13] These risings gave the verdict of the Roman governing classes on their Emperor's rapacity and cruelty. As Tacitus makes Galba say, 'It was not Vindex with his unarmed province or I with one legion that freed the people from Nero's yoke, but his own monstrousness and extravagance'.[14] Nero might have averted disaster in 68, but his fall, if not inevitable, was not, and is not, inexplicable.

Our first presupposition, that Nero's fall can be explained to a large extent in terms of underlying causes now seems to be justified. What of the second, that his fall may in part be attributed to the nature of the Augustan Principate? The diagnosis offered by all of the ancient sources is that Nero's viciousness ultimately proved his ruin. Through them we have been able to document the way in which Nero's weaknesses of character led to his offending his subjects deeply and irrevocably. Is it right to say now that this is not a sufficient explanation?

The inadequacy of the ancient diagnosis has already been suggested in connection with the initial period of goverment (chapter 6). These years were hailed as a Golden Age at Rome, described with sympathy and approval half a century later by the censorious Tacitus, and still remembered as excellent three hundred years later by writers who were no longer sure what was good about them. Nero can have been in no doubt about the appreciation and popularity his conduct brought him; yet he found it impossible to continue as he had started. The sheer difficulty of the role, with its unresolved contradictions, put a strain on the young Emperor's weak character and intellect. It seems legitimate to consider the possibility that this interaction of system and personality eventually led to his fall.

The only reason to doubt the validity of this type of explanation lies in the fact that the ancient sources do not explicitly analyze the performance of Nero, or indeed of any Princeps, in terms of institutions, even in combination with character. Yet an answer can only be produced if the question is asked, and the idea that their own system of government could contribute to political disaster was the last one the Romans were likely to entertain. For them, the Republic was an excellent and much-lamented institution: even Tacitus could find nothing to criticize in the celebrated mixed constitution to which the Republic was likened, except the fact that it lacked durability.[15] In the Roman view this admirable system had to be abandoned because the body politic was infected with the vices of envy, greed and ambition, while Caesar's ruthless and successful bid for autocratic power had set an irresistible example for imitation.[16] The Principate was accepted as a *pis aller* for the Republic which could no longer be maintained without civil strife. The system was resented for its falsity, in that sovereignty was said to reside in the Senate and People, whereas frank observation showed that the system was really monarchy.[17] Yet even Tacitus chose to present this falsity as intentional hypocrisy on the part of the *principes*, particularly the founders, Augustus and Tiberius.[18] The only hint of substantial criticism of Augustus' new system, as a system, concerns the practice of hereditary succession, and this criticism, as we shall see, was principally inspired by the fact that it allowed evil *principes* to come to the throne.

The Roman idealization of the Republican constitution does not deter us from thinking that the unrestrained violence and ambition of the Late Republic were encouraged by a political and financial system not geared to the strain of a world empire. Therefore, in studying the Julio-Claudian Principate, we should be similarly prepared to see weaknesses in the system Augustus created, however blind to them our sources are.

Difficulties concerning the imperial freedmen, the Senate, ideology and the succession have been used to explain Nero's failure to maintain his initial style of government. The last of these problems, in particular, acquired increased importance as the reign went on, while other strains imposed by the Principate were clearly manifest by the end. The rest of this study forms an extended post-mortem on Nero's fall from the institutional point of view, that is, an examination of problems inherant in the Augustan Principate which contributed to his *immanitas* and *luxuria*.

TWELVE

The Problem of the Succession

The chief problem presented by the method of succession was that there was no method to speak of. As the Principate was not an overt monarchy, there could be no acknowledgement of the hereditary principle, dominant as it was in practice and, *a fortiori*, no law of succession to regulate hereditary claims. In theory, the choice belonged to SPQR, but the uncertainty went deeper, for there was no obligation on SPQR to choose a Princeps at all. The office died with each incumbent: between the death of the old Princeps and the conferment of the traditional powers on the new, there was not even a formal interregnum, as existed when there were no consuls in the Republic, to suggest that a replacement was needed.[1] The view of the Princeps that Augustus had promoted, namely a man exercising various magisterial functions according to the mandate of the sovereign Senate and People, not only justified Tiberius in throwing open for senatorial decision the matter of scope and duration of the Princeps' power: it also sanctioned the attempt of the consuls and Senate, after Gaius' assassination, to dispense with a Princeps and revert to the Republic. The fear of renewed civil war and the connivance of elements like the Praetorian Guard and the palace staff, who had a vested interest in the new system, was enough to stifle the last idea in 41 and, effectively, forever.

In practice, then, a Princeps must be found for SPQR to invest with the traditional powers. When Galba, in making his bid for power, declared that he was only the legate of the Senate and Roman People, he was paying lip service to the actual theory of the Principate itself, according to which SPQR (the Senate, in effect) conferred the powers that made a man Princeps. Though no more than the appearance had been maintained in the accession of Augustus and his successors, the years 68 and 69 showed that many still attached importance to that appearance. Two prominent generals took their stand on the principle that allegiance could only be given to an Emperor so chosen or at least approved.[2] The Senate demonstrated that the theory of senatorial approval could sanction a rejection of the hereditary claim, when it deposed the descendant of Augustus, the adopted son of Claudius, and acclaimed Galba Princeps. Then two Upper German legions, borrowing a slogan from their revered ex-commander Verginius Rufus, repudiated their oath of allegiance to Galba and swore loyalty to SPQR, to whom they left the choice of another Princeps.[3] But the oath, as Vitellius saw, was vacuous: a new Emperor had to be put up for approval. For there was no recognized mechanism for election, no agreed rules of eligibility, only a procedure for conferring powers.[4] The weakness and danger inherent in the very theory of the Principate could not be better revealed. If any ruler approved by SPQR was legitimate, however his selection had come about, then no Princeps need be tolerated for long. Continual armed usurpations could be justified on constitutional grounds. It is in this sense that Mommsen was right to describe the Principate as 'not only in practice, but in theory, an autocracy tempered by legally permanent revolution'.[5]

It is in a utopian passage of Flavian date that we find the idea of truly elective monarchy. The Elder Pliny dates to the reign of Claudius the arrival of some envoys from Ceylon whose account of their society he purports to give. The whole is clearly a form of indirect criticism of Roman society. The king is said to be elected by the people on grounds of old age, clemency and childlessness. If he produces children while in office, he is deposed, to prevent the monarchy from becoming hereditary. The fact that this is an unrealistic dream is revealed not only by accompanying statements that the Ceylonese are all early risers, long-lived and hard-working, but by the remark that the king, if he misbehaves, is condemned to death and apparently commits suicide or accepts social annihilation, for all shun him but there is no executioner.[6] This world where a king fights neither to retain his throne nor to pass it on to his children is clearly one without imperial armies and a heritage of civil war. In Rome it was recognized that the best means of providing stability was for the incumbent to designate his own successor, securing powers for him that would put him in a strong position to carry on the government and be recognized as Princeps when he died, and/or signifying his intentions through the instruments of private law, namely, adoption and the will. Despite many exceptions, this may be regarded as the norm in the early Principate: the alternative was for the praetorians, as with Claudius and Otho, the legions, as with Galba, Vitellius and Vespasian, or the minions of the palace, as with Nerva, to support a candidate for senatorial recognition.

If the incumbent must choose, selection based on ties of blood rather than selection based on merit or favour, had the advantage of stifling ambition and softening envy. As the younger Pliny admitted in his panegyric on Trajan, 'Men tolerate with greater equanimity the evil progeny fortune has given an emperor than the bad choice he himself has made'.[7] To be sure, the childless Nerva had adopted Trajan, who was not of his kin, and Pliny's encomium duly expatiated on the advantages of selection by merit. Yet he concluded with the hope that the new Princeps might have a son of his own to succeed him.[8] Thirty years earlier Galba, the first to hold Augustus' place without a family claim and himself childless, decided to strengthen his own position by adopting a man of suitable Republican descent. In the speech

Tacitus gives him, probably not inaccurate on this point, he claims to be repudiating the family monopoly that has prevailed since Augustus and choosing the man whom he judges the best for the sake of the state. Yet his own choice followed the traditional pattern of adoption in that Piso had long been a personal favourite of Galba's and had been designated his son in his will.[9] In fact, adoption had long been a standard way of continuing a line when nature failed, and these speakers, Galba and Pliny, were just making a virtue of necessity. Recent memories of Nero and Domitian, who had gained the throne by dynastic descent, no doubt lent a momentary plausibility to the idea of selection by merit.

Aside from the opportunistic utterances just considered, there is in fact little evidence for criticism of the Augustan Principate on the score of hereditary succession. Even a man of Stoic views, like Seneca, who could have urged selection by merit, was prepared to justify the practice on the grounds that gratitude was thereby shown to the outstanding man who had established the dynasty.[10] Nonetheless, the theory of the Principate precluded formal recognition and regulation of the hereditary principle.

The transmission of absolute power is a natural focus for intrigue, but the Principate encouraged fear on one side and ambition on the other because there were no clear criteria for eligibility or primacy. Since it was not even clear that a relative of the reigning Princeps must succeed him, descendants of noble families that had been equals in birth, office and status of the Julii and Claudii while the Republic lasted, might now cherish imperial ambitions. Seneca has Augustus address the traitor Cn. Cornelius Cinna, the grandson of Pompey, in these words: 'If I alone am the obstacle to your hopes, will Paulus and Fabius Maximus and the Cossi and Servilii and the great line of nobles, those who do not merely parade empty names but are worthy of their ancestors, tolerate you?'.[11]

Augustus, however, had slowly prepared the ground for a dynastic succession and, after many vicissitudes, he had won. His example was followed, so that Galba could say, in the words of Tacitus: 'Under Tiberius and Gaius and Claudius we were the inheritance, so to speak, of one family'.[12] Augustus had first built up his own following by exploiting the will of Julius Caesar and the provision for his adoption that it contained. He established both will and adoption as instruments of dynastic designation, adopting first Gaius and Lucius, and then Tiberius whom he also made his heir to the major portion of his estate in his will. But the mandate he left his successor was ambiguous. He appeared to have made clear his preference for his own blood descendants in 17 BC when he adopted Gaius and Lucius, grandsons by his daughter Julia, rather than his own grown stepsons, Tiberius and Drusus. After their death, he had Tiberius adopt Germanicus prior to his own adoption by Augustus, thus showing that he wished the succession to return to his blood descendants: for Germanicus, himself the grand-nephew of Augustus, had children by his granddaughter Agrippina. On the other hand, the fact that Germanicus was made Tiberius' son seemed to imply that direct descent from the *reigning* Emperor was at least as important as descent from Augustus. It is not surprising that the indecisive Tiberius, who made Augustus' example his creed, dithered to the end about the succession.

When Gaius was assassinated, Claudius became the candidate of the Praetorian Guard as the nearest surviving male relative of the dead Emperor and the brother of the popular Germanicus, grandson of Augustus. But Claudius was not himself in the direct line of descent from Augustus by birth or adoption, and he thus lacked the family names, Iulius and Caesar. He was the first Princeps in this position, and he promptly remedied the defect by calling himself Tiberius Claudius Caesar.[13] Claudius' son inherited from his mother as well as his father the blood of Augustus' sister Octavia. But he faced, as potential rivals, direct descendants of the first Princeps, who were also older: the Junii Silani, progeny of Augustus' great-granddaughter, Aemilia Lepida; Rubellius Plautus, the son of Tiberius' granddaughter Julia; and Agrippina's son himself. Then, through his adoption by Claudius, the latter acquired direct descent from the reigning Emperor as well. The young Nero now outshone both Britannicus and the others: his filiation, as we have seen, advertises the double claim.[14]

The difficulties caused by the lack of a law of succession to regulate dynastic claims were exacerbated by the marriage policy of the imperial house. To have embarked on dynastic marriages with foreign royal houses would have been to avow the monarchical nature of the new system. In any case, the Roman claim to world rule was accompanied by a contempt for foreign rulers, whether civilized or not. Antony's charge that Octavian wanted to marry the daughter of Cotiso, king of the Getae, who would receive his daughter Julia in exchange, was not only slanderous, but ludicrous.[15] The Princeps was a Roman aristocrat whose family married within the Roman governing class. The result was an ever-increasing number of senators having some tie of kinship with the ruling family, a tie which often inspired enough respect or fear to lead to more marriage connections with that family. The longer the Julio-Claudian dynasty continued, the greater the number of people there were with some claim to the throne: the Junii Silani multiplied, the surviving descendants of Tiberius grew up, and Claudius, with his multiple marriages, brought more families within the circle.

Like any monarch, the Princeps could only be removed against his will, as there was no temporal limit on his tenure and no retirement age. But unlike a monarch, no matter how long the throne had remained within his family, men of comparably ancient pedigree or dynastic descent could all feel that they had a legitimate claim to succeed him. Yet, while the Princeps remained in possession of his reason, he would see that he could not destroy or disgrace them all, at least until he produced an heir to ensure stability. If it began to appear that he would not have a direct heir, he would know that one of them must be chosen as his successor. As a result, there was bound to be factional strife at court, organized around rival claimants and involving high-ranking senators, many of whom might reasonably expect to command armies. Freedmen intrigued on either side and the imperial women plotted on behalf of their offspring. Praetorian Prefects were hired and fired. Other knights and senators lost their lives through involvement in real or alleged plots concerning the imperial succession.

The pressure of this insecurity and uncertainty made great demands on the character of the Princeps. The issue of the succession accounts in large measure for the aristocratic blood-baths in which the reigns of Tiberius, Gaius and Claudius had ended. It is true that after the fall of Sejanus (which, on any theory, was connected with the succession), the loftier *nobiles* survived, but many perished under Gaius as a result of the Gaetulican conspiracy which aimed at putting M. Aemilius Lepidus on the throne. Messallina's attempt to make Silius Emperor to protect the claims of Britannicus brought down senators and highly-placed knights.[16] Claudius is credited with the deaths of thirty-five senators and over two hundred knights, many of them related to the imperial house or involved in intrigues concerning the succession.[17]

Nero's Rivals

The three factors leading to uncertainty over the succession: lack of an acknowledged hereditary principle, lack of a law of succession and the habit of intermarriage with aristocratic Roman families, meant that Nero was faced with a frightening number of potential rivals and heirs.

The possibility of restoring the Republic was not seriously mooted at this date, except in the sentimental form that we find in Lucan's poem on the great civil wars.[18] Instead the lack of a recognized hereditary principle showed itself in threats, real or supposed, from *nobiles* outside the ruling house, such as the conspiracy to put C. Calpurnius Piso on the throne.[19] There were also dynastic rivals. Tacitus notes that Piso feared competition from Lucius Junius Silanus in his bid to usurp the throne, but rejects a story in the Elder Pliny that Piso was to be accompanied by Claudius' daughter Antonia when he entered the praetorian camp after Nero's murder.[20] Yet the two ideas belong together and point to the fact that, by the latter part of Nero's reign, kinship with the imperial house was common enough among the nobility to put mere Republican lineage in the shade. L. Junius Silanus was a direct descendant of Augustus: the marriage with Antonia would have given Piso too a dynastic claim. But Tacitus objects to the story, stating that Piso loved his wife and that Antonia would not have given her name to such a dangerous venture. Even more telling is the fact that Antonia was not punished with the other conspirators. So it is possible that the tale was a rumour not credited by Nero at the time but resurrected some time later when he put an end to her life 'as an instigator of revolution', in the words of Suetonius.[21]

Suetonius goes on to say that Nero's real reason for punishing Antonia was that she refused to marry him after Poppaea's death. This story probably relates to Nero's concern with rivals whose claim rested on kinship with his predecessor. After the death of her two husbands, Antonia remained a widow: any man she espoused would have been immediately suspect to Nero. The child of Claudius' second wife, Antonia was some eight years older than Nero. Yet she may well have seemed a natural choice as spouse after the death of Poppaea and his unborn heir in the summer of 65. For Poppaea too had been older than he, and Antonia was still capable of bearing a child. Moreover, Nero's concern about his dynastic claim that had been weakened by the divorce of Octavia may have been heightened by the recent Pisonian conspiracy. In the event, Nero married Statilia Messallina, a woman with whom he had a liaison of long standing, going back to the period before Poppaea's death. (In April of 65 her husband Vestinus Atticus lost his life because he had dared to marry the Emperor's mistress.)[22] That does not rule out Nero's having once contemplated a political union with Antonia. The marriage with Statilia took place sometime before mid-May of 66 after the visit of Tiridates.[23] Antonia's death too should fall after Tacitus' account ends, for he would certainly have mentioned it. Nero may have construed the rejection of his suit as treasonable in itself, the link with Piso now being credited or created for palliation. In any case, he was unwilling to leave Antonia, unattached in Rome, when he set sail for Greece with his new bride, and the Vinician conspiracy in June will have hardened his resolve.[24]

Claudius' connections illustrate how quickly the supply of potential rivals could be increased by imperial marriages. His first wife, Plautia Urgulanilla, had given him a son whose betrothal to a daughter of Sejanus encouraged early and excessive hopes in the Prefect, according to Tacitus.[25] The boy died young, but the relations of Urgulanilla prospered, even after her divorce in bitter circumstances.[26] One of her brothers was made a patrician by Claudius himself, and the adopted son of another reached the consulship in 45. In the older branch of the family, A. Plautius led the invasion of Britain in 43, and through his influence his nephew Plautius Lateranus escaped the death penalty, though implicated in Messallina's intrigue with C. Silius in 48.[27] Nero made the recall of Plautius Lateranus his first act of clemency, but Urgulanilla's closer relatives were to fare less well. Her adopted nephew, Ti. Plautius Silvanus Aelianus, suffered a setback in his career that can plausibly be ascribed to Agrippina's influence, but he managed to survive his six year governorship of Moesia in the latter years of the reign, though his great deeds went unrecognized.[28] The son of the patrician brother eventually lost his life because Nero believed that Agrippina had encouraged his ambitions. It is perhaps not surprising that Plautius Lateranus, who was designated consul for 65, nonetheless joined the Pisonian conspiracy, though Tacitus gives his motive as pure patriotism.[29]

Nero still faced formidable descendants of Claudius' predecessors on the throne, notably Rubellius Plautus and the clan of the Junii Silani. As with the Plautii, Agrippina did what she could to destroy them and Nero continued her work. As Tacitus says of Marcus Junius Silanus whom Agrippina destroyed on her son's accession, 'He was the great-great-grandson of Augustus: that was the cause of death'.[30] There were also men more remotely connected with the first Princeps by marriage. Agrippina's sister Julia Livilla had married M. Vinicius: the sons of his relative Annius Vinicianus both perished through alleged involvement in conspiracies against Nero.[31]

The proliferation of rivals that faced the young Emperor may explain the point of a curious story that Tacitus recounts under the year 61 as part of the obituary of P. Memmius Regulus. When Nero was ill and courtiers were predicting the downfall of Rome if anything happened to him, the Princeps is said to have remarked that the state had its reserve in Memmius Regulus. Nonetheless, says the historian, he survived, protected by his inactivity, his undistinguished ancestry and his wealth which was not enough to provoke envy.[32] The story of the dying Emperor who names someone the state can rely on is a standard one that recurs at different times and with different names. This version, in particular, forfeits its historicity because of its careless chronology: of Nero's three illnesses mentioned by Suetonius, only one can be placed before 61 and that belongs in 60, which scarcely allows time for Regulus' survival to merit comment.[33]

The story might, nonetheless, be there to make an important point, namely, that Memmius Regulus, consul in AD 31, was the eldest surviving consular Nero could trust. Of the senior consulars known to be alive in 61, L. Calpurnius Piso, consul in 27, came from a distinguished family whose dignity had been enhanced by the marriage of his son to Licinia Magna, one of the doomed descendants of the great Pompey.[34] C. Cassius Longinus, consul in 30, was also descended from Republican nobility including Caesar's assassin whose memory he revered. In addition, he was married to Junia Lepida, sister of the two Junii Silani already destroyed by Agrippina.[35] Also still on the scene, perhaps, was the conqueror of Britain, Aulus Plautius, consul in 29. Through Claudius' first wife he had a link with the imperial house, and his wife made no secret of her devotion beyond death to the mother of Rubellius Plautus.[36] Memmius Regulus presents a great contrast. Certainly the first consul in his family, he may also have been the first senator from Narbonensis to attain that rank.[37] He was a man of peace, refusing to press the persecution of Sejanus' partisans in his consulship or his quarrel with his colleague when invited to do so the following year. Having survived his tenure of the highest office in the fateful year of Sejanus' fall, he was subsequently on good terms with Tiberius' successor. When Tiberius Gemellus was murdered, it was Regulus whom the Arval priests chose to co-opt in his place, and when asked by Gaius himself to surrender his betrothed, he complied, escorting her to Rome and uttering no protest when the Emperor set her aside shortly afterwards.[38] Such a man could clearly have been left to manage the state during the Emperor's illness, without seizing imperial power for himself.[39]

Nero's own marriage had continued the process of multiplying possible contenders for the throne. Suetonius reports that he had Rufrius Crispinus, Poppaea's child by her first marriage, drowned by his slaves because it was said that he played at being a general and an emperor.[40]

The system encouraged fears to which Nero was prone in any case. But his obsession with comets, which were thought to portend a change of ruler, and his general tendency to paranoia, which he shared with his mother, become more intelligible when it is realized that he did face a greater problem than any of his predecessors. For he was still surrounded by descendants of Republican families as old and illustrious as the Julii and Claudii, but the number of men who could claim descent from past Emperors naturally increased as the dynasty continued. He was also worse off than his successors, for few of the Republican nobility, and few of the relatives of past Principes survived his own reign of terror. Yet it is instructive to observe the terror inspired in Vitellius by allegations that a young noble, carrying the blood of the Republican Antonii and that of the imperial family, was ambitious for the throne.[41] Also revealing is the way Nero's treatment of the Licinii Crassi and Calpurnii Pisones, descendants of great Republican *nobiles* and, through Augustus' wife Scribonia, of the great Pompey himself, belongs to a pattern of imperial persecution that continues after his time. Claudius destroyed M. Licinius Crassus Frugi with his wife; his son Pompeius Magnus was first married to Antonia and then destroyed by her father;[42] Nero removed another son, M. Licinius Crassus Frugi, and probably exiled a third, the unlucky L. Calpurnius Piso Frugi Licinianus who was killed with Galba in 69.[43] Before Vespasian's return to Rome, his confederate Mucianus disposed of the three remaining adult male members of the clan, all of them regarded as active or passive rivals to the new Emperor.[44] Under the virtuous Nerva, a son of Nero's victim was suspected of conspiracy and relegated, under Trajan the Senate sent him to an island, and on Hadrian's accession he was mysteriously killed.[45] It is only fair to note that a slave who claimed to be this man's brother had attracted a large following until his seditious activities were ended by Vitellius.[46] Nero was not the last Princeps to fear this great clan, natural rivals and victims of the Caesars.

When Nero died the Julio-Claudian dynasty was nearly a hundred years old: no other was to last so long. By the time Vespasian established the Flavian line, the remnants of the Republican nobility had been mostly destroyed – by Nero, by the Civil War, and by Mucianus. The link with the first Augusti too was broken. The policy of intermarriage with the governing class still remained to cause trouble, but it would take a long dynasty to bring the number of potential rivals to the level it had reached under the last of the Julio-Claudians. Yet it is worth noting that Domitian, the last of the Flavians, was compared with Nero for his cruelty and had a tendency to suspect and persecute his own relatives.[47]

THIRTEEN

The Problem Of Finance

There were other similarities which justified the satirist Juvenal in describing Domitian as 'the bald Nero'. Both Emperors were accused of being not only cruel through fear, but rapacious through need. Both were lavish spenders on buildings, shows and largesse.[1] We must now consider to what extent the financial system of the Principate encouraged that heavy spending which Galba regarded as a prime factor in Nero's downfall.

The ancient authorities perceive all imperial expenditure and exaction in primarily moral terms: rational spending in an appropriate manner on appropriate persons and things shows *liberalitas* (the virtue of generosity); spending of the reverse kind manifests *profusio* or *luxuria* (the vice of extravagance); the Emperor can balance his budget by exercising *parsimonia* (the virtue of frugality) or *avaritia* (the vices of meanness and greed). Those Suetonian biographies that make a sharp division between their subject's good and bad conduct reflect this type of analysis most clearly. Thus Nero's economic activities are divided, his liberality being treated in the early chapters, remote from the examples of his extravagance and rapacity.[2]

It is Tacitus who provides evidence that Nero and his advisers had a serious interest in financial matters and saw careful management of them as part of their responsibilities. Thus Nero put older and more experienced officials in charge of the state treasury when instances of injustice were brought to light; he made a contribution to the treasury to maintain public credit; he attempted to reform the collection of indirect taxes and he appointed a commission to investigate the failure of revenue to equal public expenditure. It was in this context of financial stringency, when a large number of grain ships had been destroyed in a storm in the year 62, that Nero contrasted his regular spending on behalf of the state with the irresponsible management of state resources by his predecessors.[3]

Yet it is difficult to deny the copious testimony of the ancient authors that Nero eventually found himself in grievous financial difficulty which led him to exact money and seize treasure from Italy and the provinces. Aside from the evidence in these same authors for the poor financial circumstances that Galba found on reaching Rome,[4] two undeniable facts confirm the difficulties of Nero's last years.

First there is his reduction in the weight of the precious metal coinage. After the last dated gold and silver which belongs to December 63/4 (*trib. pot.* x), the weight of the *aureus* was reduced by about 4 per cent from his earlier issues. Examination of the Julio-Claudian gold coinage as a whole confirms the statement of the Elder Pliny that the Emperors had gradually reduced the weight of the *aureus* from the Republican standard of 40 to the pound, until Nero brought it down to 45. But his reduction in AD 64/5 was of a different order of magnitude from the earlier gradual ones that can be explained as a way of maintaining parity with older coins which had suffered wear. At the same time the *denarius* was also reduced in weight and, in addition, its silver content was lowered by a greater admixture of copper, which reduced the intrinsic value of the silver coinage by more than 10 per cent from the pre-reform *denarius*.[5] Pliny does not mention this change explicitly[6] nor does he offer an explanation of the change in the gold coinage, but his discussion of the Republican coinage shows clearly that he thought the purpose of such reductions was to help the state meet its obligations in periods of financial stress, such as war. The date of Nero's reform and the fact that most of the *aurei* seem to have been issued before mid-66 suggest that the Great Fire of July 64 was the cause of these changes.[7]

Other explanations have been offered: that Nero wished to accommodate Rome's coinage to the standard current in the eastern provinces;[8] that he wished to check the export of silver to the Middle and Far East for the purchase of luxury goods;[9] that he was trying to adjust the relative weight of gold and silver to fit the price on the open market.[10] These explanations are vulnerable in themselves, and none of them fits the date as well or harmonizes with the literary evidence for Nero's financial problems. It is better to assume that the reform was intended to enable the government, either by extensive recoinage or by more profitable use of existing bullion stocks, to achieve more with the same resources. The changes Nero made, like those in the token coinage, were well thought out. His weights for the *aureus* and *denarius* were maintained by the next dynasty, except for a brief period when Domitian tried to return to the Augustan standard.[11] Nero also took care not to diminish confidence in his new coins and precipitate hoarding of the old: by reducing the percentage of silver in the *denarius* he avoided a greater reduction in the weight of the coin, which would have been far more obvious to the general public.[12]

The second fact that attests to Nero's financial difficulties is the support his rebellious governors found in their provinces. Vindex could call on the Gallic notables, Galba on the many Roman citizens in his province, Clodius Macer on the landowners of Africa. They rose in arms against the Princeps whose officials were told, or acted as if they had been told, 'You know what my needs are'.[13]

Though the effect of the Great Fire was appreciated,[14] the general verdict of antiquity was that Nero's extravagance caused his financial difficulties, especially as he maintained his lavish scale of expenditure until the end of his reign. One line of defence still found occasionally in modern accounts is to say that Nero's extravagance would have affected only his private wealth, and that the link made by Suetonius between his extravagant building and the eventual shortage of funds to pay soldiers and reward veterans is to be dismissed as malice.[15] This is to misunderstand the intimate connection between the Emperor's wealth and the state's resources. The precise relationship between the Emperor's *fiscus* and the *aerarium* is obscure, but certain facts are clear. Nero's adviser wrote in *De Beneficiis* 'Caesar possesses everything, but his purse (*fiscus*) holds only his private and personal fortune; and all things are under his control, but only his own things are included in his patrimony'. He thereby indicated that imperial direction covered all aspects of the state, including its finances, though imperial ownership was a separate matter, concerning only the Emperor's private wealth.

If the Senate traditionally authorized disbursements from the *aerarium*, the Emperor often took the initiative in its deliberations. When Nero appointed the members of the senatorial commission to investigate public revenue, he was following good Augustan precedent.[16] Accounts covering the public treasury in Rome and the provincial chests that held tax money were kept by imperial freedmen under Augustus and probably continued to be kept later by the *a rationibus*, the same official who was also responsible for supervision of the Emperor's resources. The publication of these accounts is not mentioned after Gaius, a factor which must have added to the uncertainty men felt about which funds were being employed on which projects, those of the *aerarium* or the *fiscus*.[17]

Cassius Dio, when speaking of Augustus' road-building schemes, admits that he cannot be sure whether the cost was borne by the Emperor's own funds or the public funds because 'the people and the Emperor use each other's monies freely'. Tacitus, noting the diversion of money on one occasion from *aerarium* to *fiscus* comments 'as if it mattered'.[18]

Not only were the two funds used for similar projects: they had never really been financially independent of each other. As long as the tribute from all provinces went to the *aerarium* (and that was certainly true of the Early Principate),[19] the Emperor must have been entitled to grants from the state treasury as a proconsul, and there are occasional references to grants made to him by the Senate for specific expenses. Thus Nero is said to have been voted in 67 an annual allowance of 10,000,000 HS for his expenses.[20] But, from the beginning of the Principate, the Emperor also made contributions to the *aerarium*, and on a large scale, such as the 40,000,000 HS that Nero handed over in AD 57 to support public credit.[21]

When Lucan wrote in his poem on the Civil War, 'And then for the first time, Rome was poorer than Caesar', he was describing Julius Caesar's forceful removal of funds from the state treasury, but his epigram relates to the great size and importance of the imperial wealth in his own time, when examples of appropriation of existing state revenues by the Emperor are in fact hard to find.[22] Instead, the Emperor's generosity was large in relation to state resources. The annual grant of 10,000,000 HS Nero is said to have been voted in AD 67 hardly compares with the 60,000,000 HS he claimed to have spent on the state *annually* since his accession. This is on the same scale as Augustus' donation of 2,400,000,000 HS to the public treasuries, plebs and soldiers during his reign of about forty years, the equivalent of nearly five years' annual income of the *aerarium*.[23] Moreover, it was the imperial wealth, resting principally on properties initially acquired by Augustus as booty and constantly augmented by legacy and confiscation, that was the dynamic element in the resources that maintained public services and benefits. Proper management and a privileged position in law meant that the imperial properties provided a growing income and capital reserve, whereas holdings of state land were small and the *aerarium* was dependent, as in the Republic, on taxes.[24] Except for Egypt, most of the new provinces acquired under Augustus and his immediate successors will have used up most of their revenues on garrisons for some years. It is not surprising to find that Nero, like Augustus, is represented by the Elder Pliny as taking a keen interest in the yield of the crops on imperial estates.[25]

It should now be clear that an Emperor who spent his own resources unwisely could seriously affect not only the level of public services and amenities but the ability of the state to meet its basic obligations. Given the regularity of imperial subventions, a shortage in the *fiscus* was eventually liable to cause trouble in the *aerarium* too. In addition, the Emperor's influence on policy meant that *aerarium* funds could be misapplied or eroded because he wished to receive credit for a policy of liberality.[26]

The view of antiquity that Nero's lavish spending caused the financial difficulties in his latter years is therefore not implausible. But it is unsatisfying as a complete explanation. Liberality was expected of and praised in the Princeps, and Nero had already displayed it in those early years that were so acclaimed. Indeed this was one of the respects in which Nero justly claimed that he was following the example of Augustus.[27] But why did the early policy eventually cease to be viable? Before we blame the entire fiasco on the Great Fire, we should see if the pattern laid down by Augustus had inherent difficulties.

The Augustan Pattern

In the record of his achievements displayed at his mausoleum, Augustus' expenditure on the state and the Roman people occupies ten chapters, nearly a third of the whole. The spending recorded is in the Republican tradition whereby leading senators acquired popularity by erecting public buildings, giving shows and making distributions of corn and oil. The help Augustus gave to impoverished senators and other *amici*, including poets and artists, also belongs to that tradition of private generosity accepted as an obligation by the upper orders since the mid-second century BC.[28] Augustus' allegiance to the Republican tradition is clear, not only in his attempts to encourage its survival among the senators themselves, but in his designation of his spoils as the source of his spending on public buildings and of his largesse to the soldiers and plebs. Also traditional was his indication that his gladiatorial games and nautical exhibitions (*munera*) were given as a private citizen, whereas it was as a magistrate that he gave the official games (*ludi*).[29] Augustus' munificence exceeded that of his Republican predecessors in scale, and not in that alone. He boasted that he was the first to buy land on which to settle veterans. Republican magnates had only been able to use political influence to release public funds for this purpose, though it is notable that Nero's great-great-grandfather, L. Domitius Ahenobarbus, had at least promised land to his soldiers in the Civil Wars.[30]

The Roman state had never been rich, even for its commitments which were not very great. If we ask why a great imperial power continued to rely to such an extent on private generosity, the answer must be respect for tradition reinforced by the deliberate wish of the founder of the Principate to secure for himself the popularity, and ultimately the immortal reputation, such liberality earned.[31] It is true that Emperors could and did claim credit for generosity when they initiated public spending, but true liberality had to come from their own resources. Augustus recorded only liberality of this sort in the *Res Gestae* and Vespasian was notorious for saying at every possible opportunity, 'I am paying for this out of my own purse'.

To preserve his right to gratitude, the Emperor naturally resisted the institutionalization of his largesse into regular payments: thus Tiberius was quick to point out that Augustus' generosity to an ancient senatorial family did not give them the right to make further claims on the imperial purse.[32] Nonetheless, custom tended to harden and create specific expectations. Augustus set the pattern not only for Tiberius who regarded his example as law, but for later Emperors. It was the Princeps on whom cities struck by natural disaster, provinces unable to pay their taxes, senators unable to maintain the census requirement, the *aerarium* overburdened by its obligations all relied for relief.

Where did the Princeps find the money to meet all these expectations? The *Res Gestae* mentions several kinds of private wealth on which Augustus drew: his family inheritance (*patrimonium*), his booty (*manubiae*) and vague categories such as 'my own money'. It is generally agreed that his inheritance from Caesar, his adoptive father, and his natural father would not have exceeded 100,000,000 HS. The major sources of his wealth were his booty, particularly that of Egypt, and the legacies he received from his friends and freedman. In his will he claimed to have received 1,400,000,000 HS in this form during the last twenty years of his life.[33] Yet Augustus left to his heirs and legatees, the Roman plebs, the soldiers and his friends, a total of about 240,000,000 HS, a fortune easily surpassed by other wealthy men of the period, and soon to be eclipsed by the fortunes of the imperial freedmen under Claudius and Nero. In his will Augustus apologized for the smallness of his property, saying that he had spent his inheritance and the legacies he had received mostly for the benefit of the state.[34]

A rough estimate ascribes to his booty about half of the largesse Augustus was able to record in the *Res Gestae*. It is therefore important to note that, of his dynastic successors, only Claudius, through his conquest of Britain, can have accumulated any booty worth mentioning.[35] The principal way in which the Julio-Claudian Emperors coped with the lack of booty and steady or rising imperial expenditure was the acquisition of property, particularly mines and landed estates which, as we saw, could bring a large return.[36] Hence they tended not to abide by Augustan principles of refusing legacies from strangers or from men with children, and they gradually intruded on the *aerarium*'s right to *bona vacantia* and *bona caduca* (property to which no one was entitled to claim under a valid will or under the laws governing intestacy) and *bona damnatorum* (the property of those whose sentence involved total or partial confiscation). It is in this financial light that we must see the frequent allegations in the ancient sources that bad Emperors instigated serious accusations when short of cash.[37]

Each of Augustus' successors played his own variation on Augustus' theme. Tiberius inherited 100,000,000 HS from the first Princeps and managed to amass twenty-five times that amount in his twenty-three years as Emperor. It is in his reign that, our evidence suggests, *bona vacantia* and *bona damnatorum* were first claimed for the *fiscus* in some cases, rather than the *aerarium*.[38] Since there was no effective check on the power of the Princeps, only the decision of a good Princeps could reverse such innovation and his financial obligations would usually make it difficult for him to do so completely.[39] But the principal source of Tiberius' capital was his meanness. He did follow the Augustan pattern of generosity to a limited extent, giving *congiaria*, donatives, subsidies, tributes and hardship relief.[40] But he built very little and gave very few games.[41]

The undesirable effects of this frugality were partly economic. In AD 33 the shortage of money in circulation caused a crisis of credit with interest rates running very high. Finally Tiberius provided money for interest-free loans. It is interesting to note that this situation was allowed to become so severe, although the link between cause and effect was understood.[42] For imperial spending, though in fact an economic necessity, was in theory a free exercise of imperial virtue. Tiberius' parsimony also had political consequences: the plebs gave their verdict at his death by shouting 'The Tiber for Tiberius' and threatening to burn his body in an amphitheatre to ensure that he at last provided some entertainment.[43]

These lessons were not lost on Tiberius' successor. According to Suetonius, in one year Gaius ran through the surplus of 2,700,000,000 HS that Tiberius had accumulated in one year, a sum comparable with the total of Augustus' largesse throughout his long reign. In his four years of power he made up for over twenty years of Tiberian frugality in buildings and games.[44] Though he honoured the traditional obligations of helping the victims of natural disaster, showing generosity to favoured subjects and distributing money to the plebs and soldiers, his main expenses were elaborate spectacles and personal extravagance. Seneca claims that he spent 10,000,000 HS on one dinner, a sum which he describes, with some exaggeration, as equivalent to the tribute of three provinces.[45] Gaius increased the yield in legacies by abandoning the principle of refusing legacies from strangers, and initiating the custom of invalidating the wills of men he thought owed him something if they disappointed his expectations: his loose definition of ingratitude extended to all senior centurions who had not named Tiberius or himself among their heirs.[46] Gaius also raised money by auctioning off imperial treasures and inventing minor taxes, including one on prostitutes, the proceeds of which went to the *fiscus*.[47]

Claudius has a better financial reputation in our sources. He reverted to the Augustan pattern of spending on congiaria, donatives, hardship relief, games and constructions of public utility, which he initiated on a grand scale.[48] His plans for Ostia and his attempt to drain the Fucine Lake encountered the traditional resistance to very expensive engineering projects which aimed to improve or reverse nature, but his reputation in this respect was restored by the Flavians for whom the personal extravagance of his hated successor eclipsed any excesses of Claudius.[49]

The circumstances of Claudius' accession made it expedient for him to follow the example of Gaius in rewarding the Praetorian Guard handsomely. In fact, whereas Gaius had given 1,000 HS each, a donative on a recognizably Augustan scale, Claudius gave 15,000 HS each and reminded the Guard annually of his munificence by a gift of 100 HS each.[50] Gaius had spent his resources, and Claudius had little in the way of personal fortune,[51] so how did he finance his generosity? He recovered some of Gaius' less discriminating gifts and was fortunate in deriving some booty from the conquest of Britain. He was possibly the first Emperor to receive wreaths of solid gold, a traditional Eastern type of gift, from the western provinces of Gaul and Spain.[52] The venality of his favourites and freedmen must have resulted in profitable legacies, and the long list of senators and *equites* convicted in his reign, albeit for political reasons, must have produced enough confiscated property to make a serious difference to his budget.[53]

These were the precedents that Nero inherited. His father's inheritance should have been ample for a private citizen, but Claudius himself cannot have left a great surplus, nor do we know if Nero took it all when he suppressed his predecessor's will.[54] Agrippina's wealth was considerable and would have been available to him in the early years when their relations were good and after her death in 59.[55] Booty, however, must have been negligible. In Britain the cost of suppressing the great rebellion of 60–1 would have balanced any profits of Suetonius Paullinus' earlier victories. On the eastern frontier, the war dragged on for years, ending in a diplomatic settlement; the resulting visit of Tiridates and his retinue was a burden to the *aerarium* and the *fiscus*.[56] In addition Claudius had made things difficult for his successor. He had replaced at least two of the three legions lost with Varus in Augustus' last years, thereby increasing the military burdens on the *aerarium* and the need for the generous imperial subventions Nero gave: he may also have been the Emperor who increased the number of praetorian cohorts from nine to twelve.[57] As Nero, like Gaius and Claudius, had become Princeps largely through the support of the Guard, he felt obliged to follow their example in the way of generosity, and Claudius had raised the level of expectation to 15,000 HS each for the accession donative. The cost of Nero's largesse in 54 was thus 180,000,000 HS, one-third again as much as the triumphal doative Augustus had given to all of his veterans out of his Egyptian spoils. The Guard was also rewarded for its loyalty in 59 after his mother's murder and in 65 after the Pisonian conspiracy when they received 2,000 HS each.[58] Each time the change in the number of cohorts, from nine to twelve, meant that Nero's largesse was automatically one-third again as costly as it would have been for Augustus and possibly for all his predecessors. It is worth noting that Vespasian returned to the Augustan number of nine cohorts, and precisely on financial grounds.[59]

The evidence already adduced makes it likely that Nero would have difficulty in balancing his budget from the very beginning of his reign. In addition, his nature was free of the meanness that had characterized his father and his aunt, while the circumstances of his accession inclined him to generosity as a means to popularity. Seneca, as we have seen, encouraged him to give games and help individual senators ungrudgingly.[60] He was the first Emperor we hear of to give annual pensions instead of the more usual capital sum, and he generously made the annual grant half the required senatorial census, the amount usually granted once and for all. Later, after the Pisonian conspiracy, Nero was to extend the principle of regular subventions to a monthly corn allowance for the praetorians.[61]

Nero fulfilled his obligation to distribute *congiaria* (the one recorded by Tacitus was on the Augustan scale),[62] to build works of public utility, including an extension of the Claudian aqueduct, a market and baths, and to relieve hardship by corn subsidies and disaster relief.[63] In addition, he gave lavish games, at which Gaius' precedent of showering gifts on the spectators was maintained.

It is therefore not surprising to find that Nero took steps to maximize his income from legacies. By 65 it had become the custom for those who had enjoyed the friendship of the Emperor to protect their legacies by leaving him a large share.[64] Nero ultimately made formal the practice initiated by Gaius of confiscating the estates of the 'ungrateful', adding provision for the punishment of the lawyers who drafted their wills. He also laid down that any freedman who usurped the name of a family connected with his own had to pay for the privilege by leaving him five-sixths rather than the usual half of his estate that a freedman owed his former master.[65]

As for *bona damnatorum*, it is difficult to separate the motives of fear and rapacity, but Tacitus seems to indicate 66 as the turning point when men realized they could use the Emperor's greed as an instrument for punishing their enemies. Dio alleges that Nero eventually took to claiming all the property of those executed and those living in exile, and the last is confirmed by Tacitus.[66] These last excesses belong to the period after the Fire when there were also voluntary and compulsory contributions throughout Italy and the provinces.

Some of these measures might have been necessary even if there had been no Fire and Nero had stayed within the Augustan limits of liberality. Yet the financial system can hardly be blamed for the fact that Nero inclined more and more towards the extreme example of Gaius who had erected extravagance into a guiding principle, 'A man ought either to be frugal or to be Caesar'. Seneca may have praised liberality in a prince but he can hardly have presented Gaius as a model, for his philosophical works consistently represent him as a monster and castigate not only his cruelty, but his luxury. Suetonius notes Nero's admiration of his uncle and attributes to him the reflection that only mean and niggardly men account for their expenditure, while it is a mark of the elegant and truly magnificent to waste and squander.[67]

The Magnificent Monarch

As with Gaius, Nero's extravagant standard of living and his enormous personal gifts were bound up with the vision he eventually adopted of what the Princeps should be. These young Emperors with no clear mandate from their predecessor to rule, no achievements to justify their assumption of power, had difficulty in finding a *persona*. To behave as one among equals shows that one is secure in one's greatness; as Pliny was to tell Trajan, and Nero did not feel secure.[68] Therefore he sought to assure himself and his subjects that he was greater than they and hence had a right to rule them: more and more he pursued the image of the super-aristocrat, the magnificent monarch, rather than that of the *civilis princeps*. He wished to excel in splendour and magnanimity, and he wished to do so in a period when the standards for magnificence were particularly high. Tacitus remarks on the revolution in manners that came after 69 following a period of great and growing luxury under the Julio-Claudians. He also notes the dangers wealth had brought to the upper orders, for this was one aspect of Nero's increasing intolerance of rivals and of the link he made between high living and the imperial position. Seneca was accused of trying to surpass the Princeps in the wealth and magnificence of his villas and gardens out of political ambition; D. Junius Silanus found that his lavish gifts were construed as a sign of imperial aspirations.[69] Gifts to supporters, favourites and dependants were central to Nero's conception of his own munificence. The sources naturally emphasize the freedmen, actors, athletes, gladiators and usurers among his beneficiaries, and it was probably only from the lowly that Galba could hope to recall the nine-tenths of Nero's gifts that he demanded. Many of the senators and *equites* who had profited from imperial munificence were in any case dead by then, their properties having passed to the *fiscus* already. But the total mentioned by Tacitus in the context of Galba's exactions is 2,200,000,000 HS, a sum of the same order of magnitude as Augustus claimed to have spent on the treasuries, plebs and veterans throughout his reign.[70]

The same theme of magnificence and grandeur underlies the plans for the Domus Aurea, the residence in which Nero would at last live like a man and which cost Otho 50,000,000 HS just to add the finishing touches.[71] The Elder Pliny notes with indignation the craze for myrrhine vessels at Rome, revealing the authentic Flavian attitude in his remark, 'Nero, as was proper for a Princeps, outdid everyone by paying 1,000,000 HS for a single bowl. It is worth recording that an Emperor and Father of his Country drank at such expense.'[72] It only remained for Nero to aggravate the effect of his extravagance by depriving the *aerarium* of the tribute from Greece (admittedly a poor province): by then he had clearly lost any trace of the financial sense he had once possessed.[73]

The example of Nero was not lost on Vespasian. He found both *aerarium* and *fiscus* sadly depleted and claimed, according to Suetonius, that 40,000,000,000 HS were essential to put the state on its feet again.[74] This figure seems so out of proportion to all that is known of imperial largesse and state income that it is often emended to 4,000,000,000 HS. Otherwise we would have to assume that Nero had long left the armies unpaid, a supposition that accords ill with the reluctance of the German legions and the Praetorian Guard to desert him. The fact that the idea of raising a public loan from private individuals of 60,000,000 HS was mooted under Vespasian but dropped would also be harder to understand.[75]

Vespasian took some drastic economy measures: he reduced the size of the Guard, raised tribute assessments, abolished the exemption of Greece and other eastern states from tribute as well as other immunities, established new minor taxes and sold the scraps of public land which had not been assigned when colonies in Italy were founded.[76] He also found a way of increasing the revenue from the rich province of Egypt. In contrast with the methods of Nero's penultimate Prefect, Caecina Tuscus, namely, compulsory tax-farming and rent-collection, Vespasian reorganized the rich imperial estates in the province so as to produce more taxes for the *aerarium* and rent for the *fiscus*. Under the Julio-Claudian Emperors, many of these were in the hands of Roman senators, members of the imperial family and other imperial favourites. With Vespasian and Titus, the evidence for estates listed as the personal property of individual Emperors disappears, and the names of local landlords and tenants appear. Rostovzeff concluded that the extraction of taxes and rents from highly-placed Roman absentee landlords had become too difficult for the local administration, so that now, as the estates returned to imperial hands by legacy and confiscation, they were either sold to more tractable local land-owners or leased from a central bureau through tenants-in-chief.[77]

Vespasian also deemed it necessary to change the whole Neronian style of life. Tacitus credits the move away from luxury in Roman society after 69 to his example. As a successful soldier, Vespasian had enough prestige to reduce the Guard, be niggardly with donatives and maintain a general reputation for meanness and avarice.[78] He did continue the Augustan tradition of beneficence, helping impoverished senators, practitioners of the arts and victims of natural disasters, putting on games and constructing roads, temples and the Colosseum.[79] Yet in his liberality there is a new spirit, less personal, less aristocratic. There is less of the magnificent aristocrat distributing largesse according to whim and claiming personal gratitude, and more of the executive of the Roman people giving or restoring to them what they should have by right. The conversion to general public use of the site and constructions belonging to the Domus Aurea was much publicized. Similarly, inscriptions on the Aqua Claudia record the Emperor's restoration to the city of Rome, at his own expense, of portions of the aqueduct built by Claudius and afterwards neglected. Inscriptions also record the restoration of roads 'ruined by the neglect of an earlier age'.[80] The implicit rebuke to his predecessor suggests that such public liberality should be regarded as a duty by the Princeps. Whereas Nero with a grand gesture ceded public lands to squatters, Vespasian diligently went about reclaiming such lands for the state.[81] Martial's phrase about Vespasian returning Rome to itself clearly echoes the Emperor's own propaganda.[82] It is not surprising to find him adopting the principle of guaranteed annual grants and extending it to the establishment of salaried posts in Greek and Latin rhetoric, thus involving the *fiscus* in a permanent obligation not limited to a single favoured individual or a single generous Emperor.[83]

The Augustan financial pattern was not easy to continue successfully without substantial booty. But a self-confident military Emperor could pretend to antique parsimony, manage without the goodwill earned by lavish donations and forgo the distinction of a more magnificent style of life than his potential rivals. The example of Gaius and Nero tended to regain ground whenever an Emperor was young and without military repute. Vespasian's son Domitian was the next to accede with this handicap, which he failed to make good. Instead he raised legionary pay, gave lavish games, built an enormous palace, and after living down his family's reputation for meanness, became rapacious through lack of funds.[84]

FOURTEEN

The Temptation of Philhellenism

Nero's philhellenism seems particularly difficult to elucidate in terms of the pressures imposed on him by the political system, for the tendency was deeply rooted in his personality. Nero was a philhellene from his earliest years and, as we have seen, pursued his tastes and notions, despite strong opposition, from the start of his Principate. Yet we have also noted manifestations of his enthusiasm for things Greek which seem akin to the displays of cruelty and extravagance that we have analysed in institutional terms. Just as Nero could brook no rival in pedigree or largesse, so he set great store by his victories in the Greek contests which, in Rome, were to involve the defeat of his social peers. Just as he compensated for his lack of traditional achievements by ascendancy in magnificence and luxury, so he clearly conceived the celebration for his victories on the Greek tour as an answer to the Roman triumph. Is it possible that Nero's philhellenism, like much of his cruelty and extravagance, was, in part, a response to features of the Augustan Principate?

The notion of philhellenism is a complex one. At least two elements have to be considered: the Greek tastes which Nero was determined to pursue and to inculcate in others, and the practical benefits he conferred on individuals, cities, and provinces in the eastern Empire.

Nero's Greek Tastes

Nero's passion for music and athletics was dramatically displayed in his shows. Already in 57 the entertainments he presented in his new amphitheatre included pyrrhic dances (akin to pantomime) performed by Greek youths.[1] There followed the Juvenalia and the two celebrations of the Neronia. Tacitus makes Nero defend his Greek pursuits by pointing out that chariot-racing and singing were accomplishments of ancient heroes. That this is authentic is suggested by the appearance of the same idea in a poem of the period, the *Laus Pisonis*, where lyre playing is justified by the example of Achilles.[2] Yet Nero did not despise the contemporary heirs of that culture, as is shown by his eager acceptance of crowns sent from the

Greek festivals of his own day, followed by his visit to Greece to participate in these same festivals.[3] Rather, like the Greeks of the Roman period themselves, he thought them justly proud of their past, for which they still deserved respect, but he acknowledged that Old Greece, at least, was in decline.

In his speech at the Isthmus in 67 Nero lamented that his gift of liberty could not be conferred when Hellas was at its peak, so that more people could enjoy it; and he alluded to that internal discord which the Greeks themselves blamed for their decline.[4] In fact trouble was already brewing, but though Nero punished the authors of *stasis* in Sparta, he allowed Greece to retain its freedom. Vespasian, at the start of his reign, was able to cite internal dissension as justification for putting the province once more under a direct rule. His judgment that Greece had forgotten how to be free was a bitter disappointment after the sympathy of Nero.[5]

That his philhellenism extended to the contemporary Greek world fits with a fact we have already noted, namely that in the visual arts and in literature Nero was not favouring any particular Greek forms, Classical or Hellenistic. He was advancing along paths artists and writers had already taken in Rome, where Greek models of various kinds had been acknowledged and assimilated long ago. Thus Nero patronised current Greek epigrammatists and had a taste for Alexandrian verse, but he also cultivated the classical Greek genres of epic and tragedy.

Nero could speak Greek, and made at least two public speeches in the language, one of them in the Roman Senate. This was not in itself an innovation: Claudius had set a precedent there, just as he had anticipated Nero's attitude to Greece by recommending Achaea to the Senate as 'a province dear to me through our sharing of cultural pursuits'.[6] What distinguished Nero from earlier Roman *graeculi* was his wholehearted subscription to Greek values. It was not only the degree of his enthusiasm for music and athletics that set him apart, but also the overriding value he attached to the arts in general.

His aestheticism found a comfortable milieu not only in Greece itself, but in Magna Graecia. Naples, in particular, was a Greek city which had traditionally afforded the Romans relaxation and entertainment, and Nero was a frequent visitor. There he gave his first public performance, there he sought solace after the death of Poppaea, there he brought Tiridates before escorting him to Rome. Naples was the scene of his triumphal return to Italy from Greece, and the place where he lingered after hearing the news of the Vindex rising.[7] But the Greek city of Alexandria also attracted him. Twice he planned a visit, in 64 and later as part of the Greek tour, and it was to Alexandria that rumour imagined his final flight.[8]

In his systematic study of Nero's philhellenism Schumann distinguished Greek elements, such as Nero's Greek games and his tour of Achaea, from Hellenistic ones, in which he included Nero's Alexandrian plans and his advancement of men from Egypt and other eastern provinces. This is an artificial distinction in this period, when 'Greek' was a linguistic and cultural classification embracing the inhabitants of Greek cities in Asia Minor, Syria, Palestine, Egypt and Cyrene. It was not only the Greeks of Achaea and Asia that looked to the ancient cultural tradition: the great Greek festivals, including the one at Naples, attracted participants from all over the Greek world. The history of ancient Greece, too, was celebrated by writers from all over the Greek diaspora. After all, that history included the conquests of Alexander which had brought the diaspora to its height.[9]

Practical Benefits

Just as Nero did not despise contemporary Greece proper (he assures them that his generosity springs from goodwill, not pity), so his practical munificence acknowledged no such barriers as Schumann defined.[10]

It was in the context of his grant of liberty to Achaea that the priest of the imperial cult hailed Nero as 'the mightiest emperor, philhellene, Nero Zeus god of freedom'. This was only the climax of his generosity to Greek cities, which started with his successful plea to Claudius on behalf of Rhodes in 53.[11] That island had enjoyed a privileged position under the Principate until AD 44, when Claudius punished the Rhodians for crucifying some Roman citizens. Rhodes appealed: an inscription honouring the ambassadors who brought back a favourable reply from Claudius particularly notes the good offices of the young prince. In a letter written after his accession, Nero alludes to the goodwill he has shown the city since his earliest youth.[12] His early services to Rhodes are further celebrated in an epigram by Antiphilus of Byzantium, who draws a parallel between them and the blessings conferred by the Sun-god, their ancient patron. A Rhodian coin repeats the theme, representing Nero with the Sun's rayed halo. Nero protected the island to the end: his freedman Acratus, when he was collecting treasures for Nero's palace, reassured the terrified Rhodians, telling them that he had no authority to touch any of their possessions. It is not surprising that, in Suetonius' story about Nero's plan to escape from Agrippina's scolding, it is Rhodes that figures as his place of refuge.[13]

At Alexandria a new system of tribes was introduced in the first year of Nero's reign, with names commemorating his deified father and his mother. A papyrus attests his generosity to Greek settlers in the Arsinoite name, including the remission of crown gold which he grants, 'not wishing to burden you at the start of my Principate'. Nero speaks elsewhere in the letter of continuing Claudius' generous policy, but this and other documents may suggest exceptional zeal on his part in protecting the exclusiveness of the Greek population in Egypt. Even the new tribes have been construed as a means of restricting tribal membership, so that those who were not authentic citizens of Alexandria would not share in the tax privileges and other benefits that Augustus, here as elsewhere, had conferred on the Greek population.[14]

After the Fire of 64, and probably even earlier, Nero's agents had taken treasures from the shrines at Athens, Delphi, Olympia, Thespiae and Pergamum. Though what he did was regarded as sacrilege, the Emperor's motives were clearly aesthetic and financial;[15] his respect for the Greek gods, voiced in the speech delivered at the Isthmus, is confirmed by the offerings he personally deposited in the Greek temples. Pausanias records the gift of a golden crown and purple robe to the Heraeum at Argos, while Olympia received three crowns, clearly commemorations of Nero's artistic triumphs. He also presented the Pythian oracle with 400,000 HS.[16]

The crowning act of the Greek tour was the liberation of the whole province of Achaea from direct rule and tribute obligations. Plutarch interrupts his biography of Titus Flamininus, who had proclaimed the freedom of Greece in 197 BC, to recall the glorious occasion: 'It was in Corinth that Titus at this time, and at Corinth that Nero again in our own day – both at the Isthmian games – made the Greeks free and self-governing, Titus by the voice of a herald, but Nero in a public address which he delivered in person on a tribunal in the market-place amidst the multitude'. The inscription recording his address, which was delivered in Greek, shows that the Emperor had ordered as many as possible to come to Corinth for the occasion.[17] It is not clear whether or not compulsion is here envisaged: it is certainly attested in connection with the games in which Nero participated.[18] On this occasion, however, it was probably not necessary. Even Greek writers like Plutarch and Philostratus, whose Roman connections and sympathies lead them to view Nero's artistic performances with contempt, celebrate his liberation of Greece with warm feeling.[19] Plutarch, who regards him as a criminal and a tyrant who nearly destroyed the Empire, never mentions his depredations at Delphi where he himself was a priest. Moreover, in recounting the vision of Thespesius of Soli he represents Nero as finding mercy in the next world, for 'he had paid the penalty for his crimes and was owed some kindness from the gods because he had freed those of his subjects who are noblest and dearest to them'. Instead of being reincarnated as a viper which eats its way out of its mother he would become a frog singing in the marshes and lakes.[20] Philostratus writes that 'Nero restored the liberty of Greece, showing an uncharacteristic wisdom and moderation', and describes this act as rejuvenating Greece and instituting peace and concord such as ancient Hellas had not enjoyed. Yet elsewhere he represents the Emperor as a tyrant and a matricide.[21] Even Pausanias, who catalogues Nero's thefts from the temples of Greece and notes his mistreatment of his mother and his wives, regards his liberation of Greece as proof of Plato's theory 'that the greatest and most daring crimes are committed not by ordinary men but by the noble soul corrupted by improper education'.[22]

Nero's contribution to the advancement of individuals from the eastern provinces is more difficult to document and assess. The infiltration of provincials into the Roman governing class was a process that the Romans themselves liked to see as continuous with their ancient tradition of converting the vanquished into allies and citizens. Under the Principate that process is clearly visible, the western provinces of Baetica in Spain and Narbonensis in Gaul leading the way.

By comparison with the western élites, the upper classes of the eastern provinces make considerably slower progress. Some of this is to be ascribed to the linguistic problem, for the Greeks were reluctant to speak and read any other language than Greek. Moreover, in deference to the age and superiority of Greek culture, Rome had accepted Greek, alone of the languages of the Empire, as an official language co-ordinate with Latin in the east. Though Philostratus represents the philosopher Apollonius advising Vespasian to send out to the Greeks governors who can understand their language, and complaining of one in the past 'who knew as little of the Hellenes and their tongue as they of his', the Romans normally respected their sensibilities: the letters of Cicero and Pliny permit us to trace a continuous tradition whereby Romans in charge of the Greek provinces were expected to show knowledge of and respect for Greek culture.[23] Yet to become a senator or hold a post in Rome or the West, one had to know Latin.[24] Another reason suggested for the comparative slowness with which prominent citizens of Greek cities enter the Roman governing class is that they were initially content with local and provincial politics, even if they had the Roman citizenship.

Neither this last consideration nor the language problem, however, applies to descendants of Roman veterans living in Roman colonies, or to the descendants of other Italian families living in enclaves within the Greek cities. Admittedly they advance to senatorial rank before other easterners, but incomparably slower than the Gauls and Spaniards. The latest research yields, at most, three Roman senators from the eastern provinces before Nero's reign, two of them from this category, the first, Q. Pompeius Macer, being a native of Mitylene whose family enjoyed exceptional advancement through a close connection with Pompey in the late Republic.[25]

On present evidence five eastern senators started their career under Nero. Three of them are descendants of Italians: L. Servenius Cornutus from Acmoneia in Phrȳgia, whose name suggests paternal descent from an Italian immigrant, though his mother carried the blood of Pompey's client kings; M. Plancius Varus from Perge in Pamphylia, whose name again indicates Italian descent; and T. Junius Montanus from the Roman colony of Alexandria Troas. The first two reflect informal Italian settlement; the latter official Roman colonization.[26]

The ambitions of native eastern families were stimulated by the success of western provincials. Plutarch reflects on the dissatisfaction of Chians, Galatians and Bithynians who long for the status of Roman senator.[27] The first native Greek-speaking senator after Pompeius Macer came, in fact, from Cyrene, on the fringes of the Greek world and closer to Italy. He is M. Antonius Flamma whose grandfather, we may surmise, received the citizenship from Antony when he was triumvir.[28] But the eventual triumph of Asia is celebrated on an inscription from Didyma. The name of the man is not preserved, only his claim to be the fifth Roman senator from all of Asia, the first from Miletus and the first from Ionia. Since we already know of three senators at least from Asia by Nero's reign (Pompeius Macer, Servenius Cornutus and Junius Montanus), and at least three enter the Senate under Vespasian, the nameless boaster is likely to have succeeded under Nero.[29]

How far individual Emperors can be credited with deliberate intervention in this process of provincial infiltration is difficult to determine. Where the rhythm seems to speed up it seems reasonable to make a connection with imperial patronage, if not policy, for it is the Emperor from whom Roman citizens of non-senatorial origins must seek permission to enter the Senate. Vespasian's adlection of a certain number of easterners is to be connected with the command he was holding in the east when he made his bid for power: he wished to reward his supporters, and the deaths of senators during the civil wars gave him the opportunity to do so lavishly.[30] But philhellenism could have been at work with Nero: he could have found easten aspirants particularly congenial, even if he did not consciously decide to reverse the prejudice against the Greeks, or rather the prejudice in favour of the West, that had obtained since the civil wars. That Asia succeeds before Achaea, which enjoyed Nero's particular favour, can probably be explained by its prosperity and the prevalence of Roman colonists and settlers there. That the majority of Nero's beneficiaries were of Italian descent does not weaken the case, for they were still thought of as eastern senators, as is shown by the fact that they, like the native Greek senators, tend to be employed in the Greek-speaking areas of the Empire.[31]

This thesis gains support from the fact that the introduction of true easterners into the higher echelons of the equestrian service also seems to be accelerated in Nero's reign. A start had been made under Claudius. Tiberius Claudius Balbillus from Ephesus, and Ti. Julius Alexander, an apostate Jew from Alexandria, were working their way up. Under Nero they reached the top post, the Prefecture of Egypt. Claudius Athenodorus, if he was Prefect of the Corn Supply under Nero, would be another example.[32]

Family and Imperial History

How are we to explain Nero's sympathy with Greek values and with the individuals and cities who maintained them? Family tradition is often invoked, for Nero was descended on both sides from Antony, who had frequented the palaestra and worn Greek dress in Athens; while his great-grandmother Antonia Minor had strong ties with the Jewish aristocrats of Alexandria and the client kings of Palestine. But the greatest family influences on him would have come from his grandfather Germanicus and his uncle Gaius who had travelled in the east and then lived in Antonia's house for some time in the later years of Tiberius.[33]

Germanicus had died tragically while holding a great command in the east. In Athens he had shown his respect for the city's venerable past by using only one lictor. He then paid an illicit visit to Alexandria where he paraded himself in Greek dress and spoke of the inspiration of Alexander.[34] His son Gaius had planned to visit Alexandria as Emperor but was killed before he could realise his project. From him Nero inherited that plan, along with the idea of cutting through the isthmus of Corinth.[35]

The experiences of Germanicus and Gaius are illuminating in that they show the popularity which awaited members of the imperial house who visited and favoured the eastern provinces. The Hellenistic tradition of monarchy partly explains this adulation, but it was heightened by the feeling that this part of the world had been relatively neglected and unappreciated since the Battle of Actium. The east had been Antony's, and he had lost the contest. It was Italy and the western provinces that had sworn allegiance to Octavian in the final struggle, and they had reaped their reward. In comparison, easterners were held back in political advancement, and despised for their musical and athletic activities. Germanicus' sympathy is highlighted and his popularity explained by the attitude of his enemy and suspected murderer, the legate of Syria, who criticized his free and easy manner towards the Athenians. The true Athenians, he said, had long ago perished in successive catastrophes; these people were the dregs of the earth.[36] Philo, speaking of Gaius' impending visit to Alexandria, reveals what excitement an imperial presence would generate. Nero's appearance would have had an even greater impact, for since the early reign of Augustus, no Princeps had been to the east.

One measure of the enthusiasm Germanicus aroused is the large following attracted by a youth who appeared first in the Cyclades in AD 31, claiming to be Germanicus' son Drusus, escaped from prison in Rome. It was rumoured that he would appeal to his father's soldiers in Egypt and Syria. Meanwhile he terrified the more solid elements in Achaea and then Asia, who thought his young and disreputable followers boded popular revolution.[37] Only Nero was again to inspire such appearances.

Nero resembled both Germanicus and Gaius in his paranoia and in his desire for praise. His delight in the elaborate methods of applause employed by some Alexandrians at his performances in Naples is symbolic of his whole attitude to the Greek world.[38] Suetonius tells us that it was the enthusiastic reaction of some Greeks to his singing at dinner that inspired the Greek tour. This finds reinforcement in Plutarch's complaint that flattery drove Nero to go on the stage, and Dio Chrysostom's sneer that he desired to be proficient only in the arts that bring applause.[39]

That the Greek acclaim was not entirely insincere is shown by the three false Neros that appeared in the east in 69, 80 and 88–9. Tacitus' account of the first in the *Histories* is introduced with almost the identical phrase he was to use of the appearance of the false Drusus: 'Achaea and Asia were alarmed by a false report of Nero's return'. The historian points out that the mysterious circumstances of Nero's death made the rumour credible, for only his nurses and his mistress knew of his burial. Like the false Drusus, this pretender seems to have collected slaves and impoverished adventurers; but his following continually increased, and his claim to have the loyalties of the legions in Syria and Egypt was plausible enough to merit assassination by order of the Roman governor of Galatia and Pamphylia. Aside from a certain facial resemblance the basis of his claim to be Nero was his skill at singing and playing the cithara.[40]

Ten years later an Asiatic named Terentius Maximus made the same claim on the same grounds. But he was able to add to his followers, in Asia and further east, the support of the Parthian king Artabanus. The Parthians never achieved the concord with the Flavians that they had finally established with Nero. Having requested that Vespasian honour the memory of Nero, they went on to harbour yet another impostor twenty years after his death. It would not be rash to assume that he too found a following in the Roman provinces of the east. Dio Chrysostom, writing about this time or later, states: 'Even now his subjects wish he were still alive, and most men believe that he is'.[41]

The Augustan Principate can certainly be said to have encouraged Nero's philhellenism. As will become more apparent in chapter 15, it burdened him with a need for self-justification and with doubts about his acceptability as Princeps, thus intensifying his temperamental thirst for acclaim and admiration. Then, through the western bias imparted to it by Augustus, the system made Greeks anxious to welcome any Roman Emperor willing to favour Greek sentiments and tastes. The attractions of the Greek world thus became overwhelming for a Princeps who needed applause, especially as he already felt the call as an aesthete.

The Notion of Divine Monarchy

Perhaps it is possible to go further and say that Nero found, in the eastern attitude to him as ruler, a model for the Princeps more congenial than the traditional Roman one that he found so difficult to fulfil. Seneca's adaptation of Hellenistic theories of monarchy already suggested to him an ideological alternative to the Republican mask, one which proclaimed that elevation above one's subjects which *civilitas* aimed to conceal. As Nero gave up the difficult role of first among equals, did he find in the east a more satisfactory substitute? Schumann found elements of eastern influence in Nero's view of the imperial cult; others have detected aspirations to divine monarchy on the Oriental model.[42]

There is little evidence for the notion that Nero introduced important innovations in ruler cult. Certainly, at the beginning of his Principate we find him refusing gold and silver statues of himself in Rome, while making disclaimers of divine worship and rejecting excessive honours offered in Egypt.[43] It is true that Gaius too began by following the tradition of Augustus and Claudius, but, unlike Gaius, Nero does not seem to have changed radically in this respect. The excesses of self-deification recorded by Suetonius in his biography of Gaius find no echo in his account of Nero. As late as 65 Nero refused a temple to Divus Nero in Rome, respecting the Augustan convention whereby the living Emperor was not worshipped officially in Rome or Italy.[44] What Nero had in mind in offering his sculptor gold and silver for the colossal statue of himself that would adorn his Golden House is uncertain: statues in precious metal were generally regarded as divine honours, and colossal statues had traditionally been reserved for the gods. But the statue was actually cast in bronze, and its size may have been dictated by the immense proportions of the palace and its elevated site. What does seem clear is that it was a portrait statue of Nero, not a representation of him as the Sun-god.[45]

The statue cannot therefore be invoked in support of a theory still popular with certain scholars, that Nero was founding a 'solar monarchy'. The other props of this construction are the appearance of Nero with a radiate crown on some late coins, the description of Nero as Neos Helios in some Greek inscriptions[46] and the gold trimming of the Domus Aurea. Then middle-eastern inspiration is brought in: the design of the rotating dining room in the Golden House is traced to Parthian palaces; the image of Nero driving a chariot and surrounded by golden stars on the awning over the theatre where Tiridates received his crown is interpreted as a representation of the Emperor as the incarnation of Mithras, a deity closely associated with the Sun. Finally, support is found in Apollo's comparison of Nero to the sun in Seneca's *Apocolocyntosis*, and similar adulation in Antiphilus' poem about Rhodes.

This is a singularly ramshackle structure. The last items simply echo commonplaces of Hellenistic panegyric, long assimilated at Rome. In fact, whereas the appellation of Neos Helios, already enjoyed by Gaius, does proclaim equality as a solar divinity, this is not the case with the effusions of Seneca and Antiphilus which do not go beyond flattering comparisons.[47] Similarly, at Aphrodisias in Asia Minor the image and name of Helios is simply set beside Nero's, suggesting the dawn of a new reign. As to the exotic interpretation of the Golden House, there can be added to the doubts expressed earlier the fact that Tiridates brought back workmen from Rome to help with the rebuilding of Artaxata, which suggests that architectural influence in this period might well be travelling in the other direction.[48]

As for the visit itself, it may well be, as Cumont argued long ago in an impressive paper, that Tiridates, who is called a Magus by Pliny, saw the whole ceremony of investiture as a Zoroastrian-Mithraic ceremony: he had refused to travel by sea because the Magi were not allowed to defile the element of water; after depositing his diadem at the Emperor's feet he prostrated himself in the Oriental gesture of obeisance known as *proskunesis* and addressed Nero as his god 'whom he could worship as Mithras, his Fortune and his Fate'. Dio may have garbled what was really a declaration that Nero *was* Mithras, but that would still not show that the Roman Emperor believed or even promoted the identification. After Nero had placed the diadem on Tiridates' head, the coronation was sealed with a kiss, according to the usage of the Persian court. Clearly a protocol had been worked out, probably by Corbulo and Vologaeses, the Parthian king, which would preserve his brother's dignity as much as possible. Obeisance to an incarnation of Mithras might have seemed less humiliating than grovelling to the Roman Emperor.[49]

Pliny indicates that Nero was initiated by Tiridates into the banquets of the Magi, a number of whom had accompanied him. But he says that Nero was motivated by a desire to *control the gods* by magic and that, when he failed to acquire the necessary powers, he abandoned his efforts. If Pliny's account is accurate, then Nero did not regard himself as Mithras or any other deity. Cumont may even have been right to think that Nero's reputation among the Parthians rested partly on his reputation there as Mithras incarnate, and that his popularity there did not first develop after the Flavians proved unsympathetic. Indeed Suetonius notes, as one of Nero's last desperate schemes, a plan to go as a suppliant to the Parthians.[50] But even if Nero desired to exploit such a belief, that does not prove that he shared it. He dressed for the coronation in Roman triumphal dress. Then he entertained Tiridates by playing the lyre and, afterwards, by driving a chariot in the appropriate costume, complete with charioteer's helmet. If he was represented on the theatre awning driving a chariot among golden stars, that does not prove that he *identified* himself with the Sun. At most, some association may have been intended. As Suetonius says of him, 'He was acclaimed as the *equal* of Apollo in music and of the Sun in driving a chariot'. The coins of this period show him with the coiffure appropriate to both these activities.[51]

If we discard this dubious evidence, what remains to suggest Neronian innovation in the imperial cult? First, there is Nero's identification as the New Sun (Neos Helios) in some parts of the east, to which we can add other examples of identification with specific deities in the east, such as the appellation Agathos Daimon in Alexandria, or Zeus Eleutherios (Juppiter Liberator) in Greece.[52] In fact, these effusions show us less of imperial intentions than of eastern habits.

More worthy of consideration is Nero's appearance in a radiate crown on some late coins, for these were issued at Rome. Previously the symbol of Helios, appropriated by some Hellenistic rulers, had appeared on Roman Republican coins as an attribute of the god Sol and then, on coins of Nero's imperial predecessors, as an ornament of Divus Augustus. Although Gaius is said to have worn the radiate crown as part of his Apollo costume, and portraits of Divus Claudius on Nero's coins do not feature it (fig. 13), a passage of Lucan shows that it was thought of in Nero's day as an attribute of the dead and deified Emperors.[53] Yet it is as well to remember that, in a numismatic context, the crown had long been associated with Sol and had so far only adorned one deified Princeps.

On the gold and silver coinage Nero appears with the radiate crown only on two reverse types, both of which have most recently been dated to the year 65. On one, Nero and his wife, 'Augustus' and 'Augusta', are shown standing, Nero wearing a crown (fig. 18); on the other a crowned Nero (the figure identified by the legend 'Augustus Germanicus' continued from the obverse) stands in a toga carrying a Victory on a globe (fig. 20). If the date is correct, it is tempting to connect these two types with the honours paid to Sol after the uncovering of the Pisonian conspiracy in early 65. The Sun-god was given the credit for the detection because there was an old shrine of his near the Circus where the assassination was to take place. The connection with this occasion fits well with the Victory figure, for Nero represented the suppression of the conspiracy as a military victory.[54]

On Nero's token coinage, issued in and after 64, the radiate crown adorns the Emperor's head on the obverse of some *dupondii* produced at Rome (fig. 30) and on some issues of orichalcum *asses* produced there (fig. 31). Some of these coins were probably issued before April 65 and cannot therefore be construed as alluding to the same occasion as the precious metal examples. Numismatists are agreed that, as with the globe and *aegis*, also religious symbols, the radiate crown on the token coinage 'serves to some extent the mundane purpose of differentiating issues of coins'. Indeed, in the most recent study, MacDowall claims that at both Rome and Lugdunum 'there was one representation, and one only, of Nero's head at any one time on each denomination in each substantive issue'.[55] The complexities of Nero's innovations in the token coinage brought a need for a greater variety of representation of the Emperor's head, a problem that may go a long way towards explaining the adoption of the radiate crown as an attribute of the reigning Emperor on coins. Nero's example, it is interesting to observe, was followed by the hard-headed Vespasian and the democratic Titus, who seem to have had little desire to assert their own divinity: Nero's own annexation of the ornament and its omission on representations of Divus Claudius seem to have temporarily deprived the crown of its recent numismatic association with imperial deification.[56] Nero himself, when he adopted the ornament as a distinguishing feature on his coins, may have had in mind only his emulation of Sol the charioteer and Apollo the musician.

The evidence then does not seem to point to a serious attempt on Nero's part to introduce divine monarchy. What it indicates is a taste for adulation and flattery, and a tendency to represent the Princeps' position as one that set him far above other men. That is, it points to absolutism, a conception that Nero also sought to demonstrate by a style of life grander than any other man could attain. Of the political models that the contemporary Mediterranean world afforded, and that were to some extent incorporated in the conception of the Princeps from the start, the one that appealed to Nero was that of the absolute monarch, splendid in wealth, dress and abode, adored by his subjects to whom he was both a source of awe and a fountain of benefits. To his eastern subjects, the Princeps was king (*basileus*). Like Gaius, Nero gradually ceased to moderate the extremes of their adulation, became more and more eager to promote the idea of a royal family, and came to assert in Rome the omnipotence his Greek subjects took for granted.[57]

In a passage of *De Beneficiis*, written between 56 and 64, Seneca delivered a tirade against the Emperor Gaius for holding out his foot to be kissed by a senator of consular rank whom he had acquitted on a capital charge. Gaius was a man born, he wrote, to change the habits of a free state to Persian slavery; for him it was not enough to have before him a senior consular kneeling in supplication, not enough to hear his case wearing only slippers (that they were gold and covered with pearls only made it worse).[58] This is clearly in tune with the speech Seneca had written to be delivered before the Senate on the Emperor's accession, where the emphasis had been on partnership with the Senate and the tone that of a first among equals. But that speech had intimated that Nero would also follow the example of Augustus in generosity, clemency and accessibility, qualities that presuppose the inferior position of those who benefit. Two years later Seneca had described clemency in the language of treatises on Hellenistic kingship, reminding Nero that he was virtually a king with unlimited power that only he could moderate. Now in *De Beneficiis* itself he made plain the fact that the liberality of *principes*, like that of kings, springs from their supreme position and cannot be repaid: the only recompense their inferiors can make is in terms of the service and support essential to their overriding power.[59] Yet Seneca did not actually contradict himself in *De Beneficiis*. Even where he took the monarchic strain in imperial ideology to extremes, he never suggested that kingship was a particularly commendable form of government, that Oriental despotism was anything but contemptible, or that Nero was more than a man.[60]

Had Nero followed his teaching, he would have continued to seek security and popularity by restraining and concealing his absolute power, and to justify his tenure of that power through clemency and generosity. In fact the weakness of his character and intellect proved too great to bear the considerable strains the political system placed on him, and he was led to trumpet and flaunt his ascendancy. Yet he did not follow the example of Gaius in emulating the dress or conduct of an Oriental despot, demanding *proskunesis* and claiming to be a god. He did not wish to adopt all the ideological trappings that Hellenistic kingship had devised: the Princeps was a 'master of kings', as Cicero had once called the Roman people; and Nero himself had occasion to tell Tiridates 'I have the power to take away kingdoms and bestow them'.[61]

Nero concentrated on exhibiting his superiority as an artist and his incomparable largesse and style of life, while finding pretexts for repressing potential rivals in repute. He wished at the same time to continue exercising clemency, provided the gesture could be flamboyant and the threat to his position small. His attempt to convert Roman society to a Greek view of the value of the performing arts would, if successful, have endowed his aesthetic activities with more prestige. And he never completely abandoned the more traditional ambition of winning supreme glory in war.

FIFTEEN

The Military Image of the Princeps

'I acquired complete control of affairs by universal consent', Augustus proclaims in the record of his achievements which stood before his mausoleum. This description of the period following his successful termination of the Civil Wars is followed by an account of the golden shield proclaiming his virtues, which was given to him, along with other honours, by the Senate and People when the constitutional arrangements of 28/7 BC were introduced. Augustus' original ascendancy then was justified by his victory in the Civil Wars, its continuance by his meritorious performance while in control. If the position he had carved out for himself was to continue, who had a right to it?

By the time Augustus died he had clearly marked out Tiberius as the man he wished to succeed him as Princeps: he had adopted him and seen to it that he possessed the major powers he himself enjoyed. A further claim was Tiberius' own record of service to the state, which was impressive by the traditional criteria of magistracies held and victories won. Even so, Augustus, as he asked for the crucial tribunician power to be renewed for his adoptive son, felt obliged to excuse the defects of Tiberius in justification of his choice.[1]

No other Julio-Claudian Princeps was in the situation of Tiberius. Neither Gaius, Claudius nor Nero could appeal to the clear intention of his predecessor to support his claim; and none of them had any achievements behind him to justify his installation in the highest powers and offices of state. Pliny was later to say of Trajan, 'You have two extremes combined and blended in your person, a beginner's modesty and the assurance of one long accustomed to command'. As young princes Gaius and Nero could display only the former: they lacked the assurance that comes with experience and success. Trajan possessed the *consensus* of Senate and People before his accession, so his eulogist could claim: the record of his achievements in early life had marked him out. Nero could tell the Senate, on his first appearance, that he enjoyed the *consensus* of the Praetorian Guard (just assured a handsome donative) and that he was free of political prejudice; beyond that, there were only promises.[2]

Even when imperial panegyric spoke of divine sanction for a Princeps' rule, it was always in terms of choice based on desert. Seneca suggests in *De Clementia* that the ruler must later render an account to the gods, showing that he has justified their choice, and that the consent of men must be won by virtuous performance, a young and inexperienced prince being an unknown quantity.[3]

Though virtue in the more general Greek sense was extolled as the justification of supreme power, traditional Roman *virtus* retained the highest claim to honour. Augustus did not attempt to change the old Roman view that military achievement was the highest form of service to the state. He lined his new forum with statues of the commanders of the Republic who had brought about the expansion of the Empire. There they stood in their triumphal robes in order to make the citizens demand of him and of future *principes* that they take the lives of such men as a model for themselves. So Augustus himself explained; and victory and annexation accordingly claim a large part of his *Res Gestae*. Certain innovations would assist his successors in attaining the required standard, for he had established that the Princeps acquired credit for all victories and controlled almost all the provinces in which they could be won.[4]

The public image of the Emperor, as projected in his designation and dress, was a constant reminder to himself and his subjects of the military role he was expected to fulfil. The poet Martial celebrates the replacement of the tyrant Domitian by his virtuous successor thus: 'He is not *dominus* but *imperator*'.[5] In the Republic the title Imperator was conferred on a commander by his troops after a dazzling victory. This salutation was the prerequisite for being granted a triumph by the Senate, a procession into Rome in which all the captives and booty were displayed. The title Imperator was also used more vaguely to denote a magistrate or promagistrate holding command outside Rome. During the triumviral period the first Princeps had adopted the title as a prefix to his name to advertise 'the peculiar claim of Octavianus to be the military leader *par excellence*'. His successors did not persist in this style of nomenclature, but 'Imperator' became a common term for referring to the Princeps, its military overtones remaining intact.[6]

The most tangible indication of the way the Emperor and his subjects regarded his role was his dress. In a hierarchical society like Rome dress had always been an important index of status, and Augustus was at pains to reinforce this, urging Roman citizens to wear the toga and forbidding the usurpation of magisterial dress by those not in office.[7] Change of dress marked the particular role filled at any one moment by men in public life, such as presiding over games or over a sacrifice. For anyone in the public eye how one dressed in private could attract notice: 'going Greek', for example, when in southern Italy or the East. The Emperor had less privacy than anyone. Indeed Augustus publicised the fact that the garments he wore at home were made by the women of his household, and Suetonius asserts with confidence that Nero never wore the same garment twice.[8]

The public costume of the properly dressed Princeps mirrored the Augustan emphasis on Republican tradition, but demonstrated, at the same time, how far the accumulation of Republican offices and powers he held elevated the Princeps above the ordinary magistrates. Over the tunic with the broad purple stripe (*latus clavus*) characteristic of senators he wore the purple-bordered *toga praetexta* of curule magistrates, and he was accompanied by twelve lictors carrying *fasces*, like the consuls. When he assumed his curule chair between the two consuls he must have looked like a third holder of the chief magistracy. But unlike the consuls, whose togas carried the purple border only when they were in office or afterwards when they attended festivals, the Princeps wore magisterial dress permanently, for, in a sense, he was always in office. Moreover, his *fasces* were wreathed with laurel, an honour which had belonged in the Republic to the general acclaimed as Imperator by his soldiers. He also wore a laurel wreath, which had been a privilege of the acclaimed commander at his triumph and afterwards at festivals.[9]

This military emphasis was more in evidence when the Princeps attended festivals, for, like a few of the greatest generals of the past – Aemilius Paullus, Pompey and Caesar – he enjoyed the privilege of appearing then in the gold-embroidered purple toga of the *triumphator* (the *toga picta*). He might also wear it for the reception of foreign princes, as did Nero for the visit of Tiridates.[10]

As no triumphs were now granted to those outside the imperial house, the costume of the *vir triumphalis* soon became the characteristic imperial dress for high occasions. The fact that magistrates presiding over official games continued to wear triumphal garb, as in the Republic, did not impede its identification with the imperial position. Thus Tacitus calls it *decus imperatorium* ('the trappings of rule') when the young Nero assumed the outfit at the circus games given in honour of his entry into public life. Claudius preferred to preside over the celebrations to mark the draining of the Fucine Lake in the military cloak (*paludamentum*), but this too was distinctively imperial in that the Emperor's cloak was purple in colour.[11]

Augustus and his successors continued to observe the Republican ban on military dress in the capital, even though their proconsular imperium, by express dispensation, did not lapse when they crossed the sacred boundary of the city. The way in which Republican tradition was simultaneously maintained and violated by the Principate is strikingly exemplified by the Emperor's escort. He had soldiers to guard him while he slept and to escort him in Rome, even into the Senate House. These were members of the Praetorian Guard, which had its origin in the praetorian cohort that Republican proconsuls had long had in their provinces. Within Rome, however, the praetorian soldiers who attended the Princeps normally dressed as civilians, in togas, and they kept their weapons concealed.[12]

Nonetheless, it is clear that the dress of the Princeps confirmed the predominantly military image that the designation 'Imperator' suggested. The Emperor also took imperial salutations, which were numbered and added to his titulature: by the accession of Claudius, if not earlier, the first of these was taken on his accession.[13] Tiberius was already an established general when he became Princeps, having seven imperial salutations and two triumphs to his credit. His Julio-Claudian successors could boast no military achievements at all. Aware of traditional expectations, they suffered from lack of confidence in themselves and suspicion of military talent in others. The consequences could be dire. It is not mere coincidence that the most successful of the early *principes* were Vespasian, Titus and Trajan, men who had already proved themselves in the field. Already aged fifty-four when he became Emperor, Tiberius felt no impulse to more campaigns and took only one further salutation.[14] Gaius, however, felt the need to take the field. According to Dio, he was acclaimed seven times for the expedition to Gaul in 39/40 though he fought no battle; he then announced a triumph, either postponed or abandoned the idea, and held only an ovation. The real effect of his failure was the despotic behaviour and demands for divine honours that followed his return to Rome.[15]

Claudius had a deeper sense of Roman tradition and decided to earn a genuine triumph by leading an expedition himself. A pretext was found in the expulsion of two British kings allied with Rome, and the invasion of Britain began. Claudius arrived at a crucial point in the proceedings, stayed 16 days, and, as a result, garnered several imperial salutations and the vote of a triumph by the Senate. They also conferred on him the title Britannicus in traditional fashion.[16] For the victories in Britain and others won by his legates Claudius took twenty-seven imperial salutations, six more than Augustus had for achievements of greater moment during a reign three times as long.

Neronian Foreign Policy

What would the young Nero do? The question touches the most ineluctable of the Princeps' duties. The principal justification offered to Romans for the existence and expense of the Empire had always been its role in offering military protection and maintaining peace; success in that role depended on the Roman reputation for victory in war, which needed to be kept fresh. The Emperor was heir to that tradition. He not only had to respond to invasion or rebellion: there were decisions about levying troops, appointing or deposing client kings, altering or maintaining the status and size of territories. Millar, in his impressive demonstration of the dependence of the imperial system on stimulus from below, points to the exception: 'Society demanded from the Emperor military protection, and if possible resounding victories over foreign enemies. But when he had leisure from that, it demanded not a programme of change but a willingness to listen'.[17]

Yet the impact of each Emperor on foreign policy was limited by time and circumstance. The pacification of new provinces could take years; client arrangements might prove stable for long periods, and barbarian pressures on the frontiers might only gradually be revealed as a substantial and enduring threat. Individual Emperors could initiate dramatic changes of direction, as had Augustus with his systematic conquest of the Alpine zone and the Balkans, and as Trajan was to do in the Balkans and the East. But with the exception of Gaius' mad expedition to the north and Claudius' search for glory in Britain, Augustus' immediate successors continued his projects or responded to changing circumstances by applying the solutions he had worked out: the energetic policies of the first Princeps had left them with much to complete and secure.

Until the very last years of his reign the handling of foreign policy under Nero is intelligible in these terms. In Germany, where the disaster of AD 9 had ended Augustus' earlier project of annexation up to the Elbe, Nero's governors were principally occupied with building canals and maintaining Roman authority in the border country over the Rhine. The Tiberian policy of discouraging tribal coalitions and relying on internal warfare to wear out hostile tribes was pursued.[18]

In Britain there had been a period of consolidation after the Claudian conquest of 43 and the advances made by the first two governors, A. Plautius and Q. Ostorius Scapula. The second constructed a system of fortifications to protect the new province and disarmed the tribes in the area between the Trent and the Severn Rivers. He died in 52, worn out with constant fighting on the frontiers of the new province he had delimited.[19] His successor A. Didius Gallus was not replaced by Nero for five years, during which time he continued Scapula's work, albeit in a less dramatic fashion.

The most violent resistance to Scapula had come from the Welsh tribes, particularly the Silures, and it was in the west that Nero's governors, Q. Veranius in 57–8 and then C. Suetonius Paullinus, were to make notable advances.[20] In his first two years in the province Paullinus made considerable headway against the Welsh. He also destroyed the Druid stronghold on Anglesey, which was believed to serve as an inspiration and haven for rebels. But in 60 a rebellion erupted in the east and curtailed his work. The Iceni of Norfolk had earlier, during Scapula's tenure, resisted disarmament but without success. Now, when the king died without male issue, leaving as heirs to his considerable fortune his two daughters and Caesar, it must have seemed too much of a risk to leave the tribe under female rule before the province was thoroughly pacified. Prasutagus had hoped that the generous terms of his will would induce the Romans to treat his family and subjects well. But the imperial procurator, who had been left to implement the will and annex the territory, employed cruel and rapacious methods. This aggravated the natural resistance of the tribe to come under direct rule. Thinking of what lay ahead, namely, a census followed by direct taxation, the Iceni rebelled in concert with other tribes including the Trinobantes, who resented the presence and behaviour of the veteran colonists planted in their midst at Colchester.[21]

The annexation of Prasutagus' kingdom had clearly been decided at Rome, for those in the capital who had lent money to leading Britons called in their loans in time to be accused of provoking the revolt. They no doubt calculated that widespread military operations followed by systematic taxation would make collection more difficult later. That Seneca was among those who provided money to natives intent on acquiring the costly trappings of Roman civilisation is not unlikely, though Dio's presentation of him as the sole offender is clearly an exaggeration.[22]

Paullinus dealt effectively with the revolt and was duly honoured on his return, but the new imperial procurator Julius Classicianus and Nero's freedman Polyclitus, who was sent to investigate the situation, persuaded the Emperor that a new governor with more diplomatic talents was required to establish peace in the province. Petronius Turpilianus was duly dispatched in 61, and further advances were postponed until Flavian times.[23]

The area that made the most demands on Nero's initiative, however, was the eastern frontier, where Rome's expansion in the Republic had brought her empire up to the limits of the Parthian dominions. For most of the reign Domitius Corbulo, appointed in the winter of 54–5 as special governor of Cappadocia-Galatia in eastern Asia Minor, tried by force and diplomacy to regain the hold that Rome had lost in Claudius' last years. His aim was to recover Armenia from direct Parthian control in the person of the king's brother Tiridates.[24] King Vologaeses, detained by dynastic troubles at home, responded by having his brother withdraw from Armenia, then by giving hostages. But he remained deaf to proposals of a diplomatic settlement that would allow his brother to regain the throne, on condition that he acknowledge publicly the suzerainty of Rome and receive his diadem from the Emperor. In the winter of 57–8 Corbulo, in order to make his proposal more persuasive, first established a camp in Armenia, then inflicted losses on Tiridates and finally, in the summer of 58, marched on the city of Artaxata and drove the pretender from Armenia.[25] The destruction of the ancient Armenian capital was followed in the late summer of 59 by the capture of Tigranocerta. The vacuum left by the departure of Tiridates was filled in 60 by installing a non-Arsacid client king, in the best Augustan tradition. This Tigranes was in fact a descendant of the king imposed on Armenia in about AD 6, and he had spent most of his life as a hostage in Rome. Corbulo left the king reinforcements and departed to take over command of Syria, where the governor Ummidius Quadratus had died.[26]

Tigranes was not only suspect to the Armenians because of his alien upbringing; he also turned out to be a fool. By invading the neighbouring territory of Adiabene in 61 he provoked the Parthians to reassert by force their claim to Armenia. Corbulo, by sending just enough forces to block the

Parthian advance into Armenia and by increasing Roman fortifications on the Euphrates in Syria, was at last able to persuade Vologaeses that his best hope lay in agreeing to a mutual withdrawal from Armenia, followed by diplomatic approaches to Nero on the lines that had first been suggested to him.

When Vologaeses' envoys arrived in the spring of 62 they found that the attitude at Rome had hardened. The new legate of Cappadocia-Galatia, Caesennius Paetus, arrived in Armenia about this time, speaking of direct rule and the creation of a Roman province. The Parthians attacked and Paetus, at first successful, was ignominiously defeated the next autumn and the Roman forces withdrew from Armenia. Corbulo again effected a Parthian evacuation by agreeing to destroy the fortifications he had erected on the Euphrates.[27] A new Parthian embassy arriving in Rome in the spring of 63 revealed that the Parthian king now found his previous agreement to let his brother receive the diadem at Rome too abject: Tiridates would receive his diadem before the Emperor's statue in a legionary camp but would not abase himself further. Corbulo was now put in charge of Cappadocia-Galatia again, in addition to Syria, and given authority over the surrounding territories in preparation for war, but the Parthian envoys were given to understand that the original offer of installation at Rome was still open to Tiridates. This time Parthia accepted, and, by the end of 63, Tiridates had laid his diadem before Nero's statue in the camp at Rhandeia where Paetus had once surrendered. More than two years elapsed before he finally came to Rome to resume it.[28]

The new settlement was Augustan in that it avoided direct Roman control of Armenia. But it differed from the Augustan arrangements in that the vassal king was a Parthian nominee, indeed a member of the Parthian ruling house.[29] Though this solution, like the outcome of the British revolt, was reasonably stable, if judged by the criterion of subsequent trouble, it required more military support than Rome had previously committed to the east on a permanent basis. For, with an Arsacid on the Armenian throne, there was a greater risk that Parthia would gain a military foothold in the buffer state, and that would make Roman reliance on the Syrian army for defence of all the frontier provinces hazardous.[30] Vespasian was to turn Cappadocia-Galatia permanently from a procuratorial province without a legionary garrison (as it had been since the reign of Tiberius) into a military one, as it had been temporarily under Corbulo, and reduce Rome's reliance on client kings in favour of annexation. Unfortunately, the lack of a detailed account of Nero's last years makes it impossible to be certain that Nero retained Cappadocia-Galatia as a military province, though what evidence there is points that way. If he did, the evidence for his later eastern plans obscures his purpose: was the previous arrangement retained because Cappadocia-Galatia was again needed as a base for further operations, or had Nero already seen the implications of his Armenian settlement for the permanent defence of the border with Parthia?[31]

In the first sentence of his *Res Gestae* Augustus claimed to have subjected the whole world to Roman domination. The account of his successes in the body of that document, however, makes it clear that by subjection he did not simply mean annexation. Various forms of recognition of Roman authority were allowed to count towards that claim, including the acceptance of permanent direction by petty kingdoms, and the diplomatic homage of remote principalities. The status of different areas in relation to Rome was subject to change. For example, client kings died without issue, or became unreliable or unable to handle new military pressures. Nero's annexations were few, and of this undramatic kind.

On the death of King Cottius his little kingdom in the western Alps was made into a province under an equestrian governor, just as the Iceni became part of the province of Britain. In the east the principality of Damascus once again formed part of the province of Syria after 62–3, having slipped under Gaius from the control of the Roman governor into that of the King of the Nabateans. In 64–5 the kingdom of Pontus on the southern shore of the Black Sea was removed from the rule of Polemon II and incorporated in the province of Cappadocia-Galatia. The dates of these annexations in the east are known from coins: the circumstances can only be surmised. It is likely that they have some connection with the problems Corbulo encountered in these years. From 60 to 63 he was much concerned with the security of Syria, which he believed to be under threat of Parthian invasion, and though his fortifications were along the Euphrates and in the northern part of the province, he may have been tightening Roman control of Syria in general.[32] The annexation of Pontus followed the renewal and augmentation of Corbulo's powers. It demonstrates the same concern with securing the Black Sea as the assumption of military control over the kingdom of the Bosporus on the northern shore, and the work of the governor of Moesia in freeing the Greek city of Heraclea Chersonensis when it was besieged by the Scythians of the Crimea. Though a concern for new sources of corn may play some part in Nero's desire to control the Black Sea area, the particular problems of supplying Roman troops in the area and concern for military security must have been paramount in generating this policy. For the governor of Moesia also records a defeat of some Sarmatian tribesmen, Rhoxolani apparently moving south-west towards the Danube under pressure from tribal movements in the region of the Caucasus.[33]

Nero finally made the Sarmatians the object of an ambitious project. Tacitus, Suetonius and Dio all speak of Nero's plans to lead an expedition himself to the 'Caspian Gates', but the Elder Pliny, when speaking of plans of the region drawn up by those who served with Corbulo in Armenia, explains that this was a misnomer for the pass leading through the western Caucasus from the kingdom of Iberia in the south to the Sarmatian tribes of the north.[34] Pliny indicates that Nero was aiming at the Darial Pass, not the Derbend Pass, so that when Tacitus alludes to troops sent ahead for the war being planned against the 'Albani', he should mean the more western tribe of the Alani, which first make their appearance in Roman literature of this period.[35] It may be that the movement of these northern Sarmatian tribes made the Romans eager to demonstrate their power as a deterrent and to establish forts in Iberia, a friendly kingdom whose ruler had helped Corbulo in the invasion of Armenia.[36]

According to Tacitus, the contingents sent ahead for the expedition were eventually recalled in response to the Vindex rising: some German units had actually reached Alexandria and did not return until after Nero's death; so too perhaps the Ala Siliana from Africa, though the Legio XIV Gemina from Britain never got beyond the Balkans.[37] In addition, Nero is said to have recruited especially for this eastern venture a new legion composed of Italians, a common practice in raising new units. The birthday of I Italica was 20 September, probably in 66. In the late summer of 66, several thousand soldiers had arrived in Alexandria from Africa and, by the end of the year, the legion XV Apollinaris was also in Alexandria.[38] All of this suggests that Nero had, as Dio states, made his plans for the expedition before he left for Greece on 25th September of 66, and that some detachments were sent ahead to rendezvous at Alexandria. Nero would collect them there when, at the end of his Greek tour, he took command.[39] It is notable that about May of that year the Prefect of Egypt, Caecina Tuscus, was sent into exile when it became known that he had used the special baths built for the imperial visit.[40]

It is possible that Alexandria was chosen as the assembly point, not only because Nero was afraid of making so many troops available to a senatorial governor, or because he wished to save the soldiers from the north and west a long march by land, but because he was planning an expedition to Ethiopia in parallel or in sequence with the eastern one. Dio mentions the two together, while the Elder Pliny speaks of a party of praetorians sent to explore the region of Nile between Syene and Meroe when Nero 'was contemplating an Ethiopian War among others'.[41] Seneca, writing between early 62 and late 64, speaks of two centurions sent by Nero to explore the source of the Nile.[42] The purpose of this Ethiopian expedition cannot be recovered. It may well be a mere conjecture based on the assembly of troops in Alexandria and the search for the source of the Nile, which Seneca insists was undertaken out of a thirst for knowledge.

There is little criticism in the ancient sources of Nero's handling of foreign affairs, at least down to the events of his last years.[43] Tacitus gives us a picture of the Princeps making the decisions himself in consultation with advisers. He indicates that the first decisions taken at the end of 54, when the Parthians occupied Armenia, fulfilled the expectations of the optimistic: though the Princeps was too young to fight himself, they said, much could be achieved by sound plans and a good choice of commander, and Nero had in Burrus and Seneca experienced advisers; more could be expected than from the weak and elderly Claudius, who relied on his freedmen for counsel. In fact, troops were levied to fill up the eastern legions, which were ordered into positions near Armenia; the allied kings in the area were given instructions, and the talented general Domitius Corbulo was put in charge of the conflict. Then in 57 Nero is shown rewarding Frisian envoys with citizenship but firmly ordering them out of Roman territory, their defiance being met by prompt military action.[44] As late as 63, when the embassy from Vologaeses revealed the true scale of Paetus' disaster, Tacitus shows Nero acting rationally and sensibly: as in 54, he takes counsel with leading statesmen, decides on war, appoints Corbulo, and makes arrangements about reinforcements and the alerting of neighbouring territories. He deals with Paetus in a lofty manner, saying that he would pardon him at once in order to spare a man, so prone to fear, prolonged anxiety. This is the second good joke Nero is permitted in the extant part of the *Annals*, the first being a similarly justified hit at the freedman Pallas.[45]

Nero's judgement is impugned by Tacitus only in the case of the recall of Suetonius Paullinus. For him, the Emperor's reliance on the freedman Polyclitus exposed the Romans to ridicule and a successful general to public humiliation. Tacitus' irritation is no doubt increased by the fact that Suetonius' successor was among those who received military honours for helping to uncover a conspiracy – after failing to do anything of note in Britain.[46]

The Pursuit of Glory

In the ancient sources it is not Nero's policy or appointments, for the most part, that invite censure, but his perverse conception of glory. Not that the Emperor is alone in attracting Tacitus' contempt: rival generals behave in absurd and pompous fashion; the Senate votes copious honours for scant achievement, or devalues deserved ones by absurd additions.[47] But these are common Tacitean themes. What is characteristic of his Neronian narrative is the travesty of Roman conceptions of military glory. Thus Nero's entry to Rome after the murder of his mother in 59 resembles that of a *triumphator*: tiers of seats were erected for spectators and the 'proud conqueror of Rome's servility went to the Capitol to fulfil his vows'.[48] It is clear that the analogy is the historian's, not the Emperor's, for there is no hint that Nero used the dress or vehicle appropriate to a triumph. But in 65, after the Pisonian conspiracy, it clearly was the Emperor who invented a new use for military honours, giving triumphal insignia to two senators and the Praetorian Prefect, and lesser decorations to an imperial freedman. Even without mentioning the last, Tacitus expresses profound indignation at this session of the Senate convened by Nero 'as if he were about to relate deeds of war'.[49]

Tacitus' account of Nero's return from his Greek tour early in 68 is, unfortunately, missing. If the description given by Suetonius is at all accurate, it seems to have been conceived as the answer to a Roman triumph, Augustus' triumphal car being used in a procession modelled on that of panhellenic victors. Dio has a very similar account, no doubt from the same source. He also bears witness to a similar mixture of elements at the reception of Tiridates in 66, Nero presenting a complicated image: first the Roman Imperator surrounded by military standards, then the virtuoso lyre-player and charioteer.[50]

Though it is difficult to distinguish report from interpretation in the ancient writers, especially Tacitus and Dio, who are intrigued by the travesty theme,[51] it would not be surprising to find that Nero's response to the expectation of military success, inherent in his office, changed as his reign went on. Certain facts are revealing for his early attitude. Whereas Gaius and Claudius each felt impelled to take the field personally after two years in office, Nero seems to have resisted the temptation until 66, or possibly 64, if his abortive eastern visit was planned to include military operations. Then again, Nero only accumulated 12 or possibly 13 imperial salutations, while Claudius, who reigned for the same number of years, achieved a total of 27.[52] A glance at the occasions on which Nero took his salutations might reveal something of his changing attitude.

Nero was hailed as Imperator in the praetorian camp on his accession. He seems to have waited until late 55 or early 56 to take his second salutation in honour of the diplomatic victory over the Parthians when they gave hostages, for Tacitus reports that Nero then added laurel to his *fasces* 'in honour of the achievements of Quadratus and Corbulo'. It follows that Nero did not exploit the Senate's willingness to vote him the most extravagant personal honours a year earlier, when the Parthians had abandoned Armenia because of internal problems.[53] He waited for a more substantial token of their submission, and he expressly gave credit to his legates. It was in no way contrary to tradition to accept a salutation for a diplomatic success, especially one involving the eastern frontier, for Augustus had become Imp. IX for the return of the standards captured by the Parthians. Indeed it was important that war be represented as necessary and just: peace through intimidation could be represented as more admirable even when praising an Emperor in no way shy of fighting.[54]

By late 57 inscriptions proclaim Nero as Imp. III, probably for the action of Duvius Avitus in enforcing the Emperor's orders to the Frisii to vacate Roman territory over the Rhine.[55] In that year Nero despatched Q. Veranius to institute a more active policy in Britain, for with stalemate in the east, glory needed to be sought in a new area. But between late 57 and January of 59 Nero had acquired three more salutations, two for military successes in Armenia: one is plausibly traced to Corbulo's first successes against Tiridates, another belongs to the destruction of Artaxata, for which Tacitus explicitly records a salutation. The third probably celebrated the work of Duvius Avitus again, this time in breaking up a coalition of German tribes formed to occupy the same lands.[56] Armenia yielded another in 59, for the seventh salutation can most plausibly be assigned to

Corbulo's capture of Tigranocerta in the late summer of that year.[57]

Between July of 61 and late 62 Nero's count had risen to Imp. IX. The eighth occasion was probably furnished by the victories of Suetonius Paullinus in Britain, including the suppression of the revolt early in 61,[58] and the ninth[59] by the early successes of Caesennius Paetus in the autumn of 62.[60] In between these two salutes Nero had accepted the need for conciliation in Britain and decided on a more aggressive policy in Armenia.

An inscription from Armenia shows Nero still described as Imp. IX at the end of 64 or in 65.[61] The implication is clear: Corbulo's final diplomatic settlement with Tiridates at Rhandeia in the latter part of 63 was not marked in this way; the fact would certainly have been known in Armenia if anywhere. This has proved very difficult for scholars to accept, but it is not so hard to understand. Even if Caesennius Paetus' intimations of direct rule had gone beyond Nero's actual plans, it is clear that the end of his hopes for impressive results in Britain had made the Emperor eager to achieve something dramatic in the east.[62] But in the spring of 63 Nero reappointed Corbulo, to try again for the face-saving plan originally devised.[63] The ninth salutation was by then known to be based on the empty boasts of Paetus: it was legitimised by Corbulo's work, but the next salutation for Armenia would celebrate Nero's own crowning of Tiridates.[64] A year later Nero was issuing coins to celebrate the closing of the gates of Janus which would take place when the claimant reached Rome (fig. 21).[65]

Tiridates was in no hurry to abase himself, and the visit may have been postponed because of the Great Fire of July 64 and then again because of the Pisonian conspiracy and the death of Poppaea in 65.[66] Nero's notions of personal glory were maturing in the interval. Even before the Fire Nero may already have conceived his idea of a great military expedition to the east, though he postponed the venture after a supernatural warning in the temple of Vesta.[67] To be sure, an excerpt of Dio notes that Nero had intended to accompany the expedition against Tiridates in person when Corbulo was reappointed in 63, but that is plainly incompatible with the Emperor's insistence that Tiridates make obeisance to him in Rome, and there is no hint of such a plan in Tacitus.[68] There is no reason to put his dreams of a personal victory earlier than 64.

The new emphasis on personal glory was, however, first to be exhibited in a more shocking way. Between the end of 64 and mid-66, when Tiridates arrived in Rome, Nero acquired a tenth salutation.[69] It is too late to be a celebration of Corbulo's successful negotiations at Rhandeia,[70] and it is therefore presumed to mark the detection of the Pisonian conspiracy. Nero then proposed triumphal insignia and statues for his loyal bloodhounds, while the Senate responded with honours for the Emperor. This was certainly an innovation in the concept of military glory!

At last Tiridates reached Rome. His visit was marked by a salutation (clearly XI) and the depositing of a laurel wreath on the knees of Jupiter's statue on the Capitol.[71] Nero does not appear to have held a triumph, though he dressed up in triumphal garb. He now closed the gates of Janus, an event which continued to be celebrated on coins in 66–7. This is the only Neronian salutation mentioned by Suetonius after the one he took on his accession, and the special significance it was meant to have is shown by Nero's setting Imperator before his name now for the first time.[72] Suetonius, in showing that Claudius was restrained and unassuming in adding to his own dignity, adduces the fact that he did not assume Imperator as a *praenomen*.[73] Therefore we can assume that the assumption of this prefix by Nero and its retention ever after would not only single out this salutation from his earlier ones and assert the personal nature of his diplomatic victory over the Parthians.[74] The Emperor now departed on the Greek tour which was to culminate in his eastern expedition.

Nero's love of applause, his natural exhibitionism, and his sense of insecurity had all conspired to make him at last aspire to personal victories. His preparations and presence seem to attribute an importance to the expedition out of keeping with any rational conception of its purpose. No doubt his principal motive was to win glory in a region where his predecessors on the throne had not been conspicuously successful.[75] The Greek tour allowed him to escape from Rome. Surrounded by flatterers and freed from reminders of the Augustan tradition he could indulge in a different kind of glory. Yet he did not abandon thoughts of leading a Roman army into battle himself. It was the Vindex rising which finally made him recall the advance troops for the eastern expedition to Rome. Then, too, in the summer of 66 revolt broke out in Judaea, the fruit of Claudius' decision to renew the policy of Augustus' latter years and return the heartland of Judaism to direct Roman rule. A disastrous policy in itself, its effects had been aggravated by the appointment of some unsuitable procurators to govern it, the last being the notorious Gessius Florus.[76] The Jewish War remained a serious military commitment through 67 and would have necessitated the postponement of Nero's venture. Then followed his recall to Rome by Helius in the winter of 67–8, and the news of the Vindex rising which finally put an end to his plans.

Nero reverted once more to the idea of taking command when, probably after the news came that Galba was in revolt, he took over one of the consulships with the intention of defeating the rebels himself. In Suetonius he is portrayed as more concerned with composing victory hymns and disproving Vindex' taunt that he was a bad instrumentalist than with fighting.[77] It would help to gauge the value of this tradition about his state of mind if we knew the occasion for his twelfth salutation, assumed in 67 (and his thirteenth if it existed).[78] Did Nero dare to celebrate his victories in the Greek games in this way? It is more likely that it was a tribute to Vespasian's first successes in the Jewish War.

What does seem clear is that Nero came to find the burden of expected military glory as hard to bear as Gaius and Claudius had, and that he dealt with the problem in both orthdox and unorthodox ways. Despite the celebration of the Pisonian conspiracy and of his Greek victories in ways that suggested a disregard for traditional Roman values, he never had the confidence to defy that tradition entirely. Nero's growing anxiety about his standing shows in the increasingly grudging attitude he adopted towards the achievements of his legates.[79] Just as the uncertainty of his claim to the throne led Nero to persecute his rivals in pedigree, so the pressure to justify his ascendancy set him against those who achieved greatness in the field. For, as Tacitus says, 'Good generalship is the Emperor's virtue'.[80]

The historian aims this remark at Domitian and his growing fear of rivals. As we have already seen, with regard both to the succession and to the financial system Domitian's reaction to the pressures inherent in the Principate bears a strong resemblance to Nero's. Even his philhellenism and desire for literary pre-eminence find a parallel.[81] But Tacitus makes it clear that Domitian's chief anxiety was military glory. For, like Nero, he was relatively young and inexperienced in military matters. As Princeps he led expeditions himself, celebrated two triumphs and took a total of twenty-two imperial salutations, one more than Augustus. He also assumed the prefix Imperator and took to wearing triumphal dress in the Senate House.[82] Like Nero too, he took to putting provincial governors to death while in post and became grudging with military honours.[83]

Time and the strong-mindedness of Hadrian were eventually to bring about a change in the military image of the Princeps. Antoninus Pius was the first respectable Emperor whose prevailing image, in the literary sources at least, is that of a peace-loving prince who did not win military glory. Dio Chrysostom, in addressing Trajan, could already say that it is the task of an Emperor 'to marshal an army, pacify a district, found a city, bridge rivers', thus adding to the Roman picture the Greek conception of a monarch's task as advancing civilisation through the foundation of cities.[84] Under Pius, Aelius Aristeides could speak of law-making, tax-arrangements, and the founding of cities, as the central achievements of a ruler. Marcus Aurelius and Commodus could be hailed as 'Armenian victors, Sarmatian victors and, above all, philosophers'.[85] It is an irony of history that the necessity for constant warfare should fall on such an Emperor as Marcus. There was to be no opportunity for the concept of the Roman Emperor as a man of peace to prevail.

Nero had never achieved a satisfactory and consistent image as Princeps. By the end he knew that his failure in that role had been complete. The confidence that he craved had come to him only as an artist: of the insults that appeared in the edicts of Vindex, he disputed only the criticism of his lyre playing.

Sources for the Neronian Material in Tacitus *Annals*, Suetonius *Nero* and Cassius Dio

Tacitus is the only author to name his sources, all of which are lost. In fact, it is only in the Neronian books of the *Annals* (13–16) that he does name his major authorities, perhaps because these books were never put into final form (Syme, *Tacitus*, 291, n4). He mentions Cluvius Rufus (13.20; 14.2), the Elder Pliny (13.20; 15.53) and Fabius Rusticus (13.20; 14.2; 15.61), while his unique reference to his use of the *acta senatus* occurs at 15.74,3. He also mentions Corbulo's memoirs (15.16,1) and the testimony of those who survived the suppression of the Pisonian conspiracy (15.73). Suetonius and Dio claim to have used several sources but do not name them (Suet. *Nero* 34.4; Dio 61.12,1).

The many similarities in Tacitus, Suetonius and Dio are usually traced to the use of common sources, given that there are strong reasons for rejecting the alternative possibility of mutual dependence. First, the composition of Suetonius' biography, which was probably published either between 119 and 122, or in the late 120s, was too close in time to that of the *Annals* (113– after 117) for systematic direct use, though Tacitus may be the target (unnamed) of Suetonius *Nero* 52, where the biographer rejects, on the basis of personal examination of Nero's papers, the view about Nero's poetic plagiarism that appears in *Ann.* 14.16,1. Second, Dio is unlikely to have made serious use of Suetonius who fails to provide the chronological indications he needed for his annalistic account. Third, the passages in Dio that are parallel to parts of the *Annals* often contain details lacking in Tacitus (e.g. *Ann.* 13.4, cf. Dio 61.3,1; *Ann.* 14.15, 4–5, cf. Dio 61.20, 3–5; *Ann.* 14.32, cf. Dio 62.1,2).

Of the sources named by Tacitus, only the history of the Elder Pliny 'a fine Aufidii Bassi' (Pliny *Ep.* 3.5) is easily traced in both Suetonius and Dio. That is because these authors contain remarks about Claudius and Nero that closely resemble statements in the Elder Pliny's extant work, the *Natural Histories*, which was composed at much the same time as his History and adopted the same eulogistic tone to the reigning Flavian house, on the author's own confession (*NH* preface 20). The fullest collection of these parallels was made by A. Gercke in *Fleckeisen Jahrbucher* Supplement 22 (1896). Some examples are:

Suetonius	Pliny *NH*	Dio
Nero 11.1	8.21	
51	11.144	
27.2	31.40	
	33.63	60.33,3
	33.90	63.6,3
	33.140; 11.238	62.28
20.1	34.166	

Cluvius Rufus or Fabius Rusticus may be responsible for Dio's adoption of the version that held Agrippina alone responsible for the murder of M. Junius Silanus in 54 (61.6, 4–5), for we know that Pliny, at least in the *NH*, blamed Nero (*NH* 7.58). Otherwise there is no proof that Dio used Cluvius Rufus, despite the attempt of G. Townend to show it (*Hermes* 88 (1960), 98ff.; 89 (1961), 227ff., on which see my note in *Seneca*, 429, n2). The version of the Nero-Agrippina incest story, adopted by Suetonius (*Nero* 28.2), may derive from Fabius Rusticus (*Ann.* 14.2).

All three of Tacitus' main literary sources seem to have been hostile to Nero. Those historians who wrote favourably out of gratitude to Nero, according to Josephus (*AJ* 20.154) were clearly writing while he was alive, and may, in any case, have been Greek writers: *BJ* 4.9,2 shows that Josephus knew of Greek sources at least for the years 68/9, perhaps back to 62. Tacitus' sources were probably writing under the Flavians and supported the contemporary verdict on Nero. The hostility of the Elder Pliny is manifest in the *NH* (see p.15). Though Cluvius Rufus had been a courtier under Nero's régime (see p.247, n47), *Ann.* 14.2 shows only that his attitude to Nero was slightly less hostile than that of Fabius Rusticus. This is confirmed by the fact that he was still regarded as respectable after Nero's fall and when Tacitus was writing the Histories (*Hist.* 4.43; cf. Pliny *Ep.*9.19 which is best explained on the hypothesis that he criticized Verginius Rufus for not helping the rebel Vindex against Nero).

Apart from the remarks of Suetonius about Nero's poetry in the *Nero* 52, only Tacitus shows any scepticism of his sources. The *acta senatus* could have provided a check on the negative bias of the historians, as did the evidence of eye-witnesses (*Ann.* 15.73). Tacitus alone records the favourable tradition about certain alleged enormities: Nero's examination of his dead mother's body (*Ann.*14.9,1 cf. Suet. *Nero* 34.4; Dio 61.14,2); Nero's responsibility for the Great Fire (*Ann.* 15.38,1, cf. Suet. *Nero* 38; Dio 62.16). He was also on the alert for evidence of bias, as is shown by his remark about the partiality of Fabius Rusticus towards his patron Seneca (13.20,2). On the other hand, his principle of following the *consensus auctorum* where his authorities agreed (13.20,2) was clearly no defence against the predominantly hostile historical tradition, especially as there is no evidence that Tacitus consulted the favourable accounts mentioned by Josephus.

Tacitus did not adhere to his promise at 13.20,2 to give the views of his authorities under their names, where they diverged (discrepant versions are noted anonymously at 14.9,1; 15.38,1; 15.53,2; 16.3,2; 16.6,1; note also *Ann.* 16.17 where Tacitus ignores the whitewashing of Anicius Cerealis which is preserved by Dio 59.25,5b). As to how Tacitus decided which version to adopt, he gives only rare indications: rejection of the version showing favourable bias at 13.20; adoption of the version supported by tradition (*fama*) at 14.22. Probability based on consistency of character and on his general conception of human nature prompts rejection of the testimony of the Elder Pliny at 15.53.

The scholarly literature on the source question is immense. Of particular interest, aside from Gercke, and Syme, *Tacitus*, are:

K. Heinz, *Das Bild Kaiser Neros bei Seneca, Tacitus, Sueton u. Cassius Dio*, Diss. Bern, 1948

C. Questa, *Studi sulle fonti degli Annales di Tacito*, (Rome, 1963)

K.R. Bradley, *Suetonius' Life of Nero, An Historical Commentary*, (Brussels, 1978)

Nero's Later Coinage

In the discussion of Nero's later coinage I have been guided by the thorough treatment of D. W. MacDowall in his monograph 'The Western Coinages of Nero', *American Numismatic Society Notes and Monographs* no.161 (1979), but I have paid more attention to the indications in the text than to the schematic chronological charts on pages 134 and 152 which tend to show earlier dates for the initial issues. These discrepancies are attributable apparently to Macdowell's ultimate view, expressed in the charts, that each major issue can be assigned to one calendar year in accordance with the annual tenure of office by the *tresviri monetales* at the Roman mint (pp. 151–2). This is an odd assumption, given MacDowell's own view (p. 130) that the central government (Nero and his advisers) made the decisions for both mints on the very points that largely govern his own classification into issues.

For the gold and silver, after the first dated EX S C series ending with trib. pot. x (December 63–December 64), MacDowall distinguishes five separate issues, all undated and all struck at the reduced weight and, for the silver, at reduced fineness as well. Three of these (1a, 1b, 1c) belong before Nero's adoption of the praenomen Imperator in the course of 66, probably about mid-year (pp. 4–6), and are characterised by a very heavy production of aurei (p. 139), while 1b exhibits a marked expansion in the number of reverse types attributed by MacDowall to the redeployment of the *officinae* or workshops producing the general orichalcum coinage (pp. 34, 119). Given that the trib. pot. x issue was a full issue and that there is then a significant break in weight (and fineness for the silver), portraiture and style, it is implausible to put the undated gold and silver before 65, which allows $1\frac{1}{2}$ years for 1a, 1b and 1c (as on p.139, though the tables put 1a in 64).

The chronology of the token coinage is more complex. Here MacDowall distinguishes for the Roman mint six issues in all, four of them predating the introduction of the praenomen Imperator in mid-66, and establishes their relative chronology mainly by considerations of portraiture and weight. As a result, he labels as issue I the copper asses, semisses and quadrantes without S C; as issue II the general orichalcum coinage (excluding semisses) without S C; as issue III the general orichalcum coinage including semisses, whose coins show S C and marks of value on the dupondii, asses, semisses and quadrantes, while some of them also show a reduced weight. Issue IV reintroduced the traditional bimetallism of copper and orichalcum and maintained the reduced weight of the orichalcum sestertii and dupondii while introducing a lower weight for the copper asses. These weights are maintained in issues v and vi. The Lugdunum mint began to coin in parallel with the latter part of Roman issue iii, its earliest coins being all in orichalcum and showing s c and marks of value.

The absolute chronology of the later aes issues is determined by locating the few dated Roman sestertii within these issues: those with trib. pot. xi (December 64–65) come early in issue iv and those with trib. pot. xiii (December 66–December 67) belong to issue vi (p. 78). The earlier issues MacDowall tries to date by linking their production to that of the gold and silver. Issue iii – the full orichalcum coinage with the largest range of reverse types – must overlap, at its latter end, with ia, if the reduction in weights of the two sorts of coinage are to be related. It should precede ib when mint capacity was turned over to gold and silver. Its start can be connected with the dropping of one of the three reverse types during the earlier trib. pot. ix issue of dated gold and silver and continued in the trib. pot. x gold and silver (pp. 32, 117). Issues i and ii of the aes would earlier have required some conversion in mint capacity and so i is best linked with gold and silver marked trib. pot. ix (December 62–December 63) (pp. 72, 118–9), which also suits the portraiture (p. 42).

The following is a rough chart of these developments.

Nero's trib. pot.	Gold and Silver	Aes
ix (Dec. 62–Dec. 63)	Coins with EX s c dated TR.P.IX	Issue i: copper asses, semisses, quadrantes without s c
x (Dec. 63–Dec. 64)	Coins with EX s c dated TR.P.X	Issue ii: general orichalcum coinage without s c
Fire at Rome in July 64		Issue iii: general orichalcum coinage with marks of value and s c
xi (Dec. 64–Dec. 65)		
Early 65	Issue ia: reduced weight, EX s c omitted	Reduction of weights in orichalcum coinage Opening of branch mint at Lugdunum
Mid-65	Issue ib: reduced weight, EX s c omitted, more reverse types	
Later 65		Issue iv: bimetallic coinage with reduced weights
xii (Dec. 65–Dec. 66)	Issue ic: same but return to limited number of reverse types	
Mid-66	Issue 2: praenomen Imperator	Issue v: praenomen Imperator
xiii (Dec. 66–Dec. 67)		Issue vi
xiv (Dec. 67–Dec. 68)	Issue 3	Last issue
Death of Nero in June 68		

Notes and References

1 Introduction   *(pages 15–17)*
1 C. Merivale, *History of the Romans under the Empire*, vol 6 (London, 1858), 311
2 Tacitus, *Annals* 1.1,2; Josephus, *Antiquities of the Jews* 20.154
3 *Natural History* 7.45; 22.92
4 Nero is so classed with Caligula or Domitian or both by Herodian (I pref.3.4) and the *Historia Augusta* (e.g. *Marcus* 28.10; *Avidius Cassius* 8.4; *Commodus* 18). On the Quinquennium Neronis in Aurelius Victor and the *Epitome de Caesaribus*, see p.37 and p.84
5 *Sibylline Oracles* 4.119–24; 138–9; 5.137–521 362f. On the false Neros in the East, see pp.214–5
6 *Sibylline Oracles* 8.70f; 88–90; Tertullian *Apol.*5; Lactantius, *de mortibus persecutorum* 2; St. Augustine *Civitas Dei* 20.19; St. Jerome, *Dial.* 21.4; *Sacred History* 2.29. On the Nero Legend see B. Henderson, *Life and Principate of the Emperor Nero*, (London, 1903), 415f; B. Walter, *Nero* (Paris, 1955; English translation 1957), Appendices II–V
7 M. Praz, *The Romantic Agony* (Oxford, 1933), especially 208–9. Notable adherents of the cult of Nero were Flaubert, Gautier, and Lorrain
8 General Bertrand's report of a conversation with Napoleon on St. Helena, cited by Georges-Roux, *Néron* (Paris, 1962), 77. 'Le peuple aime Néron. Néron lui inspire attachement et respect. Il y a une cause à cela. Tacite ne la fait pas connaître. Qu'il opprime les grands et ne pèse jamais sur les petits, on entrevoit une raison de ce sentiment populaire. Mais Tacite n'en dit rien. Il parle de crimes. Il en parle avec passion. Dès lors, on le sent prévenu; il n'inspire plus la même confiance; on est porté a croire qu'il exagère; il n'explique rien, il semble ne chercher qu'à faire des tableaux'

2 The Making of a Princeps   *(pages 18–33)*
1 Suet. *Aug.* 28
2 *Res Gestae Divi Augusti* 34; Cassius Dio 53. 11–13
3 The fact that in 23 BC two ostentatious Republicans (Tacitus *Annals* 2. 43,2; Dio 53. 32) succeeded the conspirator Murena and himself in that office shows that Augustus' resignation of the consulship was primarily conciliatory
4 Tacitus *Ann.* 3.74
5 *ILS* 244, lines 16ff

6 For Augustus' dynastic arrangements, see pp.191–2

7 Suet. *Nero* 1–4

8 Tacitus *Ann.* 4. 44; Vell. Pat. 2. 72, 3 (also in Tacitus *Ann.* 6. 47); 2.102

9 As his mother, Antonia Maior, was born c. 39 BC, he could have been born in the penultimate decade of the first century BC and hence have been old enough to accompany Gaius Caesar to the East in 1 BC, but Suetonius (*Nero* 5. 1) is usually thought to have confused Gaius with Germanicus who went there in AD 17 (*PIR*² D 128), or this Domitius with an older brother, also to be identified with a child on the Ara Pacis frieze, who died young (R. Syme, *AJA* 88 (1984) 583f). For his interest in declamation see Elder Seneca, *Controv.* 9. 4, 18

10 Tacitus *Ann.* 6. 45; 47–8; Suet. *Nero* 5. 2 (where allegations of incest with sister Domitia Lepida are also mentioned)

11 The day is certified in the *Acts of the Arval Brothers* for 58 (Smallwood, *Documents illustrating the Principates of Gaius, Claudius and Nero* (Cambridge, 1967) no. 21). Each of the major sources contradicts himself on the year, but the most explicit statements point to 37 (Suet. *Nero* 6. 1, cf. 8 and 57. 1; Dio 63. 29, 3; cf. 61. 3, 1; Tacitus *Ann.* 13. 6, 2, cf. 12. 58). See P. Gallivan, *Historia*, 23 (1974), 300–1

12 Vell. Pat. 2. 10, 2, though cases of two sons in the same generation are known in the Republic, and see n 9 above for the possibility that Nero's father had an older brother

13 Caesar *BC* 1. 17, 3; Dio 41. 11. 1, on which see P. A. Brunt, *Latomus* 34 (1975), 619ff.; Quintilian 6. 1, 50

14 Suet. *Nero* 5. 2; Quintilian 6. 3, 74

15 Tacitus *Ann.* 13. 10; Suet. *Nero* 9. 'Pietas' was one of the virtues celebrated on the honorific shield presented to Augustus in 27 BC (*Res Gestae* 34. 2). The absence of celebrations for the birthday of his adoptive father Divus Claudius from the *Acts of the Arval Brothers* cannot be accorded significance as no sessions in the right month (August) are preserved

16 Tacitus *Ann.* 15. 23

17 Shaving of the beard: Dio 61. 19, 1; Suet. *Nero* 12; clean-shaven on the Greek tour of 66/7: Dio 63. 9, 1. The beard appears on gold and silver coinage of AD 64–8 (*BMC Imp.* Nero, nos. 52ff) and on *aes* (token) coinage of AD 64–6 (e.g. *BMC Imp* 1 Nero, nos. 122; 196–7) and AD 66/7 (e.g. *BMC Imp.* 1 Nero, no. 116; *RIC*², no. 354). Some apparently unbearded examples are *BMC Imp.* 1 Nero, (nos. 111; 135; 159; 120), though wear may sometimes account for its absence. The Worcester bust (fig. 3) which is dated to the period after 64 is clean-shaven (see U. Hiesinger, *AJA* 79 (1975), 119f). Cn. Domitius Ahenobarbus' *denarii* with bearded ancestor are dated to 41 BC by M. H. Crawford, *Roman Republican Coinage* (Cambridge, 1974), 527

18 Suet. *Nero* 41. 1; Lucan 2. 508–25; 7. 219–20; 7. 597–616

19 The Elder Pliny frequently calls him 'Domitius Nero' (*NH* 2. 92; 4. 10; 7. 45; 11. 238) and in the *Octavia* (see p.100) he is 'Nero insitivus, Domitio genitus patre' (line 248). Juvenal 8. 224–230. The discreditable version of Lucius Domitius Ahenobarbus' conduct at Corfinium is not found earlier than Pliny *NH* 7. 186; Plutarch *Caesar* 34 and Suetonius *Nero* 2

20 Strabo 5. 232 C; Cicero *Ad Att.* 4. 8, 1; Suet. *Nero* 6. 1; 9; Tacitus *Ann.* 14. 27; 15. 23; 15. 39. M.E. Blake, *Roman Construction in Italy from Tiberius through the Flavians* (Washington D.C., 1959), 40 surmises that the sumptuous villa was an enlargement of the house where Nero was born
21 Suet. *Gaius* 8; Dio 58. 25, 2; Suet. *Nero* 6. 2; Dio 61. 2, 3
22 Pliny *NH* 7. 46; Suet. *Nero* 6. 1; Tacitus *Ann.* 11. 11, 3; Pliny *NH* 7. 71. R. Syme (*Tacitus*, (Oxford, 1958) 277) suggests that Agrippina's threats to expose all the scandals of the dynasty noted by Tacitus at *Ann.* 13. 14, 3 (under the year 55) convey a hint of the family chronicle she went on to write
23 Tacitus *Ann.* 14. 9. The prediction is probably one of the 'dire prophecies' that were made soon after Nero's birth, according to Suetonius (*Nero* 6. 1)
24 Tacitus *Ann.* 3. 2
25 Tacitus *Ann.* 2. 84; 3. 31; 3. 56
26 Tacitus *Ann.* 4. 4
27 Tacitus *Ann.* 4. 8; 4. 17
28 He was depressed by Drusus' death and talked of retirement into private life (Tacitus *Ann.* 4. 9)
29 Tacitus *Ann.* 4. 53
30 Suet. *Gaius* 10; Josephus *Ant. Jud.* 18. 182; Tacitus *Ann.* 6. 3, 4
31 Tacitus *Ann.* 4. 59
32 Suet. *Tib.* 53
33 Dio 58. 8, 4; Tacitus *Ann.* 4. 60; 6. 24; 6. 25
34 Tacitus *Ann.* 6. 27; cf. 4. 12 'pudicitia impenetrabilis'
35 Elder Seneca *Controv.* 2. 4, 13; cf. Suet. *Gaius* 23. 1
36 Tacitus *Ann.* 4.75
37 Tacitus *Ann.* 6. 46
38 Suet. *Tib.* 76; Dio 59. 1; Philo *Legatio ad Gaium* 23; Tacitus *Ann.* 6. 46, 1
39 Tacitus *Ann.* 6. 46, 4
40 Dio 59. 3, 8
41 Dio 59. 3, 5; Suet. *Gaius* 14; *ILS* 180, 183
42 Dio 59. 3, 4; 9, 2; Suet. *Gaius* 15. 3; coins: *BMC Imp.* I, p.154, no. 44; the two extant inscribed oaths: *ILS* 190 from Lusitania, *IGRR* IV, 251, from Assos in the Troad do not give the form of words ('Gaius and his sisters') in Suetonius, but there was considerable regional variation: Suetonius could be right about Rome (cf. *AFA* for 12 (?) January 38 – Smallwood, *Documents*, no. 2
43 Dio 59. 22, 8, Tacitus *Ann.* 6. 48, 2
44 Dio 59. 22, 5–9; Smallwood, *Documents*, no. 9
45 *Ann.* 14. 2, 2, cf. 4. 12
46 Dio 59. 23, 7. The date is suggested by J.P.V.D. Balsdon, *The Emperor Gaius* (Oxford, 1934), 48
47 Smallwood, *Documents*, nos. 9–10; Suet. *Nero* 5
48 Suet. *Nero* 6. 3
49 Dio 60. 4, 1
50 The discrepancy between Tacitus' birth date for Britannicus of 41 (*Ann.* 13. 15, 1) and Suetonius' of 42 (*Claudius* 27. 2) is resolved in favour of Tacitus by an Alexandrian coin (Smallwood, *Documents*, no. 98a); Dio 60. 4, 1; 60. 27, 4

51 Suet. *Galba* 5. 2 says that he never received the bequest, but Plut. *Galba* 3 remarks on his wealth, while Claudius' grant of *ornamenta triumphalia* to him and divinisation of Livia are suggestive

52 Suet. *Nero* 6. 3; cf. Dio 60. 34, 4; 62. 14, 3; Seneca *Ben.* 2. 27, 1

53 Schol. Iuv. 4. 81. The date of his death is not known, but the rumour is best explained on the assumption that he died around 48. The absence of an obituary notice in the surviving Claudian books of Tacitus' *Annals* suggests that he actually died before late 47 (Syme, *Tacitus*, 328, n12)

54 Dio 60. 8, 6

55 Dio 60. 31, 6; Seneca *Cons. Polyb.* 13. 2; Tacitus *Ann.* 12. 8, 2, where Tacitus' description of Seneca as 'loyal to Agrippina because he remembered her kindness, hostile to Claudius because he resented the injury to himself' points to a favour done him by Agrippina in the past, like the injury

56 Suet. *Nero* 6. 4; Tacitus *Ann.* 11. 11–2

57 If Messallina's half-brother Faustus Sulla Felix, born to her mother by her second marriage, reached his consulship in AD 52 at the minimum age of 32, Messallina will have been born before AD 20. Moreover, her father is not recorded as *consul ordinarius* which, given his lineage and connections with the imperial house, is best explained by early death, and as his father died in 12 BC, he must then have been dead by AD 21 and Messallina therefore born c. AD 20. Tacitus is then exaggerating when he says that her mother was close in age to Agrippina, who was born in AD 15 (*Ann.* 12. 64, 3): they were at least a decade apart

58 Suet. *Claudius* 27

59 Tacitus *Ann.* 11. 5: Silius disapproved of the power of accusers like Suillius Rufus during Claudius' reign; 11. 12

60 Tacitus *Ann.* 11. 26

61 Tacitus *Ann.* 11. 28–38

62 Tacitus *Ann.* 12. 4; Suet. *Claudius* 29; *Ann.* 12. 9

63 Tacitus *Ann.* 12. 25; *ILS* 224; *BMC Imp.* 1 Nero, nos. 84, 90. Suetonius *Nero* 7. 1 erroneously gives his age as ten: he was in fact twelve

64 Suet. *Nero* 7. 2; Tacitus *Ann.* 12. 41. See below, p.223

65 M. Grant, *Nero* (London, 1970), 30; Smallwood, *Documents*, no. 105a

66 Dio 60. 33, 2

67 Tacitus *Ann.* 12. 4; 12. 1; 12. 67

68 Tacitus *Ann.* 12. 41–2

69 Heisinger, *AJA* 79 (1975), 115f

70 Suet. *Nero* 51

71 Suet. *Nero* 51, cf. 1.2 where the biographer remarks that a large number of the descendants of Ahenobarbus had the characteristic beard

72 See p.73 on the protection Nero gave to the procurator Celer

73 Tacitus *Ann.* 13. 19, 4; 21, 3; Suet. *Nero* 23. 5

74 Suet. *Nero* 34. 5; Dio 61. 17, 1: Nero inherited her estates at Baiae and Ravenna

75 On Tacitus *Ann.* 12. 64 see n57. For the granaries on her estates near Pompeii that earned her profits from the storage of grain in transit, see *AE* 1978 no. 139; see p.103

76 Tacitus *Ann.* 12. 65, 1; Suet. *Nero* 7. 1

77 Suet. *Claudius* 32; cf. Tacitus *Ann.* 13. 16, 1

78 Suet. *Otho* 2. 2; cf. Tacitus *Ann.* 13. 12, 1

79 Tacitus *Ann.* 12. 41, 3; Suet. *Nero* 7, 1, who differs from Tacitus in making Britannicus call him 'Ahenobarbus', attributing the mistake to habit and making Nero himself complain to Claudius. Cf. Dio 60. 32, 5 who agrees with Tacitus in making Agrippina responsible for having Britannicus' tutors changed. Nero's later attitude to his name (p.22) favours Tacitus' account

80 Tacitus *Ann.* 12. 26, 1; 11. 38; 12. 53; Suet. *Claudius* 28

81 Tacitus *Ann.* 6. 20, 1; Seneca *Ben.* 1. 15, 5

82 Josephus *Ant. Jud.* 20. 183; Tacitus *Ann.* 14. 3, 3; Suet. *Nero* 35. 2

83 Tacitus *Ann.* 12. 8; Suet. *Nero* 52. For the date when Seneca's instruction began, see Griffin, *Seneca* (Oxford, 1976), Appendix C1

84 Tacitus *Ann.* 12. 41 (see above, n79); cf. 13. 15, 4

85 Suet. *de Rhetoribus* 1. 6–7; *Nero* 7, 2

86 Suet. *Nero* 7, 2; Tacitus *Ann.* 12. 58 (whose date for these requests is here preferred). *CIL* XI. 720 may be connected with the consequent reconstruction of a bath in Bononia

87 Suet. *Nero* 7, 2; Tacitus *Ann.* 6. 11, 1 stresses the role of Prefects in taking over consular duties

88 Tacitus *Ann.* 12. 69 (Nero preferred to Britannicus); Dio 61. 1, 2 (the will was in favour of Britannicus and Nero); Suet. *Claudius* 44

89 Tacitus *Ann.* 12. 65–7; Suet. *Claudius* 43–4; Seneca *Apoc.* 2. 2

90 Tacitus *Ann.* 12. 69; Suet. *Claudius* 45

91 Tacitus *Ann.* 12. 69; 13. 2–3. The date from which Nero reckoned his *tribunicia potestas* is problematical. For Gaius and Claudius, the reckoning appears to start from the *dies imperii* which, for Nero, was 13 October, 54, when the Arval Brothers sacrificed *ob imperium Neronis Claudii Caesaris Augusti Germanici*. But the Acts of the Arval Brothers also record during Nero's reign, and for the first time, sacrifices *ob tribuniciam potestatem*, presumably celebrating the formal *comitia tribuniciae potestatis* at which the popular assembly ratified the Senate's conferment. These sacrifices, preserved for AD 57 and 58, were carried out on 4 December. There is no conclusive evidence to show whether Nero reckoned his *tribunicia potestas* from 13 October or 4 December (though *ILS* 8794, which appears to show trib. pot. XIII in November of 67, favours the December date). If Nero did count his *tribunicia potestas* from 4 December 54 (as I assume throughout), he was stressing the importance of the purely formal *comitia*, as part of the attention to form he showed in the early reign. The problem is discussed by M. Hammond in *MAAR* 15 (1938), 36–52; T.B. Mitford in *ABSA* 42 (1947), 219f. Hammond also successfully disposes of Mommsen's idea that Nero changed the method of his reckoning to 10 December from trib. pot. VII, on which see also Griffin, *Scripta Classica Israelica* 3 (1976/7) 138–9, briefly summarizing the evidence of new inscriptions

3 The New Ruler *(pages 37–49)*

1 Aurelius Victor *Liber de Caesaribus* 5.2–4: Qui cum longe adolescens dominatum parem annis vitrico gessisset, quinquennium tamen tantus fuit, augenda urbe maxime, uti merito Traianus saepius testaretur procul differre cunctos principes Neronis quinquennio; quo etiam Pontum in ius provinciae Polemonis permissu redegit, cuius gratia Polemoniacus Pontus appellatur, itemque Cottias Alpes Cottio rege mortuo. Quare satis compertum est neque aevum impedimento virtuti esse; eam facile mutari corrupto per licentiam ingenio, omissamque adolescentiae quasi legem perniciosius repeti. Namque eo dedecore reliquum vitae egit, uti pigeat pudeatque memorare huiuscemodi quempiam, nedum rectorem gentium fuisse. *Epitome de Caesaribus* 5, 2–5: Iste quinquennio tolerabilis visus. Unde quidam prodidere Traianum solitum dicere procul distare cunctos principes Neronis quinquennio. Hic in urbe amphitheatrum et lavacra construxit. Pontum in ius provinciae Polemonis reguli permissu redegit, a quo Polemoniacus Pontus appellatur, itemque Cottiae Alpes Cottio rege mortuo. Eo namque dedecore reliquum vitae egit, ut pudeat memorare huiuscemodi quemquam.

The anecdote is generally held to have been found by these authors in their common source (known as 'Enman's *Kaisergeschichte*') who took it from a biography of Trajan written by Marius Maximus, a contemporary of Cassius Dio. For further discussion of the problems in the tradition of the Quinquennium, see p.84

2 Calpurnius Siculus 1. 42 f; cf. Seneca *Apocolocyntosis* 4. 1, vv 8–32; *Carmina Einsidlensia* 2. 22 f. On Calpurnius Siculus see pp.64, 147f. The contrast he draws between Nero's peaceful accession and the civil wars in which the Principate was born becomes in Seneca's *De Clementia* 1. 11 a reason for rating Nero above Augustus, an idea that may lie behind the praise of the Quinquennium Neronis attributed to Trajan

3 Suet. *Nero* 9, cf. Tacitus *Ann.* 13. 3; 13. 4; 13. 10

4 The restrictions on the public sale of food are dated by Dio 62. 14, 2 to 62; the persecution of the Christians belongs to 64 (*Ann.* 14. 44); Agrippina died in 59; Seneca partially retired and Burrus died in 62. Note also that when Suetonius wishes to indicate Claudius' control by his minions he is quite explicit (*Claudius* 25. 5; 29. 1)

5 Dio 61. 7, 1

6 Dio 61. 3, 3–4, also reported by Tacitus *Ann.* 13. 5, 2; the Claudian episodes are in *Ann.* 12. 37; 56

7 Dio 61. 4; see p.248, n7

8 *Ann.* 13. 1; Dio 60. 34, 4–5 and 61. 6, 4 for the same version: Pliny *NH* 7. 58 blames Nero for the death of Silanus (see p.254, n32). According to Dio 62. 3, 2 Agrippina also sent letters to kings and governors in the early days

9 *Ann.* 13. 2, 3; 13. 5, 1; Dio 61. 3, 2, cf. Suet. *Nero* 9; *BMC, Imp.* 1, 200, no. 1; *Ann.* 13. 6, 2; *BMC, Imp.* 1, 201, no. 7

10 *Ann.* 13. 3–4. Tacitus does not explicitly note Seneca's authorship of the accession speech, as does Dio 61. 3, 1, but he implies it, as the account of the speech follows directly on his general remarks about Nero's use of Seneca's eloquence

11 *Ann.* 13. 5, 1. The comparison with Livia is made explicitly in *Ann.* 12. 69, 3. See also the similarity of 12. 68, 3 to 1. 5, 4

12 *Ann.* 13. 14

13 See pp.59ff. *Ann.* 13. 2; 13. 13–14; 13. 6–8; 13. 11. For Tacitus' portrayal of Nero's control of foreign policy, see pp.229–30

14 See Appendix 1

15 Suet. *Nero* 10. 2; *ILS* 8794. For the literary quality of the address to the Greeks, see M. Holleaux, *BCH* 12 (1888), 523–5; H. Bardon, *Les empereurs et les lettres latines d'Auguste à Hadrien*[2] (Paris, 1968), 213

16 Tacitus *Ann.* 16. 6, 2; Suet. *Nero* 47

17 Tacitus *Ann.* 13. 3; 14. 14

18 Cicero *Rep.* 4. 10; *de Oratore* 3. 87; Seneca *Ep.* 88; Quintilian 1. 10

19 *Apocolocyntosis* 4

20 Suet. *Nero* 20; Dio 63. 1

21 Tacitus *Ann.* 14. 16, 2. The names of two philosophers who taught him, Alexander Aegaeus and Chaeremon, are preserved by the *Suda* s.v. Alexandros

22 Suet. *Nero* 10. 2; 53; 54

23 Horace *Epistle* 2. 1, vv 156f; Plutarch *Quaestiones Romanae* no. 40 (274 D); Cornelius Nepos *Vitae*, pref. 1. 1

24 Titus and Britannicus were skilled in music (Suet. *Titus* 2.1; 3.2; *Nero* 33.2; Tacitus *Ann.* 13.15)

25 Sallust *Catiline* 25. 2; Pliny *NH* 19. 108; 28. 237

26 Nepos *Vitae*, pref. 5; Suet. *Gaius* 54; Dio 59. 29

27 L. Friedländer, *Roman Life and Manners* (English translation of the seventh edition), vol II, 17f; 48

28 Suet. *Aug.* 43. 3; Dio 54. 2, 5; 56. 25, 7–8; 57. 14; Suet. *Tib.* 35. 2; Dio 60. 7. The renewal by Tiberius noted in Suet. *Tib.* 35. 2, which is dated to AD 19 by Tacitus *Ann.* 2. 85, 1, is now better known from the inscribed text of a senatorial decree (M. Malavolta, *Sesta Miscellanea Greca e Romana* (Rome, 1978), 347f and now Levick, *JRS* 73 (1983), 97f)

29 Pliny *NH* 21. 7

30 Seneca *NQ* 8. 32; Juvenal 8. 197; Gaius *Institutes* 1. 13 (on the Lex Aelia Sentia of AD 4). Yet gladiatorial contests between free youths seem to have been included among the games of the Roman *iuventus*

31 Tacitus *Ann.* 14. 14

32 Suet. *Nero* 12; Dio 61. 19, 1; Tacitus *Ann.* 14. 15

33 Suet. *Nero* 40. 2; Dio 63. 27; Suet. *Nero* 49. 1. For *artifex* as an instrumentalist, Seneca *Ben.* 4. 21, 3; *Ep.* 87. 14. In Suetonius it always means 'artist', but is not confined to musicians (*Nero* 20. 1: 'generis eius artifices'; *Divus Julius* 84. 2; *Vesp.* 18) and see K.R. Bradley, *Suetonius' Life of Nero, An Historical Commentary* (Brussels, 1978), 122; 277

34 Suet. *Nero* 22

35 Tacitus *Ann.* 14. 14–5, cf. 14. 21; Dio 61. 17; Suet. *Nero* 11. 1. Both Tacitus and Dio place these events just before the Juvenalia in 59. Dio connects the games with Agrippina, recently murdered, but he also mentions, as one episode, an elephant ride which sounds like the one connected with the Ludi Maximi by Suetonius (*Nero* 11. 2). Yet these games seem to belong in spring or summer of 57, if 'maximis' is correctly restored after 'ludis' in the inscription recording the career of Q. Veranius (Smallwood, *Documents* no. 231c, see p.113), and the alternative proposal of Bradley, *GRBS* 3 (1975), 308 seems ruled out by the fact that 'Augusto principe' here cannot be Claudius who is given his full name several times in the inscription. Dio 61. 9 appears to place participation by *equites* in the arena in 57 when Nero's amphitheatre was built (*Nero* 12. 1, cf. Tacitus *Ann*. 13. 31)

36 Suet. *Nero* 11. 1 speaks of only one gladiatorial show, dated apparently to 57 (12. 1, see note above). Tacitus *Ann*. 15. 32, 3 reports a gladiatorial show with participants of the senatorial order in 63 (cf. Dio 62. 15, 1, dated to 64) and Dio notes games he gave in 66 at Puteoli (63. 3). The charge by Philostratus *Life of Apollonius of Tyana* 4. 36 that Nero fought as a gladiator has no support in any of the historical sources, hostile as they are

37 Dio 61, 19, 3

38 *Ann*. 14. 14, 1

39 Suet. *Nero* 12, 3–4, cf. *Aug*. 44. 3: Augustus strictly excluded all women from gymnastic spectacles

40 Tacitus *Ann*. 14. 21, 4

41 Tacitus *Ann*. 14. 20, 4; Lucan *Bellum Civile* 7. 270–2

42 Seneca *Epp*. 15. 2; 88. 18; Pliny *NH* 15. 19; 35. 168; *ILS* 212, col. 2.15

43 Dio 61. 17, 1

44 Tacitus *Ann*. 14. 47; Dio 61. 21, 2 says that the gymnasium was built and used for the Neronia in 60; Suet. *Nero* 12. 3 associates the dedication of the baths and gymnasium with the Neronia. It is possible that Tacitus' date refers to the dedication of the whole complex, the gymnasium alone being finished by the Neronia. It is clear from *Ann*. 14. 20, 4 that members of the upper orders were not expected to take part in athletic contests at festivals. Tacitus is disappointingly silent on public reaction to the destruction of the gymnasium in 62 by a bolt of lightning which melted Nero's statue within (see p.263, n66)

45 For the importance of the games see below, chapter 7. Aside from military and foreign policy it could be claimed that the Emperor was primarily expected to ensure justice, continue those essential services, such as the corn supply, for which the Roman government had traditionally been responsible, and to maintain tactful relations with the governing class, generosity and responsiveness to all subjects. The importance of the last aspect and the large extent to which ordinances of the Emperor were initiated from below form the thesis of F. Millar's *The Emperor and the Roman World* (London, 1977)

46 Seneca *Clem*. 2. 2, 1; cf. Tacitus *Ann*. 3. 55, 4

47 Dio 63. 20, 2–3. The senior consular Cluvius Rufus, who announced Nero's later performances, published a work on actors (*histriones*), see p.277, n81

48 Suet. *Nero* 53

49 Calpurnius Siculus 4. 157f; 1. 59–62; 4. 117–121

50 See pp.96f; *Apoc*. 4. 1, vv, 22–3

51 *Ann*. 13. 45–6, which gives the second version, is usually thought to contain Tacitus' final thoughts on the Otho – Nero – Poppaea triangle, whereas *Hist*. 1. 13, 3 agrees more with Suet. *Otho* 3, Plut. *Galba* 19 and Dio 61. 11, 2

52 Plut. *Galba* 20, 1; Suet. *Otho* 3, 2

53 Josephus *AJ* 20. 183. The context is the recall of Antonius Felix, a notorious chronological riddle involving the chronology of Paul's life, as revealed in the *Acts of the Apostles*

54 Suet. *Nero* 35, 2; Tacitus *Ann.* 14. 3, 3
55 Tacitus *Ann.* 14. 62; Suet. *Nero* 42. 2; 50; Tacitus *Ann.* 13. 10, 1
56 Tacitus *Ann.* 13. 15; *CIL* x. 7952; Tacitus *Ann.* 13. 30, 1
57 Tacitus *Ann.* 13. 2, 1; Seneca *De Ira* 2. 21, 3 (the work dates from the reign of Claudius, before AD 52)
58 The date, as indicated in 1. 9, is Nero's nineteenth year, i.e. between 15 December 55 and 14 December 56
59 Seneca *De Clementia* 1. 1; 1. 3, 2–3; Pliny *Pan.* 4. 1. Note that Tacitus, in *Ann.* 13. 11, 1, attributes to the Neronian Senate the aim of encouraging good behaviour in major matters by praising profusely for minor ones
60 *Clem.* 1. 1, 5; 1. 11, 3; 1. 1, 6; 1. 9
61 Ibid. 1. 1, 6–7; 2. 2, 2; 1. 8, 6–1. 13
62 Tacitus *Ann.* 13. 11, 2, *Clem.* 2. 5, 2
63 Tacitus *Ann.* 13. 50; *ILS* 8794, lines 10f; see pp.199–200
64 One of the arguments advanced against Nero's proposal is that 'abolition of the indirect taxes would be followed by demands to abolish direct taxation also'
65 Tacitus *Ann.* 13. 34; Seneca *Ben.* 2. 7–8
66 Tacitus *Ann.* 14. 48–9
67 Tacitus *Ann.* 13. 10, 2. The role of the consuls in deciding to accept cases brought before the Senate can be seen in *Ann.* 1. 73, 3 and 3. 10, 1. For the implicit repudiation of such *maiestas* charges in Nero's opening speech to the Senate, see pp.52–3
68 *Ann.* 15. 35, 3; cf. the similar conduct of Tiberius in *Ann.* 2. 31, 3

4 **The Golden Age**   *(pages 50–66)*

1 Dio 61. 4, 2
2 *Ann.* 13. 4–5
3 *Nero* 10; 7. 1; 35. 5; 52
4 E.g. *Ann.* 13. 31, 3; 15. 20–2, but compare 13. 33; 13. 43; 13. 52
5 Gaius 2. 255; *Digest* 36. 1, 1. Bradley, *Historical Commentary* 107–8 is justly sceptical of the arguments of A. Honoré, *Tijdschrift voor Rechtsgeschiednis* 30 (1962), 473f who sees strong Senecan influence behind this decree and another, cited by Gaius 2. 197, also on legacies
6 *Ann.* 13. 42, cf. *Ann.* 13. 5
7 Dio 52. 19–41, on which see Millar, *A Study of Cassius Dio,* 107f. Anachronistic thinking may also lie behind Dio's implausible conception of Nero as entirely passive in government, which resembles closely his first-hand account of the behaviour of Commodus, an idle playboy whose advisers did the work (72. 9, 1; 72. 10, 2). In portraying Nero in this way Dio could have been influenced by the view currrent in his day that Commodus was a second Nero (*SHA Commodus* 19. 2: Commodus likened to Nero by the Senate, according to Marius Maximus; Herodian 1. 3, 4)
8 *Ann.* 13. 4. The mention of Augustus as a precedent is made explicit by Suetonius *Nero* 10
9 Josephus *Ant. Iud.* 19. 246; Dio 59. 6, 1; 7; Dio 59. 3, 8; Tacitus *Ann.* 12. 11
10 Dio 61. 3, 1

11 *Ann.* 13. 5, 1

12 Dio 60. 4, 4; Suet. *Claudius* 12. 2; Tacitus *Ann.* 11. 5–7. See p.60 and n60

13 Calp. Sic. 1, vv. 69–73

14 *Ann.* 14. 28 (see n47); *Ann.* 13. 48; *Ann.* 14. 17, on which see p.56

15 *Ann.* 14. 62, 4 (trial of Anicetus in 62); 15. 58, 3; 15. 61, 2. That these later proceedings, involving suspected members of the Pisonian conspiracy of 65, were trials and not police investigations, as has been suggested, is shown by 15. 69, 1 where 'non crimine, non accusatore existente, quia species iudicis induere non poterat' is clearly meant to point a contrast with the preceding account

16 Suet. *Nero* 15. 1. This procedure is later attested under Trajan, when its efficacy in revealing the truth is noted by Pliny (*Ep.* 6. 22, 2)

17 Suet. *Nero* 15. 1; cf. Seneca *Clem.* 1. 15, 4; Suet. *Aug.* 33. 1

18 This last is the reason given for recommending the practice in the speech of Maecenas to Augustus in Dio 52. 33, 4. The first is suggested by Suetonius' previous statement that Nero only gave a decision on the following day and in writing, thus 'non temere'

19 Dio 55. 33, 5; cf. Suet. *Aug.* 33. 1

20 Tacitus *Ann.* 11, 1–3; Dio 60. 29, 4–6. The trial of Cassius Chaerea, Gaius' chief assassin, took place in the palace (Jos. *AJ* 19. 268), but this was during the upheavals attending Claudius' accession, and members of the Senate may be among the ἑταῖροι who were asked for their verdict

21 Suet. *Claudius* 37; Dio 60. 14, 3–4. Cf. Tacitus *Ann.* 11. 29, 1 'Appianae caedis molitor Narcissus'

22 *Ann.* 13. 43: Lusius Saturninus and Cornelius Lupus. Some of the *amici* named in *Apoc.* 13. 5, may have been dealt with in a similar way

23 Tacitus *Ann.* 13. 10 on which see p.248, n67; Seneca *Ben.* 3. 26, 1

24 Dio 59. 4, 3 (Gaius); 60. 3, 6 where it is stated that Claudius' promise was kept. But *Ann.* 12. 42 shows that the charge was a possibility in 51 and earlier the trial of Valerius Asiaticus involved a treason charge, no matter what it was called. In 42 Claudius was faced with real treason in the form of armed revolt: those brought to trial must have been charged with *maiestas*. The cases of Appius Silanus in 41 and of Pomponius Secundus, driven to join the rebellion in 42 by Suillius' accusations (*Ann.* 13. 43), suggest that political charges, even of the nebulous sort, started to be countenanced right away, under whatever name

25 *Apoc.* 6. 2; 15. 2; Juvenal 14. 329–31

26 *Ann.* 13. 43, cf. Seneca *NQ* 4, pref. 15

27 *Ann.* 12. 1; 13.14, 1; Dio 60. 19, 2; Suet. *Vesp.* 4; *Ann.* 12. 53

28 A. Momigliano, *Claudius: the Emperor and his Achievement*² (Cambridge, 1961), chapter 3, has been the most influential. Cf. also A. Garzetti, *From Tiberius to the Antonines* (1960; Eng. trans. 1974), 587

29 Polybius, the *a studiis*, and for a time *a libellis*, was killed in 48 (Dio 60. 31, 2); Callistus, his successor as *a libellis*, in 52 (Dio 60. 33, 3a); Narcissus – *Ann.* 13. 1; Dio 60. 34, 4–6; Pallas – *Ann.* 13. 23

30 Tacitus *Ann.* 14. 65; Dio 61. 5, 4; Josephus *AJ* 20. 183–4

31 Tacitus *Ann.* 13. 21; 14. 3. Suet. *Nero* 35. 2 (see p.46)

32 *Ann.* 14. 39: Pliny *Ep.* 6. 31. 9 attests the influence of Polyclitus with Nero. Epaphroditus: *ILS* 9505, discussed by W. Eck in *Historia* 25 (1976), 381f; Epictetus 1. 1, 20; 1. 26, 11–12; and see p.166

33 Dio 64. 3, 4: his mention of Narcissus may be an error, if the famous Narcissus is meant, for he died in 54; Plut. *Galba* 17. According to Tacitus *Hist.* 1. 49 Galba's head was later exhibited before Patrobius' tomb

34 *Hist.* 1. 76, 3

35 For the limited significance of the division of the provinces in general, see Millar, *JRS* 56 (1966)

36 Tacitus *Ann.* 13. 31; on 13. 50, 1, see pp.47-8. Cf. *Ann.* 14. 18, on which see Griffin, *Seneca*, 114

37 Tacitus *Ann.* 13. 48, on which see J. D'Arms, 'Tacitus *Annals* 13. 48 and a new inscription from Puteoli', *The Ancient Historian and His Materials*, 155. The conferment of colonial status by Nero two years later may be the occasion of the games in honour of Nero mentioned on the inscription. But D'Arms' suggestion that the honour marked a change from senatorial to imperial control seems unwarranted. The problem is that, as is shown by S. Panciera, *Atti dei convegni Lincei* 33 (1977), 194f, Puteoli already had colonial status and had indeed enjoyed the title Colonia Iulia Augusta from the time when Augustus sent new colonists there. Tacitus implies, at *Ann.* 14. 27, that no new colonists were sent in 60 and that the new status was meant to help the town out of difficulties. Panciera suggests that some internal reorganisation of the town's constitution was involved

38 Tacitus *Ann.* 14. 17, where it is stated that the Emperor referred the case to the Senate. See *CIL* 4. 2183; 1329 for Pompeian inscriptions expressing the hostility of the two towns

39 Tacitus *Ann.* 13. 49; *IG* 5. 1. 1449. On these see Millar, *Emperor and the Roman World*, 347, n38; 388

40 *Hist.* 4. 45; *Ann.* 3. 60, 1-2

41 *Ann.* 13. 30, 1; 14. 28. The venue is not explicitly stated but the context is senatorial; it is possible that P. Celer the procurator of Asia was also tried (*Ann.* 13. 33) before the Senate (see Griffin, *Seneca*, 111-2). *Dialogus* 7. 1

42 Tacitus *Ann.* 13. 29; Dio 53. 2, 1; 53. 32, 2

43 *ILS* 966-7; Tacitus *Ann.* 13. 29; Dio 60. 10, 3; 60. 24, 1

44 *Ann.* 13. 28-9. Nero is sometimes also held responsible for the change, with regard to the praetorian *praefecti* who managed the *aerarium militare*, from the Augustan method of selection by lot to direct selection attested by the early third century. Dio 55. 25, 2-3 says merely that the old arrangement endured 'for many years'

45 Tacitus *Ann.* 13. 23, 2

46 Suet. *Nero* 17 who gives no date, but the change might have been prompted by the misbehaviour of Obultronius Sabinus which precipitated the change to *praefecti* (Tacitus *Ann.* 13. 28)

47 Suet. *Nero* 17, who, however, may just be oversimplifying the development reported by Tacitus *Ann.* 14. 28 under the year 60, whereby caution money was now required for appeals to the Senate. Alternatively, the provision in Suetonius might have increased the number of appeals to the Senate and made necessary the discouragement of frivolous appeals through the measure in Tacitus

48 *BMC Imp.* 1, Nero, nos. 1-51

49 For a clear discussion of the problem see C.H.V. Sutherland, *The Emperor and the Coinage: Julio-Claudian Studies* (London, 1976), 11f; cf. *RIC* I², 135, 149 (4-5)

50 Sutherland, *Emperor and Coinage*, 21–2, explains the difficulty by combining his explanation about metal control with that of Konrad Kraft about types (see note below)

51 K. Kraft, *Jahrbuch für Numismatik und Geldgeschichte* 12 (1962), 7f = *Wege der Forschung* 128 (1969), 336f with additions (402–3). For an attempt to disprove Kraft's theory and return to Mommsen's dyarchy interpretation see A. Burnett, *NC* 17 (1977), 37f

52 Kraft (n51) thought the EX S C, going clearly with the type at first, was retained on the Neronian coins with allegorical figures as a fossil, but the time involved (six years) seems too short for fossilization

53 Tacitus *Ann.* 14. 28; Suetonius *Nero* 15. 2

54 *Ann.* 15. 73, 2

55 *Dialogus* 41. 4

56 Tacitus *Ann.* 1. 12; cf. the abdication of senatorial initiative at *Ann.* 2. 35

57 Tacitus *Ann.* 11. 5–7; 13. 5, 1. Suet. *Nero* 17 may record a subsequent modification (see B.H. Warmington, *Suetonius: Nero* (Bristol, 1977) *ad loc*). The Claudian rule seems to be in force in Pliny *Ep.* 5. 9

58 Tacitus *Ann.* 11. 22, 2–3. Suet. *Claudius* 24. 2 has the games given by the quaestors when already in office

59 Tacitus *Ann.* 11. 5; 14. 11, 1; see p.38

60 The Lex Cincia was a *lex imperfecta*, that is without sanction. According to Dio 54. 18, 2 Augustus in 17 BC tried to attach a penalty to the operation of the law. The renewal, as originally proposed in 47, subsumed charges of violation of the law of extortion (*Ann.* 11. 6, 3) and this may have been the technical charge brought against Suillius in 58, when it was decided to drop the question of his conduct as proconsul of Asia and concentrate on his *urbana crimina* (*Ann.* 13. 43, 1). Suillius' outburst against Seneca preceded his trial (Griffin, *Seneca*, 74–5)

61 Vacca *Life of Lucan*, but the Vacca *Life* is probably no earlier than the fifth century AD and may be inaccurate in regarding Lucan's practice as customary. For the date of his quaestorship see pp.157–8

62 Suet. *Aug.* 29; Tacitus *Ann.* 2. 37

63 Tacitus *Ann.* 13. 5; see p.38

64 Pliny *Pan.* 44. 6; cf. 45. 1; *Meditations* 1. 16, 6

65 Tacitus *Ann.* 13. 8. See pp.226f

66 *PIR²* A 776

67 Tacitus on Tiberius' practice at *Ann.* 4. 6, 2; Pliny *Pan.* 58. 3; 69. 4, *Ben.* 4. 30–1

68 Suet. *Nero* 14; 43. 2. Of the first four consulships, I was in 55 and ran for the first two months, as Suetonius says; II was in 57 and ran, not for six months as he claims, but for the whole year, as is known from *CIL* 4. 3340 (34, 36–40); III was in 58 and probably ran, as Suetonius says, for four months; IV was in 60 and probably did last for six months, as in Suetonius, for Nero was still in office in May (*CIL* 4. 3340 (144)). On his fifth consulship in 68 see below, p.286, n92

69 Suet. *Nero* 15. 2; P.A. Gallivan, *CQ* 24 (1974), 290f

70 Tacitus *Ann.* 13. 11

71 Suet. *Nero* 15. 2

72 Tacitus *Ann.* 13. 41, 4

73 Suet. *Nero* 8: coins show that the title *pater patriae* was accepted between late 55 and late 56; Tacitus *Ann.* 13. 10

74 On the significance of the adjective *civilis* and the emergence of the noun *civilitas* in the second century see A. Wallace-Hadrill, *JRS* 72 (1982), 42–4

75 Suet. *Nero* 10

76 Suet. *Nero* 10. 1; Tacitus *Ann.* 13. 31, 2. Coins record a second *congiarium* (*BMC, Imp.* I, pp. 225–6; 261) which cannot be dated. See p.293, n62

77 *Ann.* 12. 69, 2; Dio 61. 14, 3; Suet. *Nero* 10. 1. There was also another *donativum* to the Guard after the exposure of the conspiracy (*Ann.* 15. 72). See p.204

78 See p.48 and p.204

79 Suet. *Nero* 10. 1; Tacitus *Ann.* 13. 31; 13. 51, see pp.47–8 and p.56

80 Suet *Nero* 10. 1; Tacitus *Ann.* 3. 25; 28. See Millar, *JRS* 53 (1963), 34–6. The *fiscus* had begun to share the profits with the *aerarium* in some way by Domitian's time (Pliny *Pan.* 42. 1)

81 Calp. Sic. 4. 117–21. According to Juvenal 4. 54–6, Domitian had finders prosecuted on the ground that the treasure was originally imperial property. Eventually fiscal claims were common (*Digest* 14. 1, pref.). See Millar, *JRS* 53 (1963), 36 and D.C. Braund *Greece & Rome* 30 (1983), 65f who points out the implied contrast with Claudius but thinks the allusion more general: 'Calpurnius' point is that, under Claudius, men had feared the discovery of treasure, because that would bring about their execution by the cruel emperor who wanted their new-found wealth'

82 Amphitheatre: Tacitus *Ann.* 13. 31, 1; the market: Dio 61. 19, 1; the baths: see p.44

83 B.M. Levick, *Tiberius the Politician* (London, 1976), 87–8. Compare the similar senatorial manoeuvre under Gaius (Dio 59. 16, 10)

84 Josephus *AJ* 19. 246; Seneca *Apoc.* 14. 1; cf. 10. 4; 12. 3, vv 19f; Suet. *Nero* 33. 1

85 Calp. Sic. 1. 59f

86 Tacitus *Ann.* 13. 11, 2; 14. 11–2

87 Seneca *Clem.* 2. 3: the final definition of *clementia* as 'quae flectit citra id quod merito constitui posset'. Tacitus *Hist.* 1. 77, 3 implies that Otho and others held that convictions for *maiestas* under Claudius and Nero were not disgraceful, i.e. evidence of criminality, in the sense that convictions for extortion were

88 Tacitus *Ann.* 13. 11, 2; 13. 43, 5

89 *Ann.* 14. 40, 3; 13. 33, 1; 13. 52: Pompeius Silvanus had been governor of Africa in 53–6, an exceptional term now revealed by *AE* 1968, no.549. This long term will have necessitated the collection of a great deal of evidence, which may explain why his trial came up at the same time as that of Sulpicius Camerinus, who was probably proconsul in 56/7. Tacitus does not comment on the guilt of Camerinus, who was also acquitted, perhaps softened by the knowledge that he later fell victim to the odious accuser Aquillius Regulus in 67 (Dio 63. 18. 2; Pliny *Ep.* 1. 5, 3)

90 Jos. *AJ* 20. 182: for the date of 56 for this episode see Griffin, *Seneca*, Appendix D5

91 Tacitus *Ann.* 13. 33, 2; 14. 48, 1

92 Pliny *Ep.* 9. 13, 21; *Pan.* 70; cf. the speech of Thrasea Paetus in Tacitus *Ann.* 15. 20, 3–21. See *Seneca*, 147–8 (but see n89 on Pompeius Silvanus)

93 *Ann.* 13. 43; *Agricola* 6.2

94 Suet. *Nero* 10. 2; Seneca *Clem.* 2. 1, cf. *Gaius* 29. Compare the mean Nero chose between cruelty and pity in the case of the slaves of the murdered Pedanius Secundus in 68: see p.80

95 Suet. *Nero* 10. 2; *Aug.* 53. 3

5 Partners in Power   *(pages 67–82)*

1 *ILS* 1321

2 Tacitus *Ann.* 1. 7, 5; 4. 2, 2; 12. 69, 1

3 *RE* 22. 2 (1954) 2391f; Millar *ERW*, 61–3; 122f. See p.204

4 Gaius may originally have replaced Macro with one (Dio 59. 11, 2) but there were eventually two (Dio 59. 25, 8; Suet. *Gaius* 56. 1): perhaps he appointed a second to accompany him when he marched north in September of 39. Seneca, *Apoc.* 13. 5; Dio 60. 18

5 Tacitus *Ann.* 11. 1, 3 (Crispinus active in prosecution of Valerius Asiaticus); 33 (Geta not trusted in crisis of Messallina's marriage to Silius); 12. 42

6 *Ann.* 12. 41, 2

7 *Ann.* 12. 42

8 At *Ann.* 16. 17 Tacitus notes that he possessed these, but he does not record their conferment; *Ann.* 12. 69

9 *Ann.* 13. 14, 3; 13. 18

10 *Ann.* 14. 7, 4; 13. 15, 3; 15. 67, 2; Faenius Rufus: *Ann.* 13. 22; 14. 51, 2; 57; 15. 50, 3. Tacitus also indicates his popularity with the people.

11 See p.75

12 *Ann.* 12. 42; 13. 14, 3: on the problems and different interpretations of 'egregiae militaris famae', see Griffin, *Seneca*, 82, n5.

13 *Ann.* 14. 51. Seneca recounts Scipio's last words in *Ep.* 24, 9

14 *Acts* 18. 17

15 *Ann.* 16. 17; Elder Seneca, *Controversiae* II, pref. 4

16 Illness: Seneca, *Ep.* 78, 1–4; Dio 59. 19; Pliny *NH* 31. 62; Novatus' disposition: Seneca, *NQ* IV, pref. 10f

17 Seneca, *Ep.* 108. 22f

18 *PIR²* G 25; Seneca, *Cons. Helv.* 19. 2, 6. Seneca cannot have held the praetorship before his exile in 41, as he received it on his recall (*Ann.* 12. 8, 2)

19 Suet. *Gaius* 52; Seneca *Ep.* 49. 2; Dio 59. 19, 7–8. See pp.26–7

20 See p.28 and p.243, n55

21 Seneca, *NQ* 6. 4, 2

22 It attacks Gaius and is addressed to Seneca's brother Novatus. It thus belongs between 41 and 52, by which date his brother had taken the adoptive name Gallio (as *SIG³* 801D shows) which Seneca thereafter used. A statistical study of the figures of speech and variety of vocabulary used in the three books supports the old hypothesis that I and II are considerably earlier than III which could belong c. 50 (A. Nikolova-Bourova, *Eirene* 13 (1975), 87f)

23 Suet. *Nero* 52; Seneca *Cons. Polyb.* 18. 9; cf. Ovid *Tristian* v. 7, 57–8; *Ex Ponto* IV.2, 15f

24 Seneca, *Cons. Helv.* e.g. 8. 2; *Cons. Polyb.* 13. 3

25 *SIG³* 801D

26 Tacitus *Ann.* 13. 6, 2; 14. 52, 4; 15. 62, 2

27 *Ann.* 14. 7, 4; 14. 15; Dio 62. 13

28 See p.47. Plut. *Mor* 461F–462A; Seneca, *Ben.* 6. 32, 2–4

29 Tacitus *Ann.* 14. 2

30 *Ann.* 13. 13

31 *Ann.* 13. 2, 2

32 See above p.39; p.65. Although the Emperor condoned the deed later, no doubt is thereby thrown on this version, for, by that time, there had been a quarrel and reconciliation during which Agrippina recited her criminal services to her son (*Ann.* 13. 14, 3; 21, 5)

33 Seneca and Burrus must be, or be among, the *seniores amici* mentioned in *Ann.* 13. 12, 2; 13, 3

34 *Ann.* 13. 12–14

35 *Ann.* 13. 15–17; Dio 61. 7, 4; Suet. *Nero* 33. 3; Josephus *BJ* 2. 250; *AJ* 20. 153. Note also the omission of this crime from the list at *Ann.* 15. 67, 2. Tacitus hints at Seneca's knowledge by making him name Britannicus' murder among Nero's crimes, in his death scene (*Ann.* 15. 62, 2)

36 *Ann.* 13. 18; 17, 1

37 *Ann.* 13. 18–23; Suet. *Nero* 34. 1

38 *Ann.* 13. 20; 13. 21, 1

39 *Ann.* 13. 23. Tacitus reports the presence of Burrus as *iudex* at his own trial, which must be a distortion. Perhaps he served on Nero's *consilium* during Pallas' trial, or when the accuser was tried later for *calumnia*

40 *Ann.* 13. 42, 3; Dio 61. 10, 1. See pp.97–8

41 *Ann.* 13. 25; Suet. *Nero* 26

42 Suet. *Nero* 34. 2; Tacitus *Ann.* 14. 1, 3; 13, 2; Dio 61. 11–12. Tacitus and Dio make much of Poppaea's role in driving Nero to murder; the argument commonly used against this, viz. that it was three years before Nero actually married Poppaea is not unanswerable (see pp.98–9). Dio alone suggests the instigation of Seneca and Burrus

43 Tacitus *Ann.* 14. 3–8; Suet. *Nero* 34; Dio 61. 12, 2–13

44 Tacitus *Ann.* 14. 10; Dio 61. 14, 3 indicates that the enthusiasm of the Praetorians was kindled by a donative

45 *Ann.* 14. 11; Quintilian 8. 5, 18 states Senecan authorship as a fact

46 *Ann.* 14. 13, but it is a difficulty that Tacitus refers to Nero's comforters, who wished to be sent ahead to Rome, as *deterrimus quisque*. The ground had clearly already been prepared, perhaps by some senators

47 *Ann.* 14. 53–6. For Tacitus' familiarity with Seneca's works, apparent in this dialogue, see *Seneca*, 442

48 *Ann.* 12. 5–7; 9

49 *Ann.* 13. 3; Dio 61. 3, 1; *Ann.* 13. 11, 2

50 *Ann.* 14. 8

51 *Clem.* 1. 1, 8; 1. 4, 2–3

52 *Clem.* 1. 1, 4. See p.95

53 *Ann.* 13. 6–7 and see p.61

54 See above, p.45–6. Only Plutarch *Galba* 20. 1 records Seneca's role in the appointment. As Suetonius (*Otho* 3. 2) confirms Tacitus' date of 58 for the appointment by noting that Otho was governor ten years before 68, it seems reasonable to reject his report (*Otho* 3. 1; Suet. *Nero* 34. 2) that Otho played host to Nero and his mother before her murder in 59, as a colourful but inaccurate tradition

55 *SEG* 19. 384; see p.209

56 The elder Paullinus' post is attested in Seneca's *De Brevitate Vitae* 18–9, written after mid-48 and before mid-55. See *JRS* 52 (1962), 104f. The younger Paullinus was legate of Lower Germany in 55 (*Ann.* 13. 53), hence already suffect consul. He was young enough to be an active member of the Senate in 62 (*Ann.* 15. 18, 3) and so may only have reached the consulship after his sister married Seneca following his return from exile in 49 (see *Seneca*, 57–9). But an earlier date, some time in the 40s, cannot be ruled out. Eck, *ZPE* 42 (1981) now proposes him for the colleague of M. Junius Silanus in *CIL* 14. 3471 (only 'A.' survives of his name), because a document from Ephesus now shows that Paullinus' praenomen was Aulus

57 Tacitus *Ann.* 16. 17. In 37 or thereabouts, Mela was still devoting himself to philosophy and rhetoric (Elder Seneca, *Controv.* II, pref. 3.). In *Cons. Helv.* 18. 2, a work Seneca wrote from exile, Mela is described as still enjoying *otium*

58 His colleague was T. Cutius Ciltus (see *Seneca*, 73, n6)

59 See pp.157–8

60 See n56; Tacitus *Ann.* 13. 22

61 *Ann.* 13. 53; Pliny *NH* 33. 143

62 Duvius Avitus: see Syme *Tacitus*, 591; Annaeus Serenus: Pliny *NH* 22. 96; see *Seneca* Appendix D 3, and on his predecessor Laelianus, Dio 61. 6. 6 (with Boissevain's note) and *Seneca*, 86, n3

63 Seneca *Epp.* 49. 1; 53, 1; 70, 1; *NQ* 4, pref. 1, 3. On his career see H.G. Pflaum, *Carrières procuratoriennes* vol I, no. 30, 70; III, 961–2

64 Tacitus *Ann.* 14. 48, 2; Seneca *Ep.* 99 (dramatic date late summer or autumn 64; publication date perhaps late 64); see *Seneca*, 92; 400. See p.93

65 Pliny *NH* 14. 51 (see p.81); Juvenal 8. 212

66 *Ann.* 14. 52; 15. 45

67 See pp.50–1; 93–4; Tacitus *Ann.* 13. 26, 2

68 The whole theme is argued in detail in *Seneca*, e.g. p.11. Games by provincial governors: *Ann.* 13. 31, 3; 15. 22; *Seneca*, 247–9. Gladiatorial games: Suet. *Nero* 12. 1 (with Warmington *ad loc*). Slaves and freedmen: Paulus *Sent.* 3. 5, 5; *Digest* 29. 5. 3, 17 = *Ann.* 13. 52 (as suggested in *Seneca*, 271, n6); *Ann.* 14. 42–5. (See *Seneca*, 280–1; Appendix E3)

69 *Ann.* 13. 36–7, on which see *Seneca* 281–4

70 *Ann.* 13. 50; see pp.47–8; p.92

71 Dio 61. 7, 5; 61. 10, 6; 61. 12, 1

72 *Ann.* 14. 53–6

73 See pp.27, 31; pp.103–4 and *Seneca*, Appendix D3: T.K. Roper, *Hist.* 28 (1979), 346f doubts my suggestion there that the conviction of Cossutianus Capito in 57 would not have taken place had Tigellinus already been *praefectus vigilum*. Her idea that Tigellinus owed that post to Seneca's influence runs counter to the ancient evidence: for Nero's patronage early in his reign, see pp.45–6

74 *Ann.* 14. 51

75 *Ann.* 14. 56, 3

76 *Ann.* 15. 45; Dio 62. 25, 3 attests his surrender of money at this point, confirmed indirectly by Tacitus at *Ann.* 15. 64, 4

77 Pliny *NH* 14. 51; for date see *Seneca*, 289, n4

78 *Epp.* 49. 1; 57; 62; 77; *Ann.* 15. 33–4. The possible allusions to official duties occur in *Epp.* 62, 72 and 106 (see *Seneca*, 358–9)

79 Nomentum (*Epp.* 10. 4, 110); Alba (123). He travelled to Campania in spring of 65, according to Tacitus *Ann.* 15. 60

80 Lucilius: Seneca *Ep.* 79; 19. 8; Paullinus: *Ann.* 15. 18, 3; Mela: *Ann.* 16. 17, 3 implies that he remained a procurator until his death. For other possible cases, see *Seneca*, 93–4

6 The Turning Point   *(pages 83–99)*

1 Suet. *Nero* 26. 1, cf. Tac. *Ann.* 13. 25; *Nero* 10. 1, cf. *Ann.* 15. 72, 1

2 Suet. *Nero* 38; 16, 2

3 Scholars are divided on the question of whether there is implicit criticism, in e.g. *Nero* 11. 1: participation of upper classes in games; 13. 2: closing of temple of Janus 'as if no war remained anywhere'; perhaps 10. 2: honours for poetry recitations

4 *Ann.* 14. 51, 1; 52, 1; 56, 3; 57, 1. The two *maiestas* trials, the death of Burrus, and the withdrawal of Seneca, are all dated to the early part of the year by the fact that Octavia's death which followed them is dated to the same day as Nero's death, viz. 9 June (Suet. *Nero* 57)

5 *Ann.* 13. 2 where Tacitus follows the account of Silanus' murder with the words 'A succession of murders would have followed had Seneca and Burrus not prevented them'

6 Dio 61. 4–5 (general survey of his character); 61. 7, 5; 61. 11, 1

7 Boissevain chose this point: grammarians' citations from Dio show that the break falls between 51 and 59 (after the murder)

8 For the text of these passages, see pp.244–5, n1. Pontus was annexed in 64; Jerome's date of 65 for the annexation of the Cottian Alps is plausible, given Nero's concern with another part of the Alpine region around this time (Tacitus *Ann.* 15. 32: Latin rights granted to the Maritime Alps in 63): see p.228. Of the buildings mentioned by the Epitome, the amphitheatre was completed in 57, the baths in 60 or 61 (see p.44); Victor's phrase 'augenda urbe' may not refer to the embellishment of the city by buildings but to an extension of the sacred boundary of the city (the *pomerium*), carried out to mark the two extensions of the Roman Empire (Syme, *Antiquitas* 4: *Beiträge zur Historia-Augusta-Forschung* 13 (1978), 217f)

9 *Ann.* 13. 20, on which see p.78

10 Tacitus has Acratus sent to collect treasures for the Domus Aurea at *Ann.* 15. 45 (64), but compare 16. 23 where his exactions are tied to the proconsulship of Barea Soranus, who must have held that office before 63, as the list of governors is full after that. The year 61/2 fits his consulship of 52 nicely. Bradley, *Commentary on Life of Nero* suggests collections for the earlier palace, the Domus Transitoria (p.172)

11 The consul of 61 had the full name L. Junius Caesennius Paetus, as is now known from *AE* 1973, 141f, see Syme, *JRS* 67 (1977), 38f. His adoption by a Junius before his consulship may have improved his social status. The *consules ordinarii* for 62 were P. Marius and L. Afinius Gallus

12 See p.247, n44. Though Suetonius (*Nero* 12. 3, cf. 19. 3) puts the item among the blameless acts, Tacitus is unambiguously hostile to Nero's Hellenisation programme

13 Tacitus *Ann.* 15. 35

14 *Ann.* 14. 65, cf. 15. 52, 1 and Syme *Tacitus*, 745

15 Suet. *Gaius* 6; Dio 57. 7, 1; 57. 19, cf. Suet. *Tib.* 39 where the deaths of both sons play a part and *Tib.* 41–2 marking Tiberius' retreat to Capri in 27 as a further point of decline

16 *Clem.* 1. 1, 6. But it is not the case that Seneca and Tacitus would have been unfamiliar with the idea of character-change (C. Gill, *CQ* N.S. 33 [1983], 469f)

17 See pp.54–5

18 Note Tacitus *Ann.* 15. 54, 4 implying that a freedman would be particularly prone to perfidy, and his surprise at 15. 57, 2 that a *libertina* should show more loyalty than *ingenui*. Note too the sentiment 'ex-slaves are slaves at heart' ascribed to Germanicus at 2. 12, 2

19 *Ad Q.F.* 1. 1, 17–8

20 *Germania* 25

21 Millar, *ERW*, 70. Tac. *Ann.* 15. 35, though only the title *a manu* is actually attested for the Republic (Suet. *DJ* 74): see Millar *ERW*, 73. For an analogous charge, cf. Dio 63. 18, where Sulpicius Camerinus is punished for *retaining* his ancestral cognomen Pythicus after Nero's victory at the Pythian games

22 Suet. *Aug.* 67; 72. 2; Tac. *Ann.* 4. 6, 4

23 *Ann.* 13. 14, 1

24 It was Augustus' personal correspondence, *epistulae amicorum*, which the Emperor had been writing in his own hand, for which he wished to have the assistance of Horace (Suet. *Horace*, 19f)

25 Statius *Silvae* 3. 5, on which see P.R. Weaver, *Familia Caesaris* (1972), 284f

26 See Millar, *ERW*, 89f. Weaver, 'Social Mobility in the Early Empire', *Past and Present* 37 (1967) = *Studies in Ancient Society*, ed. M.I. Finley, 121f discusses the evidence in terms of 'status dissonance'

27 Pliny *Pan.* 88. 1–2

28 See p.55. Note Tac. *Ann.* 14. 65 noting the opposition of Doryphorus, Nero's *a libellis*, to the marriage with Poppaea, in the old Claudian tradition. (Suet. *Nero* 29 names Doryphorus as one of Nero's sexual partners, which might suggest jealousy as a motive, but the name here seems to be a mistake for Pythagoras as in Dio 62. 28, 3; 63. 13, 2 and Tac. *Ann.* 15. 37, 4)

29 *Ann.* 14.39; see pp.118, 226

30 Suet. *Nero* 37. 3

31 Penalties: Dio 54. 18 (17 BC); 60. 11, 8 (AD 42); not enforced: Suet. *Galba* 3; Tac. *Ann.* 16. 22. Compulsory meetings: Dio 55. 3; quorum: Dio 54. 35 (11 BC); 55. 3, 1–2 (9BC); 55. 26, 2 (AD 6); Suet. *Aug.* 35

32 Tac. *Ann.* 16. 27

33 Suet. *Aug.* 35. 4

34 Dio 53. 21, 4; Suet. *Aug.* 35. 3

35 The purpose is well described by J. Crook, *Consilium Principis* (1955), 9–10

36 Dio 56. 28, 2–3; Suet. *Tib.* 55

37 *BGU* 611 (Smallwood, *Docs.* no. 367), col. III, 11. 10f. For the antiquity of the formula, see E. Fraenkel, *Kleine Beiträge zur klassischen Philologie*, II, 477–8

38 *Ann.* 15. 53, 1 suggests that he did not attend often by 65 (see p.140), but he is shown there after that at 15. 72–3, perhaps also 16. 4, 2; 16.11, 16. 31, 2

39 Pronouncements: *Ann.* 13. 10; 13. 11. Intervention: 13. 33, 1; 13. 43; 13. 52; 14. 40, 3; 14. 45

40 *Ann.* 13. 50; see pp.47–8

41 The surrounding chapters (13. 48–9 and 13. 52) are senatorial trials. Sometimes Tacitus seems to put trials together at the end of the year, as in 13. 30, 13. 33, but possibly as the last item of senatorial material

42 Tac. *Ann.* 3. 22; 1. 8, 4

43 *Ann.* 12. 9, cf. 12. 5

44 *Ann.* 12. 53; Pliny *NH* 35. 201; Pliny *Epp.* 7. 29; 8. 6

45 *Ann.* 14. 48–9. See pp.48–9

46 See p.79

47 Tacitus says some voted as they did to avoid exposing the Emperor to reproach, most feeling that there was safety in numbers

48 *Ann.* 3. 52

49 *Ann.* 13. 26–7

50 *Ann.* 2. 38; 13. 49

51 *Ann.* 13. 28, 2; 15. 22, cf. for consular refusal, 3. 34.

52 Tacitus speaks of it as common in the past (*Ann.* 2. 33)

53 Pliny *Ep.* 6. 19, 3. Under Claudius, in the two cases noted on pp.92, consuls designate may already have been using the privilege to say what the Emperor wished

54 Tac. *Ann.* 2. 35; 3. 51

55 *ILS* 244, clause 2

56 Tac. *Hist.* 4. 9; *Dial.* 41. 4

57 Syme, *Tacitus*, 223–5

58 *Clem.* 1. 17, 2–3; 1. 8, 1

59 *BC* 7. 444–5

60 *Clem.* 1. 4, 3

61 Tac. *Ann.* 1. 12, 3; Pliny *Ep.* 3. 20, 12. See chapter 4, for the senatorial acceptance of autocracy

62 Dio 61. 10, 2

63 Tac. *Ann.* 13. 2, 6

64 See p.244, n88

65 Tac. *Ann.* 13. 3, 1; Dio 60. 35, 2–4; Suet. *Nero* 33; Pliny *Pan.* 11. 1

66 Allusions to the Saturnalia: *Apoc.* 8. 2; 12. 2; Britannicus' song: *Ann.* 13. 15

67 For some views of this kind see the review by M. Coffey, *Lustrum* 6 (1966), 261–2; K. Kraft, *Historia* 15 (1966), 96f; B. Baldwin, *Phoenix* 8 (1964), 39f

68 Suet. *Vesp.* 9, 1

69 *Apoc.* 10. 3–4; 5. 4–6. 1

70 *CIL* 3. 346 (AD 58); *ILS* 233 (66–7); in SIG ³808, 810 and *IG* 5. 1. 1449–50. Tiberius is named before Germanicus, and Nero is described by the elastic Greek term *ekgonos* in relation to both. Nero traces his descent from Augustus via his maternal grandfather, without mentioning his mother, as Roman tradition required (cf. Tacitus *Ann.* 1. 14 where Tiberius refuses a sycophantic senatorial proposal, designed to honour his mother Livia, that he be called 'Iuliae filius')

71 Appius Silanus at *Apoc.* 11. 5, cf. Dio 60. 14; Suet. *Claud.* 37. 2; Catonius Justus at *Apoc.* 13. 5, cf. Dio 60. 18

72 *Apoc.* 11. 5; 13. 5
73 See Griffin *Seneca*, 132–3; 217, n1
74 Pliny *Ep.* 5. 3, 5; Tacitus *Ann.* 14. 52, 3. Some still doubt Senecan authorship though all the manuscripts attest it and Dio 60. 35, 3 credits Seneca with a work ridiculing the deification of Claudius
75 See pp.60, 251, n60
76 Evidence in Griffin *Seneca*, 98–9
77 *BMC Imp.* 1, pp.clxxii–iii, 200–1
78 Smallwood *Docs.* nos. 21, 22; *ILS* 228; 233 (year 66)
79 Suet. *Vesp.* 9; *Claud.* 45; Mart. *Spect.* 2; see M. Charlesworth, *JRS* 27 (1937) 57f
80 Edict of Tiberius Julius Alexander issued in July of 68 (*IGRR* 1. 1263, paragraph 4); *Acts of the Arval Brothers* for January and March 69 (Woodhead and McCrum no. 2). In conferring powers on Vespasian at the end of 69, the Senate omitted the *divus*, perhaps following its own inclination, perhaps waiting to know Vespasian's mind: *ILS* 244, on which see Brunt *JRS* 67 (1977), 105
81 T.P. Wiseman in *JRS* 72 (1982), 57f suggests that the first Eclogue of Calpurnius Siculus 'reveals a conception of Claudius' reign as usurpation' that was current at Nero's accession, but the evidence for Nero's filiation and for his attitude to Claudius at the start of his reign shows that this was not the official view of the government. Moreover, *Ann.* 6. 46 reveals that, in the view of Tacitus, Tiberius did not regard Claudius as being outside Augustus' family, while Josephus *AJ* 19. 217–220 shows that this was also not the view of the praetorians who urged him to 'seize the throne of his ancestors' in 41. It is not the 'modern phrase Julio-Claudian dynasty', but Wiseman's conception of a Julian dynasty to which Claudius did not belong, that is anachronistic, for there was no law of succession and all relatives of Augustus and of successive Principes had some claim (see pp.189f). See p.148 on the Eclogue
82 Tacitus *Ann.* 13. 23; Dio 60, 6a; see p.75
83 The child was named Rufrius Crispinus after his father: Suet. *Nero* 35. 5; Tacitus *Ann.* 13. 45; 15. 71, 4
84 *Ann.* 14. 1; Dio 61. 12
85 *Ann.* 14. 57–60, especially 59. 3–4; 13. 47; 14. 22
86 *Ann.* 14. 61, 4, cf. *Octavia* vv. 89; 188; 591. The child was born by 21 January, 63 according to *Acts of the Arval Brothers* (Smallwood *Docs.* no. 24); *Ann.* 15. 23. Poppaea probably conceived by the end of April and her pregnancy will have been known, at least to Nero, for some weeks before the death of Octavia on 9 June 62. Note the child was named *Claudia*!
87 *Ann.* 14. 64. She was actually born before Britannicus, whose birthdate was 12 February of AD 41 (see above, p.242, n50). Therefore, she was born in the early part of 40 at the latest, and her age in 62 was at least 22. See p.112

7 The Descent into Tyranny   *(pages 100–118)*

1 The play is not in the earliest manuscript of the tragedies, the Codex Etruscus of the eleventh century. The death of Nero is predicted at lines

620–31; that of Poppaea's first husband Rufrius Crispinus (who died in 66 as we know from Tacitus *Ann.* 16. 17) at line 733; perhaps that of Poppaea (who died in 65 after Seneca's death in that year, *Ann.* 16. 6) at lines 595–7

2 *Ann.* 13. 3; cf. Quintilian 10. 1, 125f. T.D. Barnes, *Museum Helveticum* 39 (1982), 215f. suggests the reign of Galba, as does P. Kragelund, *Prophecy, Populism and Propaganda in the 'Octavia'* (Copenhagen, 1982), but the sympathy for Claudius (except at 137–142) and his children might suggest the reign of Vespasian

3 On this see C.J. Herington, *CQ* N.S. 11 (1961), 18f, (and now more briefly in *Cambridge History of Classical Literature* II (1982), 34–6), who deals convincingly with the problem of authenticity

4 *Ann.* 15. 61

5 Poppaea: *Ann.* 14. 1 and Dio 61. 12; *Ann.* 14. 60–2 and Dio 62. 13, 1, 4. Tigellinus: *Ann.* 14. 57; 16. 18; 16. 20; Dio 62. 13, 3–4; 62. 28, 4 (murders); *Ann.* 15. 37; Dio 62. 15; 63. 13 (debauchery). At 63. 12, 3 Dio speaks of Tigellinus as 'a mere appendage of Nero' on the Greek tour but he means that, as the Prefect constantly accompanied Nero, his crimes were not separable from the Emperor's, as were those of Polyclitus (at Rome) and Calvia Crispinilla (in Greece)

6 Tacitus *Ann.* 13. 33; 14. 48, 1; 16. 20

7 Plutarch *Galba* 17. 4; Juvenal 1. 155

8 Plutarch *Galba* 17. 2; cf. 13. 2 and Tacitus *Hist.* 1. 72

9 Josephus *Vita* 16; *Ant. Jud.* 2. 195: Herod Agrippa was accused of violating the privacy of the Temple. See Smallwood, *Journal of Theological Studies* N.S. 10 (1959), 329f and *The Jews under Roman Rule* (Leiden, 1976), 206 n15; 278 n79

10 *Ant. Jud.* 20. 252. Josephus says he belonged to a family of Clazomenae but his name suggests ultimate Italian ancestry (Levick, *Roman Colonies in Southern Asia Minor* (Oxford, 1967), 106): a Gessius is found on Delos in the Republic (*CIL* 3 suppl. 14203)

11 Pliny *NH* 37. 50; 33. 140; 11. 238; Juvenal 6. 462

12 Tacitus *Ann.* 13. 45; Suet. *Nero* 35. 1; *Ann.* 6. 39, 3

13 Tacitus *Ann.* 11. 2

14 Suet. *Nero* 35. 5 (the date is suggested by Tacitus' silence). See pp.45–6 and p.247, n51

15 M. Della Corte, *Case ed abitante di Pompei*[3] (Naples, 1965), 72–9; A. Maiuri, *La Casa del Menandro* (Rome, 1933), 20–22; Smallwood, *Documents*, no. 433b; A. de Franciscis, 'Beryllos e la villa di Poppea ad Oplontis', *Studies in Classical Art and Archaeology – a tribute to P.H. von Blanckenhagen* (New York, 1979), 231f; *CIL* 4. 259; 1499; 6682. The ultimate origin of the family, however, may be Interamna Praetuttianorum in Picenum, according to Syme, *PBSR* 14 (1938), 7 n23, who adduces *ILS* 5671 and 6562

16 Della Corte (above, n15), 59

17 Tacitus *Ann.* 12. 27; 14. 17 and p.56. W. Moeller, *Historia* 19 (1970), 84f suggests that illicit *collegia* had provoked the riot

18 Lifting of the ban: *Notiz. d. Scavi* 1939, 307–9 discussed by A.W. van Buren, 'Pompeii – Nero – Poppaea', *Studies presented to D.M. Robinson*

(1953), 970f. *CIL* 4. 3525 (*ILS* 6444): 'iudicis Aug. felic. Puteolos Antium Tegeano Pompeios – hae sunt verae colonia[e]' certainly suggests that Pompeii became a Neronian colony like Puteoli and Antium. A. Sogliano, *RAL* ser. 5, vol 6 (1897), 389f plausibly related the imperial decision to the granting of colonial status, but other scholars prefer to connect it with the lifting of the ban on games. The term *iudicia* is baffling in either connection (see Mau on *CIL* 4. 3525 and Mommsen on 4. 1074 (addenda, p.199), G. Onorato, *Iscrizioni Pompeiane* (Florence, 1957), 151–2)

19 Tacitus *Ann.* 13. 31; 14. 27; *ILS* 6326. On Puteoli see p.250, n37. Della Corte³, 61, 259

20 *CIL* 4. 3822; 7988–9; Tacitus *Ann.* 15. 34; Suet. *Nero* 20. 2

21 *CIL* 4. 3726 (*ILS* 234): 'iudicis Augusti p.p. et Poppaeae Aug. feliciter'

22 Tacitus *Ann.* 15. 23; *AFA* in Smallwood, *Documents*, nos. 24, 25

23 *Ann.* 16. 6; Dio 62. 28, 1–2; 63. 26, 3. Van Buren (above, n18) suggests that a distich expressing the hope that a Sabina's beauty and youth may last, inscribed on a wall in Pompeii, refers to her. Her deification is attested on inscriptions (*ILS* 233; Smallwood, *Documents*, no. 25) and on an eastern coin (Smallwood, *Documents*, no. 148). See p.169

24 Tacitus *Hist.* 1. 72; Scholiast on Juvenal 1. 155; Dio 59. 23, 9; *Ann.* 12. 65, 1. See p.81

25 His acquisition of wealth: *Ann.* 15. 40; 16. 14; 16. 17, 5; Dio 63. 21, 2; Plut. *Galba* 17. 2, 5; Martial 3. 20. Cf. *Hist.* 1. 72 for his *avaritia*. His honours: *Ann.* 15. 72, cf. Suet. *Nero* 15. 2

26 Suet. *Nero* 53. 1; Tacitus *Ann.* 15. 73, 1

27 Fronto, van den Hout 199–200; Juvenal 10. 81. The priority here given to amusements by Fronto reflects the tastes of the pleasure-loving Lucius Verus to whom these remarks are addressed

28 *Brev. Vit.* 18. 5–6

29 Seneca *Ira* 2. 8, 3; *Epp.* 90. 45; 95. 33. Cf. Cicero *Tusc. Disp.* 2. 41: 'Gladiatorial shows seem cruel and inhuman to some men'; Dio Chrys. 31. 122; Philostratus *Life of Apollonius of Tyana* 4. 22

30 See p.76

31 *Res Gestae* 5; Dio 54. 1, 4, cf. 46. 39

32 Dio 55. 26, 2; 31, 4

33 The post is first attested in AD 14 (*Ann.* 1. 7, 1)

34 Tacitus *Ann.* 3. 54, 4f; 6. 13; 12. 43; Suet. *Claud.* 18

35 The identity of the *praefectus annonae* C. Turranius (Tacitus *Ann.* 1. 7; 11. 31) with the Turranius Gracilis of Baetica cited by the Elder Pliny as an authority (*NH* 3. 3; 9. 10; 9. 11; 18. 75) is accepted by Kroll (*RE* VII A (1948), 1442 n7); rejected by Stein (ibid, n5)

36 Seneca *Brev. Vit.* 18. 3–4; 19. 1; Tacitus *Ann.* 14. 51

37 Perhaps Claudius Athenodorus, though *AE* 1958, no. 236 has induced most scholars to accept a Domitianic date for him. See most recently H. Pavis d'Escurac, *La préfecture de l'annone* (Rome, 1976), 329

38 Tacitus *Ann.* 15. 18, 2, cf. 2. 87 for Tiberian subsidies to corn merchants; *Ann.* 15. 36; Suet. *Nero* 19. 1

39 Tacitus *Ann.* 15. 39; Suet. *Nero* 45. The text is uncertain but profiteering on the part of the Emperor seems also to be alleged. See, however, p.109

40 Dio 54. 1, 4; 54. 17, 1. On the role of Senate and Princeps see now G. Rickman, *The Corn Supply of Ancient Rome* (Oxford, 1980), Appendix 1

41 *Res Gestae* 15. 1; 18

42 *ILS* 6071, however, has now been questioned as evidence for an imperial freedman performing the function under Claudius or Nero, see Rickman, *Corn Supply*, 194; 215–6. The relationship between the senatorial prefects and the imperial officials was probably like that between the senatorial *curatores aquarum* and the procurators Claudius provided as assistants (Frontinus *de aquis* 2. 105)

43 Dio 62. 18, 5. See now Rickman, *Corn Supply*, 187–8

44 Tacitus *Ann.* 15. 72; Suet. *Nero* 10. 1

45 Dio 60. 11, 2; Suet. *Claudius* 20; R. Meiggs, *Roman Ostia²* (Oxford, 1973), 591–2

46 Tacitus *Ann.* 15. 18; *BMC Imp.* 1, 222, nos. 131f; Meiggs, *Roman Ostia²*, 56 and 563 favours 64 for completion but Nero commemorated earlier events of the reign on these issues (see p.122); *BMC Imp.* 1, 220, nos. 127f

47 Plut. *Caesar* 58. 10; Josephus *BJ* 2. 383, in a highly-coloured passage, gives Egypt credit for feeding Rome for one-third of the year in the reign of Nero, and it may have supplied even more corn in the reign of Augustus, according to Rickman, *Corn Supply*, Appendix 4

48 Tacitus *Ann.* 15. 46, 2; Suet. *Nero* 9. The date of the Antium harbour is not known. In theory, it could have been built before the Avernus waterway was contemplated or after it was abandoned. But Blake, *Roman Construction in Italy from Tiberius through the Flavians*, 84 suggested that the harbour was built for the use of his own villa

49 Pliny *NH* 14. 61; Tacitus *Ann.* 15. 42

50 *ILS* 207 (Smallwood, *Documents*, 312b); 5797a; Pliny *Ep.* 8. 17; Meiggs, *Roman Ostia²*, 488–9: only canals above Rome, not below, could possibly have achived that aim which, however, had immediate appeal

51 Suet. *Nero* 31. 3; 16. 1: 'Destinarat etiam Ostia tenus moenia promovere atque inde fossa mare veteri urbi inducere'. Meiggs, *Roman Ostia²*, 63–4 associates the plan with the period after the Fire. Objections to such a date have been found in Suetonius' phrase 'vetus urbs' and his use of the pluperfect 'destinarat', following a sentence about reconstruction after the Fire. But 'the old city' clearly refers to the original area of the city in contrast with the planned extension to Ostia just mentioned, while the pluperfect serves to contrast this as a plan, with the measures actually implemented

52 Suet. *Claudius* 18; Gaius *Institutes* 1. 32c; Tacitus *Ann.* 13. 51 (AD 58). The importance of such measures in encouraging the growth of *collegia* of shippers through which such privileges could be claimed is stressed by Rickman, *Corn Supply*, 89–90

53 Seneca *Ep.* 77. For the date of the Letter see *Seneca*, 400: it only provides a *terminus ante quem*

54 *ILS* 986. For the date of his governorship see *Seneca*, 244–5; 456–7

55 See now the summary by R. K. Sherk in *ANRW* II. 7 (1980), 962f. See p.228

56 Nothing seems to have come of this source of corn, as far as the city of Rome was concerned, perhaps because the Corinthian canal was never finished. Evidence for the canal project: Suet. *Nero* 19. 2; *Divus Iulius* 44.

3; Suet. *Gaius* 21. The Ps.-Lucian *Nero* 1 notes that the canal would have benefitted commerce as well as the Greek cities

57 Tacitus *Ann.* 3. 54; 6. 13, cf. Tacitus' own tribute at 4. 6, 4

58 Dio 61. 18, 3. The location on the Caelian is certified by the Notitia Dignitatum (A. Nordh, *Libellus de regionibus urbis Romae* [Lund, 1949], 75)

59 Tacitus *Ann.* 15. 39, 2. See R.F. Newbold, *Latomus* 33 (1974), 858f for the social and economic consequences of the Fire and Nero's remedies

60 Suet. *Nero* 45. 1; Tacitus *Hist.* 1. 73. For this interpretation see Bradley, *AJP* 93 (1972), 451f. Note also that the sand being carried in the ship from Alexandria would have been sent out over a month before and ordered before Macer had cut off the African supplies. For Africa as the main corn supplier to Rome in this period see Rickman, *Corn Supply*, Appendix 4

61 Suet. *Nero* 11; Dio 61. 18, 1. For the problems of dating the Ludi Maximi see p.246, n35

62 Suet. *Nero* 13; Dio 63. 4–6; Pliny *NH* 33. 54. On this event see pp.216–7

63 Tacitus *Ann.* 13. 31; Suet. *Nero* 11. 1; Pliny *NH* 19. 24

64 *Ecl.* 1. 7, vv 44f; Pliny *NH* 37. 45

65 Tacitus *Ann.* 14. 14–5, cf. 15. 33, 1; Pliny *NH* 36. 74; 37. 19

66 See above, p.247, n44. The gymnasium was destroyed by lightning in 62 (Tacitus *Ann.* 15. 22, 3). Philostratus' date of 66 for the dedication of the new gymnasium (*Life of Apollonius* 4. 42) could be that of rebuilding, perhaps started in connection with the second Neronia in 65, but cf. E. Bowie, *ANRW* II. 16. 2, 1658 who thinks the date is just a mistake by Philostratus. (Jerome's date of 63 and Cassiodorus' of 64 do seem to be errors.) It is not known if the gymnasium was rebuilt, as all later references are to the baths alone (Martial 7. 34, 5–9; 2. 48, 8; 3. 25, 4; Statius *Silvae* 2. 5, 62)

67 A. Cameron, *Circus Factions* (Oxford, 1976), 160f. Examples: Tacitus *Hist.* 1. 72, 3; Josephus *Ant. Jud.* 19. 247. Though the location is not specified at Tacitus *Ann.* 13. 50, Millar, *ERW* 372 suggests that the demand was made at the games when provincials were present

68 Pliny *Pan.* 51. 4–5; Suet. *Nero* 12; 13; Tacitus *Ann.* 13. 25

69 Suet. *Nero* 12. 2, cf. 10. 2; Tacitus *Ann.* 1. 76; Suet. *Claud.* 34. Pliny *NH* 37. 64 records that Nero watched the gladiatorial games reflected in an emerald, but whether this was to aid his vision (for which the *smaragdus* was thought to be efficacious) or was part of his arrangement for watching indirectly is not clear

70 Suet. *Nero* 22. See Cameron, *Circus Factions*, 6f and 179

71 Tacitus *Ann.* 13. 25, 4; Dio 61. 8, 2; Suet. *Nero* 26. 2; 16. 2. The actors were back by 60 (*Ann.* 14. 21, 4)

72 Tacitus *Ann.* 13. 25; Suet. *Nero* 26; Dio 61. 8, 2, cf. *Ann.* 2. 12–13

73 Tacitus *Ann.* 13. 25, 2; Dio 61. 9, 3; Suet. *Nero* 26. 2; Juvenal 3. 278–301; Dio 65. 2

74 Dio 61. 16, 2a–3 (59); Suet. *Nero* 39

75 Tacitus *Ann.* 14. 61–3

76 Tacitus *Ann.* 15. 38; 50. 44. For the whole question of responsibility for the Fire see pp.132–3

77 *Ann.* 15. 44, 5; Suet. *Nero* 57. 1; 47. 2; *Hist.* 1. 4. See p.186

78 This seems the simplest way to reconcile the evidence of Dio 55. 22, 4 (cf. Suet. *Aug.* 44. 1), 60. 7, 3–4; Suet. *Claud.* 21. 3; Tacitus *Ann.* 15. 32; Suet. *Nero* 11; Pliny *NH* 8. 21

79 Tacitus *Ann.* 13. 22; Pliny *NH* 37. 45, cf. Tacitus *Hist.* 3. 57

80 Smallwood, *Documents*, no. 231c, on which see p.246, n35

81 *Ann.* 14. 21, 1 of the first Neronia. Bribery: *Ann.* 14. 14; compulsion: Epictetus 2. 1, 12; *Hist.* 2. 62, 2 but cf. conversion of Fabius Valens (Tacitus *Hist.* 3. 62) See pp.42–4

82 Tacitus *Ann.* 15. 65; he also played the lyre, *Laus Pisonis* 165f. Dio 61. 17; 62. 19, 3

83 Tacitus *Hist.* 1. 73: 'magistra libidinum'; Crispinilla later went on the Greek tour, Dio 63. 12, 4. Suet. *Vit.*4; *Nero* 21. 2

84 Tacitus *Ann.* 14. 15; Suet. *Nero* 20; Dio 61. 20, 3–4, who gives Tacitus' date of 59 but calls the men soldiers and gives their number as already 5,000. In 63. 18 he seems to associate them with the order of *equites*. See Rostovzeff, *Römische Bleitesserae* (Leipzig, 1905), 74–5 noting the words *iuvenes Aug(ustiani)* on a lead token

85 *Ann.* 16. 4–5. See pp.160f

86 Suet. *Nero* 25. 3; 53

87 *Ann.* 3. 55. See p.205

88 Dio 61. 6, 1–3; Suet. *Nero* 22. 2. Dio apparently dates the episode to 54, but he is illustrating a general point about Nero's love of horse-racing. W. McDermott, *AJP* 91 (1970), 29f favoured 54, but now seems less certain and suggests some time before 60 (McDermott and Orentzel, *Roman Portraits* (Missouri, 1979), 12)

89 *Res Gestae* 22; Suet. *Aug.* 43; Plut. *Galba* 19. 3. cf. Pliny *NH* 13. 22: Otho introduced Nero to the custom of putting unguent on the soles of his feet

90 Suet. *Nero* 33. 2; Dio 63. 18, 1–2; cf. Quintilian 1. 6, 31. Camerinus had earlier been saved from conviction on extortion charges by Nero (p.252, n89). A possible family link with the Sulpicii Scriboniani, executed in 67, fills out Dio's story

91 Suet. *Aug.* 10; Seneca *Clem.* 1. 9. For confirmation of privileges conferred by 'the Emperors before me' in a papyrus from Arsinoe see O. Montevecchi, *Aegyptus* 50 (1970), 5f and p.210

92 *IG*² ii/iii, 3277 (61/62): *autokrator megistos* on an inscription on the Parthenon. *ILS* 8794, lines 25–6 (Nero), cf. 45–6 (the Greek priest).

93 Suet. *Nero* 35, cf. Tacitus *Ann.* 15. 36. Dio's Epitomator 63. 18, 1 dates the relegation of Caecina Tuscus to 67, but Tiberius Julius Alexander had succeeded him as Prefect by the summer of 66 (Josephus *BJ* 2. 492f) See p.161

94 Tacitus *Ann.* 15. 35; 16. 8. See p.88

95 On his connection with the Cassii Longini and the Vinicii see Syme, *JRS* 60 (1970), 27f. His wife was the daughter of Cassius Longinus (*ILS* 9518) who was at some time married to Junia Lepida; one daughter married Annius Vinicianus (Tacitus *Ann.* 15. 28, 3), a nephew of M. Vinicius, the husband of Gaius' sister Julia Livilla; another was married to L. Aelius Lamia Aelianus by 70 when Domitian acquired her

96 Tacitus *Ann.* 12. 40; *Agricola* 14. 3. Gallus had received the *triumphalia ornamenta* when legate of Moesia some ten years earlier (PIR² D 70)

97 Tacitus *Ann.* 14. 29. His father Q. Veranius had been a legate on the staff of Germanicus (*Ann.* 2. 56, 4); his daughter Verania Gemina married L. Calpurnius Piso Frugi Licinianus (*Hist.* 1. 47–8; *ILS* 240). See p.113

98 See pp.79, 61

99 Tacitus *Ann.* 13. 48; see p.56. On *ILS* 9235 see H.U. Instinsky, *JRGZM* 6 (1959), 128f who thinks a monument near Vetera in Lower Germany (*ILS* 235) served the same purpose

100 See above, n54. The stemma of the Plautii was clarified by L.R. Taylor, *MAAR* 24 (1956), 26ff. J. Ginsburg, *AJAH* 6 (1981), 51ff infers from the absence of the *consules ordinarii* of 55–60 in consular imperial provinces that Nero's policy of conciliation (above, pp.61–2) did not extend to giving the 'old governing class' military commands. She ignores the significance of the appointments just mentioned and the need to retain some Claudian appointees in the spirit of the accession 'amnesty'

101 Suet. *Galba* 7. 1; Plut. *Galba* 3. 3; see pp.27–8

102 Suet. *Vesp.* 4. In *Seneca*, App. 6, 452–3 (where *AFA* lxxxii Henzen should read lxxxvii) I argued for 61–2 or 62–3 as the date for his proconsulship, which would place it at the normal interval from the consulship. I missed *AE* 1968, no. 549 which shows Pompeius Silvanus there from 53 to 56 and thus makes it almost impossible to give the Vitellii two years there in sequence before 62–3. This makes it still more likely that one of the two dates suggested for Vespasian is correct, as the Vitellii must occupy 62–3 and 63–4 or 63–4 and 64–5

103 Tacitus *Ann.* 13. 22; 16. 14. Syme, *Historia* 31 (1982), 482 now suggests that the obscure Marinus who appears as governor of Syria on the Palmyra Tariff was a praetorian legate functioning during the lacuna between Corbulo and Cestius Gallus in 63, or during one between Gallus and Licinius Mucianus in the spring of 67

104 Tacitus *Ann.* 15. 25, 3; *Hist.* 5. 10; Josephus *BJ* 3. 1. Illness is a possibility, which Tacitus is reluctant to adduce as a cause of death, according to Syme, *ZPE* 41 (1981), 125f, who also points out that in Julio–Claudian appointments to Syria generally 'age and inertia stood on premium'

105 Dio 63. 17, 6

106 Tacitus *Hist.* 2. 5, 2; 2. 76: Corbulo's family, like Vespasian's, belonged to the municipal aristocracy of Italy, but his father was already a senator, Vespasian's only a knight. Note the hostility of Mucianus to Vespasian and to Arrius Varus, an equestrian subordinate of Corbulo who slandered his commander (*Hist.* 3. 6; 4. 11). Mucianus might have suspected Vespasian of helping to ensure his own appointment to command in the Jewish War by encouraging Nero's hostility to Corbulo

107 See pp.228–9

108 Tacitus *Hist.* 1. 7; 1. 52

109 Ducenius Geminus was legate of Dalmatia sometime between his consulate (now known to be in 60 or 61, Eck, *ZPE* 42 (1981), 227f) and his appointment as City Prefect by Galba (*Hist.* 1. 14, 1)

110 Tacitus *Hist.* 2. 86, 2; *Ann.* 13. 42. Pomponius Pius is certified in Smallwood, *Documents*, no. 384. Tacitus *Hist.* 1. 79 suggests that Aponius Saturninus, his successor, was not appointed by Otho, but Galba is just as likely to have appointed him as Nero: Syme suggests Baetican origin for Aponius (*Tacitus*, 787)

111 G.E.F. Chilver, *A Historical Commentary on Tacitus' Histories I and II* (Oxford, 1979), 6

112 Galba's caution: Suet. *Galba* 9. 1. On Pompeius Silvanus see Eck, *RE* suppl. 14, 437f: he probably came from Arelate in Narbonensis. Tampius Flavianus: *ILS* 985. Both held second consulships under Vespasian. See now Chilver, *Historical Commentary*, 248. Syme, *Historia* 31 (1982), 464–5 suggests, however, that both were appointees of Galba, which cannot be disproved

113 *ILS* 986

114 See *Scripta Classica Israelica* 3 (1976–7), 138f. But I failed to note that Rostovzeff apparently changed his interpretation of *Syll.* no. 23, the lead tessera which he originally thought was evidence for a *congiarium* in Suetonius Paullinus' honour. In *Römische Bleitesserae*, 52 he suggests, without argument, that the tessera was a token for admission to the games and the Paullinus there named the organiser of the games. But the names of *procuratores* or *curatores ludorum* seem to occur in the nominative, not the genitive, on these tesserae (when their function is clear). The 'PAULLINI' tessera seems more like that signifying a distribution in honour of the King of Armenia (*Syll.* 22: 'ARM(ENIAE) REG(IS)'). On salutations see chapter 15

115 Tacitus *Ann.* 15. 72 (for his age Plut. *Galba* 15. 2). His successor Trebellius Maximus, of Narbonensian origin, was without active military experience and possibly elderly (A. Birley, *Fasti of Roman Britain* (London, 1981), 59f)

8 The Tyranny of Art   (pages 119–142)

1 The Neronia was first held in 60 and repeated in 65, perhaps earlier in the year (Tacitus *Ann.* 16. 4; Suet. *Nero* 21): see p.161

2 Suet. *Nero* 25. 3; *BMC, Imp.*I, pp.245–6, 249–50, and 274. For Augustus' coins see *BMC, Imp.* I, pp.79, 82–3. Nero took the praenomen Imperator on the occasion of Tiridates' visit in mid–66 (Suet. *Nero* 13. 2)

3 *Apoc.* 4. 1, vv 20–3; Calp. Sic. 7. 84; 4. 159; Dio 60. 20. For other evidence in favour of imperial choice of coin types see S.R.F. Price, *CR* 29 (1979), 277–8 citing e.g. Suet. *Aug.* 94. 12; Dio 65. 6. 1; 77. 12. 6

4 *Legatio ad Gaium* 349–73; Tacitus *Ann.* 15. 42–3; Suet. *Nero* 16; 31

5 E.A. Sydenham, *The Coinage of Nero* (London, 1920), 33f

6 Pliny *NH* 34. 2: this report, given explicitly at second hand, should postdate the period when Pliny was last in Lower Germany, i.e. 56–57 or 58

7 See now on Nero's portraits Hiesinger, *AJA* (1975), 113f, who points out that Nero's entire portrait series 'reflects a self-contained development based on a style of dramatically heightened realism long at home in Roman court portraiture'

8 J.M.C. Toynbee, *NC* 7 (1947), 136–7. An approach to this style is seen in the gold and silver marked trib. pot. IX (AD 62–3) by D.W. MacDowall, *The Western Coinages of Nero, American Numismatic Society Notes and Monographs* no. 161 (1979), 31, cf. 42

9 See p.22

10 Perhaps these were the exercises on the Campus Martius that the public could see (Suet. *Nero* 10. 2)

11 The market: Dio 61. 19. 1; the triumphal arch: Tacitus *Ann*. 13. 41, 4; 15. 18, 1. Tacitus in *Hist*. 1. 43 tells us that the temple of Vesta was rebuilt by 69, yet Nero could merely have been reminding his people of his decision to remain in Rome early in the year of the Great Fire (Tac. *Ann*. 15. 36; Suet. *Nero* 19): the fire on the Caelian of AD 27 led to criticism of Tiberius' absence (*Ann*. 4. 64)

12 Suet. *Nero* 13; Smallwood, *Docs*., no. 53 (showing trib. pot. XI (late 64–5)); Tacitus *Ann*. 15. 29–31. Tacitus does not mention the closure in the extant books of the *Annals*, and according to Orosius 7. 3, 7, he stated in the *Histories* that Janus remained open from late in the reign of Augustus to that of Vespasian (Syme, *AJP* 100 (1979), 188f). (That this error was propagated by Flavian propaganda is plausibly argued by Townsend in *Hermes* 108 (1980), 233f.) Even if Tacitus had discovered his error by the time he wrote the *Annals*, the unfinished condition of the extant Neronian books makes it impossible to argue that he favoured a subsequent date

13 Smallwood, *Docs*., no. 67: its authenticity is admitted by MacDowall, *Western Coinages*, 175

14 On the location of the second mint see now Sutherland, *The Emperor and the Coinage*, chapter 3; MacDowall, *Western Coinages*, 27f. The argument for its reopening is based on the technique and distribution of coins and on the countermarking of some of these coins with SPQR, which is probably attributable to Vindex and his Gallic insurgents

15 Pliny *NH* 33. 47, on which see p.198. For what follows I am greatly indebted to the work of MacDowall, *Western Coinages*, chapter 9, 133f

16 The government appears to have succeeded in this in the case of gold, according to MacDowall, 138–9, who believes that a large recoining operation was carried out in 65

17 For other factors contributing to financial stress at this time and other suggested explanations for the reduction see p.198

18 MacDowall, *Western Coinages*, 146–7. For a discussion of MacDowall's chronology see appendix on Nero's Later Coinage, pp.238–9. For historic differences in getting this relation right see M. Crawford, *JRS* 60 (1970), 42

19 R. A. G. Carson, 'System and Product in the Roman Mint', *Essays in Roman Coinage presented to H. Mattingly* (1956), 227f. The present tense in Livy 6. 20, 13 certifies to the location of the mint on the Capitoline in the early Augustan period: inscriptions (*CIL* 6. 42–4) attest the move

20 MacDowall, *Western Coinages*, 148. But his idea that the government worried, particularly at this juncture, about a shortage of small change in the provinces may be doubted. Government spending probably required lower denominations as well as aurei and denarii: for example, although silver was the basic form of army pay, token coinage was still used, according to Crawford, *JRS* 60 (1970), 47–8

21 The Lugdunum mint was only opened for the last phase of the general brass coinage in 65, perhaps because it was damaged in a serious fire there in 64. Seneca *Ep*. 91 tells of the fire at Lugdunum, which clearly must follow the Fire at Rome as Lugdunum was able to help Rome then (Tac. *Ann*. 16. 13). As the dramatic date of the letter is late summer 64, the Lugdunum fire then belongs around August in that year (see *Seneca*, 400)

22 Suet. *Nero* 44. 2: 'exegitque ingenti fastidio et acerbitate nummum asperum argentum pustulatum, aurum ad obrussam ...', cf. Martial 4. 28, 5. Nero may also have been glad to have the lower brass denominations recalled as the experiment was abandoned

23 Tacitus *Ann.* 15. 42: Celer's non-Greek origin seems to be confirmed by *P. Ryl.* 608, a letter of recommendation from *Celer architectus* to an imperial procurator in Egypt, written in elegant Latin with Ciceronian turns of phrase, on which see H. Cotton, *Documentary Letters of Recommendation* (1981), 28f. Cf. Domitian's Rabirius (Martial 7. 56); Pliny *Ep.* 10. 40

24 Pliny *NH* 35. 120. Some scholars prefer the reading of the *editio princeps*, i.e. Fabullus, yet the name Famulus is attested (*CIL* 3. 7167: D. Haterius Famulus who made a decorated box for his wife, identified with the painter by C. Cichorius in *RhM.* (1927), 326)

25 Pliny *NH* 35. 30: the manuscript reading 'umidus' is uncertain

26 On the style of decoration: L.B. Vlad, *Bolletino dell'Istituto centrale del restauro* 29–30 (1957), 31f; R.B. Bandinelli, *Enciclopedia dell'arte antica* 3 (1960), 566–7; on the mosaic: F. Sanguinetti, *Palladio* N.S. 7 (1957), 126–7; F.B. Sear, *Roman Wall and Vault Mosaics* (Heidelberg, 1977), 25–6; 90–1: the octagonal room and the Palatine cryptoporticus also show traces of vault mosaics

27 Blake, *Roman Construction in Italy*, 33f; W. MacDonald, *The Architecture of the Roman Empire* I (1965), 17f

28 *Ann.* 15. 42

29 Pliny *NH* 3. 109; Blake, *Roman Construction*, 41. The lake was later used as an improved source for the aqueduct Anio Novus, but the credit for this is not assigned to Nero but to Trajan (Frontinus 2. 93); yet Nero did build a branch aqueduct (n33) and might have planned this one (as Nicholas Purcell has suggested to me)

30 D'Arms, *Romans on the Bay of Naples*, 98–9; a catalogue of the flasks depicting Baiae and Puteoli is to be found in K.S. Painter, *Journal of Glass Studies* 17 (1975), 45f

31 G. Carettoni, *Not. d. scavi* N.S. 3 (1949), 48f

32 Note the oracle in Suet. *Nero* 40. 3 which, as Nero interpreted it, promised that he would reach the age of 72

33 Frontinus 1. 20; 2. 76; 2. 87. For the date, see *ILS* 218 complaining that the Claudian aqueduct had suffered nine years' neglect by 71: Nero presumably checked it before building the branch. The date and the extension across the Tiber is against the idea that Nero was only concerned to supply his palaces and replace branches of the Marcian and Julian aqueducts destroyed by his constructions: E.B. van Deman, *The Building of the Roman Aqueducts* (1934), 266

34 Tac. *Ann.* 15. 39; Suet. *Nero* 31. 1; Platner-Ashby, s.v. Domus Transitoria. L. Fabbrini, *Atti della Pontificia Accademia Romana di Archeologia* Ser. III *Memorie* vol XIV (1982), 5f. She adduces traces of burning in walls and pavements of the upper storey, just discovered

35 Millar, *ERW*, 18f

36 Claudius too may have extended the Domus Augustana (Blake, *Roman Construction*, 30–1)

37 See below, n62

38 *Ann.* 15. 39; Suet. *Nero* 31. 1, *Aug.* 56. 2

39 The best account of the spread of the Fire is in *Ann.* 15. 38f. For the time: Tacitus gives six days for the first outbreak; Suet. *Nero* 38. 2 gives six days and seven nights. Inscriptions placed on the so-called *arae incendii Neronis* (*CIL* 6. 826; 30837) show that it lasted nine days in all. These altars to Neptune in special precincts were established by Domitian along the edge of the area destroyed in the Fire. They proclaim as their purpose 'the keeping away of fires': presumably the yearly sacrifice would secure divine aid, while the precincts, clear of inflammable material, would halt the spread of any fire. They also ensured that the Fire 'in Neronian times' would not be forgotten – nor the diligence and piety of Domitian

40 *Ann.* 15. 43; Dio 62. 17, 3–18, 1

41 Livy 5. 55; *Ann.* 15. 41; Dio 60. 18, 2; Suet. *Nero* 39. 2

42 *Ann.* 15. 43; Suet. *Nero* 16. 1: G. Hermansen, *Ostia, Aspects of City Life* (Edmonton, 1982), 217 proposes, on the basis of studies of buildings in Ostia, that Suetonius is in error in believing that *domus* as well as *insulae* were to be provided with *porticus* and that their roofs were to be used as platforms from which to fight fires. He suggests the purpose given in the text. Suet. *Nero* 38, gives a hostile interpretation of debris clearance as designed to facilitate looting by the Emperor

43 *Ann.* 15. 43, 3; Gaius, *Institutes* 1. 33; Ulpian 3. 1

44 Suet. *Vesp.* 8; *ILS* 245 lays blame for the bad condition of the streets on the 'neglect of earlier periods' (i.e. Nero)

45 *Ann.* 15. 43

46 Suet. *Nero* 16; *Ann.* 15. 43, 3. The complexity of the scheme suggests an earlier origin for the conception, but the language of Suetonius cannot be used to support this: see p.108 and p.262, n51

47 As argued by R.F. Newbold, *Latomus* 33 (1974), 858ff. On the areas covered by the Domus Aurea see pp.133, 139

48 *Ann.* 15. 40, 2; Suet. *Nero* 55

49 *SHA* Commodus 8. 6; *Ann.* 4. 64

50 See Bradley, *Historical Commentary, ad* chapter 55. Suetonius similarly transfers the initiative for the proposed renaming of the Caelian to Tiberius (*Tib.* 48)

51 Suet. *Nero* 31; Pliny *NH* 34. 45 (where the figure for the height is uncertain); Suet. *Vesp.* 8; Dio 66. 15, 1; Martial *Spec.* 2. 1–3; *SHA* Hadrian 19

52 Pliny *NH* 35. 51 notes a painting of Nero of the same size in the Maian Gardens on the other side of the city, which was destroyed by lightning. It was probably a sketch or painting of the statue and may never have been publicly accessible

53 Dio 62. 16, 1; Suet. *Nero* 38; Pliny *NH* 17. 5. The view is shared by the author of the *Octavia* 831–3, but neither Martial, Josephus nor Juvenal mentions it

54 *Ann.* 15. 67, 2, cf. Statius *Silvae* 2. 7, 60–1 which may show that Lucan blamed Nero in a prose work on the subject (see p.278, nn96, 103)

55 *Ann.* 15. 44f

56 Tac. *Ann.* 15. 40. 2; Suet. *Nero* 38. 1; Dio 62. 16

57 *Ann.* 15. 39, 3; Suet. *Nero* 38. 2; Dio 62. 18, 1. It may be that Nero had earlier been giving readings from his epic *Troica* (which he finally performed at the second Neronia in 65 (Dio 62. 29, 1)) on his private stage where Tacitus places this performance, and that Suetonius and Dio represent a developed tradition in which the performance has been moved out of the palace which was in flames (G. Scheda, *Historia* 16 (1967), 111)

58 See p.128 and n34. For the paintings found in the remains of the Domus Transitoria under Domitian's palace and now in the Antiquarium on the Palatine see Vlad (n26). For the two phases in the construction of the ornamental pool, now identified as a *euripus*, see Fabbrini (n. 34), 21 and *Città e architettura nella Roma Imperiale* (1983), 169.

59 Carratoni (n31), 77f. Fabbrini (n34) too emphasises the continuity of conception, despite modifications, in the two palaces, e.g. two phases in the construction of the upper floor (p.21) and of the lower floor (p.17 n17 and p.22 n.34) are discernible.

60 C. Huelsen, *AJA* 13 (1909), 45f

61 See p.112

62 Pliny *NH* 17. 5 notes that trees belonging to the house of Caecina Largus (*cos. ord.* 42) were destroyed in the Fire of 64 and speaks of the house as no longer in existence. For a house in the Palatine later: *Ann.* 15. 69 (Vestinus Atticus); perhaps also the house of Salvidienus Orfitus (Suet. *Nero* 37. 1; Dio 62. 27, 1)

63 Suet. *Nero* 38. 1. These particular buildings, however, do not seem to have been taken over by Nero, but reconstructed at an undetermined date: Blake, *Roman Construction*, 28–9; Rickman, *Roman Granaries and Store Buildings* (1971), 107

64 Martial *Spec.* 2 (cited p.138). Sanguinetti, *Bollettino del centro di studi per la storia dell'architettura* 12 (1958), 45

65 Suet. *Vesp.* 9. 1

66 Cicero *Off.* 2. 60; Dio Chrys. 47. 15 addressing the citizens of Prusa in Bithynia

67 See n51. It is not known what preceded Hadrian's temple of Venus and Rome on the site of the *vestibulum*. A. Boethius, *The Golden House of Nero* (1960), 127 suggested the construction of a temple of the Sun

68 This is the argument of M.P.O. Morford, *Eranos* 66 (1968), 158f

69 B. Tamm, *Auditorium and Palatium* (1963), 101–6; van Deman, *MAAR* 5 (1925), 115f. The remark is by J. Ward Perkins, *Antiquity* (1956), 214

70 Suet. *Nero* 31; *Ann.* 15. 42

71 Nepos says of Atticus' house in the city that its charm lay in its park rather than its building (*Atticus* 13), but Atticus aimed, he says, to be 'elegans non magnificus' whereas Nero aspired to be both, the magnificence showing partly in the size of his palace and grounds

72 The rural villa view is that of Boethius, *Golden House* and Ward Perkins, *Antiquity* (1956), 209f who agree with Toynbee, *JRS* 38 (1958), 160–1 and Charlesworth, *JRS* 40 (1950), 71–2 in dismissing the ideas of H.P. L'Orange, *Symbolae Osloenses* (1942), 68f. See p.216

73 The point is made forcibly by Morford in *Eranos* 66 (1968), 158f, citing Elder Seneca *Controversiae* 2. 1 and 5. 5, 1–2 in particular. For Neronian authors: Lucan 10. 110–121; Petronius 120. 87–9; Seneca *Epp.* 88. 6–7; 88. 22; 90. 7; 90. 9; 90. 15; 90. 43; 115. 8–9 (size is stressed at 90. 43 and 115. 8).

Letter 90 is the one in which covert allusions to the Golden House are most commonly discerned, but in fact the parallels are not close enough: at 7, high buildings are the target (not a feature of the palace); at 9, panels heavy with gold are noted which may have been a feature of the palace though the main dining room had ivory panels, while 15, which is taken to refer to that room, has moving panels but they are not said to be of ivory and they display different scenes rather than sprinkle flowers (cf. Suet. *Nero* 31. 2). The pipes sprinkling saffron to great heights in section 15 do not suit what Suetonius says of pipes sprinkling unguents *desuper*. Cf. Plut. *Galba* 19. 3 for such pipes elsewhere

74 The remains are carefully catalogued by C.C. van Essen, 'La Topographie de la Domus Aurea Neronis', *Medelingen der Koninklijke Nederlandse Akademie van Wetenschappen*, Afd. Letterkunde 17. 12 (1954), 371f. Of the remains he attributed to Nero, the great cistern called the Sette Salle, east of the major remains on the Oppian Hill, is now thought to be wholly Trajanic, despite the fact that its orientation fits the Domus Aurea (L. Cozza, *Atti d. Pontif. Acad. di Archeologia*, Ser. III *Rendiconti* 47 (1974–5), 79). New excavations now show that the Oppian complex included an upper storey and extended further to the east (see p.141)

75 Van Essen (see note above), 4–13

76 A.M. Colini, *Atti d. Pont. Accad. Rom. di Arch.* Ser. III *Memorie* vol VII (1944), 137f

77 Pliny *NH* 36. 162. I owe this reference and many of the ideas here about the purpose of the Domus Aurea to a paper and subsequent discussions with Nicholas Purcell

78 Suet. *Gaius* 22. 1; Vell. Pat. 2. 81. On the public quality of temples see Pliny *Pan.* 47. 4–5

79 Tacitus *Ann.* 15. 37

80 *Ann.* 15. 44. The idea of privacy lies behind the interpretation of Lucillius' epigram on a theft of golden apples from the garden of Zeus as an allusion to some theft from the gardens of the Domus Aurea, but that interpretation is, in any case, implausible (see p.273, n31)

81 *Ann.* 15. 52–3; Josephus *Ant. Jud.* 19. 76

82 Tacitus *Ann.* 15. 55 attests his living in the Servilian Gardens in 65

83 Tamm, *Auditorium and Palatium*, 72–5

84 Suet. *Nero* 41; MacDonald, *Architecture of the Roman Empire*, 31

85 Dio 65. 4; G. Zander, *Bollettino del centro di studi per la storia dell'architettura* 12 (1958), 47f

86 This is the reconstruction of Fabbrini (n34) who notes the possibility that the octagon represented a modification of an earlier conventional plan. Her suggestion that Nero's MAC AUG dupondii (fig. 28) celebrate the design and mechanical ingenuity (*machina*) of his new palace is not unlikely but untenable if MacDowall, *Western Coinages*, 59 is right to assign the earliest coins depicting this building to his Issue II: it predates the Great Fire which stimulated the final redesigning of Nero's palace

87 H. Storz-S. Prückner, *MDAI (R).*, 81 (1974), 323f

88 Dio Chrys. 71. 5–9; Suet. *Nero* 24; 54; Dio 63. 9; 18. 1; see pp.114; 162–3

9 **The Artistic Tyrant**   *(pages 143–163)*

1 *Vita Persi* ascribed to Valerius Probus, a contemporary grammarian. It is there stated that Cornutus thought only this one work should be published

2 For Calpurnius Siculus the most precise indications of Neronian date are 'maternis causas qui vicit Iulis' vv 44–5 of Eclogue I alluding to Nero's speech on behalf of Ilium in 53 (Tacitus *Ann.* 12. 58, 1) and the celebration of the new amphitheatre in Eclogue VII, identified with the one finished in 57 (*Ann.* 13. 31, 1). For the two Einsiedeln Eclogues, the allusion to Nero's epic, the *Troica*, in II is the clearest evidence. But both of the latter poems and I, IV VII of Calpurnius' Eclogues also show thematic similarity to Seneca's *Apocolocyntosis, De Clementia* and the accession speech. For recent vindication of a Neronian date for Calpurnius Siculus, see G. Townend, *JRS* 70 (1980), 166, R. Mayer *JRS* 70 (1980), 175, T.P. Wiseman *JRS* 72 (1982) who, however, challenges the usual interpretation of vv 44–5, on which see n48 below

3 *Ann.* 16. 18–19 (C. Petronius). Pliny *NH* 37.20 tells us of a T. Petronius consularis who broke a valuable vase to prevent the Emperor acquiring it after his death; Plutarch *Mor.*60e mentions a T. Petronius who flattered Nero by pretending to criticize his meanness. For a recent discussion of the identifications, M. Smith, *Cena Trimalchionis* (1975), 213–4. Now W. Eck, *ZPE* 42 (1981), 227 adduces a new document from Ephesus that dates the consulship of P. Petronius Niger and Q. Manlius Tarquitius Saturninus to July of 62. Tablets from Herculaneum show a T. Petronius Niger in office with the same colleague in July of an unidentified year. Though the tablets are not very reliable, it is tempting to prefer their praenomen here

4 *Satyricon* 119–124; see pp.153, 157, 277 n90

5 The most complete study of lost Latin works of the early Empire is H. Bardon, *La Littérature latine inconnue* II (1956). Celsus is mentioned by Quintilian at 10. 1. 124. Papirius Fabianus' style is discussed by the Elder Seneca *Contr.* II, pref.2 and by his son in *Ep.* 100

6 Quintilian 10. 1, 102–3; Tacitus *Dial.* 23. 2; *Ann.* 4. 34–5. Cf. Seneca's celebration of Cremutius Cordus in the *Consolation to Marcia*

7 Quintilian 10. 1. 98; Tacitus *Ann.* 12. 28; Pliny *Ep.* 3. 5, 3. Seneca may have written some of his tragedies before Nero's accession: Quintilian 8. 3, 31 shows he was writing tragedy while he and Pomponius were both in Rome c.51: Pomponius probably died in the 50s, as Pliny *Ep.* 3, 5, 3 suggests. *Ann* 14. 52 implies that Seneca continued to compose tragedies after Nero's accession (see p.154)

8 Quintilian 10. 1, 38–42; 45; 104

9 Epic: 10. 1, 89–90; satire. 10. 1, 94; Menippean satire 10. 1. 95; Seneca: 10. 1, 125–131

10 Quintilian 10. 1, 96; Martial 8. 70

11 Juvenal *Sat.* 7. 1: 'et spes et ratio studiorum in Caesare tantum'

12 *Ann.* 13. 3

13 Suet. *Aug.* 78; 98. 4; 89. 2; 86; 89. 3

14 Ibid, 89. 3

15 Burning of history of T. Labienus and of the works of Cassius Severus: Elder Seneca, *Controv.* 10, *pref.* 4; Suet. *Gaius* 16. 1; Tacitus *Ann.* 1. 73, 3; 4. 21, 3. Ovid was exiled in AD 8 and his works banned from the public libraries in Rome (*Tristia* 3. 1, 59–82; 3. 14, 5–18)

16 Suet. *Tib.* 70; Tacitus *Ann.* 6. 20, 3; Suet. *Tib.* 14. 4. Note also the dedication to him of a Greek commentary on the work of a Greek lampoonist (Diog. Laert. 9. 109). Valerius Maximus expresses a distaste for hearing Greek spoken in the Senate (2. 2, 3) which must have pleased the Emperor (Suet. *Tib.* 71)

17 Horace *Epist.* 1. 3; 1. 8; 1. 9. Velleius Paterculus 1. 16–7 is elaborating a general theory of the rise and fall of genres: Livy's death in AD 17 seems to be the terminus of the 80 years Velleius has in mind

18 Seneca *Ep.* 1.22, 11; cf. Elder Seneca *Controv.* 7. 1, 27

19 Tacitus *Ann.* 3. 49f; Suet. *Tib.* 70

20 For other upper class victims or near-victims: Dio 57. 22; *Ann.* 4. 31; 6. 9. Suet. *Tib.* 56

21 Phaedrus, Bk. III pref., Tacitus *Ann.* 4. 34; 6. 29, 3

22 Syme, *AJP* 99 (1978), 45f against recent attempts at rehabilitation

23 Jos. *AJ* 19. 208f; Suet. *Gaius* 34; 53. For his envy: Dio 59. 19, 4; 7; cf. Suet. *Gaius* 53. 2

24 Pliny *Ep.* 1. 13

25 Seneca *Cons. Polyb.* 14. 2f; *Apoc.* 5. 1; *Brev. Vit.* 13 (even if written in 55 after Claudius' demise)

26 *Cons. Polyb.* 6. 3; 11. 5; 8. 2

27 Largus' work is dated to between 44 and 48 by his reference to Claudius' British expedition which Largus had joined (163), and by his mention of Messallina as living (60)

28 *Anth. Pal.* 9. 572; 11. 75; 11. 116

29 *Anth. Pal.* 11. 254, cf. Suet. *Nero* 21. 2–3; Dio 63. 10, 2

30 *Anth. Pal* 11. 185, cf. Suet. *Nero* 39. 5

31 *Anth. Pal.* 11. 132. The arguments for dating Lucillius' work are those of C. Cichorius, *Römische Studien*, 372–4, opposed by L. Robert, *Entretiens de la Fondation Hardt* 14 (1967), 208–9, who wishes to connect *Anth. Pal.* 11. 184 with the Domus Aurea (see p.271, n80). His interpretation, presented in *CRAI* 1968, 280f goes against the other indications of date and would be the only example, according to Robert himself, of an epigram by Lucillius in which the situations and names were not imaginary

32 For the date of Septimius and his possible identification with the poet Septimius Serenus, see A. Cameron, *Harvard Studies in Classical Philology* 84 (1980), 172f and E. Champlin, *Harvard Studies in Classical Philology* 85 (1981), 189f who goes on to suggest the identification of both with the antiquarian scholar Serenus Sammonicus

33 Dictys Cretensis, ed. Eisenhut (1973), who discusses the Greek version in *RhM.*, 112 (1969). On the papyri, see also *Oxyrhynchus Papyri* vol 31 (1966), no. 2539. The governor of Crete is called 'the consular Rutilius Rufus', although Crete (and Cyrene) was a province regularly held by ex-praetors. If the name has any basis in fact, it could be a distortion of T. Atilius Rufus who reached the consulship under Vespasian (*PIR*² A 1304),

but it is more likely to be an allusion to the famous consular who ended his days in exile in Asia. On Dido's treasure, Tacitus *Ann.* 16. 1; on Nero's *Troica*, see p.151

34 The grounds for identification are principally metrical: see G.E. Duckworth, *TAPA* 98 (1967), 85f; R. Verdière, *Études prosodique et métrique du De Laude Pisonis et des Bucolica de T. Calpurnius Siculus* (Rome, 1971). The hexameters are particularly Ovidian, a fact to which there may be an allusion in Calp. Sic. IV. 151. What the poet says of his own circumstances in the eulogy and the eclogues does not conflict with such identification. The further identification of Meliboeus, the patron addressed by Calpurnius Siculus, with Piso is not a necessary consequence

35 *Laus Pisonis* vv 109–37; 260–1; Birthday ode; vv 159–60, cf. 212–3; parallel with Maecenas: vv 230–42; 246–8

36 The dramatic date of the poem is early autumn (vv 1–3) when the shepherds find Faunus' prophecy, recently carved on a tree, which mentions the comet heralding the change of ruler as being in the sky for the twentieth night (vv 77–9). This is the comet that appeared from 9 June to 9 July 54 and was taken to portend Claudius' death on 13 October (Suet. *Cl.* 46; Pliny *NH* 2. 92)

37 *Ann.* 15. 48, 2–3; 15. 65. D'Arms, *Romans on the Bay of Naples*, 150, 206 suggests that Piso performed in the Sebasta, the Greek games at Naples, but vv 89–92 where Naples is mentioned seem to be about Piso's skill at declamation, not included in the games. Declamations were, however, one of the features of Neapolitan society, e.g. A. Gellius *NA* 9. 15, 2

38 Juvenal 5. 109; *Ann.* 13. 34, 1

39 Martial 12. 36, vv 8–9; cf. 4. 40 Vibius Crispus: Tacitus *Hist.* 2. 10; *Dial.* 8. The date of his suffect consulship is not known, but c.61 is most likely (U. Weidemann, *Die Statthalter von Africa und Asia in den Jahren 14–68* AD (Bonn, 1982) 219; Syme, *Historia* 31 (1982), 480. A date in the 50s has been proposed by A.B. Bosworth, *Athenaeum* 51 (1973), 70f

40 On Seneca's younger admirers and imitators, see Quintilian 10. 1. 126–7

41 Fabius Rusticus: Tacitus *Ann.* 13. 20. On Lucilius, see p.79; Seneca *Epp.* 79. 5–7; 8. 10; 24. 19; 46. Seneca's friend Annaeus Serenus (*Ep.* 63) may also have been a writer (*Tranq. An.* 1. 13)

42 *De Re Rustica* 9. 16, 2. He speaks flatteringly of Seneca at 3. 3, 3

43 For this problem and a defence of the idea of 'literary patronage', see R.P. Saller, *CQ* 33 (1983), 246f

44 Seneca's criticism of Virgil's inclusion of lines reminiscent of Ennius shocked Aulus Gellius (*NA* 12. 2) but is trivial in comparison with Seneca's great admiration of the *maximus vates* (*Brev. Vit.* 9. 2) whose works he often cites

45 Robert *CRAI* 1968, 284f

46 *A.P.* 9. 178; Gow-Page *Garland of Philip* I, 94; II, 119–120; see p.210. In the poem, Nero is called 'Caesar' and although he was called 'Nero Claudius Caesar' from the time of his adoption, the fact that Claudius is not mentioned makes it likely that Nero was already Emperor when the poem was written. But a time soon after his accession in 54 is plausible

47 *A.P.* 7. 379; Gow-Page, *Garland of Philip* I, 92 and II, 118 suggest that this poem must have been written before 42 when Claudius enlarged the

harbour at Ostia so as to overshadow Puteoli. But Puteoli remained the principal harbour for traffic from the East even after Trajan's new harbour at Ostia allowed the Alexandrian corn ships to dock there, perhaps until the reign of Commodus (Meiggs, *Roman Ostia*, 56–61; cf. D'Arms, *JRS* 64 (1974), 104f). Like *A.P.* 9. 178 this would then be another poem in the *Garland of Philip* later than the reign of Gaius, when the work is usually said to be published. For other such poems see Cameron, *GRBS 21* (1980), 43f who suggests publication under Claudius or Nero

48 *Ecl.* 1. 44–5: 'Blessed ages attend the young prince who won their case for his mother's Iulii'. That this is an allusion to Nero's speech that won perpetual tribute exemption for Ilium in 53 is shown by Tacitus' testimony that the descent of the Julian gens (to which Nero belonged on his mother's side) from Aeneas was stressed in the speech (*Ann.* 12. 58, 1), cf. Smallwood, *Docs.*, 101a, an inscription at Ilium calling Nero 'kinsman of the city'. Martial success is mentioned in *Ecl.* 4. 90–1 and 7. 84 (comparison with Mars)

49 *Eins. Ecl.* 1. 36f. Metrical analysis now suggests that this may be written by a poet different from the author of the second Eclogue celebrating the Golden Age and that neither poet is identical with Lucan or Calpurnius Siculus (Duckworth (above n34) 141–3)

50 *Ann.* 14. 16 (the text is corrupt at the beginning of the second sentence, *hi cenati* being Halm's conjecture)

51 Suet. *Nero* 52

52 Martial 8. 70; Suet. *Vit.* 11. Philostratus, *Life of Apollonius* 4. 39 is probably an allusion to this book, said to contain a hymn, songs from tragedies and other songs. For a survey of evidence about Nero's compositions see Bardon, *REL* 14 (1936), 337f

53 Dio 61. 20. Since Dio's comments concern Nero's singing voice and the prize earned was for cithara-playing, it seems a rash assumption

54 Both Attis and the Bacchants were favourite themes for this kind of learned poetry (Catullus 63; 64. 253–66; Martial 2. 86, 4–5)

55 Pliny *Ep.* 5. 3, 5; Martial 9. 26, 9; Suet. *Dom.* 1; Tacitus *Ann.* 15. 49

56 Suet. *Nero* 24. We do not know the subject of the poem nor which King Mithridates is meant

57 Pliny *NH* 37. 50; Tacitus *Ann.* 15. 34, 1

58 No credence can be given to the scholiasts on Persius who assign various whole or partial hexameter lines ridiculed by the poet to Nero (*Sat.* 1. 93–5; 99–102): they seem to see Nero everywhere, spotting allusions in 1.4; 1.29; 1.28 and 1.121 (on which see p.157)

59 *Grammatici Latini*, ed. Keil, 6. 209; 'vir doctus atque eruditus'; 6. 555: 'Bassus ad Neronem de iambico sic dicit.' Martial 8. 70, 1: 'carmina qui docti nota Neronis habet'

60 Tacitus *Ann.* 14. 52 using the vague word *carmina*, used of the tragedies of Pomponius Secundus at 12. 28, cf. Quintilian 10. 1, 128 who includes the tragedies under the equally vague term *poemata*. The scholiast on Persius 1.128 may reflect a tradition that Nero wrote tragedies and Philostratus *Life of Apollonius* 4. 39 speaks of songs from tragedies composed by Nero as well as songs he composed for tragedies by others

61 See p.132 and pp.269–70, n57

62 Servius on *Aeneid* 5. 370: 'This Paris, according to Nero's *Troica*, was the bravest, to the extent of surpassing everyone, even Hector, in the prize competition at Troy. When Hector was drawing his sword on him in anger, Paris said he was his brother and proved it by bringing tokens, though he was still disguised in rustic habit.' The lines quoted by the scholiast on Lucan 3. 261 are:

> Quique pererratam subductus Persida Tigris
> deserit et longo terrarum tractus hiatu
> reddit quaesitas iam non quaerentibus undas.

Seneca cites in *NQ* 1. 5, 6: 'colla Cytheriacae splendent agitata columbae'

63 Dio 62. 29, 2–4

64 Suet. *Vit.* 11

65 Martial 8. 70, 7; Suet. *Dom.* 1; Juvenal 8. 221. For Quintilian's silence, compare Pliny *Ep.* 5. 3, 6 on light verses: 'I pass over Nero, although I know that what is done by evil men is not corrupted by them, but is kept honourable by being practised often by the good'

66 Suet. *Nero* 20. 1; Dio 61. 20, 2. Tacitus says that Nero resented Seneca's ridicule of his voice (*Ann.* 14. 52), but for Vindex the target was his lyre-playing (Suet. *Nero* 41. 1)

67 Pliny *Ep.* 5. 3, 5. If the epigrams ascribed to Seneca are his, some of them clearly date from his exile (2, 3, 18 Prato) and some are addressed to Claudius as conqueror of Britain (28–34 Prato). Lucan also wrote light epigrams (Vacca Life; Martial 10. 64)

68 See pp.96–7

69 *Sat.* 1–5 on the faults of rhetorical training; 85–7 on decadence of the arts; 118 on epic poetry

70 *Sat.* 89f; 119f. For a sceptical view of the relation of Petronius' *Bellum Civile* to Lucan's, see Smith, *Cena Trimalchionis*, 214–7 and P. A. George, *CQ* 24 (1974), 119f. The view I have adopted is exemplified by G. Luck, *AJPh* 93 (1972), 133f

71 *Iliacon*: Statius *Silvae* 2. 7, 54f; Vacca Life of Lucan. For the metre of the *Ilias Latina*, see Duckworth (n34), who supports the view that Silius Italicus is the author. Persius in *Sat.* 1.50–1 mentions a translation of the *Iliad* by Attius Labeo

72 Calpurnius Siculus 4. 158–9; 4. 57; *Laus Pisonis* 163–5. To this period also belongs the grammarian Remmius Palaemon who wrote in varied and recherché metres (Suet. *Gramm.* 23)

73 Suetonius *Life of Lucan*

74 On Silius Italicus, Pliny *Ep.* 3. 7, especially 3 and 9. Valerius Flaccus and two other epic poets were dead by the mid-nineties when Quintilian was writing (10. 1, 89). Saleius Bassus was well-known by 74/5, his talents being recognized by a gift from Vespasian (Tacitus *Dial.* 5. 9)

75 Vacca *Life of Lucan*; *Vita Persi*. Persius' was a youthful work, destroyed after his death. A garbled sentence of the latter Life states that Cornutus was a 'tragicus sectae poeticae.' The text has defied emendation and may be an unreliable gloss: there is no other evidence that Cornutus was a tragic poet. The tragedies of Curiatius Maternus mentioned in *Dial.* 3. 4

and 11. 2 (which perhaps include the work which broke the power of Vatinius) probably belong after Nero's death

76 *Ann.* 14. 16. See p.41
77 See p.160
78 Tacitus *Ann.* 15. 49; 60; 71; 16. 18; 21; 28
79 Pliny *Ep.* 3. 7, 3; cf. Thrasea's reluctance (Tacitus *Ann.* 16. 22, 1)
80 Tacitus *Ann.* 15. 72, 1. cf. ILS 273
81 Suet. *Nero* 21. 2; Dio 63. 14, 3; Tacitus *Hist.* 4. 4; Plut. *Mor.* 107
82 The extreme proponent is E. Cizek, *L'époque de Néron et ses controverses idéologiques* (Leiden, 1972): see my review in *JRS* 66 (1976), 229
83 *Ann.* 3. 54, 1 (though the talk here is moral and political); *Ann.* 16. 19, 2; Seneca *Ep.* 64. 1
84 The acquaintance with Piso is presupposed by Natalis' story of Piso's message to Seneca and by Seneca's version offered in defence (Tacitus *Ann.* 15. 60, 2; 61, 1). On the question of Seneca's involvement in the conspiracy, see pp.173–4
85 According to the Vacca Life, Lucan joined Nero's circle shortly after assuming the *toga virilis* between 54 and 56 (see p.157)
86 *Vita Persi* which dates the start of Persius' association with Cornutus to AD 50–1
87 Dio 62. 29, 2–4; Gellius *NA* 2. 6, 1; Charisius *Gramm. Lat.* 1. 125; *Vita Persi*. On Thrasea's relations with Nero, see pp.165, 170, 176–7
88 The tortuous Persius subscribes to all these clichés in Satire 1. Augustus had criticised the exotic style of his friend Maecenas in much the same terms as Seneca was to do. (Suet. *Aug.* 86. 2; Seneca *Ep.* 114. 4f)
89 On this characteristic of Roman literature of this period and earlier, see G. Williams, *Change and Decline* (1978), chapter 5
90 For example, we cannot date the composition of Petronius' *Satyricon*. It was a long work, to judge from the fact that the parts we have come from Books 15 and 16. As Petronius died in the spring of 66, some of it may have been written before he joined Nero's circle after his consulate in the summer of 62. This is often forgotten by scholars finding allusions in the work to Seneca's Letters, which cannot have been composed before their dramatic date of autumn 63 – late 64, and of which the first 7 books (1–69) cannot have appeared before late spring 64 while the later letters will have been published shortly before his death in 65 (see *Seneca*, 349, 400, 418). A similar problem arises in detecting echoes from the later books of Lucan's epic in Petronius, for Lucan was working on the poem right up until his death on 30 April 65 (Statius 2. 7, 100–4). See on the problem of echoes, M. Smith, *Cena Trimalchionis*, 214–9
91 On Petronius' and Piso's alleged Epicureanism, mistakenly inferred from their high-living, see *JRS* 66 (1976), 229–30. Persius: Satire IV, 1–15
92 On imperial misconstruction, see Pliny *Pan.* 3. 4 alluding particularly to Domitian. For tragedy: Tacitus *Dial.* 2. 1; 3. 2; history: *Ann.* 4. 33, 4; 14. 14; Pliny *Ep.* 5. 12; 9. 27
93 Thrasea's biography of Cato, a genre related to history, could have been a provocative work, since it probably included the account of his last campaign against Caesar and of his heroic suicide, but we do not know when it was composed. The mention of it by Thrasea's accuser

Cossutianus Capito occurs in a long recital of charges and is not among those things that Tacitus thought had most provoked Nero over the years (*Ann.* 16. 22, 2; 21). Heroizing Cato cannot have been regarded as 'patent defiance' in the earlier part of the reign (*pace* J. Geiger, *Athenaeum* 57 (1979) 69) as Seneca was always prone to it and Lucan practised it even in the early books of his epic

94 On the possible allusions to the Golden House in Seneca's Letters see pp.270–1, n73. On the general difficulty of detecting allusions in Seneca see *Seneca*, 5, 12–20, 360. Though, no doubt, delightful for his readers, the hostility to gymnastics and theatrical performances at Naples that Seneca expresses in his Letters 15 and 76 can hardly count as 'literary opposition', for Seneca had been openly expressing his views on these subjects to the Emperor for years (cf. Tacitus *Ann.* 15. 61, 1 on Seneca's *libertas*)

95 See Villeneuve's edition of Persius (11), for comments by scholiasts on *Satire* 1.4; 29; 99; 120; 121; 128

96 Statius *Silvae* 2. 7, 60–1: 'You will tell how the impious fires of the guilty tyrant spread through the roofs of Remus.' The notion of Nero's guilt could be Statius' idea, as in his description of Lucan's *Laudes Neronis* (the work for which he was crowned at the Neronia in 60) as praise of 'ungrateful Nero'. On the other hand, by mid-64 Lucan was estranged from Nero and the work may have been written after the ban was imposed (see n103)

97 He compared himself to Virgil, according to Suetonius, a comparison credited by Statius (2. 7, 74). The ban: Tacitus *Ann.* 15. 49; Dio 62. 29, 4. The Vacca Life alone mentions that pleading cases was also forbidden; Suetonius omits the ban altogether

98 The death of Thrasea Paetus, dated to 66 by Tacitus (*Ann.* 16. 34–5) is put in 65, earlier than the ban, by Dio's Epitomator (62. 26)

99 Dio 52. 20; Ulpian in *Digest* 50. 4, 8; *Digest* 4. 4, 2

100 Pliny *Pan.* 69; *CIL* 3. 21; 12. 316 (see Mommsen, *Staatsrecht*[3] I, 577). K. Rose's idea (*TAPA* 97 (1966), 394, n35), followed by Ahl (*Lucan*, 347, n24) that a one year remission is the most Lucan could have won, seems too rigid

101 See pp.45–6, 78, 254, n54. In 63 we find Corbulo allowed to take out with him his son-in-law as *pro legato* of a legion when he was not yet of senatorial age: legionary legates were usually ex-praetors (Tacitus *Ann.* 15. 28; Dio 62. 23, 6)

102 *Ann.* 15. 49, cf. Suet. *Life of Lucan*: 'paene signifer Pisonianae coniurationis'

103 Ahl, *Lucan*, 333f implausibly suggests that the *de incendio urbis* mentioned by the Vacca Life in a sentence beginning 'prosa oratione' is identical with the 'famosum carmen' mentioned by Suetonius. Statius, who claims to be praising Lucan for prose and verse, mentions no other work that could be prose. Nor is there any reason to think that the *famosum carmen* necessarily preceded and caused the ban (Ahl, 350–2)

104 Suetonius mentions recitations, and the Vacca Life definitely mentions publication as among the things that made Nero jealous

105 It is not ironic: see the verbal parallels for such excesses in Lebek, *Lucans Pharsalia*, 89f and compare also Seneca's *Ad Polybium*

106 I.670–2; II.62–3

107 Especially VII.440f; 455f; 641f and 696 ('the eternal pair of gladiators, Freedom and Caesar')

108 Tacitus *Ann.* 15. 52, 3

109 Tacitus *Ann.* 15. 49, 3

110 Tacitus *Ann.* 15. 70. One of the passages proposed is III.635–646 from one of three books published when he was still in favour

111 Tacitus *Ann.* 16. 28, 1 cf. 29, 2 (Curtius Montanus); *Ann.* 16. 19–20. The friend was Flavius Scaevinus (see 15. 49, 4)

112 Williams, *Change and Decline*, 289 suggests that the list was a key to the *Satyricon*. If it needed a key, it can hardly have been composed as a *roman à clef*, unless we assume that, of those most likely to catch the allusions, Nero was very stupid and his friends, including Petronius' rivals, very discreet

113 The August date depends on accepting Tacitus' testimony that the comet of 60 appeared during the first Neronia (*Ann.* 14. 22, 1): it was observed by Chinese astronomers on 9 August (R. S. Rogers, *TAPA* 84 (1953) 237f)

114 Tacitus *Ann.* 14. 21; Dio 61. 21, 2; Suetonius *Nero* 12. 3 who writes 'The crown for oratory and Latin verse for which all the most distinguished men had competed was offered to him with their consent and he accepted it', whereas the Vacca Life of Lucan says that the poet was crowned on this occasion for his poem, the *Laudes Neronis*. The solution adopted in the text is in essence that of J. Bolton in *CQ* 1948, 87 n4. For encomia (prose and verse) as providing distinct categories at Greek festivals, see e.g. *IG* 1773, *SEG* 3. 334; *MAMA* 8, no.240 and *IG XIV* add.755e (Naples) as restored by G. Civitelli. For discussion see L. Robert, *Études épigraphiques et philologiques* (Paris, 1938), 21f

115 Tacitus *Ann.* 15. 23. If the model was the Aktia at Nicopolis, music would have been included (Dio 51. 1, 2); if the celebration at Rome was followed, only horse-raising and athletics would have been appropriate (Dio 53. 1, 4–6; these are the games mentioned in *RG* 9. 1)

116 The character of Naples is noted in Cicero *Rab. Post.* 26; Dio 55. 10, 9; see D'Arms, *Romans on the Bay of Naples*, 83. See p.294, n7

117 *Ann.* 15. 33; Suet. *Nero* 20. 2. Seneca's Letters show him to have been in Campania in the spring and summer of 64 (*Epp.* 49–87): in *Ep.* 76 he mentions the theatre at Naples, claiming to prefer the philosopher's lecture-room

118 Suet. *Nero* 20. See p.113; *Ann.* 15. 34, see pp.102–3 and 151

119 Tacitus *Ann.* 15. 33–5; Suet. *Nero* 19. 1; 35. 5, cf. Dio 63. 18, 1; 62. 22, 4. On Suetonius, see Bradley, *Historical Commentary* on 19. 1 and 21. 1

120 As Caecina Tuscus was still Prefect of Egypt in July of 64 (P. Mich. 179) and his successor is not attested before May 66 (Josephus *Bellum Iudaicum* 2. 309), the baths that he built and used, thus incurring banishment, could have been prepared for a visit on the occasion of the Greek tour of 66/7 in which context Dio 63. 18, 1 reports his punishment. There were troop movements to Alexandria in 66, see p.229

121 Tacitus *Ann.* 15. 37. Dio 62. 15 dates to 64 before the Fire Nero's chariot-driving in public, but he could really be referring to the games (which he does not appear to mention) after the Fire (*Ann.* 15. 44). The performance in the Circus Maximus mentioned by Suet. *Nero* 22. 2 is probably the same as that noted by Dio 63. 1, 1 under the year 66

122 *Ann.* 16. 4–5; Dio 62. 29. Bolton, *CQ* 1948, 82f suggested, on the basis of Suet. *Nero* 21, that Nero planned the Neronia for 64 despite his intention to be in Greece himself, but then decided, after his Naples success, to participate personally and so held the contest early (Suetonius' *ante praestitutam diem*), performed on the lyre on the first day, then postponed the rest of the festival to the next year. His supporting argument from the semisses celebrating the festival was demolished long ago by MacDowall in *CQ* 8 (1958) 192f. But recently Bolton's view of the chronology has been revived by Bradley (*Commentary on Suetonius' Life of Nero*, 129–131) and M. Malavolta, *Sesta Miscellanea Greca e Romana* (Rome, 1978), 395f

123 The *certamen ad exemplar Actiacae religionis* (pp.160–1), if based on Augustus' games at Rome (last held in AD 9) should have followed the Greek five-year cycle and been due in 65, not in 63 or 64 when they were to have taken place

124 Tacitus *Ann.* 16. 21–2 (charges made to Nero but clearly repeated in the Senate, 16. 28, 2); Dio 62. 26, 3. On Nero's chariot-racing, see n121

125 Suet. *Nero* 22. 3; 23. 1; Bradley, *Commentary*, 140–1

126 Philostratus *Life of Apollonius* 5. 7; Eusebius ed. Schoene, 154, 157. Though the connection of these vows (Smallwood, *Documents* no 26) with Nero's departure for Greece means that he sailed late in the sailing season when there was some risk (Vegetius 4. 39), that is not a good reason for doubting it; the Arval records also show that a conspiracy was uncovered some time between 19 June and 25 September (see p.178), which would have delayed departure. The Arval vows could relate to Nero's departure from Rome or to his departure from Italy. In the former case, he would not have left Italy until about 12 October, still arriving before the close of the sailing season on 11 November. (G. Schumann, *Hellenistische und griechische Elemente in der Regierung Neros* (1930), 70 estimates the time for the crossing as three days from Brundisium to Corcyra, 14 days to Corinth)

127 Suet. *Nero* 19. 2; 24. 2; Plut. *Flam.* 12. 8; *ILS* 8794. The year is not given on the inscription but Suetonius' 'decedens' indicates 67, not 66. The only objection to the dating is based on *ILS* 5947 which seems to show that Sardinia began to be governed by a proconsul instead of a procurator in June 67 at the latest, for Pausanias 7. 17, 3 says that Nero handed Sardinia over to a senatorial governor to compensate for the loss of Achaea whose liberation meant freedom from direct Roman administration. But the inference that Achaea was already freed in 66 is unnecessary: arrangements for the change of administration in Sardinia could have been made in advance

128 Suet. *Nero* 23. 1; cf. Philostratus *Apollonius* 5. 7. Three to four months' labour was spent on the canal (B. Gerster *BCH* 8 (1884), 225f), and Nero left Greece in December. But the cutting of the canal could have been inaugurated at another visit, in between the normal and special celebrations of the games

129 Dio 63. 14, 3 mentions city festivals; 63. 21 the winning of 1808 crowns. Philostratus *Apollonius* 5. 8–9 mentions only the Olympic and Pythian

victories in that order. Eusebius, ed. Schoene, 156–7 gives the Olympic
victory first and later, in an entry headed 'rursum', notes Nero's victories
at the Isthmian, Pythian and Actian games. 'Again' here clearly alludes to
the Olympic victory and does not mean that the games mentioned
thereafter were repeated, as argued by Bradley *Latomus* 37 (1978), 61f. For
detailed discussion of the chronology of the tour, see Schumann,
Hellenistische und griechische Elemente, 67f. Gallivan, *Hermes* 101 (1973),
230f; Bradley, op. cit.

130 Suet. *Nero* 24–5; Dio 63. 14; 20; on the custom of breaching the walls,
Plut. *Mor.* 639E. On the route, see E. Makin, *JRS* 11 (1921), 25f. Dio, not
Suetonius, says that he did ascend the Capitol before going to the
Palatine. His route could have been the Porta Capena, Circus Maximus,
up the Vicus Tuscus through the Velabrum, then to the Capitoline temple
from which he could have doubled back into the Forum, up the Sacra
Via and the Clivus Palatinus and round the east side of the Palatine to the
Temple of Apollo

10 'What an Artist Dies with Me' *(pages 164–182)*

   1 Dio 61. 12, 2; see p.127. Various episodes of his life have been interpreted,
   not always convincingly, as re-enactments of tragedies by Baldwin in
   Mnemosyne 32 (1979), 380–1 and R.M. Frazer Jr., *Classical Journal* 62
   (1966), 17f

   2 Tacitus *Ann.* 15. 67; Dio 62. 24, 1–2

   3 Tacitus *Ann.* 15. 37; Dio 62. 15, 2f; 62. 28, 3

   4 Tacitus *Ann.* 15. 35, 3; he was still performing the travesty of clemency in
   65 (*Ann.* 16. 11 fin.)

   5 Suet. *Nero* 29; *Ann.* 16. 20; *Ann.* 15. 73, 1

   6 Initial guilt: *Ann.* 14. 10; Dio 61. 14, 1. The Furies: Suet. *Nero* 34. 4; Dio
   63. 14, 3

   7 *Ann.* 13. 49; 13. 33, cf. 16. 21, 3; 16. 21, 1–2 Dio 62. 26, 4; *Ann.* 14. 48;
   15. 20–2, 1

   8 *Ann.* 15. 23

   9 Tacitus' account of the conspiracy occupies chapters 48–74 of Book xv.
   He mentions his sources of information at 15. 53, 3–4 (Elder Pliny), 15.
   61, 3 (Fabius Rusticus) and 15. 73, 2 (the participants, whose testimony he
   could have received at first hand)

   10 Gaius' assassination: Josephus *Ant. Jud.* 19. 184; Lateranus: *Ann.* 15. 53, cf.
   13. 11; Epictetus 1. 1, 20 (the attribution of the remark to Lateranus
   requires a commonly accepted emendation of the text)

   11 *Ann.* 15. 51, 3; 15. 67

   12 Josephus *Ant. Jud.* 19. 162f; 212f

   13 Suet. *Gaius* 25, 1. The exile was in 40, not 37, as Dio 59. 8, 7–8 has it
   (*PIR²* C 284)

   14 *Ann.* 15. 48, 1, cf. p.85 on Tacitus' proleptic notice at 14. 65. Subrius
   Flavus' attempt: *Ann.* 15. 50. Praetorians had accompanied Nero when he
   sang at Naples (*Ann.* 15. 33), but some earlier performance on his private
   stage may be in question (*Ann.* 15. 33, 1): it is not necessary to suppose
   that the Juvenalia of 59 is meant

15 *Ann.* 14. 7, 4

16 Josephus *Ant. Jud.* 19. 200; Suet. *Gaius* 59; Dio 59. 29, 7

17 *Ann.* 15. 59, 4; 72, 1

18 *Ann.* 15. 71; 60; 61

19 *Ann.* 16. 1–3; Suet. *Nero* 31

20 Suet. *Nero* 32. In *Ann.* 16. 7 the wealth of Cassius Longinus only harms him by adding to his pre-eminence; cf. 16. 14, 1; 17, 4; see pp.205–6

21 *Ann.* 15. 62, 1; 16. 14, 3; 17; 19, 3. Dio's Epitomator 62. 28, 4 dates to the period after Poppaea's death the practice of buying safety from Tigellinus

22 Deification: *Ann.* 16. 6–7; 21; see p.103. Sporus: Dio 62. 28, 3; 63. 13, 1, cf. Suet. *Nero* 29

23 Statilia Messallina became his wife in 66, see p.194

24 Tacitus *Ann.* 16. 7, 2; 10, 4

25 Tacitus *Ann.* 16. 7–8; Suet. *Nero* 37; *Dig.* 1. 2, 2, 52 mentions that Cassius was sent to Sardinia, whence he was recalled by Vespasian

26 Examples are Pompeia Paullina (Seneca's widow), Fannia (Thrasea's widow) and Polla (Lucan's widow: Statius *Silvae* 2. 7; not, I believe, identical with Polla, the wife of Pollius Felix, of *Silvae* 2. 2; 3. 1; 4. 8)

27 Tacitus *Ann.* 16. 10. Thrasea's absence at the senatorial sessions when Lucius Silanus and Antistius Vetus were condemned was unusual and remarked (*Ann.* 16. 22, 1)

28 *Ann.* 16. 14; cf.14. 48; 12. 31

29 *Ann.* 16, 17–9, 21f

30 Plutarch *Cato Minor* 25, 37 notes Thrasea's biography as a source: the mention of Cato and of Favonius, an obscure follower of Cato, by Cossutianus Capito at *Ann.* 16. 22, 2 and 4 strongly suggests that a reference to the biography is intended

31 Helvidius' Stoicism is certified in Tacitus *Hist.* 4. 5; Paconius' philosophical ideas are celebrated by the Stoic Epictetus in 1. 1, 28–30; 1. 2, 12–3; frags. 21 and 22. Barea Soranus, according to the Scholiast on Juvenal 3. 116 was a *discipulus* of the Stoic philosopher Egnatius Celer whom Tacitus calls his *cliens* and *amicus* (*Ann.* 16. 32, 3). Barea's memory was later vindicated by Musonius Rufus (Tacitus *Hist.* 4. 10, 1 and 40. 3). Musonius Rufus, represented as an associate of Thrasea by Epictetus 1. 1, 27, is found with Rubellius Plautus in Asia at *Ann.* 14. 59

32 *Ann.* 14. 57, 3; 15. 71, 4

33 *Ann.* 16. 26, 4; Rusticus, later Thrasea's biographer, is attested as a Stoic in Pliny *Ep.* 1. 5, 2, cf. Dio 67. 13, 2. At *Ann.* 16. 34 Thrasea is shown discussing the immortality of the soul with Demetrius, a philosopher who appears frequently in Seneca's Neronian works as the ideal Cynic demonstrating the direct way to virtue (e.g. *Ben.* 7. 8, 2; *Ep.* 20, 9, cf. *Brev. Vit.* 14. 1 and Epictetus 3. 22 on the relationship of the true Cynic to Stoic teaching). The evidence for Demetrius' banishment by Nero rests on Philostratus' unreliable *Life of Apollonius of Tyana* 4. 42; 5. 19, but Epictetus 1. 25, 22 does show Nero threatening Demetrius, though the episode cannot be dated. Exile some time after Thrasea's suicide in 66 is possible

34 Heliodorus: Scholiast on Juvenal 1. 33; Cassius: Cicero, *Fam.* 15. 16–8. Cassius' grandfather Q. Aelius Tubero (the eminent jurist) was the son of

L. Aelius Tubero, whom Photius 169 Bk. describes as a devotee of the
Academics, and the grandson of Quintus, the well-known Stoic

35 On Petronius and C. Calpurnius Piso see p.277, n91

36 Julius Canus under Gaius (Seneca *Tranq. An.* 14. 4; Plut. *Mor.* frag.
211 S); Julius Graecinus (Tacitus *Agric.* 4; Seneca *Ep.* 29. 6)

37 Tacitus *Ann.* 16. 22, 4

38 Seneca *Ben.* 2. 20, where Seneca also misleads in implying that Brutus was
a Stoic when in fact he was a member of the Old Academy (Cicero *Fin.*
5. 8), whose doctrines were close to those of the Stoa (Cicero *Acad.*
2. 132). For the view of Stoics such as Panaetius current in Brutus' day,
see Cicero *Rep.* 1. 34; 61; 65; 69, cf. Seneca *Ep.* 90. 6 for the Stoic
Posidonius' view on the degeneration of kingship into tyranny

39 Diog. Laert. 7. 131; Aristotle *Pol.* 2. 1265b. Zeno's disciples Persaeus and
Sphaerus wrote works on the Spartan constitution (Diog. Laert. 7. 36;
178; Plut. *Lyc.* 5); Sphaerus advised King Cleomenes to restore the
'Lycurgan' institutions (Plut. *Cleom.* 2. 2; 11. 2)

40 Treatises *On Kingship* were written by Cleanthes, Persaeus and Sphaerus
(Diog. Laert. 7. 175; 36; 178). Persaeus was an adviser of Antigonus
Gonatas (Diog. Laert. 7. 36) and Sphaerus of King Cleomenes (note
above)

41 Note Tacitus' ironic comment on the instability of the mixed constitution
(*Ann.* 4. 33); Musonius Rufus, frag. 8 Hense

42 Cicero *Leg.* 3. 14. On Seneca's purpose in discussing the Principate in
these terms see pp.77–8, 95

43 Proposed by Rostovtzeff, *SEHRE*[2], 115f. What Seneca says at *Ben.* 4. 31,
1 and what Marcus did about his son must count forcibly against this
view. It was probably Helvidius Priscus' criticism of the moral character
of his sons Titus and Domitian which drew from Vespasian the remark
'My son will succeed or no one' (Dio 66. 12)

44 Tacitus *Ann.* 16. 22, 2; Suet. *Nero* 37. 1; contrast Pliny *Ep.* 8. 22, 3; Dio
61. 15, 3 and the advice to avoid empty gestures that Thrasea gave to
Arulenus Rusticus at *Ann.* 16. 26, 4. Dio 66. 12, 3 contrasts Thrasea's
reasonableness with the provocative behaviour of Helvidius Priscus
towards Vespasian

45 Cassius: Cicero *Fam.* 15. 19, 2–3 (clemency praised in Epicurean terms);
15. 19, 4 (45 BC); Plut. *Caesar* 66. 2 on the assassination, cf. the view of
Statilius the Epicurean in Plut. *Brutus* 12. Brutus: Seneca (*Cons. Helv.* 8. 1,
cf. Cicero *Brutus* 250) testifies to the importance he gave in his work *On
Virtue* to our independence of external circumstance; *Brutus* 330f seems to
urge him away from acquiescence to higher goals

46 Demetrius: Seneca *Ben.* 7. 11; Epictetus 1. 25, 22; Suet. *Vesp.* 13; Dio 66.
13, 1–2. Tradition of free speech: Seneca *Ben.* 5. 6, 2–7; *Epp.* 28. 8
(Socrates); 9. 18 (Stilpo). Seneca claimed that he had exercised *libertas* in
his relations with Nero: Tacitus *Ann.* 15. 61, 1; Thrasea showed it,
according to Tacitus *Ann.* 16. 24, 2

47 Socrates: Epictetus 4. 1, 160; passive resistance, e.g. Epictetus 1. 29;
Thrasea at *Ann.* 16. 22, 1; Dio 66. 12, 3

48 Suicide as guaranteeing the freedom of the wise man, *SVF* 3. 768; 363;
Epictetus 1. 25, 18–20; 4. 1, 30–2; Plut. *Cato Minor* 67, 1–2

49 The Panaetian doctrine of the *personae* (roles) is set out by Cicero in *De Officiis* I. 107 and traces of it are found in Seneca *Tranq. An.* 6; *Ben.* 2. 17, 2; Epictetus I. 2; I. 6, 15; 3. 23, 4–5. Classification of duties by social role was older (Seneca *Ep.* 94. 35): Panaetius thought inborn talents and the type of life one had chosen should also be considered. See Brunt, *PCPhS* 19 (1973), 9f; *PBSR* 43 (1975), 7f; Griffin, *Seneca*, 341f. Cicero on Cato: *Off.* I. 112

50 Thrasea Paetus and Helvidius Priscus celebrated the birthdays of Brutus and Cassius (Juvenal 5. 36–7): others, not known to be Stoics, revered them; Seneca, who disapproved of the assassination of Caesar, did not: *Ben.* 2. 20; *Ira* 3. 30, 4. Tyrannicide is an 'ex tempore officium' in Cicero *Off.* 3. 32, perhaps following Posidonius (*Att.* 16. 11, 4). For such duties in general, Diog. Laert. 7. 109

51 Tacitus *Ann.* 15. 68. For a fuller discussion of the question of Seneca's participation in the conspiracy see 'Imago Vitae Suae' in ed. C.D.N. Costa, *Seneca* (London, 1974), 25–8

52 Dio 62. 24, 1; Tacitus *Ann.* 15. 60, 4; 51; Polyaenus *Stratagems* 8. 62: it is also stated there that Epicharis was persuaded to join the conspiracy by Seneca

53 Tacitus *Ann.* 15. 60, cf. 15. 56, 2. For the wording of the imperial oath, *ILS* 190; Suet. *Gaius* 15. 3; Epictetus I. 14, 15

54 *Ann.* 15. 65. Cf. Juvenal *Sat.* 8. 211–4: 'If a free vote were given to the people, who would be so depraved as to waver in his preference for Seneca over Nero?'

55 *Ira* I. 6, 3; *Ben.* 7. 20, 3. Caesar's murder: n50. Gaius' murder: Seneca's references show he had no direct knowledge: *Ira* I. 20, 9; *Const. Sap.* 18. Civil War: *Ben.* I. 10, 2; *Ep.* 73. 9–10

56 Plato *Gorgias* 473–80, 525b and elsewhere, cf. Cicero *Fin.* 4. 56

57 Tacitus *Hist.* 4. 5; Epictetus I. 1, 28ff, cf. *Ann.* 16. 10 (Petronius' panache)

58 *Ann.* 14. 57, 3, cf. 22, 1; 14. 52, 4

59 *Ann.* 14. 57, 3; 16. 22, 1–2

60 Seneca *Otio* 8. 1; *Tranq. An.* I. 10; Pliny *Ep.* I. 10, 10. Contrast with Epicureanism: Seneca *Ep.* 90. 35; Horace *Ep.* I. 1, 16–7; Epictetus 3. 7, 21

61 Plut. *Mor.* 1033 B–E; Seneca *Tranq. An.* I. 10; *Otio* I. 5; *Ep.* 68, 1; Dio Chrys. 47. 2

62 Seneca *Otio* 3. 2; Cicero *Rep.* I. 10; Diog. Laert. 7. 121

63 *SVF* 3. 611; Seneca *Otio* 3. 3–4; 8. 1; *Ep.* 68. 2

64 Tacitus *Ann.* 16. 28, 2; 13. 28, 3, cf. *Hist.* 2. 91, 3: Helvidius as praetor (the next office) in 70. Note that his biographer, Herennius Senecio, refused to rise above the quaestorship, thereby offending Domitian (Dio 67. 13, 2) and that his son, the younger Helvidius, withdrew from politics after his consulship under that same Emperor (Pliny *Ep.* 9. 13, 3)

65 Cicero *Phil.* 12. 14; Tacitus *Ann.* 2. 34, 1; 2. 43, 2

66 Cicero *Att.* 9. 18, 1; Tacitus *Ann.* 6. 27, 3; 16. 27, 2

67 Tacitus *Ann.* 16. 26, 4; Plut. *Cato Minor* 66. 3

68 Tacitus *Hist.* 4. 6; 9; 43; Suet. *Vesp.* 15; Dio 66. 12; Epictetus I. 2, 19–24

69 Tacitus *Ann.* 16. 26, 5; Epictetus I. 2, 12–18

70 Helvidius Priscus was put to death by Vespasian who also expelled Demetrius and others (Dio 66. 12, 3–13). In 93 Arulenus Rusticus and Herennius Senecio were condemned and there was an expulsion of philosophers including Artemidorus, Epictetus and possibly Plutarch (Tacitus *Agric.* 2; Pliny *Ep.* 3. 11, 2; Suet. *Dom.* 10. 3; Dio 67. 13, 3)

71 Tacitus *Hist.* 4. 42; 1. 48, 1; Dio 63, 18, 2. See p.196, on the Crassi

72 Tacitus *Ann.* 14. 57–8; 16. 23. For the date of Barea's proconsulship and attendant problems see p.256, n10

73 Josephus *Ant. Jud.* 19. 49; 52; Dio 60. 15, 1; Pliny *Ep.* 3. 16, 7

74 On Corbulo's wife and family connections see Syme, *JRS* 60 (1970), 27f. The two sons of his half-brother were: Glitius Gallus (*Ann.* 15. 71, 3) and Ser. Cornelius Salvidienus Orfitus (Suet. *Nero* 37. 1 and Dio 62. 27, who connect his fate with that of Cassius Longinus in 65; but he was still alive after that (*Ann.* 16. 12, 2), so that a date after the *Annals* breaks off is indicated)

75 Suet. *Nero* 36; *AFA* Henzen, LXXXIV (= Smallwood, *Documents*, no. 26). Henzen, LXXX note and 115 suggested that the entry '[ob det] ecta [nefariorum consilia]' earlier in the year (LXXXI = Smallwood, *Documents*, no. 25), before the notices relevant to Tiridates' visit, also refers to this plot, but then the detection of the conspiracy should be in the *Annals*: such a slow unravelling of it seems in any case unlikely. The entry more likely concerns an anniversary of the Pisonian conspiracy. If it is reasonable to expect three sets of consuls in AD 66, then the thank-offerings belong to September, not earlier (Gallivan, *CQ* 24 (1974), 303)

76 See p.161

77 Tacitus *Ann.* 15. 28, 3; Dio 62. 23, 6; *Ann.* 16. 23, 2: as for the date, the *AFA* record the dedication of laurel on the Capitol and thanksgivings probably before mid-May (Henzen, LXXXI = Smallwood, *Documents*, no. 25). See Henzen, 78–9 and (for the date) Henzen, LXXXIII (= Smallwood, *Documents*, no. 26), n3

78 Suet. *Nero* 37. 3; Tacitus *Hist.* 4. 42. Aquillius' victims: *Hist.* 4. 42, 1; Dio 63. 18, 2; Pliny *Ep.* 1. 5, 3

79 Dio 63. 15, 1; Suet. *Nero* 37. 3

80 Dio 60. 21, 2. Of the men who went with Claudius, D. Valerius Asiaticus, M. Vinicus and Cn. Sentius Saturninus had all played a prominent part in the attempt to prevent Claudius assuming the purple in 41; others were Roman *nobiles* like Ser. Sulpicius Galba, Cn. Pompeius Magnus and L. Junius Silanus (see A. Birley, *People of Roman Britain* (London, 1981), 23). For Nero's entourage see Bradley, *Illinois Classical Studies* IV (1979), 152f

81 Dio 63. 12; 63. 14, 3; 66. 11, 2, cf. Josephus *BJ* 3. 8; Suet. *Vesp.* 4. 4; Tacitus *Hist.* 4. 41. The counter-charge made by Paccius against Vibius Crispus in 70 might suggest that the latter was also present in Greece and similarly occupied

82 C.P. Jones, *HSCP* 71 (1966), 209 adducing IG 2/3² 4184; Gallivan, *CQ* 24 (1974), 304–5

83 Statilia Messallina is honoured in the Boeotian inscription celebrating the liberation of Greece (*ILS* 8794) and her name is plausibly restored in the records of the Arval Brothers where sacrifices are being offered on 25 September 66, probably to be connected with the Emperor's departure for Greece (Smallwood, *Docs.*, no. 26). It is in any case unlikely that Nero, who wanted an heir, would have left his newly-married wife behind when he was to be away for some time (Bradley (n80) 154)

84 Letters: Suet. *Nero* 23. 1; embassies: Josephus *BJ* 2. 558. Phoebus: Dio 63. 10, 1a; Sporus: Dio 63. 12, 3–4; Pythagoras: Dio 63. 13, 2. Calvia Crispinilla: Dio 63. 12, 3–4; *Hist.* 1. 73, see Bradley, *AJPh* 93 (1972), 451f

85 Josephus *BJ* 2. 555; 3. 3f

86 Dio 63. 19, 1, cf. Suet. *Nero* 23. 1. Presumably Polyclitus was left in charge when Helius made his lightning seven day journey to Greece (Dio 63. 12, 3)

87 Vindex was (*legatus*) *pro praetore* of a Gallic province (Plut. *Galba* 4. 2) which was unarmed (Tacitus *Hist.* 1. 16, 2): Gallia Lugdunensis seems most likely, but for the possibilities see Bradley, *Historical Commentary*, 245–6. D.C.A. Shotter, *Hist.* 24 (1975), 61 suggests that Helius was anxious about Vindex' early moves, namely his letters to provincial governors (Plut. *Galba* 4. 2; Suet. *Galba* 9. 2) and to exiled senators (Joann. Antioch. fr. 91 Muell.)

88 Suet. *Nero* 40. 4; the anniversary of his mother's death fell in the period 19–23 March

89 Fonteius Capito, the governor of Lower Germany, was also a recent appointment as he was *consul ordinarius* in 67, leaving office before 20 June. The governor of Aquitania proved loyal, if that is the correct interpretation of Suet. *Galba* 9. 2

90 Suet. *Nero* 41; Dio 63. 26, 4

91 Suet. *Galba* 10. 2; 14. 2; Plut. *Galba* 5; Dio 63. 23; 64. 6, 5[2]; Tacitus *Hist.* 1. 13, 4; 1. 53

92 Nero's consulship: Suet. *Nero* 43. 2 says he replaced both consuls but Pliny *Pan.* 57.2 mentions only one, and the Fasti still record one consul, i.e. Galerius Trachalus, with Nero: but that may be conventional, according to Bradley, *Historical Commentary*, 264. The date was probably in April as Suetonius has only just reported Galba's defection at this point and Gaul is shown as uppermost in Nero's mind (42. 2 *prosperi quiddam* need not be Vindex' defeat at Vesontio): see p.301, n77. Galba a public enemy: Plut. *Galba* 5. 4. Troops summoned home: Tacitus *Hist.* 1. 6; 9; 31; 70. Troops recruited: Tacitus *Hist.* 1. 6; Suet. *Nero* 44. 1; Dio 63. 27, 1a. On these arrangements see Chilver, *Historical Commentary on Tacitus' Histories I and II*, 6–7

93 Clodius Macer: Plut. *Galba* 6; Tacitus *Hist.* 1. 73; 2. 97, 2; 4. 49, 4

94 Plut. *Galba* 6 has Verginius' army offer him the purple before *and* after Vesontio but Dio's view (63. 25, 1) seems to be supported by Tacitus *Hist.* 1. 8, 2 where he says of the German troops: 'tarde a Nerone desciverant, nec statim pro Galba Verginius'. The second phrase there suggests that Verginius delayed in putting down the Vindex rebellion as long as he thought this compatible with his duty as commander of Upper Germany (Plut. *Galba* 6. 2; 10. 2; Dio 63. 25; Pliny *Ep.* 9. 19, 5). *Hist.* 4. 69, 2 shows that Tacitus thought Verginius did ultimately *lead* his army against Vindex. Verginius' epitaph and his reply to the historian Cluvius Rufus suggest he himself told the story that way, though Dio 63. 25 and Plut. *Galba* 6. 3 claim he lost control of his troops who attacked Vindex on their own initiative. But it is most unlikely that a man who had failed to maintain control of his own troops would be offered the Empire, or be regarded as too dangerous by Galba either to leave in command or to punish (*Hist.* 1. 8, 2). It is a story that Galba, who removed Verginius 'under the pretext of friendship', might have sponsored

95 Dio 63. 27; Tacitus *Hist.* 2. 27; 1. 9, 2. On these events see Chilver, *Historical Commentary*, 11–12

96 Tacitus *Hist.* 1. 6; Plut. *Galba* 15. 2; 17. 3; Dio 63. 27, 1a

97 Suet. *Nero* 47. 1–2; Plut. *Galba* 2. 1; Dio 63. 27, 2. The Prefect of Egypt Tiberius Julius Alexander issued an edict (Smallwood, *Documents*, no. 391) proclaiming support for Galba on 6 July, only a week or so after he could have received news of Galba's proclamation by the Senate. Indeed, it was probably drafted earlier (see Shotter, *Hist.* 24 (1975), 63, n39)

98 Suet. *Nero* 47; 48. 2; Plut. *Galba* 2. 2; 14, 2; Tacitus *Hist.* 1. 5

99 Tacitus *Hist.* 1. 72, 1–2

100 Suet. *Nero* 49. 2; Plut. *Galba* 7. 2; Dio 63. 29, 1

101 Suet. *Nero* 49. 1 and 4

11 Why Did It Happen?   (pages 185–188)

1 *Histories* 1. 89

2 *Hist.* 2. 11, cf. 2. 27, 2. For Nero's sake, they were quick to join Otho against Galba

3 *Hist.* 1. 5, 1, cf. 1. 30; Plutarch *Galba* 2; 7; 14

4 Suet. *Nero* 48. 2. He left Rome by the Via Nomentana

5 *Ann.* 15. 72

6 This may be what Dio Chrysostom means by his rather obscure remarks in *Or.* 21. 10: 'It was solely on account of his abuse of the eunuch Sporus that he lost his life. For the latter in anger disclosed the Emperor's designs to his retinue, and so they revolted from him and compelled him to make away with himself as best he could'. Compare Suet. *Nero* 49: Sporus was one of Nero's companions on his last night

7 *Hist.* 1. 78; Plut. *Otho* 3; Suet. *Otho* 7; 10; Dio 64.8; 65.7, 3; Suet. *Vit.* 11

8 *Hist.* 1. 4, 3: cf. *Ann.* 14. 60–1 where Poppaea claims that those who protested against the deposition of Octavia were only her own clients and slaves calling themselves the Roman Plebs. Suet. *Nero* 57. 1

9 Plut. *Galba* 4. 3; 6. 4, cf. *Hist.* 1. 51 where Tacitus says that Vindex lost all his men. It is not necessary to assume that the 100,000 included the Rhine legionaries, given the numbers of the Gallic tribes as given earlier by Strabo (e.g. at 4. 3 he gives 200,000 for the Arverni, one of the tribes which joined Vindex (*Hist.* 4. 17)): Vindex was no doubt counting the total following he thought his chieftains could command (Josephus *BJ* 4. 440 refers to his supporters as 'the chiefs of the land')

10 Suet. *Galba* 10; Tacitus *Hist.* 1. 11; 2. 97, 2

11 C.M. Kraay, *NC* (1949), 129f; Dio 63. 22

12 Dio 63. 22, 1a; Plut. *Galba* 4; Pliny *NH* 18. 35; Josephus *BJ* 2. 293 (Judaea); Smallwood, *Docs.* no. 391, para. 1 and 4 (Egypt); *Ann.* 15. 45; 16. 23; Dio 63. 11 (Greece). Tacitus *Hist.* 4. 74, 2

13 See pp.180f. On the more remote allies that Galba collected before his recognition by the Senate, see Chilver, *JRS* 47 (1957), 29f and his *Commentary*, 12

14 *Hist.* 1. 16

15 *Ann.* 4. 33. Tacitus does not appear to share the view that the mixed constitution had been realised in the Roman Republic
16 E.g. Seneca *Ben.* 2. 20
17 Tacitus *Ann.* 1. 1–2; 4. 33, 2; Dio 53. 17
18 But note *Ann.* 6. 45, 3 showing that Gaius too was charged by Tacitus with simulation

12 The Problem of the Succession *(pages 189–196)*

1 Herodian 2. 21, 4 can say of the time when the short-lived Princeps Didius Julianus was dethroned in AD 193 that the consuls normally take over business when there is a succession crisis. This had certainly happened after the assassination of Gaius when the consuls convened the Senate, gave orders to the Praetorian Guard and took charge of public funds (Jos. *AJ* 19. 160; Dio 60. 1, 1; Jos. *AJ* 19. 186; Dio 59. 30, 3)
2 Verginius Rufus and Petronius Turpilianus: see p.182
3 Tacitus *Hist.* 1. 12; 55. Suet. *Galba* 16
4 *Hist.* 1. 56, 2–3. Note the different *ad hoc* arrangements for senatorial election in AD 238 concocted by Herodian (7. 10, 3) and *HA Max. et Balb.* 1. 1. Cf. the method of imperial nomination envisaged at *HA Hadrian* 4. 9
5 *Staatsrecht*³, vol II, 1133
6 Pliny *NH* 6. 84–91
7 *Pan.* 7. 7
8 Pliny *Pan.* 7. 4–7; 94. 5: Pliny explicitly states that the Princeps will adopt only if fate denies him a son of his own
9 *Hist.* 1. 16–17, cf. Suet. *Galba* 17. Galba did not follow the normal legal procedure for adoption. He chose Piso in the praetorian camp, at what Tacitus ironically terms 'comitia imperii': there were, of course, no 'imperial elections'
10 *Ben.* 4. 31, 1; see p.173
11 *Clem.* 1. 9, 3–9
12 *Hist.* 1. 16, 1
13 The poet Thallus possibly celebrates the new cognomen Caesar and describes Claudius as Augustus' grandson in *AP* 6. 235, according to Cameron, *GRBS* 21 (1980), 43f
14 See pp.97; 257, n70
15 Suet. *Aug.* 63. 2
16 *Ann.* 11. 35, 6; see pp.26–7, 29
17 Seneca *Apocolocyntosis* 10. 3–14. 1
18 *Ann.* 15. 52, 3; see pp.158–9
19 See p.196 and n43 for M. Licinius Crassus Frugi and his brother; p.114 for Sulpicius Camerinus and his son; p.170 for Antistius Vetus
20 *Ann.* 15. 52, 2–3; 53, 3–4
21 Suet. *Nero* 35. 4, cf. Dio 61. 1, 2
22 Tacitus reports the death of Vestinus Atticus at *Ann.* 15. 68, 3, before the death of Lucan, dated to 30 April by the Vacca Life
23 Smallwood, *Documents* no. 26, l. 8 (= Henzen lxxxiii and 172)
24 See p.285, n83. The story of Antonia is astutely treated by P. Fabia, *RPh* 19 (1895), 228f who is sceptical of the Pisonian involvement; the chronology is analysed by Bradley in *Symbolae Osloenses* 52 (1977), 79f

25 *Ann.* 3. 29

26 Suet. *Claud.* 26, 2. On the family, see Taylor, *MAAR* 24 (1956), 26f

27 Tacitus *Ann.* 11. 36, 4

28 *Ann.* 13. 11, 2; see p.116f

29 Suet. *Nero* 35. 4; Tacitus *Ann.* 15. 49, 3

30 *Ann.* 13.1. At *Ann.* 13. 14, 3, Tacitus makes Agrippina invoke the spirits of the Silani in listing the crimes she has committed to effect her son's elevation. See pp.39, 73, 115, 169–70

31 Tacitus *Ann.* 6. 15, 1; see pp.178–9

32 *Ann.* 14. 47

33 Three illnesses: Suet. *Nero* 51. One was in 60 (*Ann.* 14. 22, 40); one in 68 (Suet. *Nero* 41. 1; Dio 63. 26, 1) and one possibly in 66 (Philostratus *Life of Apollonius* 4. 44), but the passage is chronologically confused, for the thunderbolt and gymnasium mentioned in the context belong in 60 (*Ann.* 14. 22) and 601 (*Ann.* 14. 47 with p.247, n44): see p.263, n66

34 I have used J. Willems, *Musée Belge* 6 (1902), 140f for the surviving consulars. L. Calpurnius Piso survived Cassius Longinus, as can be inferred from Pliny *Ep.* 3. 7, 12; on his son's connections by marriage, see p.196 and n44

35 See pp.170 for his exile in 65

36 Aulus Plautius is last attested in AD 57 (*Ann.* 13. 32)

37 Syme, *Tacitus*, 787, adducing inscriptional evidence

38 Tacitus *Ann.* 12. 22; Dio 59. 12, 1; Suet. *Gaius* 25. 2, *AE* 1967, no. 448

39 The Prefect of the City, murdered in this year, was Pedanius Secundus: he might not have inspired respect (*Ann.* 14. 42), though he was the obvious stopgap

40 Suet. *Nero* 35. 5. Tacitus' silence might favour a date after mid-66, where his account breaks off

41 Tacitus *Hist.* 3. 38–9

42 Seneca *Apoc.* 11. 2, 5; Suet. *Claud.* 29; Tacitus *Hist.* 1. 48

43 Tacitus *Hist.* 1. 48, 1; 4. 42; 1. 43

44 They were: a fourth son of Claudius' victim, named Licinius Crassus Scribonianus: *Hist.* 1. 47; 4. 39 (apparently dead by 4. 42, 1); the husband of their sister Licinia Magna, L. Calpurnius Piso, consul of 57: *Hist.* 4. 49; his cousin ('consobrinus') Calpurnius Galerianus, son of the conspirator of 65: *Hist.* 4. 11; 4. 49. Vespasian himself used his absence as an excuse for such murders (Suet. *Vesp.* 15)

45 Dio 68. 3, 2; 68. 16, 2; *SHA Hadr.* 5. 5 and 6: his name was C. Calpurnius Piso Crassus Frugi Licinianus. One of his two brothers may be the Libo Frugi mentioned as a consular in 101 by Pliny (*Ep.* 3. 9, 33), see *PIR²* L 166: possibly the maternal great-grandfather of Marcus Aurelius

46 *Hist.* 2. 72

47 Tacitus *Agric.* 45. 2. For the murders of Flavius Sabinus and Flavius Clemens, Suet. *Domitian* 10. 4; 15. 1

13   The Problem of Finance   *(pages 197–207)*

1 Juvenal 4. 38; Suet. *Dom.* 3. 2

2 Suet. *Nero* 10 (which runs into chapter 11 on games); 26. 1; 30–2; cf. *Gaius* 17–21; 37–42; *Dom.* 4–5; 12

3 *Ann.* 13. 29 (on which see p.57); 13. 31; 13. 50–1; 15. 18

4 See pp.186–7 *Ann.* 15. 45, 1–2; *Hist.* 1. 20; Dio 63. 14; Suet. *Galba* 15. 1

5 Pliny *NH* 33. 47. MacDowall, *Western Coinages of Nero*, 135f. His estimate of the change in value of the silver (5–10%) is less than that of D. Walker (14.4%) in *The Metrology of the Roman Silver Coinage, Part I, BAR* 5 (1976), p.45

6 Pliny writes at *NH* 33. 132 (where the text may be corrupt): 'Forgers put an alloy of copper in silver coins, while others reduce the weight, the proper coinage being 84 denarii from one pound of silver'. After the Neronian reform, the denarius was struck at 96 to a pound of silver, but it is not clear that Pliny's disapproval is directed at Emperors rather than producers of spurious coin

7 Pliny discusses the purpose of the Republican reductions at 33. 44–5. See pp.123–4; MacDowall, *Western Coinages*, 135f who discusses the alternative explanations mentioned below

8 It is true that the new weight of the denarius did improve the relationship between it and eastern silver, but an easier way of achieving this would have been to improve the eastern silver coinages rather than affect such a drastic change in Roman gold and silver

9 The drain of money to India is attested by Pliny *NH* 12. 84; that to Arabia in *NH* 6. 162. The scarcity of post-Tiberian coins on a great trade route in India has been explained as the result (intended by the Emperor) of a crisis of confidence in Roman coins after the debasement of the denarius. But the Roman way of dealing with such a currency drain would have been sumptuary laws and bans on the export of bullion (cf. Cicero *Pro Flacco* 67). Nero's proposal to cancel indirect taxes including import and export duties certainly suggests no concern with such a problem in AD 58 (Tacitus *Ann.* 13. 50). Moreover, it has been suggested that the trade went on via a new route around the southern tip of India, for coins of Nero and Vespasian have been found in Ceylon (see C. Starr, *CPh.* 51 (1956), 27f)

10 In its latest form (E. Lo Cascio in *JRS* 71 (1981), 80) the argument is that high production of gold in Dalmatia, attested for Nero's reign by Pliny *NH* 33. 67, required the greater reduction in the precious metal content of the silver than of the gold. But Pliny gives no date and, in any case, imperial control of mines in the Empire was so close that a new find need not automatically have affected the market price of gold. Most important, there was no need to reduce the weight of the gold also if the only aim was to achieve the correct relative value of gold and silver: a lesser reduction of the denarius would have sufficed

11 Walker, *Metrology Part I*, 111f

12 MacDowall, *Western Coinages*, 138; Walker, *Metrology Part I*, 119 notes that Galba's mints in Spain and Gaul struck at the Augustan standard of fineness rather than the Neronian one used in Rome and suggests that the officials told to strike there at Nero's weight did not know of his simultaneous reduction in fineness

13 See pp.186–7; Suet. *Nero* 32. 4

14 Tacitus *Ann.* 15. 46 has the collections in Greece and Asia initiated in 64 as a direct result of the Fire

15 Suet. *Nero* 32. 1. See most recently Bradley, *Historical Commentary*, 165–6

16 Seneca *Ben.* 7. 17, 3; see pp.57, 63f; Tacitus *Ann.* 15. 18, cf. Dio 55. 25, 6

17 Suet. *Aug.* 101, 4; Tac. *Ann.* 1. 11; Suet. *Gaius* 16. 1. Pliny *Ep.* 8. 6, 7 calls the *a rationibus, custos principalium opum*; see his role in *FIRA²* 1 no. 61

18 Dio 53. 22; cf. Tacitus *Ann.* 6. 2, 1

19 On this vexed question, see Millar, *ERW* 197f

20 Jerome *Chron.* ed. Helm; cf. Orosius 7. 7, 8; Dio 7. 33 reports a request of Marcus Aurelius for a grant of money from the *aerarium*

21 Tacitus *Ann.* 13. 31, 2. Cf. *RG* 17; Dio 58. 21, 5 (AD 33): he clarifies the accounts in Tacitus *Ann.* 6. 17, 3 and Suet. *Tib.* 48

22 *BC* 3. 168. Frontinus *de aquis* 2. 118 records the diversion of the rentals on water-rights from the *aerarium* to Domitian's coffers, which were restored by Nerva. But, as they had been inefficiently collected, Domitian may have had as his chief aim to improve the revenue. On the Emperor's share of unclaimed and confiscated goods, see below p.202

23 In 62 BC after Pompey's eastern conquests, the annual income of the *aerarium* was 340,000,000 HS (Plut. *Pomp.* 45. 4). Since then Gaul and Egypt had been organized as provinces and other provinces had been increased in size (see T. Frank, *ESAR* vol v, 6–7)

24 On the importance of the imperial wealth, see Millar, *JRS* 53 (1963), 29f

25 Pliny *NH* 18. 94–5: the procurator writing to the Emperor about the Byzacium plain in Africa

26 Cost of the Neronia: *Ann.* 14. 21, 2; *Ann.* 14. 18 shows Nero allowing odd bits of state land to be usurped by squatters with a loss of rents. The great example is the liberation of Greece, on which see n73 below

27 See pp.63–4f for Nero's lavishness before 62. Suet. *Nero* 10: 'ex Augusti praescripto'

28 Val. Max. 4. 4, 1; 4. 8, 1. Cicero *Off.* 2. 56; 62; *Brutus* 164

29 Dio 53. 22, 1; *RG* 15. 1, 3; 21. 1–2; 22–3

30 See p.21

31 Suet. *Aug.* 71 on the 'caelestis gloria' his generosity would earn

32 Dio 66. 10, 3; Tacitus *Ann.* 2. 38, 3

33 See T. Frank, *ESAR* vol v, 14–17. Suet. *Aug.* 41 shows the inflationary impact of the arrival of the Egyptian treasure in Rome; Suet. *Aug.* 101. 3 on the legacies he had received

34 Suet. *Aug.* 101, 3; Dio 56. 32, 2

35 Tacitus *Agricola* 12. 6

36 After Claudius made the procurators who looked after his properties judges in their own cases, the already privileged position of the *fiscus* in law must have been enhanced (Tacitus *Ann.* 12. 60) at least for a time (Pliny *Pan.* 36)

37 Suet. *Cal.* 38. 3; *Domitian* 12. 1–2, cf. Pliny *Pan.* 42

38 *bona vacantia*: Tacitus *Ann.* 2. 48: in this case, the claim of the *fiscus* could have arisen because of the kinship between the Aemilii Lepidi (to which family the intestate freedwoman seemed to belong) and the imperial house, but see Millar, *ERW* 158f for the Hellenistic background; *bona damnatorum*: the notion of ingratitude for former imperial generosity was

invoked in the first cases; Tacitus *Ann.* 4. 20, 6. 19, cf. Dio 58. 22, 2; *Ann.* 6. 2

39 Thus under Trajan *fiscus* and *aerarium* still share *bona vacantia* and *bona damnatorum* (Pliny *Pan.* 42. 1). Pliny also mentions goods which the Augustan inheritance laws prevented legatees from taking and which originally were forfeit to the *aerarium* (Tacitus *Ann.* 3. 28)

40 Tacitus *Ann.* 2. 42; Suet. *Tib.* 54. 1; 48; 46; *Ann.* 4. 64; 2. 47; 4. 13; 6. 45; 2. 48; 1. 75

41 *Ann.* 4. 62, 2; 6. 45, 1; Suet. *Tib.* 47

42 See above, n21 and cf. Suet. *Aug.* 41. 1

43 Suet. *Tib.* 75. 1, 3

44 Suet. *Gaius* 37. 3; 21; Dio 59. 14, 6; Pliny *NH* 16. 201; Suet. *Gaius* 22. 4

45 Suet. *Gaius* 16; 18. 2–3; Dio 59. 6; 59. 2. 2; 2. 3; Seneca *Helv.* 10. 4

46 Suet. *Gaius* 38. 2; Dio 59. 15, 2

47 Suet. *Gaius* 39–40; Dio 59. 14, 1–2

48 Suet. *Claud.* 20–1; 18

49 See p.108. Tacitus is hostile to the Fucine Lake project (*Ann.* 12. 57) and neutral about the aqueduct (11. 13, 2). Dio 60. 11, 1–5 is favourable: the text of the opening sentence of Suet. *Claud.* 20 is disputed, but the reported hesitations of Caesar and Augustus strike a negative note. The Flavian attitude appears in Pliny *NH* 36. 122–5, who praises the aqueduct and harbour and reproaches Nero for neglecting the Fucine Lake project

50 Dio 59. 2, 3; Suet. *Claud.* 10. 4; Dio 60. 12, 4

51 Suet. *Claud.* 4. 7; 9. 2

52 Dio 60. 17, 1; Pliny *NH* 33. 54

53 Suet. *Claud.* 28; 29. 2; Seneca *Apoc.* 14. On Calp. Sic. 4. 117–21, see above p.252, n81

54 Suet. *Claud.* 28 (Claudius complaining of shortage of funds): see p.32 on his will

55 Tacitus *Ann.* 12. 7, 3; 13. 13, 2; 13. 18; 14. 6

56 The period 54–63 was one of great activity in the eastern minting of silver which is reasonably connected with the war with Parthia: Walker, *Metrology of the Roman Silver Coinage Part III, BAR* 40 (1978), 112; MacDowall, *Western Coinages*, 141. On the expenses of Tiridates' visit: Dio 63. 2, 2; 5. 4–6. 6; Suet. *Nero* 30. 2. The provinces also suffered from the obligation to support him in transit (Pliny *NH* 30. 16)

57 There were 9 cohorts under Tiberius in AD 23 (Tacitus *Ann.* 4. 5). The evidence for the increase is epigraphic, *ILS* 2701, showing 12 cohorts by the reign of Nero. *AE* 1973, no. 286 now provides evidence for an eleventh cohort under Augustus and/or Tiberius. If this increase was made after AD 23 under Tiberius, no change need be attributed to his successors, but the order of posts on the inscription more naturally suggests that this increase was made by Augustus and that Tiberius effected a reduction some time before AD 23

58 See p.63; Dio 61. 14, 3; Tacitus *Ann.* 12. 69

59 Tacitus *Hist.* 4. 46: 'The cost of retaining such a large number of men was immense'. By 69 Vitellius had raised the number of cohorts to sixteen and others were claiming places in the Guard. Vespasian was no doubt

thinking of donatives as well as annual pay. *ILS* 1993 dated to AD 76 shows the reduction to nine cohorts

60 Seneca *Ben.* 2. 7–8; *Prov.* 4. 4; see pp.21, 48

61 Tacitus *Ann.* 13. 34, 1; Suet. *Nero* 10. 1 where the *frumentum menstruum* clearly balances the *annua salaria* and must similarly indicate a recurrent payment (*pace* Bradley *ad loc.*). Tacitus *Ann.* 15. 72 is even less explicit about this but the contrast he makes with previous practice of buying corn at the market price suggests an innovation in the regular arrangements, not a single gift

62 See p.63. Tacitus *Ann.* 13. 31, 2 gives the amount as 400 *HS* each (cf. *RG* 15). A second congiarium recorded on coins of AD 64 cannot be dated. Others are likely given the great abundance of *tesserae* that survive (Rostovtzeff P-W IV (1900), 877). See p.266, n114 on the one issued in honour of Suetonius Paullinus

63 See pp.127, 106–9; *Ann.* 16. 13, 3 on his help to Lugdunum

64 *Ann.* 15. 59; 16. 11; 16. 19

65 Suet. *Nero* 32. Though Nero may have been aiming to curb the arrogant behaviour of new *liberti*, the financial penalty was not the obvious way to do this (cf. Suet. *Claud.* 25. 3)

66 See p.169 and *Ann.* 16. 14, 17 and the review of cases by Bradley in his commentary on Suet. *Nero* 32. Dio 63. 11, 3; *Hist.* 1. 90

67 Suet. *Gaius* 37; *Nero* 30. 1

68 Pliny *Pan.* 71. 4, cf. *Pan.* 2. 4

69 Tacitus *Ann.* 3. 55; 14. 52; 15. 35. See p.114

70 *Hist.* 1. 20; Suet. *Galba* 15; Plut. *Galba* 16; Dio 63. 14

71 See p.141f; Suet. *Otho* 7. 2

72 Pliny *NH* 37. 20

73 Pausanias 7. 17, 3: his reference to Nero compensating the Roman people by transferring the *prosperous* province of Sardina to their control probably does not show that the tribute of imperial provinces went to the *fiscus* rather than the *aerarium* at this date: the prestige and profits of governors appointed by the Senate could have been Nero's concern. Nero may also have been responsible for freeing Lycia, another decision reversed by Vespasian (Suet. *Vesp.* 8. 4)

74 Suet. *Vesp.* 16

75 Tacitus *Hist.* 4. 47. Suet. *Nero* 32. 1 reports that Nero had to postpone the pay of the soldiers and rewards for the veterans, the period after 65 being indicated, but there is no support in other sources. At most it could have been an aggravating factor right at the end

76 *Corpus Agrimensorum Romanorum* (ed. Thulin) 1. 1, 41: see Millar, *ERW*, 444. Suet. *Vesp.* 8. 3; 16; 23. 3

77 Smallwood no. 391, ll 14; 26f; Rostovtzeff, *SEHRE*² 292f. D. Crawford, 'Imperial Estates', *Studies in Roman Property*, ed. M.I. Finley (1976), 53

78 Dio 65. 22 (a mere 100 *HS* each); Suet. *Vesp.* 8; 23; Tacitus *Hist.* 2. 82; 84; Dio 66. 2, 5

79 Suet. *Vesp.* 17; 8. 5; 9

80 See p.137; McCrum and Woodhead nos. 408a; 413 (cf. 408b and 409 where Domitian and Titus repair constructions whose poor condition is attributed to age)

81 *ILS* 249; *SEG* 9. 166; *SEG* 9. 165; 9. 360
82 *Liber de spectaculis* 2
83 Suet. *Vesp.* 18. 1
84 For a partial vindication of the ancient tradition about Domitian's rapacity, see Levick, *Latomus* 41 (1982), 50f

14 The Temptation of Philhellenism   *(pages 208–220)*

1 Suet. *Nero* 12. 2
2 *Ann.* 14. 14; *Laus Pisonis* vv 169f (see pp.147–8)
3 See pp.162–3
4 Decline: Plut. *Flam.* 12. 6; *Mor.* 414A; *ILS* 8794, vv 16f. Discord: *ILS* 8794, v 15; Plut. *Mor.* 401C; 824C
5 *SEG* 11. 408 shows that the privilege of freedom was saved under Nero. It seems natural to connect this with Plutarch *Mor.* 488A on troubles in Sparta (see C.P. Jones, *Plutarch and Rome* (1971), 19, 52; *JRS* 56 (1966), 70). Vespasian's remark is given by Pausanias 7. 17, 4, cf. Philostratus *Life of Apollonius* 5. 41 where Vespasian's reason is regarded as a pretext. Doubtless Vespasian was largely concerned with the loss of revenue, but internal discord was a standard reason for imposing direct control and Vespasian was probably moved also by the threat to peace posed by the false Nero who appeared off the Attic coast in 69 (Tacitus *Hist.* 2. 8)
6 See p.32; Suet. *Claud.* 42. By the late Republic Greek envoys had been allowed to address the Senate in Greek and not, as previously, through an interpreter (Val. Max. 2. 2, 2; Cicero *Fin.* 5. 89). But neither Augustus nor Tiberius had made speeches in Greek in the Senate (Suet. *Aug.* 89; *Tib.* 71)
7 See p.161; *Ann.* 16. 10; Suet. *Nero* 20; 25, 1; 40, 4; Dio 63. 2, 3. Even Augustus approved Greek dress for Romans in Naples (Suet. *Aug.* 98. 3) and Claudius wore it himself there (Dio 60. 61–2)
8 See p.161; Plut. *Galba* 2. 1, cf. Suet. *Nero* 47. 2
9 Schumann, *Hellenistische und griechische Elemente in der Regierung Neros*
10 *ILS* 8794, v. 20: 'not through pity but goodwill'
11 Tacitus *Ann.* 12. 58, 2; Suet. *Claud.* 25. 3; *Nero* 7. 2. The classic treatment of Nero's relations with Rhodes is P. Fabia, *RPh* 29 (1896), 129f
12 Dio 60. 24; *IGRR* IV. 1123; *IGRR* IV. 1124: the occasion of the latter, some alarming letters received in Rhodes, is obscure
13 *AP* 9. 178 on which see p.149; Dio Chrysostom 31. 148–9; Pliny *NH* 34. 36 notes 3,000 statues in Rhodes; Suet. *Nero* 34
14 Montevecchi, *Aegyptus* 50 (1970), 5f; *PdP* 30 (1975), 48f
15 For the date of the collections see above, p.256 n10. Athens: Dio Chrysostom 31. 148, Delphi: Dio Chrysostom 31. 148; Pausanias 10. 7, 1, cf. 10. 19, 2; Olympia: Dio Chrysostom ibid., Pausanias 5. 25, 8; 26, 3; Thespiae: Pausanias 9. 27, 3; Pergamum: Dio Chrysostom ibid.; possibly Plutarch *Mor.* 815D is to be construed as an allusion to the confiscations. See in general Pliny *NH* 34. 84. Sacrilege: Pausanias 9. 27, 4; Tacitus *Ann.* 15. 45, 3
16 *ILS* 8794, vv 22–4; Pausanias 2. 16, 6; 5. 12, 8; Dio 63. 14, 1–2 who records that he also took away temple lands from Delphi. Suet. *Nero* 24

notes a grant of citizenship and money to *iudices*, presumably the same judges at Olympia, though he has the gifts announced at the Isthmian games, which shows confusion about the location of Nero's address (see n17). But see Bradley *ad loc.* who defends Suetonius and thinks the Isthmian judges received these awards

17 Plut. *Flam.* 12. 8. The inscription, noting that he is speaking before an assembly, confirms Plutarch's account of the venue, as opposed to Suetonius who says Nero stood in the middle of the stadium. For the speech see p.41 and p.246, n15

18 Philostratus *Life of Apollonius* 5. 7; Dio 63. 15, 2–3. Plutarch and his teacher Ammonius witnessed the Pythian games then, perhaps under duress (*Mor.* 385B: see Jones, *Plutarch and Rome*, 17)

19 Disapproval of his performances: Plutarch *Mor.* 56F; Philostratus *Life of Apollonius* 5. 7; Dio Chrysostom 71. 9

20 Plutarch *Antony* 87, cf. *Mor.* 505C; *Mor.* 567F

21 Philostratus *Life of Apollonius* 5. 41, cf. 4. 38

22 Pausanias 9. 27, 4; 7. 17, 3

23 Philostratus *Life of Apollonius* 5. 36; Cicero *ad Quintum fratrem* 1. 1; Pliny *Ep.* 8. 24. In selecting Pliny for his special governorship of Bithynia, Trajan no doubt considered his knowledge of Greek language and literature

24 Claudius removed citizenship from a Greek who proved ignorant of Latin, but the case only received his attention because the man was on the jury album at Rome (Suet. *Claud.* 16. 2). Dio 60. 17, 4 records his similar treatment of an ambassador from Lycia who proved ignorant of Latin during a senatorial hearing: see Levick, *Roman Colonies in Southern Asia Minor*, 104, n2

25 Levick, *Roman Colonies*, 106f; H. Halfmann, *Die Senatoren aus dem östlichen Teil des imperium Romanum bis zum Ende des 2. Jahrhunderts n. Chr.*, Hypomnemata 58 (1978). The two of Italian descent are M. Calpurnius Rufus of Attaleia and, less certain, L. Sergius Paullus, proconsul of Cyprus under Claudius (*Acts* 13. 7), who, Halfmann surmises, was an Italian settler of unusually high rank among the veterans settled at Pisidian Antioch, perhaps an equestrian officer (*IGRR* III. 935 which attests a Q. Sergius Paulus is now assigned an Antonine date by T.B. Mitford in *ANRW* II. 7, 1301). But other scholars regard the Sergii Paulli, more plausibly, as Roman landowners who acquired estates in the Anatolian plateau in the proconsul's time or later; see now S. Mitchell, *ANRW* II.7 (1980), 1073–4

26 Servenius Cornutus: McCrum and Woodhead, no. 270; Halfmann, p.102; Plancius Varus: Tacitus *Hist.* 2. 63; Halfmann, p.104; Junius Montanus: *AE* 1973, n500; Halfmann, p.103. J. Devreker, *Latomus* 41 (1982), 495 adduces also D. Junius Novius Priscus (*cos. ord.* 78) of Pisidian Antioch, but the doubts of Levick, *Roman Colonies*, 115–6 still seem convincing

27 Plutarch *Mor.* 470E

28 Tacitus *Hist.* 4. 45; Halfmann, pp.103–4

29 *AE* 1930, no. 4; Halfmann, pp.108–9. Another possible Neronian senator of native origins is Ti. Julius Candidus Marius Celsus, ex-praetor by 75, adduced by Devreker, *Latomus* 41 (1982), 495, but regarded as Vespasianic by Halfmann. Many of Devreker's suggestions for Neronian recruits rest

on the dubious assumption that all of these new men had held the vigintivirate and received the *latus clavus* early, a particularly rash assumption to make of a period of civil war

30 Suet. *Vesp.* 9. 2, with hindsight, describes Vespasian's action as a policy of putting the best of Italians and provincials into the Senate

31 Note Elder Seneca *Controversiae* 7. 1, 27: Cestius Pius, whose name proclaims Italian origin, speaks poor Latin and is thought of as a Greek. For prejudice see Levick, *Roman Colonies*, 104. Halfmann, pp.27f denies that there was any anti-Greek feeling at work

32 See *Seneca* 95–6. See p.261 n37

33 Balsdon, *Romans and Aliens* (1979), 51–2; Josephus *Antiquities* 18. 143; 19. 273 (Antonia Minor); see pp.23–4

34 Tacitus *Ann.* 2. 53; 2. 59; *P. Oxy.* 2435 recto. Senators required imperial permission to enter the province of Egypt, and Germanicus had not secured it

35 Philo *Legatio ad Gaium* 172–3; Suet. *Gaius* 21. It has been argued that Gaius observed Greek forms in his marriage with Lollia Paulina (Dio 59. 12) by Oliver, *Hesperia* (1966), 150f, but L. Robert, *REG* 80 (1967), 477 is sceptical

36 Tacitus *Ann.* 2. 55

37 *Ann.* 5. 10

38 Suet. *Nero* 20. 3

39 Suet. *Nero* 22. 3; Plut. *Mor.* 56E-F; Dio Chrysostom 71. 9

40 *Hist.* 2. 8; Dio 64. 7, 3. For the chronology of the false Neros see Gallivan, *Historia* 22 (1973), 364f

41 Dio 66. 19, 3b; Suet. *Nero* 57, cf. *Hist.* 1. 2. Syme, *Some Arval Brethren*, 88 connects the execution of Civica Cerialis, proconsul of Asia, with this last pretender. Dio Chrysostom 21. 10. For the Jewish version of this hope, as expressed in the Sibylline oracles, see p.15

42 Schumann, *Hellenistische und griechische Elemente*, 21f; H.P. L'Orange, *Apotheosis in Ancient Portraiture* (1947); E. Cizek, *L'Époque de Néron et ses controverses idéologiques* (1972), 242–3

43 Tacitus *Ann.* 13. 10; above p.294, n14. For Seneca's attitude see *Seneca*, 220–1

44 Tacitus *Ann.* 15. 74, 3; Suet. *Aug.* 52; Dio 51. 20, 8

45 See p.131

46 *IGRR* III. 345 (Smallwood, no. 146): Sagalassus in Pamphylia; *SEG* XVIII. 566: Prostanna; *ILS* 8794: Boeotia. In Curtius Rufus 9. 3, 'huius <novi sideris> hercule non solis, ortus lucem caliganti reddidit mundo', the Emperor is not being identified with the sun, but is said to be the source of light, *not* the sun, that actually dispels the shadow, that is, the comparison is taken a stage further and the Emperor is better than the sun. Such a commonplace cannot help us to identify the reigning Emperor or his predecessor who is implicity criticised

47 Seneca *Apocolocyntosis* 4. 1 (Phoebus speaking) 'ille mihi similis vultu similisque decore' (v 22), cf. v 30. On Antiphilus see p.210. Against the solar monarchy theory see J. Rufus Fears in *Historia* 25 (1976), 494–6, and *Princeps a Diis Electus* (Rome, 1977), 325f

48 J. Reynolds, *ZPE* 43 (1981), 317f. On the Domus Aurea see pp.137–8 and Dio 63. 6, 6

49 Dio 63. 5; F. Cumont, *RFIC* 11 (1933), 45f. Tiridates as a *magus*: Pliny *NH* 30. 16; Tacitus *Ann.* 15. 24. For the notion that Tiridates' dignity was being saved, G. Charles-Picard, *Auguste et Néron, le secret de l'Empire* (1962), 171f

50 Pliny *NH* 30. 15; 17. Suet. *Nero* 47. 2

51 Dio 63. 4, 3; 6, 3. Suet. *Nero* 53. On the Apollo coins see pp.120–1

52 *P. Oxy.* 1021 (Smallwood, no. 47): Agathos Daimon, on his accession in 54; *ILS* 8794, cf. *BMC, Imp.* I, 214, no. 110: coins of Corinth (?) with Iuppiter Liberator on them

53 On the significance of the radiate crown see S. Weinstock, *Divus Julius* (1971), 382f. The portrait of Claudius is always laureate on Neronian coins, but gold and silver coins of 55 show the radiate statues of *divi*, usually identified as Augustus and Claudius, being drawn in a car (fig. 15). Lucan 7. 457–9: 'bella pares superis facient civilia divos/fulminibus Manes radiisque ornabit et astris/inque deum templis iurabit Roma per umbras'

54 *BMC, Imp.* I, 208, nos. 52f; 56f. These are assigned by MacDowall, *Western Coinages*, 34 to Issue Ia (see pp.238–9). Fears, (above, n47) makes the connection with Tacitus *Ann.* 15. 74 but suggests that the 'Augustus Germanicus' coins and the token coins recall primarily Nero's status as heir of three *divi*. For the repression of the conspiracy as a military victory, *Ann.* 15. 72 and pp.230, 232

55 *BMC, Imp.* I, lxxi; MacDowall, *Western Coinages*, 114

56 Vespasian and Titus have the radiate crown on *dupondii*, a practice abandoned by Domitian (*BMC, Imp.* II, xiv, xliii). Vespasian and Titus as *divi* appear on coins with the radiate crown (*BMC, Imp.* II, xix)

57 Suet. *Nero* 37. 3, cf. pp.90, 95; Suet. *Gaius* 29. Royal family: Germanicus, in an edict preserved on papyrus and apparently addressed to the Alexandrians (E-J² 320b) deprecates divine honours for himself but says that they are appropriate for Tiberius and Livia; Suet. *Gaius* 24. 2: deification of Gaius' sister Drusilla; see also p.26 on the honours enjoyed by Gaius' sisters. Nero allowed elaborate honours to be given to his mother; later Poppaea and his daughter were deified on their death (Tacitus *Ann.* 13. 2, 3; 15. 23, 3; above, p.261, n23)

58 Seneca *Ben.* 2. 12

59 *Ben.* 5. 4, 2–3

60 On the sophistry of *Ben.* 2. 20 where the superiority of kingship seems to be asserted see above p.172; contempt for Oriental despotism: *Ben.* 5, 16, 6; *Brev. Vit.* 18. 5; the Princeps as a man: *Clem.* 1. 1, 2; 1. 7, 1–2; 1. 19, 9; 1. 26, 5

61 *De Domo* 90: 'ille populus est dominus regum, victor atque imperator omnium gentium'; Dio 63. 5, 3

15 The Military Image of the Princeps *(pages 221–234)*

1 Tacitus *Ann.* 1. 3, 3: by Augustus' death Tiberius was 'filius, collega imperii, consors tribuniciae potestatis'. *Ann.* 1. 10, 7; Suet. *Tib.* 21; 68. 3

2 Pliny *Pan.* 24. 1; 10. 1–2; 14f; Tacitus *Ann.* 13. 4

3 Pliny *Pan.* 1.3f contrasting selection by Fortune; Seneca *Clem.* 1. 1. 2; 4; 7–8

4 Republican tradition: Cicero *Pro Murena* 22; *Imp. Cn. Pompei* 6; *Off.*
1. 74. Suet. *Aug.* 31. 5. *RG* 34. 2 lists what he regarded as his highest
honours: bay leaves, a sign of victory; the civic crown traditionally given
for bravery in saving the life of a fellow citizen; the shield on which *virtus*
was listed as the first of four virtues, hence not 'virtue in general' but
'courage', or something similar. On his monopoly of triumphs, see p.19

5 Martial 10. 72

6 Syme, *Historia* 7 (1958), 180 = *Roman Papers* I, 370. Dio 53. 17, 4,
writing in the third century, says 'the name Imperator is held by them all
for life, *not only by those who have won victories in battle* but by those who
have not, to make clear their absolute authority, and this takes the place
of the title of king or dictator'

7 Suet. *Aug.* 40. 5; Dio 49. 16: he seems to refer to the purple toga worn by
promagistrates when presiding over the games (Mommsen, *Staatsrecht* I,
414, n1)

8 Suet. *Aug.* 73; *Nero* 30. 3

9 Dio 49. 15, 1; Pliny *NH* 15. 137. On the whole subject of imperial dress,
see Mommsen, *Staatsrecht*[3] I, 408–435; A. Alföldi, *Die monarchische
Repräsentation im römischen Kaiserreiche* (1934–5), 121–186

10 Though this might suggest that the old association of triumphal and royal
dress (e.g. Dion. Hal. 5. 35, cf. Tacitus *Ann.* 4. 26; Dio 44. 6) was being
made here, Augustus' refusal to be called Romulus, and his habit of
wearing triumphal dress only on ceremonial occasions and not
consistently (as did Caesar), suggest that the military and magisterial
associations of this garb were paramount under the Empire. Dio's
evidence that the privilege was a surrogate for a triumphal celebration
(53. 26) points in the same direction

11 Tacitus *Ann.* 12. 41; *Ann.* 12. 56: 'insigne paludamentum'

12 See pp.67–8; Tacitus *Ann.* 16. 27, 1; *Hist.* 1. 38; Pliny *Pan.* 23. 3

13 Suet. *Claud.* 10. 2

14 Tacitus *Ann.* 2. 18, 2. See Syme, *Phoenix* 33 (1979), 308f

15 Dio 59. 22, 2; 25. 3; 25. 5; Suet. *Gaius* 47; 49

16 Suet. *Claud.* 17. 1; Dio 60. 21, 2–22, 2. Tacitus notes his comparison of
the capture of Caratacus to that of hostile kings in the Republic (*Ann.*
12. 38): he may well have made similar remarks to the Senate when his
triumph was decreed; Dio 60. 23, 1 notes his strict adherence to ancient
precedent at its celebration

17 Millar, *ERW*, 11

18 See pp.21; 115–16. Tacitus *Ann.* 13. 53–7 recounts the events of 54–8. For
the engineering labours of the Roman army in this region under
Claudius, see *Ann.* 11. 20, 3

19 Tacitus *Ann.* 12. 31–9. His *praenomen* appears to be Quintus, not Publius
(as in Tacitus), if the evidence of a wax tablet is reliable: see A.E. Hanson,
ZPE 47 (1982) 243f

20 See p.115

21 Tacitus *Ann.* 14. 29f; *Agricola* 14. 3–15. *Ann.* 14. 31 leaves it unclear how
the king intended his inheritance to be divided: D. Braund, *PBSR* 51
(1983), 43–4; 53–4 suggests that he left his kingdom to Nero and legacies
to his daughters

22 Dio 62. 2, 1; cf. Tacitus *Ann.* 13. 42, 4. See *Seneca*, 232

23 See p.89
24 See p.61; *Seneca*, 234f
25 Tacitus *Ann.* 13. 6–9 (recounting events down to 55); 13. 34–41 (events to AD 58)
26 *Ann.* 14. 23–6 (events down to 60)
27 *Ann.* 15. 1–17 (events down to 62)
28 ILS 232 (Corbulo's position); *Ann.* 15. 24–31 (events of 63). See p.285, n77 and pp.232–3
29 E. Luttwak, *The Grand Strategy of the Roman Empire* (1976), 105 underestimates the difference between the Augustan buffer state and Neronian condominium
30 There was a scuffle worthy of triumphal decorations in 75 (Pliny *Pan.* 14; 16; Victor *de Caesaribus* 9. 10; *Epit. de Caesaribus* 9. 12)
31 See *Seneca*, Appendix F
32 Cottian Alps; Suet. *Nero* 18. A date of 65 is provided by Jerome *Chron.*, 184. For Corbulo's concern for Syria, Tacitus *Ann.* 15. 2–3; 9; for Damascus, see *R-E* IV (1901), 2046
33 See Anderson in *CAH* x, 265f; 774–6. Above, pp.108–9
34 Tacitus *Hist.* 1. 6; Suet. *Nero* 19; Dio 63. 8, 1; Pliny *NH* 6. 40
35 Lucan *BC* 8. 223; Seneca *Thyestes* 630, cf. Josephus *Ant. Jud.* 18. 97
36 Anderson, *CAH* x, 776f thinks the expedition could have no sensible purpose, but it was Roman practice to impress hostile tribes bordering on the provinces with Roman might (e.g. *Res Gestae* 30. 2). Chilver, *Historical Commentary* ad 1. 6 (pp.55–6) suggests that the Iberians resisted the idea of Roman fortifications in their territory and the Albani were to support Rome in accomplishing its goal; but that does little to save the credit of Tacitus, who clearly thinks that Nero's expedition was directed *against* the Albani. Mommsen's emendation 'Alanos' may be correct, as is now argued by Sherk, *ANRW* II.7 (1980), 992–4
37 *Hist.* 1. 6; 1. 31, 3; 1. 70; 1. 9, cf. 2. 11
38 Josephus *Bellum Judaicum* 2. 494; 3. 8
39 I follow here the analysis of Chilver, *Historical Commentary*, Introduction 9–11
40 See pp.161–2
41 Dio 63. 8, 1; Pliny *NH* 6. 181, 184
42 Seneca *NQ* 6. 8, 3
43 Suetonius lists his annexation of Pontus and the Cottian Alps and the eastern expedition among his respectable acts, even though he reports, in connection with the latter, that his new legion (I Italica) was restricted to Italians of uniform height and called the 'phalanx of Alexander' (Suet. *Nero* 18; 19. 2, cf. Suet. *Gaius* 52)
44 *Ann.* 13. 6–8; 13. 54, 4
45 *Ann.* 15. 25, cf. 13. 14, 1
46 *Ann.* 14. 39. Tacitus is more sympathetic to Suetonius here than in *Agric.* 16. 3: see *Scripta Classica Israelica* 3 (1976/7), 138f. On the honours to Petronius Turpilianus, see pp.118, 232
47 *Ann.* 18. 8 (Quadratus and Corbulo); 15. 6, 3–4 (Corbulo and Paetus); 14. 29, 2 (Suetonius whom popular rumour casts as Corbulo's rival); 13. 8, 1; 13. 41, 4
48 *Ann.* 14. 13

49 *Ann.* 15. 72, 1; see p.55

50 Suet. *Nero* 25; Dio 63. 4, 3–6, 3. See p.163. Tacitus' account of the visit of Tiridates is missing; Suetonius includes the celebration among the respectable events of the reign (Suet. *Nero* 13).

51 Dio, at 63. 1, under the year 66, reports that Menecrates, Nero's lyre teacher, held a triumph for him in the Circus where he appeared as a charioteer. The word used here, 'epinikia', is used by Dio at 51. 21, 6 to describe Augustus' triumph, but this was not a true triumph, for Nero took no imperial salutation, the essential antecedent

52 The only evidence for Nero's thirteenth salutation consists in coins of Ptolemais (Acte) giving Imp. XIII with cos. IV, hence before Nero assumed his fifth consulship in mid-April of 68 (see p.181): see *PIR*² D 129; H. Seyrig, *Revue Numismatique* 4 (1962), 44 regards the number XIII on these coins as a mistake. The standard account of his salutations remains H. Stuart Jones, *Revue Archéologique* 3 (1904), 263f and 7 (1906), 141–3; later evidence and scholarship are reviewed in *Scripta Classica Israelica* 3 (1976/7), 138f

53 *Ann.* 13. 8–9

54 Pliny *Pan.* 16

55 *Ann.* 13. 54. The salutation occurs on *ILS* 5640 with trib. pot. III (56–7) and cos. II (held in 57)

56 *Ann.* 13. 37–9; 13. 41; 13. 56

57 *Ann.* 14. 24. The records of the Arval Brethren show Nero with Imp. VII in January of 60, which may be right, although the trib. pot. VII there attributed to him is generally agreed to be an error for VI. The seventh salutation was not known in Cyprus by the end of 59 (*IGRR* III. 985, republished by Mitford in *ABSA* 42 (1947), 219)

58 The eighth salutation occurs with trib. pot. VIII on *ILS* 231. The *terminus post quem* is provided by *ILS* 1987, a diploma with Imp. VII which should be dated to 61. The arguments about the occasion for Imp. VIII were set out in *Scripta Classica Israelica* 3 (1976/7), 138f

59 It is recorded with trib. pot. VIII (61/2) on *CIL* 2. 4888. The successes recorded by Ti. Plautius Silvanus Aelianus (*ILS* 986) came after his army had been depleted by a contribution to Paetus' forces (*Ann.* 15. 6): hence probably too late for this salutation. In any case, the inscription shows that he received no honours from Nero, which makes it unlikely that the Emperor took a salutation marking his achievements

60 Tacitus *Ann.* 15. 18. (Tacitus is ironic about the celebrations since the war was, in fact, still going on, but he indicates that Nero felt some disquiet. At *Ann.* 15. 25 it appears that Paetus' dispatches had remained optimistic until the end)

61 *ILS* 232

62 See *Seneca*, 229–230

63 *Ann.* 15. 25. Tacitus accordingly makes Corbulo boast now to Tiridates of Nero's achievement of total peace except for this war, whereas once he made him speak of recovering the conquests of Lucullus and Pompey (13. 34, 2)

64 Dio 62. 23, 4 (preserved here by a Byzantine excerpter) says that after the ceremony in the camp at Rhandeia, Vologaeses came to Corbulo and gave him hostages, and that Nero was saluted as Imperator a number of times and held a triumph 'contrary to custom'. Tacitus has none of this, and the point about Vologaeses actually runs counter to *Annals* 15. 31 where Vologaeses communicates with Corbulo by messenger. As the passage closes this excerpter's treatment of the subject of Armenia, it is possible that he is summing up the whole Armenian episode, noting all the salutations Nero took for successes there, including that for Tiridates' visit in 66. There is no reliable evidence for a triumph

65 See p.122 and p.267, n12
66 See on this Townend, *Hermes* 108 (1980), 237
67 *Ann.* 15. 36; Suet. *Nero* 19; see p.161
68 Dio 62. 22, 4. It is possible that this is a garbled version of what Tacitus reports under 64 (see note above), because in it Nero is also deterred by an omen, namely, a fall while performing a sacrifice
69 The tenth salutation, attested on no inscription or coin, must fall between late 64/5 (when Imp. IX is still attested (n61)) and mid-66, on the assumption that the salutation taken by Nero for Tiridates' coronation was the eleventh (Suet. *Nero* 11). On *ILS* 233 Imp. XI appears with trib. pot. XIII (66–7), while the prefix Imperator, which seems to go with this salutation (see n72), first appears on coins with trib. pot. XII (65–6) not trib. pot. XI (64–5). Therefore it belongs to 66
70 Dio (62. 19), here preserved by Xiphilinus, says that Nero heard of a Parthian victory 'while thus engaged', the context being the Fire of 64. But Tacitus gives no hint that his account of the settlement under the year 63 extended beyond that year (the previous Armenian episodes are recounted under the terminal year) and the end of 64 requires a very long delay. Boissevain (vol III, 58) associated Imp. X with Rhandeia, but he was relying on the old chronology for Nero's tribunician power, according to which *ILS* 232 attesting Imp. IX belongs to 63–4
71 Suet. *Nero* 11; see above, n69
72 The prefix is first attested in the records of the Arval Brethren recording a sacrifice *ob laurum imperatoris Neronis* in May or June of 66; clearly Nero's deposit of the laurel wreath. See n69 for its appearance on coins
73 Suet. *Claud.* 12. 1
74 See the discussion of Townend, *Hermes* 108 (1980), 235
75 Note that Tacitus makes Corbulo allude to the Roman triumphs of Lucullus and Pompey, nothing later (*Ann.* 13. 34, 2)
76 See p.101
77 See p.181. Suet. *Nero* 43 makes Nero speak only of conquering the Gauls, but the passage in general conflates the later situation after Vesontio with that after Galba's rising (cf. Dio 63. 27. 2)
78 *CIL* 10. 8014 records Imp. XII with trib. pot. XIII (66–7)
79 See pp.117–18 The appointment of elderly men of undistinguished lineage points to the same attitude
80 *Agricola* 39. 3
81 Domitian instituted Greek games and advanced eastern senators to the consulship (see Syme, *Tacitus*, 509–10). On his dislike of being surpassed in eloquence see Tacitus *Agricola* 39. 3; Quintilian's flattery (IV, pref. 3; X. 1, 91–2) confirms it

82 Suet. *Dom.* 2; Dio 67. 4, 3

83 Suet. *Dom.* 10. 2, 3; Pliny *Ep.* 2. 7: Nerva finally rewarded Vestricius Spurinna for successes achieved twenty years earlier under Domitian (Syme, *Tacitus*, App. 6)

84 *Oration* 3. 127: the speech purports to be delivered before the Emperor; whether or not it really was, it probably presents the image of himself he favoured

85 *Roman Oration* 26; Athenagoras *Legatio* 1. 1

Bibliography

Abbreviations for Bibliography and Notes

AFA Henzen	*Acta Fratrum Arvalium*, ed. G. Henzen (Berlin, 1874)
ANRW	*Aufstieg und Niedergang der römischen Welt*, ed. H. Temporini (Berlin & New York, 1972–)
BAR	*British Archaeological Reports*
BMC Imp. I	*Coins of the Roman Empire in the British Museum*, vol I, ed. H. Mattingly (1923)
CIL	*Corpus Inscriptionum Latinarum*
ERW	F. Millar, *The Emperor in the Roman World* (London, 1977)
Furneaux	*The Annals of Tacitus*, edited with Introduction and Notes by H. Furneaux, 2nd edition, vol I (1896); vol II (1907)
IG	*Inscriptiones Graecae*
IGRR	*Inscriptiones Graecae ad Res Romanas Pertinentes*
ILS	H. Dessau, *Inscriptiones Latinae Selectae*
PIR	*Prosopographia Imperii Romani*
P. Oxy.	*The Oxyrhynchus Papyri*, ed. B.P. Grenfell *et al* (London, 1898–)
RE	*Real-Encyclopädie der Klassischen Altertumswissenschaft*
*RIC*²	*The Roman Imperial Coinage* I², ed. C.H.V. Sutherland
RP	R. Syme, *Roman Papers*, vols I & II, ed. E. Badian, (1979); vol III, ed. A.R. Birley (1983)
SEG	*Supplementum Epigraphicum Graecum*
*SEHRE*²	M. Rostovtzeff, *Social and Economic History of the Roman Empire*, ed. P. Fraser, 2 vols (Oxford, 1957)
*SIG*³	W. Dittenberger, *Sylloge Inscriptionum Graecarum* (3rd edition)
Smallwood, *Docs.*	E.M. Smallwood, *Documents Illustrating the Principates of Gaius, Claudius and Nero* (Cambridge, 1967)
McCrum and Woodhead	M. McCrum and A.G. Woodhead, *Documents of the Flavian Emperors* (Cambridge, 1961)

The titles of periodicals are, for the most part, abbreviated as in *Année Philologique*.

This list contains only the limited selection of books and articles expressly cited in the notes. It excludes reference works, editions and collections of ancient literary, numismatic and epigraphic evidence, many of which are listed under Abbreviations.

Ahl, F., *Lucan* (Ithaca, 1976)
Alföldi, A., *Die monarchische Repräsentation im römischen Kaiserreich*, Darmstadt, 1970 = *MDAI (R)* 49 (1934), 1f and 50 (1935), 1f
Baldwin, B., 'Executions under Claudius: Seneca's *Ludus de Morte Claudi*', *Phoenix* 18 (1964), 39f
   'Nero and his Mother's Corpse', *Mnemosyne* 32 (1979), 380
Balsdon, J.P.V.D., *The Emperor Gaius* (Oxford, 1934)
   Romans and Aliens (London, 1979)
Bandinelli, R.B., 'Fabullus', *Enciclopedia dell'arte antica* 3 (1960), 566–7
Bardon, H., 'Les poésies de Néron', *REL* 14 (1936), 337f
   La littérature latine inconnue, II: *L'époque impériale* (Paris, 1956)
   *Les Empereurs et les lettres latines d'Auguste à Hadrien*² (Paris, 1968)
Barnes, T.D., 'The Date of the Octavia', *Museum Helveticum* 39 (1982), 215f
Birley, A., *The Fasti of Roman Britain* (London, 1981)
   The People of Roman Britain (London, 1981)
Blake, M.E., *Roman Construction in Italy from Tiberius through the Flavians* (Washington D.C., 1959)
Boethius, A., *The Golden House of Nero* (Ann Arbor, 1960)
Bolton, J., 'Was the Neronia a freak festival?', *CQ* 1948, 82f
Bosworth, A.B., 'Vespasian and the Provinces: Some problems of the early 70s AD', *Athenaeum* 51 (1973), 49f
Bowie, E., 'Apollonius of Tyana: Tradition and Reality', *ANRW* II 16.2 (1978), 1652f
Bradley, K.R., 'A "Publica Fames" in AD 68', *AJP* 93 (1972), 451f
   'Two Notes Concerning Nero', *GRBS* 16 (1975), 305f
   'The Chronology of Nero's Visit to Greece AD 66/67', *Latomus* 37 (1978), 61f
   Suetonius' Life of Nero, An Historical Commentary (Brussels, 1978)
   'Nero's Retinue in Greece, AD66/67', *Illinois Classical Studies* IV (1979), 152f
Braund, D.C., 'Treasure-Trove and Nero', *Greece and Rome* 30 (1983), 65f
   'Royal Wills and Rome', *PBSR* 51 (1983),15f
Brunt, P.A., 'Aspects of the Social Thought of Dio Chrysostom and of the Stoics', *PCPhS* 19 (1973), 9f
   'Two Great Roman Landowners', *Latomus* 34 (1975), 619f
   'Stoicism and the Principate', *PBSR* 43 (1975), 7f
   'Lex de Imperio Vespasiani', *JRS* 67 (1977), 95f
van Buren, A.W., 'Pompeii-Nero-Poppaea', *Studies presented to D.M. Robinson*, 1953, II 970f
Burnett, A.M., 'The Authority to Coin in the late Republic and early Empire', *NC* 17 (1977), 37f
Cameron, A., *Circus Factions* (Oxford, 1976)
   'The Garland of Philip', *GRBS* 21 (1980), 43f
   'Poetae Novelli', *HSCPh* 84 (1980), 127f
Carettoni, G., 'Roma (Palatino)', *Not. d. Scavi* n.s.3 (1949), 48f

Carson, R.A.G., 'System and Product in the Roman Mint', *Essays in Roman Coinage presented to Harold Mattingly*, (Oxford, 1956), 227f

Champlin, E., 'Serenus Sammonicus', *HSCPh* 85 (1981), 189f

Charles-Picard, G., *Auguste et Néron, le secret de l'Empire* (Paris, 1962)

Charlesworth, M.P., 'Flaviana', *JRS* 27 (1937), 57f
'Nero: Some Aspects', *JRS* 40 (1950), 69f

Chilver, G.E.F., *A Historical Commentary on Tacitus' Histories* I and II (Oxford, 1979)

Cichorius, C., *Römische Studien* (Stuttgart, 1922)
'Zu römischen Malern', *RhM* 76 (1927), 325f

Civitelli, G., 'I Nuovi Frammenti d'Epigrafi Greche Relative ai Ludi Augustali di Napoli', *Atti della Accademia di Archaeologia, Lettere e Belle arte* (Napoli), XVII (1893-6), II.3

Cizek, E., *L'Époque de Néron et ses controverses idéologiques* (Leiden, 1972)

Coffey, M., 'Seneca, Apokolokyntosis 1922–1958', *Lustrum* 6 (1961), 239f

Colini, A.M., 'Storia e topografia del Celio nell'antichità', *Atti della Pontificia Accademia Romana di Archeologia*, Serie III Memorie VII (1944)

Cotton, H., *Documentary Letters of Recommendation in Latin from the Roman Empire, Beiträge zur klassischen Philologie* 132 (1981)

Cozza, L., 'I recenti scavi delle Sette Sale', *Atti della Pontificia Accademia Romana di Archeologia*, Serie III, Rendiconti 47 (1974–5), 79f

Crawford, D., 'Imperial Estates', *Studies in Roman Property*, ed. M.I. Finley (Cambridge, 1976), 35f

Crawford, M.H., 'Money and Exchange in the Roman World', *JRS* 60 (1970), 40f
Roman Republican Coinage (Cambridge, 1974)

Crook, J., *Consilium Principis* (Cambridge, 1955)

Cumont, F., 'L'iniziazione di Nerone da parte di Tiridate d'Armenia', *RIFC* 11 (1933), 145f

D'Arms, J.H., *Romans on the Bay of Naples* (Cambridge, Mass., 1970)
'Puteoli in the Second Century of the Roman Empire: a Social and Economic Study', *JRS* 64 (1974), 104f
'Tacitus *Annals* 13.48 and a new inscription from Puteoli', *The Ancient Historian and his Materials* (Farnborough, 1975), 155f

Devreker, J., 'Les Orientaux au sénat romain d'Auguste à Trajan', *Latomus* 41 (1982), 492f

Duckworth, G.E., 'Five Centuries of Hexameter', *TAPA* 98 (1967), 85f

Eck, W., 'Die Familie der Volusii Saturnini in neuen Inschriften aus Lucus Feroniae', *Hermes* 100 (1972), 461f
'Neros Freigelassener Epaphroditus und die Aufdeckung der pisonischen Verschwörung', *Historia* 25 (1976), 381f
'Miscellanea Prosopographica', *ZPE* 42 (1981), 227f

Eisenhut, W., 'Zum neuen Diktys-Papyrus', *RhM* 112 (1969), 114f

van Essen, C.C., 'La Topographie de la Domus Aurea Neronis', *Medelingen der Koninklijke Nederlandse Akademie van Wetenschappen*, Afd. Letterkunde 17.12 (1954), 371f

Fabbrini, L., 'Domus Aurea, il piano superiore del quartiere orientale', *Atti della Pontificia Accademia Romana*, Serie III, Memorie 14 (1982), 5f
'Domus Aurea: una nuova lettura planimetrica del palazzo sul colle Oppio',

Città e architettura nella Roma imperiale, Analecta Romana Instituti Danici,
   Suppl. X (1983), 169f
Fabia, P., 'Le troisième mariage de Néron. Statilia Messalina', *RPh* 19 (1895),
   218f
   'Néron et les Rhodiens', *RPh* 20 (1896), 129f
Fears, J. Rufus, 'The solar monarchy of Nero and the imperial panegyric of
   Q. Curtius Rufus', *Historia* 25 (1976), 494f
   Princeps a diis electus: the Divine Election of the Emperor as a Political Concept at
   Rome (Rome, 1977)
Fraenkel, E., 'Eine formel des Vortrags im Senat', *Kleine Beiträge zur klassichen*
   Philologie, vol II no. 70 (Rome, 1964), 477–8
de Franciscis, A., 'Beryllos e la villa di Poppea ad Oplontis', *Studies in Classical*
   Art and Archaeology – a tribute to P.H. von Blanckenhagen (New York,
   1979), 231f
Frazer, R.M., jr., 'Nero the artist-criminal', *Classical Journal* 62 (1966), 17f
Friedländer, L., *Roman Life and Manners* (English translation of the seventh
   edition) (London, 1907)
Gallivan, P., 'Nero's Liberation of Greece', *Hermes* 101 (1973), 230f
   'Some Comments on the *Fasti* for the Reign of Nero', *CQ* 24 (1974), 290f
   'Suetonius and Chronology in the "de vita Neronis" ' *Historia* 23 (1974), 297f
Garzetti, A., *From Tiberius to the Antonines* (1960, English translation, 1974)
Geiger, J., 'Munatius Rufus and Thrasea on Cato the Younger', *Athenaeum* 57
   (1979), 48f
George, P.A., 'Petronius and Lucan *De Bello Civili*', *CQ* 24 (1974), 119f
Gerster, B., 'L'Isthme de Corinthe-Tentatives de percement dans l'antiquité',
   BCH 8 (1884), 225f
Gill, C., 'The question of character-development: Plutarch and Tacitus', *CQ*
   33 (1983), 469f
Ginsburg, J., 'Nero's Consular Policy', *AJAH* 6 (1981), 51f
Grant, M., *Nero* (London, 1970)
Griffin, M.T., '*De Brevitate Vitae*', *JRS* 52 (1962), 104f
   'Imago Vitae Suae', *Seneca* ed. C.D.M. Costa (London, 1974), 1f
   Seneca, A Philosopher in Politics (Oxford, 1976)
   'Nero's Recall of Suetonius Paullinus', *Scripta Classica Israelica* 3 (1976/7),
   138f
Halfmann, H., *Die Senatoren aus dem östlichen Teil des imperium Romanum bis*
   zum Ende des 2. Jahrhunderts n. Chr., *Hypomnemata* 58 (1978)
Hanson, A.E., 'Publius Ostorius Scapula: Augustan Prefect of Egypt', *ZPE* 47
   (1982), 243f
Henderson, B., *Life and Principate of the Emperor Nero* (London, 1903)
Herington, C.J., 'Octavia Praetexta: a Survey', *CQ* N.S.11 (1961), 18f
   'The Younger Seneca', *Cambridge History of Classical Literature* II.4
   (Cambridge, 1982), 15f
Hermansen, G., *Ostia, Aspects of City Life* (Edmonton, 1982)
Hiesinger, U., 'Portraits of Nero', *AJA* 79 (1975), 113f
Holleaux, M., 'Discours de Néron prononcé à Corinthe pour rendre aux Grecs
   la liberté', *BCH* 12 (1888), 510f
Honoré, A., 'Proculus', *Tijdschrift voor Rechtsgeschiedenis* 30 (1962), 473f
Huelson, C., 'Burning of Rome under Nero', *AJA* 13 (1909), 45f

Instinsky, H.U., 'Kaiser Nero und die Mainzer Jupitersäule', *JRGZ* 6 (1959), 128f

Jones, C.P., 'The Teacher of Plutarch', *HSCPh* 71 (1966), 209
'Towards a Chronology of Plutarch's Work', *JRS* 56 (1966), 61f
Plutarch and Rome (Oxford, 1971)

Kraay, C.M., 'The Coinage of Vindex and Galba', *NC* (1949), 129f

Kraft, K., 'S(enatus) C(onsulto)', *Jahrbuch für Numismatik und Geldgeschichte* 12 (1962), 7f = *Wege der Forschung* 128 (1969), 336f
'Der politische Hintergrund von Senecas Apocolocyntosis', *Historia* 15 (1966), 96f

Kragelund, P., *Prophecy, Populism and Propaganda in the 'Octavia'* (Copenhagen, 1982)

Lebek, W.D., Lucan's *Pharsalia*, Hypomnemata 44 (Göttingen, 1976)

Levick, B.M., *Roman Colonies in Southern Asia Minor* (Oxford, 1967)
Tiberius the Politician (London, 1976)
'Domitian and the Provinces', *Latomus* 41 (1982), 50f
'The *Senatus Consultum* from Larinum', *JRS* 73 (1983), 97f

Lo Cascio, E., 'State and Coinage in the Late Republic and Early Empire', *JRS* 71 (1981), 76f

L'Orange, H.P., 'Domus Aurea: der Sonnenpalast', *Symbolae Osloenses* Suppl. 11 (1942), 68f
Apotheosis in Ancient Portraiture (Oslo, 1947)

Luck, G., 'On Petronius' *Bellum Civile*', *AJPh* 93 (1972), 133f

Luttwak, E., *The Grand Strategy of the Roman Empire* (Baltimore, 1976)

MacDonald, W., *The Architecture of the Roman Empire* I (New Haven, 1965)

MacDowall, D.W., 'The Numismatic Evidence for the Neronia', *CQ* 8 (1958), 192f
The Western Coinages of Nero, Numismatic Notes and Monographs no. 161 (1979)

Maiuri, A., *La Casa del Menandro*, (Rome, 1933)

Makin, E., 'The Triumphal route, with particular reference to the Flavian Triumph', *JRS* 11 (1921), 25f

Malavolta, M., *Sesta Miscellanea Greca e Romana* (Rome, 1978): 'A Proposito del nuovo S.C. da Larino', 347f; 'I Neronia e il lustrum', 395f

Mayer, R., 'Calpurnius Siculus: Technique and Date', *JRS* 70 (1980), 175f

Meiggs, R., *Roman Ostia²* (Oxford, 1973)

Millar, F., 'The Fiscus in the first two centuries', *JRS* 53 (1963), 29f
A Study of Cassius Dio (Oxford, 1964)
'The Emperor, the Senate and the Provinces', *JRS* 56 (1966), 156f
The Emperor and the Roman World (London, 1977)

Mitchell, S., 'Population and the Land in Roman Galatia', *ANRW* II.7.2 (1980), 1053f

Mitford, T.B., 'Roman Cyprus', *ANRW* II.7.2 (1980), 1285f

Moeller, W., 'The Riot of AD 59 at Pompeii', *Historia* 19 (1970), 84f

Momigliano, A., *Claudius: the Emperor and his Achievement²* (Cambridge, 1961)

Montevecchi, O., 'Nerone e una polis e ai 6475', *Aegyptus* 50 (1970), 5f
'Nerone e l'Egitto', *PdP* 30 (1975), 48f

Morford, M.P.O., 'The Distortion of the Domus Aurea Tradition', *Eranos* 66 (1968), 158f

Newbold, R.F., 'Some Social and Economic Consequences of the AD64 Fire at Rome', *Latomus* 33 (1974), 858f

Nikolva-Bourova, 'Observations stylistiques et lexicales des dialogues *De ira* et *De clementia* de Lucius Annaeus Seneca', *Eirene* 13 (1975), 87f

North, A., *Libellus de regionibus urbis Romae* (Lund, 1949)

Onorato, G., *Iscrizione Pompeiane* (Florence, 1957)

Painter, K.S., 'Roman Flasks with Scenes of Baiae and Puteoli', *Journal of Glass Studies* 17 (1975), 54f

Panciera, S., 'Appunti su Pozzuoli Romana', *Atti dei convegni Lincei* 33 (1977), 191f

Pavis d'Escurac, H., *La préfecture de l'annone* (Rome, 1976)

Pflaum, H.-G., *Les carrières procuratoriennes équestres sous le Haut-Empire romain*, 4 vols (Paris, 1960–1)

Price, S.R.F., 'The Divine Right of Emperors', *CR* 29 (1979), 277–8

Reynolds, J., 'New Evidence for the Imperial Cult in Julio-Claudian Aphrodisias', *ZPE* 43 (1981), 317f

Rickman, G., *Roman Granaries and Stone Buildings* (Cambridge, 1971)
   The Corn Supply of Ancient Rome (Oxford, 1980)

Robert, L., *Études épigraphiques et philologiques* (Paris, 1938)
   'Les épigrammes satiriques de Lucillius sur les athlètes – parodie et réalités', *Entretiens de la Fondation Hardt* 14 (1967), 181f
   'Bulletin épigraphique', *REG* 80 (1967), no.195
   CRAI 'Dans l'amphithéâtre et dans les jardins de Néron. Une épigramme de Lucillius', 1968, 280f

Rogers, R.S., 'The Neronian Comets', *TAPA* 84 (1953), 237f

Roper, T.K., 'Nero, Seneca and Tigellinus', *Historia* 28 (1979), 346f

Rose, K., 'Problems of Chronology in Lucan's Career', *TAPA* 97 (1966), 379f

Rostovzeff, M., *Römische Bleitesserae* (Leipzig, 1905)

Roux, Georges, *Néron*, (Paris, 1962)

Saller, R.P., 'Martial on Patronage and Literature', *CQ* 33 (1983), 246f

Sanguinetti, F., 'Lavori Recenti nella Domus Aurea', *Palladio* 5.7 (1957), 126–7
   126–7
   Boll. del centro di studi per la storia dell'architettura 12 (1958), 35f

Scheda, G., 'Nero und der Brand Roms', *Historia* 16 (1967), 111

Schumann, G., *Hellenistische und griechische Elemente in der Regierung Neros*, (Leipzig, 1930)

Sear, F.B., *Roman Wall and Vault Mosaics*, (Heidelberg, 1977)

Seyrig, H., 'Le monnayage de Ptolémaïs en Phénicie', *RN* 4 (1962), 25f

Sherk, R.K., 'Roman Galatia: the Governors from 25BC to AD 114', *ANRW* II.7 (1980), 954f

Shotter, D.C.A., 'A Time-table for the "Bellum Neronis" ', *Historia* 24 (1975), 59f

Smallwood, E.M., *Documents illustrating the Principates of Gaius, Claudius and Nero*, (Cambridge, 1967)
   'The Alleged Jewish Tendencies of Poppaea Sabina', *Journal of Theological Studies* N.S. 10 (1959), 329f
   The Jews under Roman Rule, (Leiden, 1976)

Smith, M., *Cena Trimalchionis*, (Oxford, 1975)

Sogliano, A., 'Colonie Neroniane', *RAL* ser.5, vol 6 (1897), 389f

Starr, C., 'The Roman Emperor and the King of Ceylon', *CPh* 51 (1956), 27f

Storz, H., Prückner, S., 'Beobachtungen am Oktagon der Domus Aurea', *MDAI(R)* 81 (1974), 323f

Stuart-Jones, H., 'La chronologie des salutations impériales de Néron', *Revue Archéologique* 3 (1904), 263f

'Encore les salutations impériales de Néron', *Revue Archéologique* 7 (1906), 142f

Sutherland, C.H.V., *The Emperor and the Coinage: Julio-Claudian Studies* (London, 1976)

Sydenham, E.A., *The Coinage of Nero*, (London, 1920)

Syme, R., 'Caesar, the Senate and Italy', *PBSR* 14 (1938), 1f = *Roman Papers* I, 88f

'Imperator Caesar', *Historia* 7 (1958), 172f = *RP* I, 361f

Tacitus, (Oxford, 1958)

'Domitius Corbulo', *JRS* 60 (1970), 27f = *RP* II, 805f

'The Enigmatic Sospes', *JRS* 67 (1977), 38f = *RP* III, 1043f

'Mendacity in Velleius', *AJPh* 99 (1978), 45f = *RP* III, 1090f

'The Pomerium in the Historia Augusta', *Antiquitas 4: Beiträge zur Historia-Augusta-Forschung* 13 (1978), 217f

'Problems about Janus', *AJP* 100 (1979), 188f = *RP* III, 1179f

'Some Imperial Salutations', *Phoenix* 33 (1979), 308f = *RP* III, 1198f

Some Arval Brethren, (Oxford, 1980)

'Governors Dying in Syria', *ZPE* 41 (1981), 125f = *RP* III, 1376f

'Partisans of Galba', *Historia* 31 (1982), 460f

'Neglected Children on the Ara Pacis', *AJA* 88 (1984) 583f

Tamm, B., *Auditorium and Palatium*, (Stockholm, 1963)

Taylor, L.R., 'Trebula Suffenas and the Plautii Silvani', *MAAR* 24 (1956), 26f

Townend, G.B., 'Tacitus, Suetonius and the Temple of Janus', *Hermes* 108 (1980), 233f

'Calpurnius Siculus and the *Munus Neronis*', *JRS* 70 (1980), 166f

Toynbee, J.M.C., 'Ruler-Apotheosis on Roman Coins', *NC* 7 (1947), 126f

Review of H.P. L'Orange, *Apotheosis in Ancient Portraiture*, *JRS* 38 (1948), 160

Van Deman, E.B., *The Building of the Roman Aqueducts*, (Washington, 1934)

'The Sacra Via of Nero', *MAAR* 5 (1925), 115f

Verdière, R., *Études prosodique et métrique du De laude Pisonis et des Bucolica de T. Calpurnius Siculus*, (Rome, 1971)

Vlad, L.B., 'Il distacco di due pitture della Domus Transitoria con qualche notizia sulla tecnica di Fabullus', *Bollettino dell'Istituto centrale del restauro* 29–30 (1957), 31f

Walker, D., *The Metrology of the Roman Silver Coinage* Part I (*BAR* 5 [1976]); Part III (*BAR* 40 (1978))

Wallace-Hadrill, A., 'Civilis Princeps: between Citizen and King', *JRS* 72 (1982), 32f

Walter, B., *Nero*, (Paris, 1955: English translation 1957)

Ward Perkins, J., 'Nero's Golden House', *Antiquity* 1956, 209f

Warmington, B.H., *Nero, Reality and Legend* (London, 1969)

Suetonius' Nero (Text, with Introduction and Notes) (Bristol, 1977)

Weaver, P.R., 'Social Mobility in the Early Empire', *Past and Present* 37 (1967) = *Studies in Ancient Society*, ed. M.I. Finley, 121f

Familia Caesaris (Cambridge, 1972)

Weidemann, U., *Die Statthalter von Africa und Asia in den Jahren 14–68* AD, (Bonn, 1982)

Weinstock, S., *Divus Julius*, (Oxford, 1971)

Willems, J., 'Le sénat romain en l'an 65', *Musée Belge* 6 (1902), 100f

Williams, G., *Change and Decline: Roman Literature in the Early Empire*, (Berkeley, 1978)

Wiseman, T.P., 'Calpurnius Siculus and the Claudian Civil War', *JRS* 72 (1982), 57f

Zander, G., 'La Domus Aurea: nuovi probleme architettonici', *Bollettino del centro di studi per la storia dell'architettura* 12 (1958), 47f

Index of Persons, Human and Divine

Authors, Emperors and their relations are usually listed by their conventional English names, others by *gens* with cross-references if deemed necessary. Names appearing on the Genealogical Table (pp. 12–13) are asterisked. In this and the General Index, italicized page references indicate the most important of numerous references.

Acratus, imperial freedman 85, 87, 187, 210
Acte, imperial freedwoman 38, 40, 72, 73, 75
Aebutius Liberalis, addressee of Seneca's *De Beneficiis* 79
Aelius Sejanus L., (cos. 31), Praetorian Prefect 24, 25, 68, 70, 86–7, 101, 145–6, 193, 194, 195
*Aemilius Lepidus, M., favourite of Gaius 26, 27, 193
Afranius Burrus, Sex., Praetorian Prefect 30, 33, 38, 39, 40, 45, 46, 65, 66, *67–9*, 70, 72, 74, 75, 76, 78, 79, 80, 98, 103, 104, 105, 110, 116, 167, 175
  his death 69, 75, 82, 83, 87, 104
Afranius Quintianus, senator 151, 168
*Agrippina, Julia, the Elder 20, 23, 24, 25, 191
*Agrippina, Julia, the Younger
  her childhood 23
  her marriages 21, 25, 27–8, 29, 73
  becomes Nero's mother 20, 23
  in reign of Gaius 25–7, 70–1, 103
  in reign of Claudius 28–33, 38, 64, 67, 92, 102, 103, 116
  political allies 29, 30, 73
  and the Praetorian Guard 30, 67–9
  role in government under Nero *38–40*, 60, 61, 65, 73, 84, 96, 97, 98, 103, 133, 195, 236
  her wealth 203–4
  on Nero's coinage 39, 58
  her death 41, 43, 69, 72, 75, 76, 81, 84, 89, 99, 101, 105, 109, 116, 164, *165*, 167, 230
  her memoirs 23

Anicetus, imperial freedman 32, 46, 72, 75, 77, 99, 112
Annaeus Cornutus, L., Stoic philosopher 152, 154, 155, 157, 171 272 n 1, 276 n 75
Annaeus Mela, Seneca's younger brother 70, 78, 79, 81, 170, 171, 174
Annaeus Novatus, *see* Junius Gallio Annaeanus, L.
Annaeus Serenus, friend of Seneca 72, 79, 81, 274 n 41
Annius Afrinus, M. (cos. suff. 67) 180
Annius Pollio, son of L. Annius Vinicianus 170, 178, 195
Annius Vinicianus, L., conspirator against Gaius 178, 195
Annius Vinicianus, son of L. Annius Vinicianus 178, 195, 264 n 95
  his conspiracy 178–9, 194, 280 n 126
Anteius Rufus, P. (cos. suff. before 51) 116–7, 170
Antiphilus of Byzantium, writer of Greek epigrams 149, 210, 216
Antistius Sosianus (praetor 62) 48, 49, 53, 85, 93, 165, 170
Antistius Vetus, L. (cos. 55) 61, 116, 170, 178
*Antonia Maior, niece of Augustus, paternal grandmother of Nero 20
*Antonia Minor, niece of Augustus, maternal great-grandmother of Nero 213–4, 241 n 9
*Antonia, daughter of Claudius 98, 193, *194*, 196
Antoninus Pius, the Emperor 61, 234
Antonius Felix, (M.), procurator of Judaea 65, 247 n 53
Antonius Flamma, (M.), senator from Cyrene 212–3
Antonius Pallas, M., imperial freedman 29, 30, 39–40, 54, 65, 69, 73, 75, 88, 89, 92, 93, 98, 230
*Antony (Antonius, M.), the Triumvir 20, 176, 192, 196, 213, 214
Apollo, Nero and 41, 44, 45, 120, 121, 138, 149, 163, 216, 217, 218
Aquillius Regulus, M., senator 179, 252 n 89

General Index